Water for Hartford

The Story of the
Hartford Water Works
and the
Metropolitan District Commission

Kevin Murphy

Wesleyan University Press
Middletown, Connecticut

Published by Wesleyan University Press, Middletown, CT 06459
www.wesleyan.edu/wespress

First Wesleyan edition 2010

Originally published in cloth by Shining Tramp Press in 2004

Printed in the United States of America

Library of Congress Control Number: 2010922128

ISBN 978-0-8195-7080-2

The Library of Congress has cataloged the original edition as follows"

LIBRARY OF CONGRESS CATALOGING-IN-PUBLICATION DATA

Murphy, Kevin J., 1949-
Water For Hartford: The story of the Hartford Water Works
and the Metropolitan District Commission / by Kevin Murphy.

318 p.   24 cm.
Bibliography.
Includes index.
ISBN 0-9749352-0-4

1. Hartford Water Works—History. 2. Metropolitan District Commission
(Conn.)—History. 3. Waterworks—Connecticut—Hartford—History. 4. Water-
supply—Connecticut—Hartford—History. 5. Water-supply engineering—
Connecticut—Hartford—History.
⌐HD4464.H37 M87 2004
354.366   2004400764

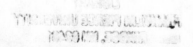

Dedicated to

Richard "Dick" Keane

Brother-in-law, friend, and confidant.

Wisdom itself,
Loyal beyond belief,
Cheerful in all weather,
Gone too soon.

Acknowledgements

A book like this requires a prodigious amount of research. Among other things, it is the result of stories, reminiscences, and anecdotes as well as historical and genealogical material supplied by hundreds of people, who surrender these priceless treasures so that a small—but important—piece of history can be preserved.

First, I would like to acknowledge the great debt that I owe to my parents, Bob and Mary Murphy for giving me life, a first-class education and a million incidentals along the way. A very special thanks goes to Bill and Rosalie Rishar who, through their great generosity, gave me the perfect place to write, with luxurious quiet and almost complete freedom from financial worries. Lastly, I must extend a heartfelt thanks to all of my family members, friends and neighbors in Wethersfield, who have read the rough drafts of my work through the years and offered important feedback. Included in this last category are: Sue Jensen, Liz Kirkpatrick, Lee Ann Forsdick, Carol and Art Bruce, Jack and Billye Logan, and Deal, Kris and Linde Aseltine.

At the Metropolitan District Commission, I owe a great debt to the company's CEO Charles P. Sheehan, the Chairman of the Board of Water Commissioners, Bill DiBella, and the firm's former Director of Community Affairs, the late Matt Nozzolio; also due thanks are engineers and employees Stanley Johnson, Jim Randazzo, Bob Kerkes, Susan McLaughlin, Dick Allen, Leland "Bud" Sanders, Sal Gozzo, Frank Dellaripa, Alan King, Fred Barbieri, Daisy Chavez and Jennifer Ottalagana, all of whom contributed mightily to this book. Credit goes as well to some retired members of the MDC, who provided anecdotes and information that could only have come from those who were there "back when"—Gerry and Paulette d'Avignon, Paul McCarthy, Richard "Dick" Phillips, Arthur Sweeton III and Mrs. Anthony Fornabi.

I am grateful for the patience of the staff at the Connecticut State Library, particularly Dick Roberts, Mel Smith, Carol Ganz, Carolyn Picciano, Jeannie Sherman, Bonnie Linck, Steve Rice, Kristi Finnan and Kevin Johnson.

Further historical and genealogical contributions were made by the able staff of the Connecticut Historical Society with generous help from Judith Ellen Johnson, Nancy Finlay, Ava Bolkovac, Martha Smart and Rich Malley.

At the Hartford Public Library, I am indebted to Bob Chapman and, also, Janice Mathews, administrator of the Hartford Collection.

Deep within the bowels of the Watkinson Library at Trinity College, warm regards go to Peter Knapp, head archivist.

At the Hartford Town Clerk's Office, I would like to recognize the aid of Winston Smith with old land deeds and at the city's Building Department, I would be remiss if I didn't mention Joseph Hewes.

For the delicate information regarding the final disposition of Caleb and Elizabeth Saville, a note of thanks is extended to D'Esopo's Funeral Home of Wethersfield and Joan Kaufman and Janet Heywood of Mt. Auburn Cemetery in Cambridge, Massachusetts.

The information about EPA regulations was generously given to me by Bill Warzecha and Bob Hurst of the Connecticut State Department of Environmental Protection.

In Barkhamsted, I was aided greatly by Town Clerk Maria Mullady as well as Harriet Winchenbaugh, Sharon Neumann-Lynes and Charles Lynes of the Barkhamsted Historical Society. For background information, generous contributions were made by the following former and present residents— Laura LeGeyt Merrill, Bertha LeGeyt Warner, Walt Landgraf, Ken Church, Nancy Winn, Robert Hart, David Gidman and Herbert Case.

In Hartland, immeasurable assistance was rendered by Town Clerk Betty Hillbrect, and by Marge Nurge and Karen McNulty of the Hartland Historical Society. This book was completed only with the assistance of the following present and former residents—Evelyn Peterson, Barb Wright, Marianne "Magi" Holtham, Joan Stoltze, Joan Schramm, Virginia Lewis, Pauline Emerick Skaret, Paul Crunden and Doug Roberts.

In Colebrook, I was aided by the kindly attentions of Town Clerk Joyce Nelson and Robert Grigg of the Colebrook Historical Society. Among the present and former residents who helped assemble the story in Colebrook were—Mildred Church, Floyd Jesperson, Katherine Doty, Eugene Carrozza, Lillian Hamilton, Agnes Harrington, Mary Gray and Juanita Dustin. A special note of gratitude is extended to another writer, Claire Vreeland, for her help.

Staffers of other historical societies around the state lent a hand as well, including Jim Bennett and Doris Armstead of the Glastonbury Historical Society and Marjorie McNulty, Town Historian of Glastonbury. For birth certificates and more genealogical information, I am grateful to Cynthia Cole of the South Glastonbury Congregational Church and Jean Green of the First Church of Christ Congregational in Glastonbury, both of whom worked hard to locate records of the Bissell family of Shingle Hollow.

I am deeply indebted to Thorndike Saville Jr.—grandson of Caleb Mills Saville—who supplied a treasure trove of background information regarding the lives and habits of Caleb and Elizabeth Saville, in Boston, the Panama Canal Zone and, later, in Hartford.

My great appreciation is extended to Atty. Austin Carey Jr.—the great-great-grandson of Hiram Bissell—and his aunt, Elizabeth "Sandy" (Carey) Smith, who were able to render first hand information about H. Bissell Carey, the industrialist who helped the MDC acquire the lands in and around Colebrook River for the Hogback Reservoir.

At Miss Porter's School in Farmington, Linda Noll and Susan Tracy are to be thanked for researching the short academic career of President Grant's daughter, Ellen (Nellie), in 1870.

The sextons of cemeteries should be commended for their assistance—Bob Harrigan of the Spring Grove Cemetery (Htfd.), F. Aldrich Edwards, Debbie Guerra and Irene McHugh of Cedar Hill Cemetery (Htfd.), Jeffrey Carstens of the Old Church Cemetery (Glast.) and Bayless Earle of the South "Still Hill" Cemetery (Glast.). Also, I would like to thank Rhoda Spencer of the Glastonbury Funeral Home, who was very helpful in chasing down the sextons of the ancient burial grounds of that town.

A great many people offered bits and pieces of information regarding the Shingle Hollow section of South Glastonbury. I am especially indebted to Francis Tryon Barker—and her sister, Shirley Tryon Fuller—whose genealogical information as well as remembrances of conversations with their "Aunt Amy" Tryon Benton were invaluable in reconstructing the daily lives of the Bissells and the Tryons of Shingle Hollow. To others in that neck of the woods—James and Barbara Morrissey, Davis and Marla Bodznick, John Heagle, Charles Tryon, Russ and William Shemstone, Sue Duffert, Marjorie McNulty, Howard Horton, Jr., Dick Chapman, Arlene Dilts and David Taylor—I am also extremely grateful. A singular word of appreciation is hereby extended to Adrien and Wendy Tetreault—present owners of the "Bissell place"—who were kind enough to give me a tour of the house and grounds.

Contents

Preface

Collectively, the oceans of the world constitute the mystical reservoir from which all life flows. Evaporation launches moisture into the atmosphere where it forms clouds, which then disperse their burden in the form of rain and snow. As this precipitation falls, it replenishes the rivers and lakes that, laterally, return this life-sustaining potion back to the seas. This is the deceptively simple hydrologic cycle that even grade school children understand. However, the history of drinking water is more complex when one considers the lives and projects of the great hydraulic pioneers, who designed the delivery systems for this precious resource.

The last few decades of the nineteenth century and the first half of the twentieth comprise the golden age of hydraulic engineering in the United States, when brilliant men seized an opportunity that comes along only once in a thousand years—to design and construct water systems for the growing cities of a budding new nation. States gave water companies unprecedented powers to seize private property in an effort to lock up vast watersheds for the future. Towns disappeared as residents surrendered their ancestral homelands to make way for reservoirs that would slake the thirst of far-off strangers. Still, as the remaining lands became more crowded, the prospects for future reservoirs evaporated.

Just as the story of water is a cycle, so too is my involvement in the subject. It begins with a simple fact: in 1960 the Metropolitan District Commission of Hartford completed its last reservoir in the northwestern hills of Connecticut—the Hogback—which impounded the waters of the West Branch of the Farmington River. As originally designed, the reservoir ensured a steady flow of water in the river, thereby satisfying the riparian rights of the mill owners downstream. Happily, by damming the West Branch, the water company inadvertently created one of the premier trout fishing streams of New England. Mayfly hatches along the river were abundant and the streambed easily wadable, but the river's principal charm for anglers was its dependable flow. Even in the parching days of August, when other streams dried up, the West Branch flowed mightily, shepherding four billion gallons of water a month past the mills along the river.

In the early 1970s, I went fly-fishing for the first time on the West Branch of the Farmington River and was, myself, hooked. The northwestern hills of Connecticut were an intoxicating place where, while waiting for a trout to rise, I watched beavers build dams and mallard ducks jet upstream only a few feet above the rising mist. Beyond these natural wonders, the soothing waters of the river endlessly massaged my body as six million gallons an hour rushed past me on its way to the sea. At that time, protozoans like *Giardia* and *Cryptosporidium* were generally unknown to the public so, to quench my thirst, I scooped up the pristine waters with my cupped hand and gulped it down hungrily. While lunching in the village of Riverton, locals told me of the water company's massive "land grab" in the 1930s and of the ghost towns at the bottom of the reservoirs.

I was mesmerized. The images haunted me and, while I fished, questions arose. Had the water company actually stolen hundreds of farms? What does it take to dismantle old New England towns? Who does one hire to move cemeteries? Eventually, I found the answers when I began to research and write about Hartford's water history. Thirty years after my first visit to the valley of the West Branch, I completed my own cycle as I returned to that fabulous trout stream to teach my godson, Patrick Keane, to fly fish.

The building years of the water works at Hartford spanned slightly more than a century, from 1854 to 1960, when its last reservoir was completed. In the early years, Hiram Bissell—a brick mason—and Ezra Clark—a steel merchant— nursed along the nascent water works but, over time, the city's explosive growth reduced their small, hand-dug reservoirs to useless, albeit charming, duck ponds. They were replaced by huge reservoirs built by the brilliant, driven chief engineer, Caleb Mills Saville, who expanded the water works beyond the wildest dreams of Bissell and Clark. However, the labors of these three men would stand in stark isolation without weaving into the story the complex social, economic and political fabric of Hartford, one of the greatest American manufacturing centers of the last two centuries. As with all good stories, each era led logically to the next until the tale crystallized as *Water for Hartford*

Introduction

Water. It's all around us, and we barely take notice. Of all our daily needs, inevitably we think of clean drinking water last. We inspect our clothing carefully and we worry about the condition of our homes and automobiles. At the same time, we are painstakingly aware of the nutritional value and freshness of our food and, should the cost of a head of lettuce go up by fifteen cents, we would gladly lead a boycott.

So why is water rarely in our thoughts? It's not as if we don't use much of it. A ten-minute shower in the morning uses twenty gallons. The dishwasher uses another twelve gallons each time it's run. The toilet is the biggest offender of all though. Every man, woman, and child in America flushes away twenty-seven gallons a day. Are you planning on driving through a car wash today? Don't ask.

The average person in the United States uses 156 gallons of water daily. In Sunbelt states, where people religiously water their lawns, the figure exceeds 200. The residents of Phoenix, Arizona each use a whopping 220 gallons daily. On a July day in 1998, the citizens of Dallas each consumed a record-breaking 372 gallons. In Florida, more than half of the treated drinking water is used for watering grass—at residences, businesses and, especially, golf courses.

There are, of course, scaremongers who don't miss an opportunity to tell us that we are running out of water. According to them, we are dangerously close to a time when either we will once again be forced to dip buckets in the nearest river or submit to some draconian form of rationing. Can that be? Are we running out of water? All the gold ever mined would fit in a twenty-yard cube, but what about water? Exactly how much is there? Better stated, how much will we be able to harvest and turn into the pure, healthful liquid that we all know so well?

The answer to these questions is both frightening and curiously optimistic. To begin with, only one percent of the water in the world is potable. Ninety-seven percent is seawater and the remaining two percent is frozen. Tell me...did the part about the one percent knot up your stomach a little?

Now for the optimistic side of the equation. There is just as much water on the face of the earth today as there was three billion years ago because water can become polluted but it cannot be destroyed. Perhaps we are so wasteful because we know that there are talented hydraulic engineers waiting patiently to rescue us from ourselves. America's history teaches us that, as a country, we can accomplish anything and providing good, clean drinking water will probably be no exception.

There are approximately 55,000 community water companies in the United States (serving 500 customers or more). In this huge collection of water utilities, the fifty largest metropolitan areas quite naturally boast the biggest water works and Hartford's Metropolitan District Commission is the thirty-ninth largest in the country. But this only tells part of the story. Based on a recent study, of the fifty largest water companies in the United States, the MDC ranks fifth for the quality of the water it produces and distributes. (Of note here also is that, of the fifty largest water works in the nation, the cost of the MDC's treated water falls smack in the middle of the pack; a little more than Richmond and Chicago and almost half the price charged in Norfolk and Seattle.)

One of the reasons for such an astonishingly good product is our state legislators. The Environmental Protection Agency classifies water sources as to quality. *Class A* supplies are those of impounded waters with protected watersheds. *Class B* sources are lakes and rivers to which the public has access—meaning that effluent can be, and is, introduced therein. Only two states in the country, by law, forbid the use of *Class B* sources for drinking water—Connecticut and Rhode Island.

A second, and more important, reason for the top quality drinking water that we enjoy in central Connecticut is the superb work of the hydraulic engineers, chemists, and other employees of the MDC. While the EPA requires tests for 111 pollutants and contaminants, the staff at the MDC routinely does 130 tests for everything from color and turbidity to protozoans, microbes and foreign elements of every description. It is stupefying to watch a whole generation of intelligent, but ill-informed, people pay outrageous prices for bottles of spring water that only undergo twenty-two tests for pollutants and contaminants, when tap water from the MDC is purer and more healthful by far. This is just one more example of people underestimating the superiority of Hartford's drinking water.

For simplicity's sake, the history of Hartford's water system—administered by the Hartford Water Works and the MDC (after 1929)—can be divided into two parts: the construction years and the refinement years. The second phase of the water company's life—a period of forty-five years—has been filled with estimable achievements. The MDC was one of the first municipal water companies in the country to use laser transits in surveying work and their GIS (geographic information system) stereo aerial mapping program is used by all the towns of the Metropolitan District to locate buildings, property lines, roads and other features of the urban and suburban landscape. Engineers at the MDC even devised a method of attaching lateral connections to 36" aqueducts without shutting down the system. In the early 1990s, a test boring project was conducted in South Glastonbury to locate additional sources of supply. By locating enough groundwater to add ten million gallons per day to the existing reserves, the future needs of Hartford and its surrounding towns have been assured for centuries to come. In addition to all this, the MDC now owns and operates two hydroelectric power facilities on the Farmington River—one at the Hogback Reservoir in Hartland and one at the Colebrook River Lake in Colebrook.

As one can see, the period from 1960 to the present has been a fruitful one for the MDC. Nevertheless, for reasons of my own, I have chosen to write about the construction years—from 1854 until 1960—when the massive reservoir projects were completed and the water system assumed the rough size and shape that it is today. Indeed since the MDC's final reservoir—the Hogback—was completed in 1960, no new catchments have been added to the system. Thanks to conservation, this is typical for water systems around the country. But it must also be understood that conservation springs not only from a newfound "waste not, want not" ethic, but from the almost insuperable hurdles associated with massive hydraulic engineering projects. One of the few reservoirs completed in the United States in the last few decades is Denver Water's tiny Strontia Springs project, finished in the mid-1980s. After a decade of red tape, lawsuits and environmental studies, Denver Water was finally able to build its new reservoir at a cost of more than $40 million. And how much water does it hold? The Strontia Springs Reservoir holds only 1.5% of Denver's total water supply.

With dazzling reservoir projects all but a thing of the past, the story of the Hartford Water Works and the Metropolitan District Commission's construction years is both informative and cautionary. It is unlikely that anything as grand as the nine-mile-long Barkhamsted Reservoir could ever be built today. Therefore, it is with a sense of nostalgia that we go back to a time when water from the Connecticut River was sweeter than anything from local wells, and a tiny pump on its banks was the state of the art in supply. Then, we travel to an era when small, feeble earthen dams and hand-grubbed reservoirs impounded enough water for a whole city. And lastly, we visit the golden age of hydraulic engineering when, after decades of intermittent water famines, Hartford's great reservoirs and aqueducts were built.

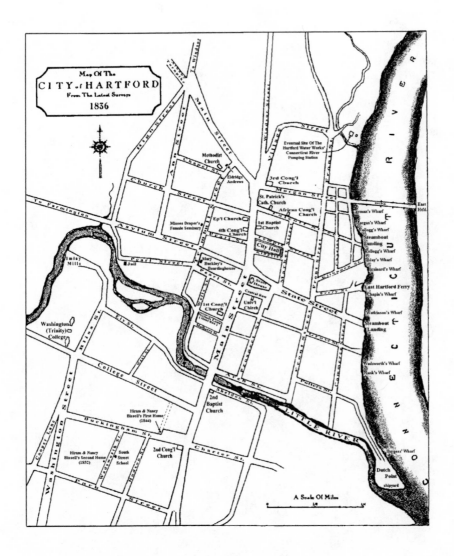

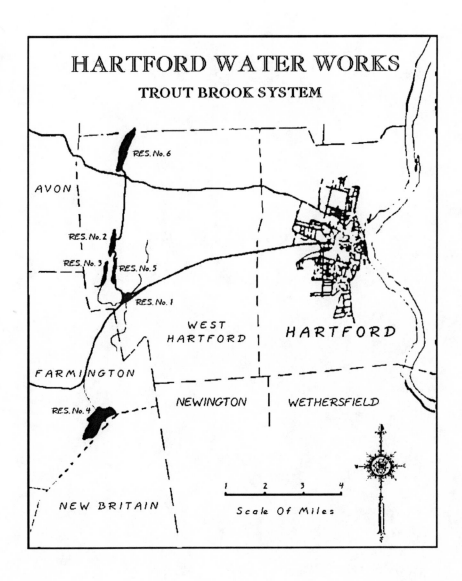

HARTFORD WATER WORKS

TROUT BROOK SYSTEM

RES. No. 6

AVON

RES. No. 2

RES. No. 3   RES. No. 5

RES. No. 1

WEST HARTFORD

HARTFORD

FARMINGTON

RES. No. 4

NEWINGTON   WETHERSFIELD

NEW BRITAIN

1   2   3   4

Scale Of Miles

WATER SYSTEM
Created By The
HARTFORD WATER WORKS
And The
METROPOLITAN DISTRICT COMMISSION

Chapter 1
The Muddling Years

In the spring of 1836, a seventeen-year-old farm boy, Hiram Bissell, arrived at the Port of Hartford to begin a four-year apprenticeship in the masonry business. Inasmuch as overland travel was difficult and the railroad had not yet reached the city, the Connecticut River was the all-important connection to the outside world. With passengers, cargo and news washing in and out on the great tidal currents, people never lost sight of this symbiosis. Thus, from steamboat pilots to the denizens of the small river towns up and down the lush valley, the rapidly expanding city on the western bank of the river was, quite naturally, referred to as the Port of Hartford.

Bissell was a wiry young man, about five-nine or five-ten in height, and the oldest of six children born to Chester and Prudence Bissell, who farmed a ten-acre parcel in a remote section of South Glastonbury known colloquially as Shingle Hollow. This tiny corner of the town—snug against the eastern shore of the Connecticut River and six miles south of the Port of Hartford—was named for a sideline business of Bissell's grandfather, William Tryon. In addition to farming, Tryon harvested the large cedar trees that thrived in the gravely soil of the surrounding hills by cutting their trunks into two-foot bolts with a whipsaw and expertly splitting off shingles with a long-handled froe and wooden mallet.

Bissell's father, Chester, was originally from East Windsor but settled in Shingle Hollow after marrying Prudence Tryon, one of six children herself. Her father had a fondness for Chester Bissell and helped him—in the early 1820s—to build a small house in the hollow. The "Bissell place"—as it was referred to on deeds extending far into the twentieth century—was a bare bones, two story affair with a total of four rooms. Resting on a stone foundation, the wooden structure measured just sixteen by twenty-eight feet, and had a lone fireplace on the first floor to supply heat in winter. A crudely built shed affixed to the back of the dwelling sheltered the family's two milking cows.

The Bissells pushed this undersized house to the limits. Not long after William Tryon's death in 1825, Prudence's mother came to live with them. By 1833, when the Bissell's last child, Sylvester, was born, there were nine people shoehorned into this little matchbox. Confronted with such a crush of humanity, the idea that the older children might strike out on their own when they reached their majority could not have been far from the thoughts of Chester and Prudence Bissell.

When Hiram finished high school, he had some decisions to make. The overcrowded situation at home dictated that he waste no time making his way in the world. With just a high school education though, his choices were limited—continue farming or learn a trade. Bissell chose the latter. Blessed with an unfailing practicality and an enviable capacity for hard work, he undoubtedly would have done well no matter which course he had chosen, but farming meant land, which he could ill afford. That left the trades and a move to the Port of Hartford where, in an effort to eliminate disastrous, sweeping conflagrations, the state legislature had mandated at the beginning of the nineteenth century that only brick and stone buildings could be erected.

For a smart young man like Hiram Bissell, the move out of Shingle Hollow was a blessing in disguise. The Tryons of South Glastonbury were as ubiquitous as cow flaps in that little corner of Connecticut, and even "a forceful character" like Hiram might have gotten lost in the shuffle. People who knew Bissell described him as a man "whose advise was sought and whose opinions were respected." For such a young man, charting his own course, as time would eventually confirm, was the wiser choice.

Finding a position as a mason's apprentice had not been difficult. Two of Hartford's five masonry contractors were from South Glastonbury and one of the men, Eldridge Andrews, was the city's largest building contractor. Owing to Andrews's penchant for paying low wages, he was always in need of new hands. Seeking to bridge this never-ending gap in his labor force, he hired Bissell for a four-year apprenticeship.

In 1836, there were a little over 11,000 people living in the Port of Hartford but, compared to Glastonbury, it was a bustling colossus. The city proper was a mere three-quarters of a mile square, with the bulk of the townspeople living on the gently sloping, quarter mile strip of land between Main Street and the Connecticut River. Since deep water schooners and brigs could navigate no farther north, the Port of Hartford became a prosperous commercial center, carrying on a lucrative trading business with every major American seaport as well as those in Europe, Africa, and the West Indies.

Initially, the port was clogged with sailing ships of every description. Many of these ships were built in towns along the Connecticut River, including a few from shipyards along the banks of the river in Hartford, but by 1836 steamers were fast replacing the older vessels. For almost a quarter of a century—beginning in 1815—steamboats enjoyed a unique monopoly. They were the most comfortable form of travel over long distances and moved passengers, raw materials and finished goods to other eastern seaports and foreign cities alike. Monopolies, however, have always been the incubators of competition and, over the powerful objections of the stagecoach and steamboat interests, the railroad came to Hartford in 1839. A decade later, the Hartford & New Haven Railroad connected to New York, enabling passengers and freight to reach all points east of the Mississippi River.

Bissell's arrival in the city could not have been better timed, for America was undergoing huge changes which would eventually play into his hands as a mason and builder. Small mills, run by waterpower and tucked in the hollows of rural Connecticut, were giving way to enormous manufactories powered by steam boilers, which would catapult production to levels never before imagined. These powerful, new steam boilers—sometimes given to catastrophic explosions because of a lack of relief valves—enabled small businesses to grow at unprecedented rates, allowing Hartford to blossom from a small backwater port into a highly efficient and productive commercial center.

One can imagine the mesmerizing effect that this bustling river port had on a farm boy from rural Shingle Hollow. At the river, more than twenty wharfs spread out like splayed fingers from the shores of the Connecticut River where thirty warehouses, owned by the city's largest merchants, were spaced out neatly along a quarter mile of the riverfront. Almost two thousand steamboats a year stopped at the Port of Hartford, creating a waterfront that roiled with seamen, dockhands, teamsters, traders, agents and travelers of every sort. While Hussar sailors tended their vessels, and white and free black dockhands offloaded cargo, passengers from every conceivable home port disembarked along the busy wharfs. The only two impediments to this fabulous trade were the prohibition against sailing on the Sabbath and the cold weather. In winter, the river froze or gathered enough floating chunks of ice to endanger vessels. As the *Connecticut Courant* reported in December 1836—

> . . .The river became completely filled with ice on Thursday night and it was with difficulty that...the schooner *Pacific* [reached this city] yesterday afternoon. The river is full of floating ice so that no vessels can move . . .

Just north of the wharfs was a covered toll bridge, about a fifth of a mile long, connecting the city with the farming enclave of East Hartford on the opposite bank of the river. Though there were dozens of ferries servicing smaller towns along the 410-mile length of the Connecticut River—from northern New Hampshire to Long Island Sound—this weather-beaten structure was one of only two public bridges across the river in the state. The Hartford Bridge sat atop six cut stone piers, the enormous pile of lumber sagging under the weight of heavily laden wagons and the sheer heft of its own timbers. Pedestrians crossed for a few cents, while a wagon pulled by a double team paid about fourteen cents and stagecoaches about twice as much. Inside, there were two roadways and a sidewalk for those on foot, the structure lighted with oil lamps every twenty feet. The sides of the bridge were partially open, allowing the river breezes to whip away the road dust and malodorous scent of horse droppings that collected inside the dank, cavernous expanse. A woman recalled taking the trip across the river in her youth and summed up the passage as "slow and tedious."

In the center of the city was the massive State House, completed in 1796, where Connecticut's General Assembly met every other year. Since the state government had yet to choose a single capital city—and would not for another four decades—the legislature assembled at the Port of Hartford only in the odd numbered years; the remainder of the time, they met in New Haven. The state house was a Federal style building overlooking the warehouses, wharfs and river. Serving as the centerpiece of a large, triangular yard that was surrounded by a black cast iron fence, it was bounded by Main Street on the west and Central Row on the south. Running along the north side—from Main Street to the river—was State Street, the widest and busiest commercial boulevard in the city. Collectively, the whole area was known as State House Square.

About a third of the way from Main Street to the river, Market Street jutted north from State Street. Filled with oxen, horses, carts and wagons, Market Street was a clamorous and exciting place, much like the waterfront. It was here that the endless din of deal making filled the air, as buyers and sellers met to haggle and dicker. Whether it was at the City Hall Market—located in the basement of City Hall, one block north of the state house—or in the open air of Market Street itself, restaurateurs, grocers, hotel agents and merchants set the price of every bushel of beans, pound of beef on the hoof, and keg of nails.

Taking up a large section of State Street on the north side of this square was the United States Hotel, which was the home-away-from-home for visiting legislators. Besides these lawmakers, out-of-town purchasing agents relaxed there as well, waiting for steamers, clients or other merchants to arrive. The cheapest room was a dollar a night. For the less well-heeled, there were two dozen other hotels and public houses nearby. Food and drink were readily available at a wide variety of older taverns and newly established restaurants, which met the needs of every purse and palate. A signature springtime meal was American shad, caught by the proprietors of small fishing businesses up and down the Connecticut River and served for twenty-five cents a plate, half the cost of beef or mutton.

While the open markets were an important point of exchange, the most prosperous merchants also had shops in State House Square. Their signs shocked the senses with their garish lettering and shameless boasts. Absent zoning laws, almost every square inch of wood, brick and stone carried advertisements trumpeting their goods and services. Merchants kept their shops open from sunrise until ten o'clock at night, slipping out for a quick dinner at noon and a similar repast in the evening. Trusted clerks managed the shops in their absences. With the whistle of riverboats, the shouts of dockworkers and the low din of shopkeepers, legislators, middlemen, jobbers and shoppers, State House Square was a kaleidoscope of noise and commotion. Hired hands herded cattle through the streets while stray dogs roamed freely and, tethered to posts around the expansive lawn of the state house were the horses, wagons and carriages of farmers and townspeople, all transacting business nearby. For most of the year, this constantly moving mélange of animals, people, carts, wagons and carriages kicked up a cloud of fine dust that settled on buildings, store awnings, stone walkways and the swirling mob of passersby with equal abandon.

The Aetna and Hartford Fire Insurance companies had erected impressive buildings in the square alongside the large brownstones of the Hartford Bank and the Exchange Bank. At street level were the shops of dealers in groceries, pastries, cast iron stoves, paints, dye stuffs, sperm oil, books, machinery, patent drugs, cigars and snuff. Housed on the upper floors of these buildings were the offices of an almost unending parade of attorneys, physicians, dentists, publishers, stationers, jewelers and bootmakers. Not to be forgotten in the profusion of rented space were brokers of real estate, lotteries, stocks and common exchange bonds.

Wedged in awkwardly on the south side of the square—and looking like Daniel in the lion's den—was the Universalist Church. Eerily quiet, this elegant, white clapboard structure with a large, open belfry astraddle its ridgepole had been built long before mammon ruled the square, when the town fathers envisioned a community where spirituality might be the handmaiden of business. The church, with its steeple towering above most other buildings in the crowded square, seemed to dominate when, in fact, it was resolutely ignored amidst the crush of commerce.

At the northwest corner of State House Square, there was a public well that supplied water to parched visitors and legislators (children called it "one-armed Billy"). Unlike Boston, New York, Philadelphia and Baltimore, all of which installed municipal pumps on street corners throughout their cities, the Port of Hartford settled for this one pump in State House Square and a couple of smaller ones along Main Street. Alternative to this facility, a thirsty shopper or traveler could ask permission to use a private well at a residence on a side street or drink freely from the waters of the Connecticut River.

The hurly-burly atmosphere and the jostle of crowds were only two of the many differences between the city and the country to which Bissell would have to adjust. His first lodging was at the boardinghouse of a widow, Mary Buckley, who lived on Trumbull Street. His employer, Eldridge Andrews, probably facilitated this arrangement, for he lived a little to the north, on the same lane. Mary Buckley's home was a tumbledown affair that housed herself, her three daughters and eight tradesmen, including Bissell. Also lodging at the same boarding house was another of Andrews' South Glastonbury apprentices and Bissell's cousin, Henry Tryon. (Since Bissell and Tryon were of the same age and from the same town, it is entirely possible that they started in the masonry trade together, although this is only conjecture. Nevertheless, it does suggest that Bissell was not completely alone and adrift in the Port of Hartford.)

Typically, room and board arrangements at the time entitled a roomer to a single bed in a shared room, a light breakfast, and a plate of simple food at suppertime, usually stew. Quite naturally, accommodations also included the use of a privy at the back of the property and water for washing and drinking—hand pumped to the kitchen from a shallow well near the house. Baths were taken at facilities like Mr. Hartshorne's warm shower baths in the western part of the city.

In fairness, Bissell's lodging arrangements with Mary Buckley were deluxe compared to the dismal tenements that most unskilled workers inhabited. Crammed together amidst the tanneries, dye works and slaughterhouses along the north bank of the Little River—a filthy tributary of the Connecticut that meandered easterly through the city—they were dingy, overcrowded and oppressive places. Bissell's new neighborhood was a cut above that. However, the cost of his room and board took every cent of his pay, forcing him to adapt to an extremely constricted social life while he learned his trade. His spare time though was not completely wasted. All the while, he soaked up the warp and weft of the city, particularly the business and municipal affairs of his newfound home.

Trumbull Street—named after Connecticut's Revolutionary governor, Jonathan Trumbull—was one block to the west of Main Street. It ran parallel to it until, in its upper reaches, it swung to the east and connected with Main, a stone's throw north of State House Square. Trumbull was like all of the residential streets of Hartford in that private homes were interspersed with small shops and businesses. Neighborhoods were, by turns, fashionable, then undesirable, only to revert back a few decades later. Some streets had reputations that defied change, like Nichols Lane—called Hotel Row—the city's notorious red light district, where dingy rooms rented for ten cents a night, and Ferry Street, teeming with unsavory "flag taverns" or sailors' haunts. These streets, however, were the exception. Flux was the order of the day, and that was Trumbull Street's lot now. There were other builders and tradesmen on Trumbull Street besides Bissell's employer and his fellow boarders, but mostly the residents were white-collar workers. Printers, tailors, jewelers, grocers and ministers made their homes on the lane, but also there were the shops of bonnet makers, joiners and rule makers. Halfway along the quarter-mile street, Miss Draper prepared young women for life in the top echelons of society at her Female Seminary, insisting that her students speak only French during the school day.

While he learned the masonry trade, Bissell's pay was abysmal, a situation compounded by the seasonal nature of the work. In the first year, he was hired to work from early spring until the work petered out in December, forcing him to find some other way to support himself during the winter months. For the whole first season, he received just $25. The second, third and fourth years were not much better, paying $30, $35 and $40, respectively. Since Bissell was a quick study, after his first year in the business, he had learned enough about masonry and plaster work to do small side jobs when the weather permitted. With this added income, he scraped by.

As a mason's apprentice, Bissell worked like a pack mule on building sites—twelve hours a day, six days a week. Starting out as an unskilled hod carrier, he mixed mortar and toted bricks for the master masons. Given his arduous work schedule, there was precious little free time for him to enjoy the excitement of State House Square.

One aspect of city life decidedly different from the long, quiet nights of Shingle Hollow were the nocturnal fire alarms, signaled by the clang of the bell atop the statehouse. More appalling still was the gross inefficiency of firefighting. Many times Bissell, along with the other men (and women) in the neighborhood, dragged themselves out of bed in the middle of the night and raced to a blaze, only to spend hours sloshing two gallons of water at a time on a blistering and out of control inferno. Other nights, he darted to the scene—half dressed and still half asleep—to discover that it was merely a false alarm.

By 1836, Hartford had been fighting fires for two centuries the same way that larger cities did—with leather buckets and axes. But getting water to the fire was the most pressing problem of all. Hartford had acquired a small, unadorned pump on wheels, which sucked water from an elaborate collection of cisterns beneath the streets. By 1836, there were about fifteen of these brick and mortar cisterns each storing 25,000 gallons of rainwater. They were recharged by the storm water runoff from nearby roofs. Still in all, they were hopelessly inefficient. After a major conflagration, the catchments closest to the blaze were left bone dry and remained that way until the next rainstorm. As a last resort, water was pumped from the river, although this was really only practicable when the blaze was near the wharfs.

Dividing the city into ten wards, patrolling fire wardens inspected chimneys, stoves and other problem areas. As one of their many duties, these wardens made lists of all the male inhabitants between the ages of fifteen and sixty, each of whom was expected to respond to alarms with a leather bucket in hand or face a fine. Penalties for citizens found in non-compliance with the fire ordinances or outright negligence were severe. The fine for neglecting to keep the requisite number of brimming fire buckets in a home was fifty cents. A dirty chimney was one dollar—the same penalty for a fireman missing an alarm. The value that the city placed on its new pump was amply demonstrated by the fine imposed for its misuse—twenty dollars (about the cost of an acre of farmland).

A conflagration erupted on Trumbull Street in the evening hours just before Christmas in 1836. Bissell had just finished his first season as a mason's apprentice and was casting about for winter work. Fires were so commonplace that the *Connecticut Courant* did not report the blaze for a whole week—

> Fire. About half past nine o'clock on Saturday night last, our citizens were alarmed by the cry of fire. It proceeded from…a frame building on the corner of Main and Trumbull Streets, occupied by Mrs. King as a dwelling and improved in the front as a market and victualizing house [restaurant]. The building was old and the fire raged

with... violence... Mrs. King, we understand, lost everything she had in the house . . .

The firemen submerged the ends of their leather hoses into cisterns under the streets and were able to play enough water on the structure to contain the blaze and save the neighboring buildings. While the city's residents struggled with these cisterns, they knew that there was a better way. Just 100 miles to the northeast, Boston had solved the two-headed problem of supplying water for firefighting and drinking purposes by allowing Abijah Wilder and Luther Eames—two entrepreneurs from Keene, New Hampshire—to build the Jamaica Pond Aqueduct, back in 1795. The ability of an aqueduct to recharge Hartford's cisterns could not possibly have been lost on the city's firefighters and denizens alike.

For drinking water, Hartford's residents relied on private wells—like the one at Mary Buckley's boardinghouse—or the river. Unfortunately, both the Connecticut River and the private wells were fickle sources. The typical well of the time was only about ten feet deep and the wells in the center and northern sections of the city delivered a barely potable liquid that had an acrid, sulfuric taste. These same wells were routinely fouled when the river swelled its banks, especially during the spring freshet, but also during periods of unusually severe rainstorms and the occasional hurricane. At such times, the water in the river became muddied with silt and debris swept from its banks. Absent their usual source, people bought water from grimy tank wagons that trundled up and down the streets selling their product either by the pail or the hogshead.

**

In spite of these rather primitive sources, Hartford was not without its own history when it came to piped water systems, for before Hiram Bissell's arrival at the Port of Hartford, there had been three separate attempts to build aqueduct companies. Though each effort sought to exploit a different source and each attacked the problem from a slightly different angle, the results were the same— all three were underfunded, unqualified disasters.

The first attempt came fourteen years after the end of the American Revolution, in 1797, when Hartford was just a small settlement of 5,000 people. The city's many newspapers published skimpy, four-page editions only a couple of times a week—and news lagged actual events sometimes by weeks. But the postal service kept the newspapers supplied with information from around the world. Consequently, the small population was reasonably well informed. In addition to Boston's great success with its Jamaica Pond Aqueduct, people knew that New York had been laying wooden pipes beneath its streets since before the American Revolution. They also knew of Philadelphia's illustrious, city-owned Central Square Water Works and Baltimore's privately-owned water company.

In theory, with the requisite effort, the accomplishments of these larger cities could be replicated in Hartford and at a tiny fraction of the cost.

The genesis of the first water effort in Hartford was in the two decades before 1800, when Elisha and Dolly Babcock pieced together a 100-acre farm on the north side of Park Street (near Lafayette Street) which included an astonishingly robust well. The origin of this spectacular source was described by a visitor to Hartford in 1781 as—

> . . .a most wonderful well...near seventy feet, without the least appearance of water, the laborers met with a large rock. [O]n the miners boring this rock...to blast it with powder, they drove the auger through it [and] the water sprouted up with such amazing velocity that...they could hardly keep the well dry until it was stoned . . .

With the help of the couple's four children, Dolly ran the farm, while Elisha printed the *American Mercury*, one of Hartford many newspapers. Considering the poor taste of the well water in the wealthier section of town by the river, the purity of the supply from the Babcock's farm was enviable. The well delivered such copious amounts of delicious, pure spring water that it achieved a mythic status, and was later referred to as the "famous well on the Dolly Babcock farm on Park Street."

Sensing that the water could be sold to the families by the river, Elisha Babcock teamed up with another wealthy Federalist businessman, William Hull, to build an aqueduct company. Accommodating the pair, the state legislature passed an act incorporating the Proprietors of the Hartford Aqueduct, which allowed the company a total capitalization of $20,000 divided over 100 individual shares. Since each share represented the purchase price of a respectable farm, the venture was clearly not for the common man. Rather, it was a private water company designed to further enrich Babcock, Hull, and a tight circle of wealthy Federalist friends.

To further their plan, the entrepreneurs hired a Vermonter, Nahum Cutler, to do the physical work of bedding the "pine logs with 2 ½ inch bores." When the aqueduct was completed, "about two hundred persons used the water for a number of years," but they used it mainly for drinking purposes because the supply was insufficient for more widespread use. Though the spring on the farm of David Clark—in the southern part of the city near Cedar Hill—was secured as an additional source of supply, the system eventually fell into disuse. This slow dissolution of the aqueduct company vexed many of the shareholders who were required to pay an annual tax of twelve dollars on each of their shares. One by one, the participants let their shares slip into default.

All the same, the idea of building an aqueduct company had staying power. As The Proprietors of the Hartford Aqueduct struggled, another pair of businessmen caught the bug. Chauncey Gleason and Elias Cowles were partners in a Hartford dry goods business, but were flexible enough to buy and sell horses, oxen and cows, if there were a profit to be made. In late 1801, they received permission from the legislature to build a water works, and the Gleason and Cowles Aqueduct Company was born. In November, the company ran the following advertisement in *The Connecticut Courant*—

A CONTRACT

The subscribers...being about to conduct water into...Hartford, by means of subterraneous [sic] pipes, from the mountain lying . . . five miles to the west . . .wish to contract...the necessary work . . .The contract . . .must be completed this fall, and the work should be begun very soon.

The following spring, the Gleason and Cowles Aqueduct Company began to lay wooden pipes near Talcott Mountain in the far western part of the city (present day West Hartford), where they would collect the pristine waters of Trout Brook. Almost from the beginning though, the star-crossed pair ran into trouble. The nub of the problem was Section 7 of their incorporation papers, which addressed the method of bedding pipes across private property. According to the 1801 bill, before Gleason and Cowles could bed such pipes, the County Court had to examine the land and assess the damages accruing to the property owner—a time-consuming process. Compounding the problem was the number of farms involved. To lay pipes five or six miles would have required a blizzard of paperwork. Moreover, if a farmer disagreed with the final damage assessment, a quick trip to the courthouse would shut down the aqueduct project indefinitely.

After suffering under the onus of Section 7 for more than a year, Chauncey Gleason sought recourse. He went back to the General Assembly and asked that the aqueduct company be given some relief from the constrictions of Section 7. The legislature obliged. Thereafter, three independent parties would assess all of the damages at one time and deliver their findings to the County Court, introducing uniformity to the settlements with the landowners. Unhappily for Gleason and Cowles, the General Assembly's May ruling came too late to save their aqueduct company. By June of 1803, the two partners threw in the towel, filing the following notice in the *Connecticut Courant*—

. . .all connection in trade between Chauncey Gleason and Elias Cowles, by the name and firm of Gleason and Cowles is by mutual consent, on the 12th instant [June 12th] dissolved . . .

The Gleason and Cowles Aqueduct Company had laid some pipes but, in the end, was stymied by a few recalcitrant farmers. The two men deserved some credit though. They may have underestimated the mulishness of the local property owners, but had shown remarkable perspicuity in their choice of a water source, for Trout Brook's waters were as pure as any in the state.

The third and final effort to bring piped water into the city before the middle of the nineteenth century did not materialize until May 1830. Two men from Massachusetts—Archippus Morgan of Springfield and Isaac Damon of Northampton—incorporated a new enterprise under the familiar sounding name of The Hartford Aqueduct Company. (Damon was not new to Hartford for, in 1818, he and another man rebuilt the covered bridge across the Connecticut River after it was destroyed by an unusually high spring freshet.)

Acutely aware of the problems of their predecessors, Damon and Morgan steered clear of the farmlands to the west and tried to tap a previously ignored series of ponds in the south end of the city. Atop Cedar Hill were three interconnected ponds, which were recharged by a small watershed to the west. There was good reason for this source to have been disregarded; it was obviously not large enough to meet the needs of a growing city. Damon and Morgan, however, viewed the three ponds on Cedar Hill as only the first of many sources that they would exploit for their water system. At completion, their system was to have different sources of supply for different sections of the city. Unfortunately, either because of a shortage of capital or the inability to arrive at agreements with the owners of the existing water sources, the would-be aqueduct never materialized. Evidence that the Hartford Aqueduct Company ever laid a single pipe simply does not exist.

The earliest water supply efforts in America were hamstrung by a crippling shortage of durable building materials. Cast iron pipes eventually supplanted the early wooden aqueducts, but not until large and efficient foundries were built in the early 1800s in and around Philadelphia. In the late eighteenth and early part of the nineteenth centuries, all American cities built their water works using wooden log conduits.

The original method of fabricating wooden pipes entailed boring out the center of logs that were anywhere from twelve to twenty feet in length, and then charring these ducts using torches. The scorching process was necessary because when the wet wood was bored, it left a ragged hole with a superfluity of burrs. To make certain that these burrs did not clog the lateral junctions, stopcocks and petcocks of the system, they were burned off. Additionally, the logs were not simply laid end-to-end but instead were either milled or cut by hand so that they had working *male* and *female* ends, as do modern concrete and cast iron pipes. The wooden pipe joints were either sealed with clay or pitch, clamped with iron bands or both.

As an etymological curiosity, the term *waterlogged* became part of the vernacular around 1770, when all of this log conduit activity began in America, and it highlighted an interesting truth. By keeping these wooden transmission pipes in constant use, the logs became gorged with water—or waterlogged— creating an anaerobic environment. Under such conditions, the water itself helped to preserve the pipes. With the problem of rot more or less conquered, the early builders of water works were left with one insoluble dilemma—leaky joints.

Laborers bedding wooden log pipes on Main Street, Hartford.

***

Due to the unlimited supply of astonishingly potable water from the Connecticut River—and the less palatable product lifted from their own private wells—until the early 1840s the residents of Hartford were not overly exercised about the failure of entrepreneurs to build water systems. From a competitive standpoint, the deficiency raised no serious issues for the average manufacturer or citizen. True, the larger—and better-capitalized—cities like Boston, New York, Philadelphia and Baltimore had more-or-less reliable water works in place by the first part of the nineteenth century, but the business of supplying water was novel enough that smaller cities were not held to the same standard. For the moment, this shortcoming did not reflect badly on the city. However, in 1842 when the engineer John Jervis finished the Croton Aqueduct and delivered fabulous amounts of clean drinking water into New York, suddenly Hartford's little shortcoming looked glaring. Businessmen and elected officials could sense that the city would quickly lose ground to other manufacturing centers and the matter became more irksome as time passed.

For four years, Hiram Bissell learned the masonry business inside out—brickwork, plastering, stuccoing, lathing, as well as the fabrication of fancy plaster ceiling centerpieces, moldings and cornices. Few of Eldridge Andrews's apprentices could afford to stay with him after they became master masons because he refused to compensate them fairly. Hiram Bissell was no exception. He went off on his own just as soon as the warm weather arrived in 1840. The great problem of working alone was that it limited him to smaller jobs, which ran counter to his plans. The bigger projects—erecting buildings for banks and insurance companies—were the most lucrative jobs and it was his intention to funnel his efforts in that direction.

In an attempt to expand his business, Bissell formed a partnership with his cousin, Henry Tryon. Unfortunately, as business partners, the two did not get along. The crux of the problem may well have rested with the leadership role within the partnership. With two ambitious men in their early twenties, each may have assumed that he would be first among equals, so to speak. However, Hiram Bissell was not one to accept a supporting role and the pair parted company after only a year.

Soured on partnerships, Bissell decided once again to go it alone, this time with more success. His business grew and it was not long before he was running a large crew of his own. Soon, he realized that laying bricks was an inefficient use of his time. With his brains, he could keep a dozen masons busy while he spent his day managing the company, bidding jobs and looking for other opportunities. It was not long before his days of handling bricks and mortar were over.

The confines of apprenticeship had kept Bissell's world small, but now that he was running his own firm, life opened up for him. Traveling about the city, meeting with potential customers and making new friends, it was natural that his thoughts would turn toward young ladies. Though the exact circumstances are lost to history, it was during this period that he met and fell in love with a young woman who worshipped at the Universalist Church in State House Square. Her name was Nancy Sheldon. The couple had similar backgrounds inasmuch as both had grown up on farms and neither was accustomed to much more than the necessities of life. Nancy Sheldon's father, Samuel, had been a farmer in the north end of Hartford until his premature death in 1836—the same year that Bissell arrived in the city. Her mother—also named Nancy—tried to continue farming, but it proved too much for her. Two years after her husband's death, for a token amount she sold the farm to her son, Richard, and together with her two daughters, Nancy and Sally, moved into rented rooms on Buckingham Street, five blocks south of State House Square.

In 1843, Bissell and his fiancée began to look for a place to build a home. Hartford had an enormous amount of buildable acreage, considering that the city proper was less than a mile square and around its periphery was nothing but farmland. A young couple could almost always secure a small building lot. Even within the built up sections of the city were smaller lots as indicated by this advertisement in the *Daily Times*—

Building Lots For Sale

Six fine building lots on Asylum Street, corner of High street... The proximity of these lots to the State House and the center of business, makes them desirable for manufacturing purposes or for dwellings . . . A small part (say 10 percent) of the purchase money to be paid on delivery of the deed. The remainder may remain on mortgage for 5, 10, or 15 years. Inquire of E.W. Bull.

Despite opportunities all around them, Bissell's mother-in-law proved to be the deciding consideration, for she needed her daughter nearby. Since Nancy's mother, in due course, moved in with the Bissells, it is most likely that they considered this eventuality from the start. In any event, the young couple concentrated their search in the Buckingham Street area.

Diagonally across from the building where the widow Sheldon and her daughters rented rooms, an unusual building lot came on the market. It had only fifty feet of frontage on Buckingham Street, but ran all the way to College Street—a distance of over four hundred feet. It was, in effect, one long bacon strip of land. For the young mason though, it was perfect. Behind a new house, he could erect an oversized outbuilding to house his buckboards, horses, scaffolding and other masonry tools. Later, the land at the back of the property— which fronted College Street—could be sold as a separate building lot or improved by Bissell himself.

For the soon-to-be Nancy Bissell, it was also ideal. It put her within earshot of her mother, walking distance of the shops in the center of the city and offered a warm southern exposure. The front parlors would be bathed in brilliant sunlight all day long. Paying $700 for the land, Bissell began construction on a house shortly thereafter. In six months time, the couple had a striking new home. Constructed of red brick, it was a fashionable three-story Italianate, its windows, doors, and eaves trimmed with ornate wooden moldings.

On July 28, 1844—and with the Reverend John Moore officiating—Hiram Bissell married Nancy Sheldon in a simple ceremony at the Universalist Church. On the Sunday afternoon of their nuptials, the bride and groom were both twenty-five years old.

By the early 1850s, the city had expanded to the point where people no longer referred to it as the Port of Hartford. Now called simply Hartford, the buzzing city was a fast-growing commercial Mecca where manufacturers and inventors were welcomed with outstretched arms. The railroad now connected Hartford to almost every city east of the Mississippi River, insuring the unimpeded flow of raw materials and the rapid and safe shipment of finished goods to a vast network of eager markets. In fact, the city's growth was powerful enough to result in a crippling shortage of tenement housing. Manufacturers were at their wits' end trying to find housing for their workers who, without lodging for their families, could not accept employment in the city. So desperate were these proprietors that they offered to guarantee the rents with their own bonds. As workers flocked to the city, they badly strained support services, including the water supply. Wells dug near the tenements delivered a product that was barely potable and gathering water at the Connecticut River became increasingly problematic as tenements sprung up farther and farther from that source.

Hiram Bissell

Increasingly it nagged at community leaders that the great manufacturing advantages that the city had amassed up to 1850 were significant but not self-perpetuating. Such advantages were maintained with great vigilance and careful planning. Characteristic of that planning were a host of amenities including passable roads, clean sidewalks, safe neighborhoods and good schools. The one final ingredient that would ensure growth was a reliable water system which, of course, Hartford did not have.

Bissell's masonry business, at mid-century was small compared to, say, Colt's Patent Fire-Arms, which used water at an astounding rate to power boilers, produce heat in the wintertime, fight fires and

to meet the drinking and sanitary needs of its outsized workforce. Nevertheless, Hiram Bissell needed an abundant source of clean water every bit as much as any of the city's larger manufacturers. His water needs ran along two separate, yet interconnected, lines. First, as a builder of homes, commercial buildings and factories, there would be no new business for him if Hartford were bypassed by inventors and manufacturers, like Samuel Colt, in favor of cities with an efficient water works in place. Secondly, and on a more elemental basis, Bissell's masonry business required large quantities of water for mixing mortar, washing brick and slaking the thirst of his workers. During a construction project, his masons relied on buckboards to ferry large, oaken barrels of water from the river to the building site. A three or four story brick building required as much as twenty thousand gallons of water during the course of construction. Buying water from the watermen trundling through the streets with their tank wagons was prohibitively expensive. A family could afford this but, in the quantities that a construction crew required, it was out of the question.

As it turned out, Bissell and Colt became good friends. Both were active in Democratic politics and the masonry contractor did a substantial amount of construction work for Colt over the years including the brickwork on his huge armory, built in 1855, and the stucco and plaster work on the inventor's home—*Armsmear*—completed two years later. Bissell even acted as a straw man to help Colt assemble the necessary acreage for his massive armory.

Located midway between New York and Boston, these two cities were Hartford's touchstones, stoking the embers of competition despite the obvious dissimilarities—particularly size. When the Croton Aqueduct was completed in 1842, it stood alone in the United States in sheer scope and size—for exactly six years. By 1848, the engineer Ellis Chesbrough finished the Cochituate Aqueduct, giving Boston its own marvel of hydraulic engineering—though, of course, somewhat smaller. Under Chesbrough's direction, the waters of Long Pond—renamed Lake Cochituate—were delivered to the rapidly multiplying masses of Boston. When the impact of Chesbrough's accomplishment registered with Hartford's populace, it was like a shot across the bow of a frigate.

From that point forward, businessmen badgered the common council for a solution to the water impasse. Oddly enough, one of the biggest impediments to progress in the matter was the council itself. Composed almost entirely of Whigs—who viewed an aqueduct company as just another mercantile enterprise—they were not anxious to commit the city to such a venture. In their minds, the sooner a group of Whigs laid claim to the water franchise, the better.

Residents of Hartford, who traveled to distant cities, wrote to the local newspapers with their observations on the drinking water systems they encountered. This was especially true of the Cochituate and Croton Reservoirs and Aqueducts. More technically minded readers offered informed opinions as to the quality of the water in the two reservoirs. One resident even made reference to the poor taste of the water as it flowed *into* the Croton Reservoir, which would have entailed a grueling hike to the nexus of the Croton River and the reservoir itself. Hardly a week went by without some mention of the water question in the *Courant* and the *Times*.

Clearly the water issue was firmly on the front burner, but there was still a hard-to-define reluctance to fire up the stove. Some less-informed residents even ventured the opinion that water systems were for bigger cities—Boston, New York and Philadelphia—but not Hartford. This, in spite of the fact that the first community water works in the United States—completed in 1754—served the tiny Moravian community of Bethlehem, Pennsylvania and, when another small group of Moravians moved to Salem, North Carolina, they had an aqueduct system in place by 1772.

In the end, it was the specter of yet another privately-owned, for-profit water monopoly that energized the people of Hartford.

Chapter 2
The Breakthrough

Hartford might never have been settled in the first place had it not been for a falling out on religious principles between a pastor in Cambridge and his superior in the Boston church. The head of the church, Rev. John Cotton was unbending in his belief that faith came before good works. Rev. Thomas Hooker, the pastor in Newtown (Cambridge) felt otherwise.

It has often been said that reasonable men can disagree, and so it was in this case, for both Cotton and Hooker were men of excellent character and possessed of outstanding leadership ability, but their disagreement drove a wedge between them. After the predictable grousing, in 1634 the Massachusetts General Court granted Thomas Hooker and his congregation in Newtown permission "to seeke [sic] out some convenient place." Finding nothing suitable in the Bay Colony, the small congregation turned its sights toward the Connecticut River Valley. At the point where the Little River emptied into the Connecticut River, Hooker and his followers found a place that looked promising.

The area was not completely untrodden. The local—and friendly—Sukiaug Indians had been living in the area for decades and Adriaen Block, the Dutch explorer, had navigated the Connecticut River in 1614. Moreover, shortly before Hooker and his followers decided to settle in the area, the Dutch had established a trading post—the House of Hope—at the confluence of the two rivers, the same spot that interested Hooker. Other Europeans had camped in the vicinity, but it was Hooker and his followers who established the first permanent settlement there in 1636. One of Hooker's assistants, John Steele, had been born in Hertford, England and so, in deference to his trusted aide, Hooker christened the settlement—Hartford.

Seventeenth century life along the Connecticut River was primitive and provincial with almost all activities revolving around the Congregational Church. Organized religion was the very cornerstone of the early settlers' lives. Meetinghouses were the largest structures in town, hosting a least two sermons on Sunday, baptisms, weddings, funerals, political meetings and every other gathering of significance.

Generally speaking, a man achieved wealth by allying himself with three institutions—the Congregational Church, the Federalist Party and the Standing Order. To understand this last group, it is helpful to recognize that Hooker and his followers were, in reality, intolerant zealots. While they claimed to be the victims of intolerance—which was the reason for their move to the Connecticut River valley—they shunned anyone who would not join the Congregational Church. They ignored the small number of blacks and non-believers, but when faced with any kind of a challenge, a powerful group of ministers, magistrates and businessmen—the Standing Order—condemned and persecuted the upstarts. They particularly despised Roman Catholics, labeling them Papists and infidels.

In 1724, the Congregationalists engineered the passage of a law requiring elected officials to take an oath against Popery. This law remained in effect until the American Revolution.

In a sense, the smaller colonial settlements were almost all theocracies to one degree or another, while the larger cities' diverse population bases vitiated such iron-fisted religious control. Boston, with the largest population in the colonies between 1630 and 1690, was the most Puritanical of the larger cities. Rev. John Cotton and the Congregational Church exerted great influence, as the minister believed firmly in the right of Puritan magistrates to impose uniformity with regard to religious beliefs. Philadelphia, the largest city in America from 1690 until 1810, was less rigid. It was William Penn's "Holy Experiment" brought to life, where men of all races and creeds governed themselves free of religious persecution. Not surprisingly, the city became a haven for Quakers driven from other cities. New York was markedly different. By the time that the despotic Peter Stuyvesant became governor of the Dutch West Indies Company's outpost in 1647, there were Germans, Swiss, Moravians, French, English, Dutch and Portuguese people living at the southern tip of Manhattan. Under these circumstances, religious hegemony was not possible. In fact, Stuyvesant's effort in 1654 to expel the earliest Jews—twenty-three refugees from Recife, Brazil— was scotched because of the Dutch West India Company's heavy dependence on Jewish capital.

Thomas Hooker and his followers had many things to worry about as they built their settlement, but water was not one of them. Almost without exception, the budding towns of America were established along rivers for two very good reasons. Just as the Indians of North America had done 30,000 years before, the transplanted Europeans wisely camped near a source of clean drinking water. Furthermore, just as their predecessors had discovered the usefulness of rivers in transporting heavy loads of game and other materials, so too did the newly-arrived Europeans.

Throughout the 1700s, the vice grip of the Congregational Church gave Hartford a strong Puritanical sensibility, as the larger cities blossomed into freer and more diverse urban centers. The old strictures continued to demand an exclusionary society even as the colonies edged closer to war with Britain. During the American Revolution, Hartford served as a vital supply depot. However, furnishing George Washington's armies with provisions left the city impoverished. In the depression years after the war, it was uppermost in the minds of the merchant class to rebuild the thriving maritime trade that Hartford had enjoyed before the Revolution. Competition among freight handlers was fierce though, and the city had become something of a rogue's paradise, with strife on the wharfs and larceny in the streets. The answer was to incorporate the city—which the state legislature did in 1784—and build a police force to clean up the docks and the thieves' dens. Shortly after incorporation, a mayor, four aldermen and twenty councilmen were installed to run the city. Happily, thereafter things brightened for the citizenry as new wharfs were built on the river and the West Indies trade blossomed anew.

In the first half of the nineteenth century, war again cut badly into trade, as James Madison waged his unpopular replay of the American Revolution—the War of 1812. As the Federalist Party declined in importance, a new group of young Republican-Tolerationists held sway, but to their way of thinking, it was time for church and state to go their separate ways. Through the efforts of the younger members of Hartford and other towns throughout the state, the stranglehold of the Congregational Church—supported with public tax dollars— finally ended with Connecticut's new Constitution of 1818.

It was not only the protests of young Protestants that brought things to a head. Due in large part to the deluge of immigrants—particularly those of Irish ancestry—the city simply had to make way for an ever-increasing number of people from different religious and ethnic backgrounds. Still, for all the changes, Protestants controlled the political machinery throughout most of the nineteenth century. Catholics, recognizing the futility of changing things at the ballot box, took steps to preserve their culture by starting their own schools, social clubs and secret societies.

Before 1850, the city held what were called "at-large" elections, which significantly diluted the immigrant vote. This system almost guaranteed that the most prosperous and influential men—all descendants of the city's founders— would be elected to office. But at the mid-century mark, the Democratically-controlled General Assembly altered the electoral machinery slightly to "ward politics." Thereafter, four councilmen and one alderman were elected from each of the city's six wards. The mayor was little more than a figurehead, while the aldermen and councilmen fulfilled both legislative and executive functions, including the hiring and firing of city department heads. The Irish wards—the fifth and sixth—which the *Courant* took great delight in calling "Pigville," encompassed the rundown tenements along Front Street, north and south of State Street. Its voters were Irishmen—lured to the city by jobs laying railroad tracks at seventy-five cents a day—and who now exercised their franchise at the ballot box by electing the first Irish councilman, James Mulligan, a foundry worker, in 1851. Victories were hard won and it was not until a half-century later, in 1902, that the first Irish Democrat, Ignatius Sullivan, was elected mayor. (To illustrate how entrenched the moneyed Protestants were in Hartford, one should consider that New York and Boston elected Irish Catholics, William Grace and Hugh O'Brien, two decades earlier, in 1880 and 1884, respectively.)

***

Hartford, near 1850, not only afforded Hiram and Nancy Bissell a good living as the population and the masonry business grew apace, but also offered clothing and household goods that were unavailable to either of them in their youths. After their marriage, they moved into their new home on Buckingham Street and started a family. In early 1846, their first child, Isabelle, was born. Since Hiram and Nancy had both come from large farm families, it looked as though they would follow their parents' example. In July 1850, Nancy delivered a healthy baby boy, George. Sadly, the child died six months later of *erysipelas*. (Outdated medical texts characterize this ailment as "any early rash of red, dark or yellow hue, sometimes accompanied by swelling," when, in fact, it is a severe streptococcal infection. Belladonna was the drug of choice in the 1850s, although, today, it is cured with penicillin or similar antibiotics.) Two years after George's death, another boy, Samuel, was born to the Bissells, but he only lived nine months, passing away in June 1853. The attending physician noted the cause of death as *dentition*. (At that time, many ailments were accompanied by fevers and, if the child were teething, the possibility for misdiagnosis was ever-present. Children, obviously, did not die from simply cutting teeth.) Finally, in June 1855, Nancy gave birth to a girl, Ella Louise, a robust child who, by the existing record, was the healthiest of all the Bissell children.

The Bissells and their fellow citizens were enticed with a wide assortment of personal and household items as Hartford's merchants maintained a vast and diverse network of distant trading partners. In exchange for the city's exports of lumber, fabric, hardware, dried fish, salt pork, onions, and tobacco, merchants were able to import rum, sugar, molasses, coffee, spices, china, window glass, household items and the latest men's and women's fashions from abroad. There were shops of every description lining Main Street and the lapping boulevards at the heart of the shopping district, offering necessities and luxuries, both plain and fancy.

For goods of a pressing nature, Thomas Work & Company offered "Groceries and Provisions, Wood and Willow Ware, Flour, Grain, Meal, Feed, Oil Meal, Flour, Pork, Hams, Lard, and Sausages of [their] own Manufacture, Oil, Burning Fluid, Clover and Timothy Seed, Beans, Hard Seed, Hops, Malt, &c., &c." Brockett & Company sold "Hosiery and Gloves, Undershirts, Drawers . . . [also] Stocks, Cravats, Pocket Handkerchiefs, Suspenders, Shirts, Bosoms and Collars." For its part, Mrs. Hinckley's Millinery Shop on Main Street sold "A General Assortment of Millinery Goods, Straw and Silk Hats, Plain and Dress Caps, Mourning Hats, Silks and Satins for Hats, Ribbons, and Laces, &c." The last sentence of her advertisement offers a grim glimpse at life in Hartford in the 1850s—"Dress and Mourning Hats made to order at short notice."

For the ornamental, Hastings & Griswold sold—"Gold and Gilt Jewelry and Plated Ware, Watches, Clocks, &c." Lest we forget that the horse-and-buggy was the primary means of everyday transportation, in addition to selling "Men's Fur and Silk Hats," Strong & Woodruff also proffered "Bear, Wolf, Coon, and Buffalo Robes." Although women may not have understood the dangers of ultraviolet rays, they were way ahead of their time when it came to protecting their skin from the sun and Lorin Sexton & Company was right there to meet their needs. From a small shop on Main Street, they sold "Umbrellas, Parasols, Parasolettes, and Sunshades." S. A. Ensign & Company on State Street sold "Fine French Patent Leather Congress Boots, French Dancing Pumps and Gaiters," as well as "High-Heeled Kid Double Sole Buskins," and "High-Heeled Calf Congress Gaiters."

W. W. Roberts & Company on Pratt Street were "Manufacturers of all Types of Cabinet Furniture... Book Cases, Counters and Desks. Also, Coffins of all Sizes...[in] Mahogany, Black Walnut, Cherry and White Wood, Trimmed to Order at Short Notice." And Lee, Butler, & Company dispensed "Drugs, Medicines, and Chemicals," along with "White Lead and Linseed Oil, French and American Window Glass, Varnish, Camphene, Burning Fluid, Potash, Spirits, Turpentine, Emery, Glue, Borax, Sperm and Whale Oil, &c."

Another druggist had his shop on the northern edge of the business district. J. H. Woodward & Company billed himself and his shop as "Druggist and Apothecary," dealing in "Patent Medicines, Perfumery, Fancy Goods, Burning Fluid, Camphene &c., &c." Angling for more wholesale and professional business, he added, "Country Dealers and Physicians Supplied At Low Prices."

Hartford was a peaceful city of about 20,000 people in the early 1850s, but the Circus and Theater Laws of 1800—which barred such amusements—left residents starved for entertainment. People had always enjoyed simple concerts, billed as religious recitals and held in churches, but these were few. Relentlessly, the *Times* blasted the members of the common council, contending that—

> . . .the law of this state prohibiting public amusements is of no advantage to the morale or pleasure of the people. . . . This restriction is a part of the system of blue-law government [that] ought to be no longer tolerated . . .

Bowing to public pressure, the common council finally ended the prohibitions on circuses and theaters, lifting the last vestiges of puritanical restraint and making the city a much more enjoyable—even high-spirited— place. Hiram and Nancy Bissell's free time, what little there was of it, could be filled with new entertainments as the old strictures dropped by the boards. Jenny Lind, the Swedish nightingale, gave one performance at the Fourth Congregational Church on a Saturday night in July 1851. Twelve hundred people paid up to $6 for a seat in the church while, for $1, others sat on the rooftops of nearby buildings, hoping to hear the trills of P.T. Barnum's enchanting songbird. Dances were held for the sons and daughters of the city's finest families on the large upper floors of the most respectable beer halls, such as Bull's Tavern or Gilman's Saloon. Traveling orchestras gave concerts during annual visits to the city and lectures were very popular, especially those given by Ralph Waldo Emerson and Oliver Wendell Holmes (the physician and poet).

As was customary in nineteenth century America—considering that almost the entire town lay between the river and Main Street—the larger buildings, including the statehouse, faced the Connecticut River. Additionally, all of the largest and most important churches were built on the west side of Main Street so that they too faced the river. As the city mushroomed and the river lost its importance, new municipal buildings were constructed—and older ones remodeled—to face Main Street. The most important element in the birth and growth of the city—the Connecticut River—was slowly slipping from people's lives.

On the periphery of the retail section at the center of the city sat the shops and lofts of manufacturers and wholesalers. Though it was a small city compared to New York—whose population had rocketed to approximately 500,000—it had, nonetheless, carved out a name for itself as a burg where a manufacturer could prosper mightily. Hartford was home to the Jewel Belting Company, on its way to becoming the leading industrial belting producer in the world. Bidwell, Pitkin & Company fabricated a dizzying array of steam engines and boilers, and along a stretch of the Little (Park) River, the Sharps Manufacturing Company assembled the rapid-firing breech-loading rifle, for which it was justly renowned. On Pearl Street, Edwin Wesson (of Smith & Wesson fame) was producing muzzle-loading rifles. The firm that was destined to cast the longest shadow, however, was Colt's Patent Fire-Arms. Already a manufactory of considerable size, by the 1860s it would dwarf every other business in Hartford as sales of its revolvers to the Union Army made Samuel Colt one of the wealthiest men in town.

The roads were a combination of mud and manure, the city watering them several times a day to damp the dust. Main Street was cut particularly wide, allowing the horse drawn trolley cars an aisle of safety when they began service 1863. Every block had a cross walk of granite slabs laid into the street so that, even in the muddiest weather, commerce would not come to a complete standstill. Horse drawn wagons and buggies inched their way along Main Street as fashionably dressed women, in hats and hoop skirts, bustled from shop to market under the colorful, striped canvas awnings that shaded the wide bluestone sidewalks.

The overwhelming majority of buildings were only two or three stories tall. A bank or an insurance company, feeling the need to advertise its financial strength, might hire Hiram Bissell or another builder to construct a building as high as five stories but this was unusual. Pictures of the Hartford skyline in the 1850s resembled an ocean of low, nondescript buildings offset by the soaring steeples of whitewashed churches. There were twenty houses of worship, and reflecting the exclusionary bias of the city's founders, six were Congregational.

Serving a much smaller segment of the population were houses of worship for the various other Protestant denominations, a Catholic Church and a Synagogue.

Main Street in Hartford circa 1850.

Hartford was divided by a two-tiered class structure in the middle of the nineteenth century. The oldest families, who were the descendents of the earliest settlers, made up the moneyed, merchant-banker class. Overwhelmingly, they belonged to the Whig Party, which was composed of numerous factions united in opposition to the politics of Andrew Jackson. This opposition to Jackson's election in 1828 produced an amalgam of Federalists and a smaller number of Democrats, who originally rallied under the name National Republicans. Later, in 1834, they settled on the Whig appellation, borrowed from an English political party. The Whigs' hatred of Andrew Jackson was brought to a head when he established a National Bank to manage the nation's treasury. In the process, he let the charter of the United States Bank lapse. The Whigs, many of whom were deeply involved in banking, never got over this financial realignment, preferring to think of money and power as their birthright. The *noblesse oblige* that might accompany such a birthright, however, never created a class of people who felt compelled to support public projects that would benefit the masses.

The Democrats, on the other hand, favored ventures that redistributed tax dollars evenly among the populace. They also preferred that citizens decide for themselves whether alcohol should be sold freely or whether public amusements—such as theaters and circuses— should be an entertainment option.

From the time of the American Revolution until the early 1830s, there were two parties of choice—the Federalists (the earliest antecedent of the Whig Party) and the Democratic-Republicans (the precursor of the Democratic Party). Of Connecticut's eight governors between 1834 and 1850, five were Whigs, demonstrating clearly the strength of that party—at least at the state level. Nationally though, things were not quite so sanguine. The Whig Party produced only two elected presidents—William Henry Harrison (1840) and Zachary Taylor (1848)—and began a slow death spiral after the disastrous election of 1852, when the Democratic standard-bearer, Franklin Pierce, trounced Whig candidate, General Winfield Scott. As the Whig Party died, the new Republican Party of Connecticut was born. The leadership in Connecticut mirrored the chaotic times: Governor Henry Dutton, a Whig, was elected in 1854. Succeeding him was William Minor of the American (Know-Nothing) Party, followed by Alexander Holley, who ran under the Republican-American banner. Finally in 1858, William Buckingham was elected the first Republican governor of the state.

As the Whig party slowly disintegrated, these interim names sufficed until the Republican Party emerged as a collection of Know-Nothings, Whigs, Democrats and anti-slavery men. This was not always an easy transition because the Republican Party of Connecticut began life with a strong anti-slavery bias and at least some of the old-time Whigs were descendants of slave owners.

Nevertheless, from the mid-1850s forward, the Republican Party became home to the old-moneyed, merchant-banker class who adhered strictly to the canon that benefited them most—the status quo. It made little difference whether they called themselves Whigs, National Americans or Republicans; their beliefs were as rock-ribbed conservative as those of their forebears—the early Federalists. They still considered themselves the ruling class and disdained public projects that increased their taxes and distributed municipal services evenly among the inhabitants of the city. They viewed a water company as no different from any other business, whether it sold real estate, banking services or insurance. As such, they felt, the city had no right to involve itself in aqueduct projects.

The Democrats who joined the Whigs in the early 1850s were successful shopkeepers, merchants and manufacturers. By dint of ambition and desire, they often sided with the Whigs on important matters, believing that the surest way to prosperity was on the coattails of these prosperous conservative businessmen. Therefore, a sprinkling of conservative Democrats accompanied almost all Whig endeavors. Lumped together, this group recognized the usefulness of the burgeoning ranks of immigrants when labor-intensive projects arose, but otherwise held them in low regard. During this period, Hartford had twelve newspapers (five of which were religious-based publications), but the newspaper that embodied the Whig ideology was the *Hartford Daily Courant*, which could be depended upon to champion the concept of a ruling class and, of course, another larger collection of people who, for want of education and means, needed governance. The *Courant's* offices were on Main Street almost directly opposite State House Square and diagonally across from the newspaper that was antithetical to Whiggery—the *Hartford Daily Times.*

The *Courant* held tremendous sway from its inception in 1764, its editors convinced that theirs was the voice of practical politics, when, in fact, it was the gospel of exclusion. In 1840, a twenty-five-year-old compositor, who had worked his way up to foreman of the composing room, Alfred Burr, approached his employer at the *Courant,* in the hope of buying into the newspaper. His offer was met with great favor, but only if he would join the Whig party and the Congregational Church. Put off by such strong-arm tactics, Burr subsequently bought into the *Times.* In order to compete head-to-head with his erstwhile employer, he began publishing a daily edition in 1841, a year after his arrival. From its small offices across from its competitor, the *Times* became a loud— even caustic—anti-Whig citadel, issuing a crystal clear Democratic message to its subscribers. Closely aligned with the causes of the manufacturing class, as well as the smaller merchants and their employees, this Democratic bulwark fought daily to keep the *Courant* and its entrenched subscribers at bay.

The greater number of merchants and manufacturers disliked the old-moneyed Whigs and were active in Democratic politics. Though it might have helped Hiram Bissell's masonry business to join the Whigs, given his character, he simply could not do it. Ingrained deeply within him was an egalitarian sensibility and, aligning himself officially with the elite moneyed interests, rubbed him the wrong way. The Democratic Party was the place where he belonged. That said, he was businessman enough to soft-pedal his political beliefs. After all, he depended on Whig construction projects for a sizable portion of his income and he had a family to support.

As the size and variety of Hartford's industries grew, manpower needs grew proportionately. Easily the most unsettling aspects of this growth was the increased incidence of disease—especially typhoid fever, cholera, diphtheria, and yellow fever. Hartford—and for that matter all of the cities and towns in the United States—had expended very little energy on the problem of waste disposal. (It is curious how old maps show no waste disposal areas of any kind.) Consequently, in the most crowded sections of the city—particularly in the tightly packed tenement district—people dumped every conceivable type of refuse into alleys, vacant lots and even the Little River. This slow-moving watercourse became an open sewer as human waste, animal droppings, and the byproducts of tanneries and dye works polluted its waters. In short, Hartford had become downright filthy.

What few people in the city suspected—except perhaps some enlightened physicians—was that this mountain of filth was contributing greatly to the spread of disease. Even as the Little River diffused its polluted sludge into the Connecticut River—thereby slowly contaminating one of Hartford's most important sources of pure water—the link between despoiled water and disease was emerging in another part of the world.

A London physician, Dr. John Snow, made a startling—if not scientifically proved—correlation. The incidence of cholera among Londoners increased relative to their proximity to the Broad Street Pump, a public fixture used by the poorer elements of the city. The Thames had become such an open cesspool by this time that the English statesman Benjamin Disraeli, described it as "a

Drawing of the Park (Little) River in 1850.

Stygian pool reeking with ineffable and unbearable horror." Londoners who got their water from a pump farther upriver—and not despoiled by sewage—developed infinitely fewer cases of the disease. While Snow could not prove his beliefs concerning water and disease, his observations quickly spread among those in scientific circles.

In Hartford, physicians were quick to recognize the import of Snow's observations. His suspicions related solely to cholera, but those of a scientific frame of mind, suspected that contaminated water might indeed be the vehicle of transmission for other dreaded killers of the day as well. In part, they were correct. When the different bacilli were finally isolated, it became clear that cholera and typhoid fever were indeed waterborne diseases. They would only be eradicated by protecting the water supply and by cleaning up the waste and filth. Yellow fever and diphtheria, however, were not waterborne diseases. Nonetheless, the filth accumulating in Hartford provided perfect breeding grounds for pathogens of all types and only with education and the laudable efforts of the state's public health department were these areas at length cleaned up.

Besides a manufacturing Mecca, by 1850 Hartford had become an insurance, banking and publishing center. Some of the largest of New York's merchants turned to the insurance companies of Hartford for fire and casualty protection. Banks boomed as the city grew and it became quite common for publishers who specialized in reference works and subscription books—volumes presold door-to-door from a blank, dummy copy with an alluring cover—to maintain offices in Hartford. (When Mark Twain moved to Hartford in 1871, it was so that he would be closer to his publisher, Elisha Bliss, who owned the American Publishing Company.) However, unlike the tremendous strides that Hartford had made in insurance, banking, publishing and manufacturing, by mid-century it had made no lasting moves at all in the crucial business of supplying its citizens with drinking water. While the owners of livery stables, beer halls and manufactories—all of which consumed vast quantities of water—could see the desirability of a dependable supply, they were not anxious to repeat the mistakes of the well-intentioned entrepreneurs who had previously tried and failed to build aqueduct companies. None of these men had any misconceptions about the difficulty of such an undertaking.

Elected officials of all the blossoming cities of the United States were up against a confounding problem. Residents had freely dipped their buckets into nearby rivers and lakes for so long that the idea of paying for water seemed ludicrous. Convincing people that pure water, piped into their homes and businesses, was a commodity of inestimable value was an uphill battle. Moreover, large families had plenty of water bearers making the trip to the river.

Joseph Trumbull

During the long winter months of early 1851, a group of politicians, manufacturers, merchants and professional men decided that it was time to pipe water into the city. In May of that year, these thirty-six businessmen founded the Hartford Water Company. To lead them, they prevailed upon Joseph Trumbull, a former Connecticut governor, who was now a member of the legislature. (In a cruel quirk of fate, a decade later Joseph Trumbull died of typhoid fever, contracted from drinking contaminated water.) Trumbull, a Whig, had served as president of the Hartford Bank for more than a decade and was the grandson of Connecticut's Revolutionary governor, Jonathan Trumbull.

A seemingly all-inclusive ensemble of individuals signed the petition for the Hartford Water Company. Besides the Whig ex-governor Joseph Trumbull, there was a prominent Democrat—and one-time ship captain in the coastal trade—Mayor Ebenezer Flower. Joining these politicians, were the presidents of two of the city's largest insurance companies and the principals of five of the largest banks, all Whigs. The petition also included the signatures of grocers, steel and dry goods merchants, saddlers, harness makers, publishers, lawyers and druggists. Not to be branded a completely Whig enterprise, it also included the names of a few prominent Democrats. Besides Mayor Flower—and adding considerable cachet to the venture—was the signature of Alfred Burr, the Democratic publisher of the *Times*.

Ignoring the superb examples of city-owned water works in Boston, New York and Philadelphia, the Hartford Water Company—as outlined in its original hand-written document—was established as a for-profit stock company, reminiscent of the other failed water projects before it. The thirty-six original incorporators would have the right to sell shares for $25 apiece or keep them for themselves.

The men behind the Hartford Water Company were taking a calculated risk. Since no one was waiting in line for the chance to build a water works and the Whig-controlled common council was unlikely to get in their way, it was a fair bet that they could seize the water franchise with a minimum of opposition. Actually, their calculations were sound up to a point; their only misstep was in underestimating the mind-set of their fellow citizens. From the day that the charter for the Hartford Water Company was granted by the legislature, public sentiment was against it. Alfred Burr of the *Times*—one of the original incorporators of the company—later railed against private ownership of the water supply, which makes one wonder whether he originally endorsed the Hartford Water Company as a ploy to spur his fellow citizens into active opposition or merely to enrich himself.

Conspicuously absent from the Hartford Water Company's original paperwork were the names of two prominent citizens—Samuel Colt and Hiram Bissell—each for slightly different reasons. By May 1851, Colt was a thirty-six-year-old inventor and one of the largest manufacturers in the city. He stood to benefit more than anyone from the establishment of a dependable water works. His new manufactory—the largest private armory in the world—was on the drawing boards and his need for a reliable water supply was unmistakable. Still, Colt's hatred of the city's Whigs—which traced back to their shoddy treatment of the Colt family many years before—was nothing short of virulent and, accordingly, he withheld his signature.

Hiram Bissell, now thirty-two years old, was of a different mind altogether, based in part on a lesson he learned growing up in South Glastonbury. One oddity of life in Shingle Hollow was that, for the houses clustered in a semi-circle just up the hill from tiny Grindle Brook, there was only one well for drinking water. This thirty-five foot deep, hand-dug affair, sat on the east side of his grandparents' house at the top of the hill, delivering copious amounts of pure water and obviating the need for other wells. The arrangement, while seemingly very practical, had a serious downside. Living so close together, it was inevitable that small disputes would surface from time to time and, not long after a tiff got underway, the participants were forced to cross each other's property to gather water, further stoking the fires of discontent. In short, the shared well tended to exacerbate small family squabbles. For Hiram Bissell, allowing the wealthy Whigs to control the water supply was nothing more than the history of the communal well in Shingle Hollow—writ large.

Beyond this childhood memory, there were other concerns. Judging by the caliber of the men associated with the Hartford Water Company, it was clear that this enterprise was destined to be highly lucrative. Profitability, however, could mean different things to different residents of the city. Obviously, water pipes would be bedded in the wealthier neighborhoods, but the water company might be loath to lay conduits in the poorer parts of the city, where the return on investment was uncertain. It was unlikely that the common council could force a private water company to bed pipes in areas where its financial return was in doubt.

The "water question"—as Hartford's newspapers liked to refer to it—might have been jawboned to death except for a confluence of events that brought acuity to the matter. One such precipitating event was the unbearably cold winter of 1851-2. The *Times* averred that—

> . . .the winter of 1851-2 will probably be a landmark for the weather-wise...in making their comparisons of cold for many years to come. It [has] thus far proved the coldest winter known in this country since the memorable one of 1835-6 . . .

The long, cold winter was a bitter time for the people of Hartford. Deep snows blocked the roads in every direction, which caused the mails to be returned to the city undelivered. As powerful snowstorms took turns crippling the state, the trains sometimes sat in their sheds and roundhouses for three days at a time. The bone-chilling weather froze the Connecticut River to a depth of three feet, closing down steamer traffic for the winter and reducing people accustomed to accessing the river for drinking water to purchases from grimy tank wagons. People were left to ponder anew whether this outdated and unreliable method of collecting water should be continued. Ever so slowly, the appeal of piped water took hold.

By the spring of 1852, the Whigs were chomping at the bit to begin building their aqueduct system. In furtherance of their project, they explained in articles published in the newspapers that a construction firm had been engaged to do the physical work and, furthermore, they encouraged residents to—

> . . .regard a home investment in which they and their families have so deep an interest and one that at once [will] pay a fair interest and very soon become a regularly paying 7 percent stock . . .

Suddenly it was clear. The principals of the Hartford Water Company intended to procure their working capital from the residents of the city, have the physical labor performed by an independent contractor and, for their part, simply collect the water rents and skim a healthy profit for themselves. Letters poured into the newspapers wondering if this was "the forming of a Joint Stock Company of our own citizens..." and also questioning the wisdom of consigning the job "to alien hands...subject [to] foreign control... no matter [by] what *hokus pokus* a board of directors may be elected." One reader opined that "[if we] allow a heartless band of speculators or jobbers...[to] get control of this...we shall forever curse the day that we gave birth to this monstrous production." By May, a *Times* reader summed up the matter succinctly by stating that—

> . . .it was plainly to be seen by the action . . .on the question that there was a "wheel within a wheel" and that one monopoly sought to absorb within itself another that...would be antagonistic   to the prosperity of our city . . .

Now that the profiteering nature of the Hartford Water Company was exposed, the city's elected officials began to squirm. Mayor Flower was one of the original incorporators of the private company, although he could have claimed that he signed on—like his fellow Democrat, Alfred Burr—just to light a fire under the public's collective derriere. The Whig councilmen, of course, could not avail themselves of such redeeming cover. They found themselves in the awkward position of responding to the growing alarm of their constituents, while seeking to maintain close ties with their Whig friends—a crafty bit of business at best.

Resourceful in the face of tumult, they quickly acted on two fronts. First, they scheduled a meeting so that the private water company's founders could better explain their proposal. Unfortunately for Joseph Trumbull and his friends, the public departed the meeting more convinced than ever that the city should build and own the water works. As one reporter in attendance wrote—

> . . . let a corporation get the management of it [the water works] and we shall all bind ourselves at their mercy . . .We want pure water and [it] should be subject to the city's control.

The council's second gambit was to appoint a blue ribbon committee to study all of the drinking water options open to the city and, even more importantly, to recommend a course of action. The group was comprised of five men with Dr. Ebenezer Hunt, a forty-two year-old physician, acting as the chairman. The *Courant* referred to Dr. Hunt as "a man possessed of the most agreeable social qualities...fond of hearing and telling a pleasant story [and] quick to appreciate humor..." Despite the entertaining nature attributed to this Whig physician, he was also a man who had a deep interest in pure water, undoubtedly sharpened by the first-hand experience of attending to victims of waterborne diseases. A graduate of the University of Pennsylvania, without question, his medical knowledge would be useful in evaluating the relative purity of any possible source.

For the next nine months, Dr. Hunt and his committee studied assiduously the proposition of bringing pure water into Hartford and by January 1853, they were ready to present their findings. On a bitter cold night in January 1853, Hiram Bissell and hundreds of other men shuffled through the gas lit, rutted streets to attend a meeting where the findings of the study committee would be aired. The men jammed the council chambers on the second floor of City Hall. Built one block north of State House Square, it was a polished granite building with matching Greek revival porticoes on its northern and southern ends, and basement barn doors fronting Market Street on the east. These doors led into City Hall Market, an indoor bazaar where farmers rented stalls by the season and sold their produce to a hungry populace. The second floor held the council rooms and police courts. The third floor was one vast hall where speeches and public lectures were given.

The residents turned out in large numbers because, based on Dr. Hunt's findings, they would have to choose between a water franchise controlled by the prosperous Whigs or rise to the challenge and begin bedding their own pipes. The *Courant* described the meeting as, "one of the largest ever held in the city to consider measures of public good..."

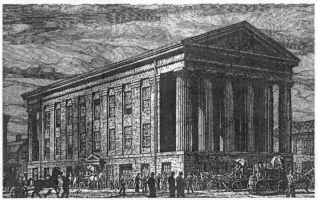
Hartford City Hall circa 1850.

Mayor Ebenezer Flower presided over the gathering with Eliphalet Bulkeley acting as secretary. (A staunch Whig and Yale-educated attorney, Bulkeley was fiercely opposed to municipal ownership of the water works as we will see later.) Dr. Hunt outlined the city's options and the committee's final recommendations to his fellow citizens. His dissertation was spellbinding in its detail. First, he discussed the city's wells, displaying the results of chemical testing, which showed that there was three to five times more particulate matter in the water of the city's wells than New York's Croton water. Secondly, he enumerated four possible sources for the city to consider, showing an obvious preference for the Connecticut River water which, surprisingly, tested much cleaner than that at the Croton Reservoir.

Progressing to the city's specific needs, he explained in a concise manner how a water works was infinitely preferable to the existing wells and cisterns for firefighting, manufacturing, flushing sewers, sprinkling the streets, and for cooking and drinking purposes. Lastly, he issued the committees detailed recommendations, describing almost to the letter the configuration of the final water works. The committee suggested—

1. ...that water be introduced from [the] Connecticut River
2. ...that the water be raised by a Cornish engine
3. ...that a reservoir be built capable of holding 10 million gallons
4. ...that a substantial engine house be built at the river
5. ...that the works be owned by the city
6. ...that the works be managed by a Board of Water Commissioners...

An interesting sidebar to the whole discussion of building a water system in Hartford rested with the city's thoroughgoing competition with New Haven, forty miles to the south. Connecticut had two capital cities in 1853, but would not settle on a single one for another twenty-two years. As mentioned previously, the legislature simply alternated between Hartford and New Haven, pleasing neither as it hopscotched between venues. Both cities knew that eventually the legislature would choose a permanent home and each was determined not to be the bridesmaid. Therefore, when the following newspaper article appeared during the time between Dr. Hunt's dissertation in January and the bonding ballot in July, any doubts as to which way the public would vote were quickly eliminated—

The Water Project In New Haven
The water project has been carried by the people of New Haven. The proposition was whether an application should be made to the legislature for power to furnish pure water by the city, at the expense of $325,000. The people voted to apply.

As was expected, Hartford's public ballot produced an 80 percent majority in favor of accepting the recommendations of Dr. Hunt's study committee and, ten days later, the council placed the cart squarely before the horse by authorizing the Board of Water Commissioners—which did not yet exist—to issue $200,000 worth of bonds. Three weeks later—and in accordance with the directive of the legislature—they appointed a temporary water commission until the public could elect a permanent body in April 1854.

It was at this point that the council's motives became suspect, for three of their five appointments were men who were original incorporators of the private water company— Dr. Hunt, Calvin Day, a dry goods merchant, and Thomas Belknap, one of the owners of the publishing firm of Hamersley & Belknap. Filling the last two positions on the acting board were John Carter, chief engineer of the fire department, and Elisha Root, the superintendent of Colt Patent Fire-Arms. Even concurrent with the rapidly unfolding events, it would have been impossible to fathom the true motives of Hunt, Belknap and Day. Were they legitimate converts to the proposition of a city-owned water works, or was it their intention to stalemate and ultimately derail this initiative?

Things got worse. Feeling that Dr. Hunt's group needed help in approaching the legislature, the council empanelled a committee to assist them. While this had the patina of prudence, six of the twenty men appointed were original incorporators of the private, Whig-controlled water venture. Due in no small measure to the public's thundering mandate at the polls, there were, of course, shifting loyalties but, as evidenced by letters of suspicion sent to the *Times*, citizens did not feel that the council was acting in good faith.

Just as clearly, the public's 80 percent approval of a city-owned water works had not been effected solely by the editorials in the *Times*. Assisting enormously were men who worked behind the scenes educating and persuading their neighbors, and thereby counterbalancing the Whig's daily disinformation campaign in the *Courant*. Still other backers of the city-owned water department tried an approach that was more creative—

Pure Water!
The door-keeper of the House placed a can of Connecticut River water in the lobby this noon, and cooled it with some ice. By its side stood a can of iced well water. Many of the members partook of the river water, and expressed their surprise at its excellent flavor. It so far surpasses the well water that the latter is actually distasteful by comparison, and the members are now calling for a constant supply of the river water. . . .

Frustratingly circumspect, newspapers in the 1850s almost never mentioned the names of private citizens who offered opinions before the council or championed causes behind the scenes, referring in print to these people merely as "A citizen." In fact, so guarded were the newspapers that when a steam boiler exploded at the Fales & Gray Car Works, a railroad car manufacturer—killing twenty-one people in March 1854—the name of the company was never even mentioned in the original article in the *Times*. Nevertheless, the elections of

April 1854 would change this, as the champions of the new water works emerged from the shadows, assuming huge responsibilities while the Whigs persistently schemed behind their backs.

As the city's denizens waited to cast their ballots in the spring elections of 1854, they enjoyed endless performances of the stage play of "Uncle Tom's Cabin," unaware that its author, Harriet Beecher Stowe, was destined to move to Hartford in 1863. During this same period, the Hartford Bridge Company announced that they would replace the present rotting, sagging structure across the Connecticut River, although the new passageway would be another wooden bridge. And as if to highlight the city's tremendous growth, the Hartford & New Haven Railroad announced its receipts—through October 1853—showing a 51 percent increase in revenues (not including the $2000 a month it received for carrying the mail). Though the storm clouds of the coming Civil War cast an ever-darkening shadow over the country, the ultimate cataclysm was unthinkable to most people. Hartford's inhabitants enjoyed to the fullest a period of relative prosperity between the Panic of 1837 and the mid-1850s.

Just prior to the April elections, the *Times*, ostensibly to educate its readers, published a report by chief engineer Jacob Houghton of the Detroit Water Works, which detailed the progress and configurations of water projects in cities across the eastern United States. A description of the works and the costs were listed for Detroit, Cincinnati, Pittsburgh, Buffalo, Albany, New York, Philadelphia, Boston, Chicago, and Allegheny City (the northern section of modern day Pittsburgh). Of the ten cities listed, only Buffalo was served by a private water company.

On Monday April 10, 1854, the general elections were held in the city's six wards. Along with their ballots for mayor, sheriff, and a dozen other posts, for the first time, people voted for water commissioners. In the time that it took to count the ballots, the leading protagonists of the city's water works became readily apparent. Of the seven candidates running for a seat on the water board, Hiram Bissell received the second largest number of votes, outpolled only by Edward Reed, the superintendent of the Hartford & New Haven Railroad. Reed's daily work with steam was an obvious asset since the cornerstone of the new water system would be a steam engine. All the same, it was clear from the voting that Hiram Bissell's knowledge and opinions pertaining to water issues were highly respected by his neighbors. The two other men elected to the board were Samuel Woodruff, president of Woodruff & Beach, a steam boiler company, and Ezra Clark, an iron and steel merchant. The common council—as ordained by the legislature—appointed the fifth commissioner and, not a bit shy, they opted for a Whig, Daniel Phillips, the owner of Adams Express, a freight company. With the Democrats represented on the panel by only Reed and Bissell, the water board should have been able to deal with the Whig-controlled council but, in the fullness of time, this proved not to be the case.

The following day, the *Courant* lamented the choices made at the polls, opining that, "...we think it is very much to be regretted that at the elections yesterday, an *entire change* was made in the Board of Water Commissioners." The *Courant* underestimated the public's misgivings with regard to the council and the voters clear preference for men they considered knowledgeable—but more importantly—trustworthy.

The newly elected water board, recognizing that the council would scrutinize their every move, handed the presidency to a Whig that they all liked and trusted—Ezra Clark. His tenure, sorry to say, was short and tumultuous. Within four months of the election, several Whigs from the private water company, most notably James Goodwin, the president of Connecticut Mutual Life Insurance Company and Alonzo Beckwith, a securities broker, went to court and secured a temporary injunction against the sale of the city's water bonds. Precipitated by what the Whigs wanted the public to believe were gross irregularities in Ezra Clark's bond sales, they forced a city meeting where the common council could examine the matter.

In the most accusatory fashion—and entirely without foundation—the council accused Clark of malfeasance. The relationship between Clark and his fellow Whigs could best be described as testy. This can be traced directly to the Whig selection of a mayoral candidate three years earlier, when the extreme right wing of the party, sensing that the rapidly growing ranks of factory workers and immigrants called for desperate measures, allowed themselves to be duped into accepting a Trojan horse candidate. Ebenezer Flower was a middle-aged, retired sea captain whose political affiliations were murky, except of course to the Democrats who convinced him to run as a Whig. Clark who had worked his way up in the party—first as councilman, then as alderman—was unceremoniously passed over in favor of Flower, who was subsequently elected mayor. That April, Clark wrote to his brother Morton in New York—

> . . . I suppose you will see in the papers that our election is over and Capt. Flower the mayor?... The Democrats are up to their old tricks. . . . I suppose that 9/10ths of the voters have expected that I should fill the place, but the other tenth got the power by cunning management to defeat my nomination. I will give you the particulars when I see you. . .
>
> .

The Whigs harbored a special dislike for Clark, for in the eyes of most in the party, he was far too moderate, his interest in Whiggery merely a happenstance of birth. Nevertheless, Clark was the most honorable of men, conducting his business affairs with the utmost civility and displaying great courtesy to everyone, regardless of their political affiliation. In a phrase, he was the Democrats' favorite Whig.

Ultimately, Clark was vindicated but, as a result of their inquisition, the Whigs had accomplished two things. First, they managed to taint Ezra Clark—and his water board—by casting a veil of impropriety over his financial dealings. More importantly, since the Whigs on the council had handled the matter in such a heavy-handed manner, any chance for harmony between the water board and the council had completely evaporated. Clark was deeply shaken by the brazen assault on his integrity and, thereafter, circumvented the council whenever possible. This, unfortunately, made matters worse. At last, realizing that his continued presence was injurious to the infant water works, Clark decided to step aside. Altering his plans a bit, he campaigned for a seat in the U.S. Congress, which he won in November 1854. (Of the 39 towns in his district, Ezra Clark lost only 11 of them, including Hartford, where the city's Whigs abandoned him.) After the election, he resigned from the board, and Hiram Bissell was appointed president. With the water works not even half completed, Clark left for Washington, leaving Bissell and the other water commissioners with their hands full and their morale low.

Since Hiram Bissell had replaced Clark as president of the board, it was clear, that barring any further trouble from the council or unexpected calamities, he would be the man to deliver the Connecticut River waters into the city. Beyond that, he would remain at the helm of the water works for the next seventeen years, shouldering an incalculable number of burdens and, simultaneously, juggling the demands of his masonry business. His future was crowded with construction projects—office buildings for insurance companies, houses, factories and even churches. In time, his interests expanded to include the manufacture of bricks and concrete drain tiles and, still later, the buying and selling of real estate. Added to this crowded schedule now, was the tricky business of overseeing the construction of Hartford's water works while outguessing the Whigs and deflecting their destructive onslaughts.

Bissell was the only member of the board compensated for his efforts but, considering that by 1855 he had amassed almost $20,000 in real estate and investments—at a time when a typical factory worker earned $300 annually—the paycheck from the city meant little. Outmaneuvering the scheming Whigs and responding to the complaints of unhappy water customers made any monies earned, with the benefit of hindsight, seem more Pyrrhic than wind fallen.

As the Whigs' steadfast mouthpiece, the *Courant* never tired of attacking the water board, seeking small advantage by embarrassing its members. Even as the nascent water works began to organize, the most mordant editorials poured forth from the *Courant* like rain along an eave trough—

Rum and Water

. . . the establishment of expensive works to supply the city with pure water, for the use of the fire department, street sprinkling, and individuals, is "mercantile traffic," in competition with the legitimate dealings of merchants; and [now] that the city has embarked in the water project, it is right that [they] should set up in the rum trade, and monopolize that traffic, suppressing the business of merchants who [deal] . . . in that article. . . .

As sarcastic as this little barb must have seemed at the time, it was tame stuff compared with the invective from the Whigs that lay ahead. Rather than accepting the city's water works—which improved their lives and that of their neighbors immensely—they never passed up the opportunity to try to derail the project. Their feints and jabs could be merely glancing blows but, as we shall see, they could also be delivered with enough precision as to fatally damage the emerging water works. Irrespective of the sophistication of their treachery at any given moment in time, Joseph Trumbull and his friends were nothing if not relentless.

Despite the tempest at City Hall, the circumstances of Bissell's life put him in a good position to assume the leadership of the water board. First of all, in 1852 he had built a larger house for his family on Wadsworth Street, which was spacious enough so that two of his brothers— Sylvester and Martin—could come to live and work with him. Though Sylvester was the youngest of Chester and Prudence Bissell's six children, he was quick-witted and in no time at all became a full partner with his brother in H. & S. Bissell. In due course, Sylvester married, built his own home and raised a family, but Martin was an enigma. He worked steadily for his brothers, but always as a simple bricklayer. He never married and lived with Hiram until he died of heart disease in his late forties.

With Sylvester running the masonry crew, Bissell would have the freedom of movement needed to supervise the construction of the water works. He would need that freedom too, for absent any previous experience with reservoirs and water distributions systems, and hobbled by a contrary council, the building of the water works portended to be the most grueling and contentious building project he had yet faced.

Chapter 3
Building A Water Company

By dint of unlucky timing, Hartford built its water works during one of the most difficult periods in American history. From the mid-1840s, slavery dominated the political rhetoric of the United States, complicating simple social intercourse and escalating newspaper editorials to fever pitch. Springing from this tension were new political parties and many "fusions," whereby leaders of different movements concocted mutually beneficial combinations to win elections. In Connecticut, there were six major political ideologies, occasioning extended bouts of editorial fencing and, undoubtedly, plenty of heated tavern discussions—the Abolitionists, Free Soilers, Whigs, Know Nothings, Democrats and Maine Law men (prohibitionists).

The Abolitionist Party, of course, sprung up in direct opposition to slavery. In the peak year of 1774, Connecticut had 6,562 slaves accounting for 3.4 percent of the state's population and, in the late eighteenth century, a series of laws successively lowered the age at which a native-born slave became free. By 1800, more than 80 percent of the state's slaves were free and when finally the act of emancipation was passed in 1848, only a handful of slaves remained. Nonetheless, the slavery question was a red-hot issue in Hartford—as it was everywhere else in the country—all through the 1850s.

Lyman Beecher, the Presbyterian minister and father of Harriet Beecher Stowe was a prominent abolitionist and also the father of thirteen children. All seven of his sons followed him into the pulpit, including the noted preacher, Henry Ward Beecher, whose Congregational Church was in Brooklyn. He lectured regularly in Hartford and—after 1864—visited his favorite sister, Harriet, at her new home in Nook Farm, the eclectic colony of abolitionist writers, senators, businessmen and newspaper editors in the west end of the city. In Nook Farm, the barn behind the home of U.S. Senator Francis Gillette—the father of actor-playwright William Gillette—was used as a "station" of the Underground Railroad's Connecticut spur.

The Free Soil Party was another political movement that sprung up as a direct result of slavery. Members of this party believed that the western territories of the United States should be reserved exclusively for free white settlers, arousing strong emotions among Southerners who envisioned an expansion of slavery, giving their peculiar beliefs added justification and strength.

Connecticut's Whigs were of so many different stripes that a concise definition of their beliefs was not possible. As the *Times* enjoyed chiding, "...There are Union Whigs, Free Trade Whigs, Liberal Whigs, Free Soil Whigs, Maine Law Whigs, and Whigs who don't know and don't care." At least nominally, Connecticut's Whigs were anti-slavery, but by a tortuous route. The Whigs were the descendants of the wealthy Federalists, some of whom had been slave owners. However, as the Whig Party went into serious decline, the Republican Party of Connecticut beckoned with open arms, provided of course, that you were anti-slavery. Since slavery had ended in Connecticut in 1848, even Whigs with an unpleasant family heritage were free to embrace the Republican Party and its anti-slavery stance.

The Connecticut Democrats were in a tough spot, for they espoused states' rights and were strict constitutionalists. Though a pro-slavery characterization would be a little too harsh, they believed strongly that, on constitutional grounds, the Southerners could not be forced to stay with the Union; nor could they be forced to free their slaves.

In the midst all of this tumult, a secret movement to save America from the immigrant masses arose—the Know-Nothings. Angered by the new ethnic groups entering America in large numbers—particularly the Irish—the Know-Nothings emerged in 1853 as the party that would end immigration. (For a short time, the *Hartford Courant* became a mouthpiece for the Know-Nothings.) Driven either by the belief that theirs was not a particularly embraceable cause or by a conviction that concealment would give them certain advantages, its members never identified themselves publicly, instead exchanging secret handshakes and passwords. The Know-Nothings were never a particularly powerful force nationally and slowly faded away as the Civil War and slavery took center stage. All the same—and even with Hartford voting overwhelmingly Democratic—in Connecticut the Know-Nothings tapped into a virulent hatred of the Irish immigrants and were victorious in the state elections in 1855, 1856 and 1857. They even seated a governor, William T. Minor, who served a two-year term beginning in 1855.

As if this collection of parties and movements were not enough, Connecticut was in the throws of an alcohol prohibition debate, driven by Maine Law supporters. This movement swept through New England like a nor'easter, and then headed out across the Great Plains, attracting large collections of converts en route. In early April 1854, the Connecticut General Assembly passed a law "prohibiting the manufacture of spirituous liquor, ale, cider and hop beer..." For all the good the law might have done, it was a hypocritical piece of legislation, depriving working people of the right to purchase liquor while their wealthy counterparts imported spirits and circumvented the law with impunity. The *Courant* and its Whig subscribers believed in the Maine Law, while the *Times* decried the encroachment on personal liberties. During the spring of 1855, the *Times* continually observed that the crime of drunkenness continued in Hartford and the amount of liquor consumed was just as great as before the Maine Law took effect.

The most effective configuration of the Fusion Platform included the Whigs, Know-Nothings, Free Soilers and Abolitionists. As the *Times* reported in 1855—

> . . . This combination has already been made in some of the New England states and it is intended to carry it into effect in others...The people of Connecticut are . . . invited to sanction . . . the intended amalgamation of the Know-Nothings and the Abolitionists in their warfare against the constitutional guarantees of the southern states. . . .

This great political unrest weighed heavily on the country's economy and business slowly contracted as events both in New England and across the nation diminished trade. Henry Clay's Compromise Measures of 1850—designed to reconcile the antislavery and proslavery factions of the country—effectively worsened the situation inasmuch as the Abolitionists, Whigs and Free Soilers had no intention of abiding by the Fugitive Slave Law, which provided for the return of runaway slaves. Rather than soothing the national fury, the law bred rancor on both sides.

For want of frivolous entertainments—like professional sports—politics was the great outlet of the day. Unlike the meaningless outcomes of baseball and football contests though, the ideological movements of the day had the power to transform people's lives. In that context, politics was a real blood sport at mid-century, with the victors handed the power to radically alter history. Commensurate with the gravity of elections, large, festive parades were held on Inauguration Day with sumptuous dinners, parties and picnics the order of the day. Either in an open landau or on a prancing steed, the new governor would sweep up Main Street, flanked by his foot guard, and waving to tens of thousands of cheering spectators along the parade route.

Against this backdrop of political turmoil, social angst and victory parties, the Hartford Water Works began its arduous construction period. For all intents and purposes, the building of the system took a little more than two years. Some design work was done in the closing months of 1853, but the great bulk of the system was assembled in late 1854 and 1855. The first full year of construction, 1854, was not terribly productive because much time was spent correcting the mistakes of the acting water board. Further hindering progress was the common council's contemptible attack on Ezra Clark, which left the water works virtually rudderless. The embattled Clark was thrust into a campaign for a seat in the U.S. Congress at a time when personal financial troubles threatened to land him and his family in the almshouse. Accordingly—and probably just as the Whigs had intended—the physical progress of the city's nascent water system in 1854 was agonizingly slow. By late summer, Hiram Bissell was effectively in charge of the project and officially ascended to the presidency before the building season began in 1855. Bissell's ascension to the presidency of the Board of Water Commissioners was an important turning point for the water works, for he was ideally suited to complete the work. Thanks to Sylvester Bissell's agreement to take up some of the slack at H. & S. Bissell, Hiram had the requisite time to bird-dog the construction work, and was able to, at least in principle, spend full time attending to the needs of the department, as the original charter demanded. Thus, while the other four members of the board served in an almost ceremonial capacity—attending an evening meeting every other week—the lion's share of the decisions and the grinding day-to-day work of building the system fell onto the president's shoulders. No small thing.

A few months before Bissell's promotion, a local conflagration underscored the importance of his task. On Tuesday night in December 1854, James Goodwin's tired United States Hotel in State House Square caught fire. Much of the original hotel was destroyed as well as Clapp's livery stable, which adjoined the now eviscerated hulk of a hostelry. The fire department worked until eight o'clock in the morning, at last containing the blaze and limiting the damage in the most congested part of the city. The hotel's proximity to the largest of the underground cisterns, built in State House Square, saved some of the hotel, but fire hydrants connected to an aqueduct system might have reduced the amount of damage substantially.

For Hiram Bissell, thanks to a child's garden of poor decisions and outright blunders by chief engineer James Slade, overseeing the construction of the water works stole ever-increasing blocks of his time just as his masonry business was about to take a great leap forward. Until this time, he had concentrated on residential work, building and selling houses but, through his friendship with Samuel Colt, had landed the contract for all of the brickwork on the inventor's massive new armory. The outside walls of the manufactory were cut stone, but much of the other parts of the complex—including Colt's large business office—were brick. Fulfilling a separate contract the following year, he also did the stuccowork and the interior plastering of Samuel and Elizabeth Colt's new mansion, *Armsmear*, which the couple moved into in June of 1857. To say that Bissell was a busy man would be a gross understatement of the obvious.

The biggest problem at the water works though, was that before a step could be taken forward, two had to be taken backwards to unknot the skein of previous mistakes. Of paramount concern for Hiram Bissell was to figure out what chief engineer, James Slade, was doing. As an example of his bizarre calculations, Slade multiplied the horsepower of the engine (65) times $450 per horsepower to arrive at the projected cost *for the entire system*. (Where he came up with this ridiculous formula is anyone's guess.) His final figure of $29,250 was roughly $220,000 too low. Looming large in Bissell's mind were the costs associated with cleaning up after Slade. He was painfully aware these cost overruns would stick to him and his water board like flypaper. As he noted in his first annual report to the council—

The former Board, it will be remembered, had arranged all the preliminaries for the construction of the Water Works. They had an Engineer . . . had selected and purchased sites for the Reservoir and Engine House, contracted for a Cornish Pump and Steam Engine, as well as Iron Pipe, Stop Cocks, Hydrants, &c. They had also matured a plan for the Reservoir, and had selected the streets through which the water should pass. . . .

In a nutshell, the new board was stuck with a great many choices that were now cast in stone. Bissell went on to remind the common council that all of these matters had been presented to and approved by them and that the water board had no choice but to implement the plan as designed. Punctuating the problems that the water board had experienced at the hands of the council, Bissell pointed out that ". . . the Commissioners regret to have noticed an apparent desire on the part of some members of the late common council, to embarrass the action of the board." So much for setting the record straight; it was time to get to work.

Spending most of 1854 assessing the work that had already been begun and reviewing previously concluded contracts, Bissell also had many months to watch James Slade in action and, putting the most charitable light on it, one must conclude that he was entirely underwhelmed.

Slade was not from Hartford and he lodged at the City Hotel on Main Street, the most expensive place in town, during his uninspired stay. He had, on a number of occasions, employed considerable legerdemain when touting his experience, including telling the council that he had "followed this sort of civil engineering about ten years." Yet, when Bissell made a few discreet inquiries into his background, it was "ascertained that he had never before acted as chief engineer in the construction of any water works. . . ." In fact, Bissell finally came to the conclusion that Slade was so incompetent that he had to go. Bissell later wrote that the engineer ". . .did not prove to have the necessary knowledge and judgment." Given Slade's history of misrepresentations and poor decisions, Bissell dismissed him as chief engineer at the end of the 1854 construction season, November 30th—Thanksgiving Day as it turned out. (Until 1941, when Congress changed Thanksgiving to the fourth Thursday in November, it was celebrated on the last—sometimes fifth—Thursday of the month.) Accordingly, with his walking papers in hand, the hapless James Slade had little to be thankful for, as his holiday consisted of packing his bags and leaving Hartford, with winter coming on and his future uncertain.

The water system, as designed by Dr. Hunt and the acting board, was essentially three simple pieces—a reservoir, a labyrinth of distribution pipes and a steam-powered pumping engine at the river. Owing to the shortage of heavy machinery in the mid-nineteenth century, this seemingly simple trio of components represented a backbreaking and diverse market basket of labors.

Beginning with the reservoir—a glorified swimming pool and little else—the existing record illumines an oft times dispiriting and sometimes humorous record of haste, poor engineering and Sisyphean repair work. The fact that this lowly catchment managed to hold water at all was baffling, if not miraculous. Despite the litany of problems with the reservoir, its creation began harmlessly enough.

In the late fall of the previous year, the acting board agreed to purchase a two and a half acre parcel atop Lord's Hill from Rev. William Turner, a longtime teacher at the American Asylum for the Deaf and Dumb. (Actually, Rev. Turner was considerably more than just an instructor at this school, for he was elevated to provost in 1854.) The land in question was behind this school at the junction of Myrtle and Garden Streets. The great bend in the Connecticut River was clearly visible a good mile to the east and a hundred feet below Lord's Hill.

Lord's Hill Reservoir. Originally, the sidewalls were only clay.

Except for some preliminary survey work, little was done with the property until the following spring because Turner's land was not actually purchased by the board until March 1854 when, for $14,600, the transfer was effected. In approximate numbers, the land was a rectangle measuring about 275 feet on the short sides and almost 600 feet on the long. Since the proposed reservoir itself was only 150 by 300 feet and was to be excavated to a depth of thirty-five feet, this original parcel should have provided more than enough space for the catchment.

However, at the end of June, the Asylum for the Deaf and Dumb was persuaded to part with two additional—though much smaller—parcels, which helped to square off the piece of land acquired three months earlier. Since these last two parcels were meager—totaling about one acre—and the purchase made so much later than the original purchase, one wonders if a miscalculation became apparent only after the digging commenced. In any event, for $5,190, the Asylum for the Deaf and Dumb sold the board the extra land. Collectively, the site of the new Lord's Hill Reservoir—now three and a half acres—was just west of the city and, by all accounts, the only reasonable site from whence gravity could be expected to deliver water throughout the developed areas of Hartford.

By the time Bissell took command, a hundred men were crawling over the site, digging through every kind of rock and soil imaginable while they grubbed out a crater in the hilltop capable of holding almost ten million gallons of water. While the excavation was a backbreaking effort, the preparation of the walls was more exacting work and critical to the reservoir's ability to hold water. Clay was used to "puddle" the walls in a process similar to plastering except that, with the help of the sun, the final lining of the walls would have the consistency of brickwork. Chief engineer Slade had contracted with the partnership of James and Charles Collins to deliver the clay and "puddle" the walls and, by the summer of 1854, the sidewalls of the reservoir were rising apace. It was not long, however, before, the Collins brothers were reassessing their work with growing alarm.

At the bottom of this pit, the puddling proceeded with precision, but as this inner clay liner rose, its sheer weight—along with the poor quality of the clay—caused the work to slump. Though the Collins brothers rebuilt the walls a number of times, the situation was never properly corrected and persisted over the lifetime of the reservoir. (Just before the reservoir was filled in October 1855, a sample of the clay was brought to the *Times* and the substance was described thusly— "Once in about one-quarter of an inch is a layer of *quicksand*, which makes it the worst soil that can be procured for this purpose.")

As if these slides were not enough to reduce a grown man to tears, a severe drought in the summer months of 1854 brought the work on the walls to a complete standstill. Central to the puddling process was water, which—according to the Collins brothers' contract—was to come from nearby wells. Unhappily, the drought dried up these sources and the brothers took this as a sign from the Almighty that it was time for an extended rest. The Connecticut River was only a mile away and, even in the worst drought, flowed with abundant supplies, but the Collins brothers demurred. With the great gift of hindsight, this recalcitrance is almost comical—these men were building a reservoir and they could not get enough water to do their work? Finally, Bissell remedied the problem by using the wagons and barrels from his own masonry business to deliver water to the site. Thenceforth, the work progressed as intended.

The second part of the system was the hydra-like tentacles of the aqueducts that would pipe the water to the cluster of homes, offices and manufactories in the shadow of Lord's Hill. While presenting nowhere near the problems associated with the Lord's Hill Reservoir, about nine months later in the spring of 1855, this subterranean cluster of pipes raised a dilemma of a different kind, associated more with Slade's departure from Hartford than the pipes themselves. (More on this matter later.)

When comparing the innovations that allowed for the growth of the great municipal water companies, including the Hartford Water Works, the one that truly supercharged drinking water systems was the cast iron pipe. In effect, the cast iron pipe was to water systems what the ball bearing was to the wheel. By reducing leakage and allowing significantly higher pressure within the system, larger networks could be built—networks that would have been impossible with wooden pipes. When the water works chose to use cast iron pipes, another option was offered—lead pipes. In the 1850s, the cost differential between cast iron and lead pipes made the latter a tempting choice even though they were, even then, almost universally considered injurious to health.

The choice of a piping material played havoc with people's minds since they had overwhelmingly voted for a city-owned water works. Only days after that vote, the *Courant* published a series of articles on the lethal effects of lead in water pipes and, as calculated, scared the bejesus out of everyone. Recognizing the paper's true motives, Bissell decided to reassure the citizenry before the water works began operations. In the board's first annual report to the council— the highlights of which would automatically be reprinted in the newspapers—he addressed the issue of the lead pipes head-on—

> . . . The various kinds of service pipe had the careful examination of the board, and after deliberate consultation, and with the aide of the best advise they could procure, it has been decided to use the American galvanized iron pipe . . . [moreover] the commissioners recommend their fellow-citizens . . . adopt it for the inside of dwellings and other places . . . .

While a detailed explanation of the type of water pipe to be bedded beneath the streets went a long way toward stilling the anxieties of the public, it did not entirely resolve things for Hiram Bissell. There was another small problem that nagged him—the water pipes did not pass his new home on Wadsworth Street. He was expending enormous energies to help construct the water works, where his every decision blossomed into a knockdown, drag-out *battle royal* with the Whigs on the council, and his family would not even be connected to the system! How could this be?

The problem was basically one of economics. If every street, lane and highway were counted, Hartford had a grid of more than fifteen miles of roads in 1854. Bedding more than nine miles of pipes—including fifty stop cocks and sixty-two public hydrants—was a colossal expense. Had Bissell still lived on Buckingham Street—one of the wider boulevards in town—the pipes would certainly have passed in front of his home. Wadsworth Street was a different story. A relatively new street with only a few homes, it was scheduled to be connected to the system at a later date.

But Bissell found a way around this. Because the South School House was on Wadsworth Street, he had some leverage. After laying out his case before the council, surprisingly enough, even the Whigs agreed to include Wadsworth Street in the original system without the usual disputations.

Hiram Bissell's headaches should all have been disposed of with a few flourishes of copperplate lettering in an annual report and some precatory words with the council, but such was not the case. Of the three principal components of the water works, the granddaddy of all controversies, the absolute stump puller of decisions was that of the Cornish engine.

While the reservoir would never rise above the humble status of a hole in the ground and the pipes in the streets were—Poseidon be praised—buried and forgotten, the Cornish engine created an arena of dispute that elevated it to a cause célèbre. It was the marquis-cut diamond of the new water works, the whirling, chuffing, ferrous wonder that captured the imagination of young and old alike. In the final analysis, this mechanical marvel represented only a tiny fraction of the total cost of the system, but managed to cleave the city's residents into almost equal factions of squabbling dilettantes. In truth, there were only a dozen men in Hartford with enough knowledge of steam engines to qualify as experts, but every tradesman, mechanic, broker and saloonkeeper joined the fray.

The Cornish engine was a powerful steam boiler and pump, used to raise water from tin and copper mines in and around Cornwall, England. It was the British inventor, Thomas Savery who, after noting the repeated failures of others to raise the water out of the mines, licked the problem with his steam pump in 1698. Following up on Savery's success, at least a dozen French and English inventors experimented with different models of the steam engine, perfecting a wide range of refinements along the way. Of particular interest was the team of Thomas Boulton and James Watt, who worked together for a quarter of a century, with Watt supplying the brains and Boulton the business acumen. The Boulton & Watt steam engines were an improvement on the Savery design but, in time, were themselves overshadowed when another Englishman's work came to the fore.

Richard Trevithick, building on the work of Boulton and Watt, produced a most remarkable engine. By using the hot flue exhaust to preheat the water for the boiler—thus increasing its efficiency—Trevithick finally hit on the formula for the Cornish boiler in 1812. The Cornish engine was essentially a huge seesaw—or beam—mounted twenty feet in the air. While one side of the seesaw was lifted by the upward motion of the piston in the steam engine, the opposite end lowered to force water out of a housing. This simple invention—along with the inventor's other advances—allowed the Cornish engine to do many times the work of the Boulton & Watt machines.

The Cornish engine had overwhelmed the world of steam technology because it quickly built a reputation that was beyond fantastic. The largest Cornish engine built up to that time was constructed in 1846 by Sandys, Carne & Vivian of Copperhouse Foundry, Hayle, Cornwall for the Grand Junction Water Works to introduce water into the west end of London. Dubbed the Grand Junction 90 (for the diameter in inches of its piston), this monster delivered 472 gallons of water with just one bone-jarring crunch of its mighty pump. This feat was not lost on engineers and members of water boards, including those in the U.S. Therefore, although the Cornish engine was a rough brute, expelling water out of its one pump in violent, thundering spasms and, if truth be told, not particularly suited for water works, it was impossible to dismiss the engine out of hand.

One man who could have helped immensely with the dispute over the Cornish engine was Hiram Bissell's friend, Elisha Root. But although Root was considered one of the greatest mechanical minds in New England, by the time the water board needed his help, the council had already sidelined him. In early 1854, when the city was taking its first awkward steps toward building a system, Root was one of the men appointed to the post of acting commissioner. As the superintendent of Colt's Patent Fire-Arms, he was a mechanical wizard, fabricating much of the machinery in Samuel Colt's armory straight from the intricate images and configurations that materialized magically in his brain. His talents were so extraordinary that Colt offered him the astounding annual salary of $5000 to act as his superintendent, luring him away from the Collins Company, the largest producer of axes in the world. Whether he made edged tools or revolvers made little difference to Root. His interest lay in the machinery that produced these items.

Since steam engines had to be ordered—each one custom made with long lead times for production—the acting board instinctively put the engine at the top of its punch list. No sooner had the subject of the engine been broached, however, when a great brouhaha erupted. Time did nothing to vitiate this stalemate as opinions slowly stiffened and, at length, hardened to the consistency of concrete.

At a meeting of the common council in February 1854, the long and heated debate came to a head, with Root speaking for the opponents of the English machine. Root was a quiet, soft-spoken man, who had trained scores of eager young machinists in the intricacies of machine tooling. His knowledge of the Cornish engine was extensive and, more importantly, he knew that few water works in America were using it—and for good reason. Patiently, he pointed out the shortcomings of the engine—its violently pulsating nature and, almost incidentally, the fact that the sixty-five horsepower model proposed from the outset was woefully inadequate to the task at hand.

In its place, Root recommended a machine of his own design, which would run smoother by employing ten pumps and burn much less coal in the bargain. Unfortunately, he proved to be a better mechanic than a salesman, for when the final vote was taken, the council decided in favor of the Cornish engine—15 to 11. Realizing the council's folly—or perhaps willful disregard for the future of the water works—Root found himself in an awkward position. Not only was his reputation worth far more to him than an unpaid seat on a temporary water board, but now his ego was bruised. When it came to things mechanical, he had no peers and yet, unfathomably, the council had ignored his advice. Since he could not afford to have his name associated with what he perceived to be a full-fledged, ocean-going disaster, Root did the only thing he could—he resigned.

The council replaced the invaluable Elisha Root with Samuel Ward, the president of the Hartford Gas Light Company, whose knowledge of steam boilers—while not inconsequential—was that of a child compared to the highly-respected Elisha Root. A few weeks later, after tempers had cooled, the council approved a contract with R.P. Perrott & Company of West Point, New York for the production of a sixty-five horsepower Cornish engine for $21,000.

Although the matter appeared to have been settled, as early as July 1854, the water board began petitioning the council for permission to void the contract. Hiram Bissell, although not in a highly technical business himself, was a man of great conviction and a man who believed strongly in Elisha Root. If Root opposed the Cornish engine, then Bissell did not need to be a technical wunderkind; he only needed common sense.

By the beginning of September, the council chambers crackled like the ozone before a lightning storm, as tempers flared and heated exchanges forced a fresh look at the Cornish engine. Since the battle over the Cornish engine was now completely out of hand and beyond the realm of civil discourse, the opposing camps picked attorneys to make their cases before the council. In subsequent discussions, the "American engine" and the "Root engine" became interchangeable references to a low pressure, smooth running, multi-pumped machine, most likely of local manufacture. Making the case for the water board was an attorney, E.N. Dickinson of New Jersey, who had an impressive command of the principles of steam technology, an obvious familiarity with the water works in other American cities and the tireless, stentorian delivery of a fervent, Bible-thumping zealot. The members of the common council—and others who favored the Cornish engine—were represented by Hartford's city attorney, Lucius Robinson, a capable lawyer, though of a more reserved nature. At the request of the council, the case for the American engine was made first.

At seven o'clock on a Friday night in early September 1854, Dickinson delivered his attack on the Cornish engine with a precision and erudition that was as breathtaking as it was concise. His presentation, the myriad questions that followed and the lingering debate afterward lasted for more than three hours. Although Dickinson laid out the case against the Cornish engine in a series of pummeling attacks, the crux of his argument was that the physics involved in raising water two thousand feet from tin mines in England was entirely different from that of gently coaxing water up a ten degree grade to the top of Lord's Hill.

Dickinson went further. In the United States, Buffalo was the only city using the English engine at the time, and the company that supplied Buffalo with water reported a pumping efficiency that was about 25 percent below expectations. In sharp contrast, an American pump was employed at Cincinnati and was performing about 80 percent better than the Cornish engine at Buffalo.

Philadelphia, he pointed out, was using a variation of the American design. Furthermore, if the American design of engine were used at Philadelphia's Fairmount Works instead of water wheels, it would achieve the same results. Lastly, he ventured that, although the double-action pumps at Philadelphia worked well, they would behave still better with more pumps. In short, if a greater number of pumps were employed and they were arrayed in such a way as to distribute the load evenly on each pump, a greater efficiency would result.

Late in the evening and nearing the climax of his presentation, Dickinson bore down. Using a model and some diagrams, he outlined the most favorable outcome of the Cornish engine. He then proceeded to show that this "best case scenario" would produce little more than a continuing case of buyer's remorse for Hartford.

The following night, Lucius Robinson and the proponents of the Cornish engine tried to counter E. N. Dickinson's arguments, but failed to mount a convincing defense of the engine. In cautionary tones, he warned that "a failure in the engine would be a serious thing for the city [and] the Cornish engine was positively known to be successful, while the proposed substitute [was] an experiment." At ten o'clock, E. N. Dickinson rose to rebut Robinson's points, but the council postponed the discussion until the following evening.

The next night, without missing a beat, the indomitable E. N. Dickinson took the floor for another three hours of persuasion that was as welcome as ants at a picnic. Though his effect can only be surmised from a considerable distance of time, the members of the council were clearly exhausted by his genuine passion, bound as it was to a real gift for prodigious tub-thumping. Oddly enough though—according to the newspaper accounts of the day—not a single shred of new information was introduced at any of the three marathon meetings. The council, however, was dog-tired and, when at last they voted, came down overwhelmingly against the Cornish engine. Whether they were loath to chance a return engagement by the redoubtable E. N. Dickerson or had simply heard enough wrangling about the Cornish engine to last a lifetime, remains an open question.

The council's next move, however, was not in doubt. After allowing the dust to settle, they permitted the water board to abrogate the contract with R. P. Perrott and begin the search for someone to build the Root engine. The ill-fated

James Slade and the council had just cost the taxpayers of the city $750, the cancellation penalty in the agreement with Perrott & Company.

That same month, the council authorized the water board to purchase a piece of land by the river from James Ward for $1700. The parcel was in the northern section of the city about an eighth of a mile north of the covered bridge (in present day Riverside Park). Once again, the acting water board had chosen the site much earlier, and Bissell and his fellow board members were stuck with it. Soon thereafter, Henry Tryon's firm was engaged to do the construction work on the engine house. Scrambling to beat the cold weather, his men completed the foundation work by the end of the year.

When the cold weather arrived in late 1854, Hiram Bissell closed down construction for the winter and had Elisha Root assemble a set of plans for the American engine, which could be used to obtain bids. Unbeknownst to him, he wasn't the only one making preparations for the future. During December, the Whigs hatched another plot to deliver a deathblow to the water works. On January 10, 1855, the council called a special city meeting for the following Monday—the 15th of January—to "consider the subject of the water works . . . or the finances connected with them." The *Times* went on to conclude that—

> . . . it is broadly hinted that an effort is to be made to break down the important work so far as the city is concerned . . . The pretext will be that a [private] company can do it better. This pretext comes too late. The city has laid down the pipes, has expended a large sum upon the reservoir, and another large sum upon the works at the river. A large portion of the entire expense has already been incurred and the whole work can be completed [by] early next summer. . . .

Once again the public turned out in a huge throng to find out what was afoot. Not surprisingly, the water bonds were the focus of the attack but, rather than letting one man defend his honor in public—as they had forced Ezra Clark to do—this time the Whigs coerced Democratic Mayor Henry Deming to appoint a blue ribbon committee to scrutinize the finances of the water works. On a motion from the Whigs, the mayor appointed a committee of nine men to examine the books. Taking no chances this time, the Whigs overtly loaded the committee in their favor. Five of the nine men appointed were original incorporators of the private water company!

The citizens were outraged. The Whigs were in for some payback though. Astute businessman that he was, Samuel Colt sensed that the Whigs might attempt some fiscal chicanery and, energized by his extreme hatred of this bunch, he sent a communiqué to the council meeting. To the secret delight—and probable forehand knowledge—of Hiram Bissell, Colt stated that if funding were a problem, he "would buy $5000 [worth of] water bonds at par, or if necessary

$10,000, or furthermore if necessary $20,000." Stunned by Colt's sudden involvement, the Whigs turned tail. They may have done some financial studies—although no such records exist—but their latest plot to destroy the water works had failed thanks to Samuel Colt.

On a different front, an altogether unexpected conundrum surfaced involving the new engine. Finding an engine builder to fabricate the Root engine was about to turn into a house-to-house search. The verbal brawls at the city meetings between the council and the water board had escalated into such mean-spirited affairs that potential engine manufacturers were nowhere to be found. Beyond the disharmony at City Hall, they also shied away because the design of the Root engine was untried and the possibility of failure high. To fail in such a public forum was simply too much. Just as the search turned from bleak to frantic, a lone bidder emerged.

Samuel Woodruff, a Whig member of the water board, was also one of the principals of Woodruff & Beach Iron Works, one of Hartford's premier engine builders. Woodruff was an interesting character because, while at one time he was president of the Mercantile Bank, he was also an incurable shop rat. Born with lubricating oil in his veins, he was a man who loved machinery and challenges in equal measure. He had enough money and self-esteem to weather the worst of disasters and stood, therefore, in fine stead to build the engine. His firm entered the only bid.

In March 1855, the council approved a contract between the water board and Woodruff & Beach Iron Works, whereby Woodruff's firm would build the Root engine for $17,500 and they promptly handed over a down payment of $4,375. To avoid the appearance of impropriety, Samuel Woodruff resigned from the board. The battle lines had been so firmly drawn in the warfare between the council and the water board that no Whig in his right mind wanted to serve on the latter body. Lacking a better choice, they turned to an alderman and Democrat, James Bolter, a partner with the grocery firm of Charles Northam & Company. Even with the $750 penalty paid to R. P. Perrott & Company, there was still a savings of $2,750, a tidy sum in 1855, but a poor bargain if the Root engine failed. The wisdom or folly of the change would hang in the balance for nine long months.

As the spring rains fell gently across New England, Mayor Henry Deming delivered his April address to the common council. Though his speech wandered over a button box of city business, the water department got special attention— perhaps with good reason. The winter months of 1855 were the absolute low point in morale for those involved with the water venture. With the Whigs attacking like birds of prey and construction at a dead halt, there was little to do but wait for spring.

Eight of the nine-mile network of pipes had already been laid and two-thirds of the work at the reservoir was completed, leaving a jumble of pipe connections and some landscaping at the Lord's Hill site. The stone foundations at the engine house by the river had been laid, but the building itself had not yet been started. Last but not least, Woodruff & Beach was hard at work on the new engine, offering no clue as to when it would be completed. The city had already expended $177,000 on the water works and, though the mayor's prediction that the job would be completed for the allotted $250,000, his opinion was nothing but optimistic conjecture.

Adding to the existing concerns, economic times were getting tougher and the inhabitants of Hartford growing tired of the quickly-mounting expenditures and slow progress. In consequence, it was incumbent upon the mayor to give a pep talk and at least try to do a little fence-mending. A blind man could see that the relationship between the common council and the water commissioners was poor and, if the work was to be completed at all, both sides needed to bury the hatchet. The existing record paints Mayor Deming as a genial man and certainly not dim-witted but, considering the Whigs' continued assaults on the department, asking the council to embrace the city-owned water works at this point was a fool's errand. The mayor's high-minded remarks accomplished nothing.

With the advent of spring in 1855 and the chance to complete the water works at hand, Bissell made his choice for the all-important job of chief engineer to replace the now-long-gone James Slade, and it was an unusual one. Nathan Starkweather was a Hartford surveyor, with an encyclopedic knowledge of the city's many property lines and its history, but he was no engineer. In fairness though, Starkweather was in no way different from other professionals of the mid-1850s. Pretty much, a man could call himself anything he chose and, as long as he had the knowledge and skills to back it up, would be accepted as such. Truth told, the great bulk of the college-trained engineers working in the United States before 1865 were recent arrivals in America, having received their training at foreign universities. This stems from the fact that, before that date, there were only three engineering schools in the U.S.—Rensselaer, West Point and the Naval Academy.

When Starkweather entered James Slade's old office on Pearl Street, he found many drawings and designs, but a schematic for the eight miles of buried pipes was not among them. By his own account, ". . . . a large portion of the street pipes had been laid, but laid in detached pieces, and the absence of the notes and minutes, which must have been taken . . . during its progress, continued to delay the work."

Reading between the lines, it seems clear that, rather than securing Slade's office—thereby safeguarding all of his notes and surveys before letting him go— the board allowed the departing engineer to abscond with the drawings that showed where the unconnected pipes were buried beneath the streets. In the absence of these drawings, Starkweather had to reconstruct all of this information relying solely on the memories of the diggers. More time was lost, while the information was gathered and transposed onto proper surveys.

Starkweather only stayed with the water works for the 1855 season, maintaining his private surveying practice all the while. Nonetheless, he gave good value as an engineer. Either sensing that the water department represented a good career opportunity or merely because it consumed an inordinate amount of his time, he moved all of his business activities to the water board's offices. Apparently Starkweather had misjudged the situation though, for the following year, he was back in private practice and once again operating out of the Hall of Records building, farther down Pearl Street, on the corner of Trumbull. His departure was amicable though, because a decade later the water works called upon him again in an entirely different matter.

The emerging water works may have given the people of Hartford something to occupy their thoughts but, as reported by the newspapers, there were other daily concerns. With fascinating doggedness, the newspapers reported on the ebb and flow of life in small town America near mid-century—the weather, the crops, the entertainments and the conditions at the river. In early May when Messrs. Ballard, Bailey & Company's Circus came to town, the traveling performers received a royal welcome and enough inked hyperbole to warm a showman's heart. At the same time, the playbill of Dr. Wyatt's Dramatic Lyceum was regularly paraded before the public and the performances critiqued—very politely—thereafter. Underscoring the rural, agricultural nature of America at the time, the amount of moisture in the fields and the height of the corn were such common staples that editors probably left the type set on the stone, merely changing the critical numbers as the ongoing drama of farm life continued. Every freshet at the river was documented from the time the water rose an inch at the wharfs until it returned to stasis four to eight weeks later.

With startling indelicacy, privies surfaced sporadically in print for a variety of reasons. Sometimes carelessness with a whale oil lamp cost a family its facility while, on other score-settling occasions, young delinquents burned down a neighbor's outhouse for spite. The fire department responded to a number of these calls each year. Occasionally these articles told of heartrending events, demonstrating the harsh reality of everyday life before indoor plumbing. One Sunday morning in October 1855, two girls fell through the floor of a privy and drowned, just one block east of the Bissell residence, causing the *Times* to re-enumerate the basic rules of privies—

> . . . Let the seats only be placed over the vault. This is far pleasanter than the ordinary way of putting the whole building over it and in case the floor breaks through, there can be no danger.

The shape of the seats should never be circular. They ought to be elliptical [so that] the smallest child would find it impossible to get his body through them.

During the summer months, sheep owners lost some of their stock to stray dogs. The majority of these animals were "common cur dogs," some trained as house pets, but many wandering about freely, the highborn kinsmen of Hartford's low-lying meadows. Overcome by the basest instincts of their forbears—which most people assumed had been bred out of them—they made short work of a few young sheep each year. In order to compensate the owners, a dog fund was begun. To support the fund, dog licensing descended on the city and, for a registration fee of twenty-five cents, owners were given tags to be displayed on collars worn by their canines at all times. The licensing fee was nominal, but the tax was not; male dogs were taxed at $1 annually and bitches ran to $5. Registration turned out to be the most uproarious entertainment in town when it was discovered that the registration papers were a confusing mess—with dog-owners unable to figure out if the form was asking for the sex and age of the owner or the dog!

By the middle of September 1855, the work on the reservoir atop Lord's Hill was all but completed and the *Times*, in its Saturday paper, felt comfortable in predicting that water would be introduced into the city "after the middle of next week." The construction at the river was also "in such a state of forwardness that no delay will be experienced at that point . . ." Crews were even attaching the fire hydrants to pipes in various streets throughout the city. Converging like the different sections of a great symphony orchestra, one by one, the separate sections of the water works neared final assembly.

Everyone should have been ecstatic that such a laborious undertaking was about to bear fruit, but the Whigs used the pregnant pause before the triumphant finish to stir up trouble. The council meetings had degenerated into gripe sessions filled with enough harrumphing to drown out a hospital ward full of consumptives. Like some wearisome tag-team match, this time the aldermen and the councilmen took turns venting their frustrations in an evening of pointless accusations, berating the members of the water board and denigrating their efforts.

Democratic Alderman James Bolter—the appointed replacement for Samuel Woodruff on the water board—began the meeting with a list of complaints. He professed confusion over the hiring of Nathan Starkweather as chief engineer, which was done without the council's consent. Also, he was unhappy that the bottom of the reservoir had been paved (with bricks) without the authority of the council. Finally, referring to a contract for a new grade of galvanized service pipe made up specifically for the water works by the local firm of Bidwell &

Pitkin, he flatly refuse to ratify it because he "believed there was a cat under the meal."

It was obvious that Hiram Bissell had not included Bolter in any of the water board's decisions, but with good reason. Bolter was extremely ambitious and quick to align himself with the prosperous Whigs for personal gain. Without overstating the obvious, he may not have had the best interests of the water works at heart. If Bissell did not trust Bolter, his instincts were sound. Secondly, between the masonry work that Bissell was doing on Samuel Colt's armory and the time required to oversee the construction of the water works, he simply could not consult with Bolter continually. Lastly, and perhaps most importantly, the Whigs on the council had given free reign to the acting water board, but were now trying to block, or at least delay, decisions that Bissell and his board were making by imposing more stringent "advise and consent" rules. Judging by their behavior, they had definitely not earned that privilege. Under these circumstances, Bissell had decided to keep his decisions to himself and proceed with the business at hand, rather than to beg the council's blessing at every turn.

When Whig Alderman Abner Church, a rope manufacturer, took the floor, he stated that the council would have liked to have had a contract with the original engineer, James Slade, who was paid $300 a month. With this in mind, he could not understand why Nathan Starkweather was employed at $175 a month—and still with no contract. His other pet peeve was the clay slides at the reservoir that requires so much extra work—at city expense. It was his contention that, because the water board's contract with the Collins brothers was so poorly drawn, it did not force the pair to absorb the costs to rebuild the walls themselves. Consequently, the city had to pay for the repairs. (Not that it would have mattered to Alderman Church, but the contract with the Collins brothers was penned by the inept James Slade, not by Hiram Bissell or Nathan Starkweather.)

Councilman Lawson Ives, a wool dealer and thoroughly irritating man, having heard enough, made a motion that the council summarily dismiss the entire Board of Water Commissioners. Ives, without realizing it, had stumbled badly. He must have been spending too much time filling out orders for bales of wool and not enough time walking around the city, for he completely undervalued the Herculean efforts of Hiram Bissell and his board. With one ill-advised suggestion, he had put the council in an untenable position.

James Bolter, startled by the foolishness of the idea, quickly asked to have Ives's motion removed from the table. Ives had insulted Bissell and the other members of the board so thoroughly that Bolter was certain that the water commissioners would resign en masse. Seeking to lower the level of vitriol, Bolter paid some compliments to the board members and "especially the president *pro tem*, saying that he considered Bissell a valuable man."

The skirmishes between the council and the water board had been reported with great relish in the newspapers and, in the absence of legalized boxing matches or horse races, the simmering acrimony went a long way toward filling conversational voids in smoky taverns as well as the elegantly appointed parlors of private homes. Bolter knew that if all of the members of the water board resigned, there would be hell to pay. Not only would the council have a difficult time seating a new board, but the voters would most assuredly tar and feather the members of the present council. Lawson Ives may not have realized it, but Bolter saved his bacon by intervening so swiftly.

Among the many votes taken that night, the council agreed to pay about $5000 worth of bills associated with the water department but, in a childish gesture of defiance, refused to pay $962.50 in accumulated salary for Nathan Starkweather, the chief engineer.

When Bissell heard this, he was infuriated. Knowing that the water system was completed to the point that any idiot could finish the work—and also knowing that the very last thing the Whigs wanted was the job of overseeing the work themselves—he decided to act. The sickening *pas de deux* with its unrelenting brinksmanship had gone too far. When the final communication of the evening was read aloud, there was a stunned silence in the council chambers. The hastily written note was the resignation of Hiram Bissell.

The Whigs were hung by their own petard and they knew it. There was perhaps no one in the whole city who contributed more to the building of the water works than Hiram Bissell and the public was well aware of it. If the council accepted his resignation, they would be tossed out of office at the next election if they were not strung up from the nearest lamppost first. And much as they may have favored a private water company owned and run by their fellow Whigs, they had to agree with Bolter that Hiram Bissell was a good man. Therefore, at the next council meeting, and before the matter took on a life of its own, they refused to accept Bissell's resignation. In fact, a vote was passed "approving all of his acts so far as they had come to the knowledge of the council" and, once again, they reiterated their desire for him to continue in office.

Insisting on the last word, however, the council grumbled about the lack of concert existing between the water board and the council, laying the blame at the feet of Ezra Clark, the former president. As they wanted the voters to believe, even though they had accused him of malfeasance and dragged his good name through the mud, as one councilman put it, "Clark should have used the council with common civility." Now that Ezra Clark was in Congress and trying to straighten out his crumbling business affairs, he spent very little time in Hartford and, therefore, sat on the water board almost as a commissioner emeritus. In a craven attempt to pin blame on a man who was not even there to defend himself, the council recommended the removal of Ezra Clark from the board. They apparently had the last word in this shameless folderol (though there is no record of Clark's removal) for when the annual report of the water commissioners was issued in January, Ezra Clark's name was not listed.

The above-mentioned annual report was significant for another reason. While Elisha Root, and his tremendous expertise with engines, had been roundly dismissed by the common council at the outset of the construction process, he showed up as one of the commissioners for the 1855 season. Since he and Hiram Bissell were in almost daily contact as Samuel Colt's new armory arose in Hartford's south meadows, one suspects that Bissell used his persuasive powers to convince Root to "watch over" the work on the new engine at the Woodruff & Beach Iron Works. The council paid him the highest compliment by accepting his engine, so Root had no reason to balk. Besides, how could Root pass up the opportunity to assist in the creation of a brand new engine? Apparently, he couldn't.

If and when the water works was completed, it would put Hartford right in line with other cities of the time. By 1860, there were 136 water delivery systems operating in the United States. The sixteen largest cities all had water companies of one kind or another and three quarters of them were owned by the municipalities themselves. Of the sixteen largest cities in the country, all but four—Providence, Buffalo, New Orleans and San Francisco—owned their own water companies. It was unlikely that any of these systems delivered water to every last person in their respective cities, but at least the initial steps in the creation of municipal water companies had been taken.

On a Saturday night at the end of September 1855, the clay forming the north wall of the Lord's Hill Reservoir caved in and the base of the wall buckled more than a foot from its original seat, necessitating a rebuilding job destined to take weeks. Apparently, a Thursday rain had "moistened this artificial bed of clay and made it about as slippery as it would have been had it received a thorough coating of oil." The rains of the following Monday swiftly made a bad situation worse. Word of this most recent slide got around town fast, and speculation grew that water would not be introduced into the city until the following year, causing a creeping dysphoria. Doffing his public relations cap, Bissell declared that the water works meant "to supply the water by the middle of this month [September] at the farthest, notwithstanding the accident."

As workmen descended on the troublesome reservoir atop Lord's Hill, Hartfordites readied for one of the most enjoyable entertainments of the year— the State Fair. Beginning in 1817, the Connecticut State Agricultural Society began holding fairs in Hartford on a thirty-acre parcel of city land about a half mile north of Lord's Hill and just beyond the Almshouse. Occasionally, the fairs were moved to New Haven in a bid to keep peace. Hartford, however, proved more central for most of the participants and spectators and, for this reason, hosted the fairs far more often.

Each year, trains from Springfield, Willimantic, New Haven and Waterbury delivered 50,000 to 60,000 men, women and children with their prized horses, cattle, sheep, quilts, embroideries, fresh vegetables and preserves to Union Station in Hartford. From there, they walked the quarter mile up to the top of Lord's Hill and then another half mile north to the fairgrounds. Farm families took refuge in a few weather-beaten cow palaces or in their own tents for four days with the last afternoon devoted to awards. Prizes of $25 to $30 were given for the best bulls, oxen, steers, stallions, thoroughbreds, sheep, ewes and chickens; smaller cash awards were distributed for the complete cornucopia of vegetables and the finest butter, cheese, sweets and household items. Further prizes were handed out for the best farm implements and stoves.

Represented at the fair were the finest produce and livestock that Mother Nature could produce and the most up-to-date machinery and gadgetry that the minds of men could conceive. All of the largest manufacturers in the state rented booths to show off their leather belting, axes, chisels, knives and farm implements. Hardly anything of value to the average farm family of the 1850s was not displayed, judged and sold at the fair.

One of the most popular attractions was horseracing. A dilapidated quarter-mile track hosted the fastest horses in the state and wagering—though highly illegal and damned from church pulpits all over the state—was carried on with abandon. One of the most heated issues at the fair was female jockeys. Women were still trained to ride sidesaddle in the mid-1800s, with no respectable woman lowering herself to imitate a man's riding style but, increasingly, young farm girls questioned this stricture, preferring the more comfortable seating of the men.

Workmen labored daily on the north wall of the reservoir, making slow but steady progress, which caused the *Times* to alert its readers to the real possibility that the Connecticut River water was at hand. As the men ascended higher each day with the puddled clay on the north wall, it was the river's turn to cause problems, forcing the *Times* to reassess—

> . . . The high water prevents, at present, from forming a connection at the river between the pipe and the well house, but we may safely reckon upon having, in the course of ten days, the river water distributed through our streets and brought into our houses—unless the reservoir fails with its first filling.

On the eve of such a momentous event, the mood of the city was anything but celebratory. The cost of the work was burdensome and the acrimony between the common council and the water commissioners had provided plenty of fodder for the newspapers but, in the end, had dampened the spirits of the average citizen to the point where a huge and triumphant celebration was of no interest. Lamenting the sad state of affairs, the *Times*, scolded—

> The water is likely to be introduced silently, without any public demonstration or display, and no particular "puffing," except that of the steam engine that pumps it from the river. This is all wrong. The introduction of the river water—the furnishing for the first time to this city of water that is fit to drink and wash with—is a matter of too much importance to be unnoticed. We should have a grand public celebration.
> . . .

The Connecticut River Pumping Station was more than half completed but would not be finished until the following year. It was a two-story brick colossus

The Connecticut River Pumping Station circa 1860.

with an octagonal chimney poking 100 feet into the sky. In the front of the building was a foyer, nine-foot square, off of which was a large office for the water commissioners. The pump, engine and boiler rooms were on the river side of the building with each taking up about 700 square feet. The complex was located at 2 Water Street—the only building on the small dusty road running along the river.

The level of the water in the Connecticut River dropped sufficiently by the third week in October so that the connection could be made between the intake pipe in the river and the six-foot diameter well on shore. From this well, the steam engine would raise the water into the engine house and then push it through a sixteen-inch diameter ascending main for more than a mile until it gushed into the Lord's Hill Reservoir.

As the leaves on the trees around the town assumed the warm, reassuring cadmium colors of autumn, and almost two and a half years since the voters had chosen a city-owned water works, word filtered out that the waiting was over. On that afternoon, a Monday, curiosity got the better of some in the city, and they walked down to the river to inspect the engine house and its machinery. At the pumping station, machinists and their helpers readied the boiler, engine and pumps for the big event.

At noon on Tuesday, October 23, 1855, a small crowd gathered at the new Connecticut River Pumping Station to witness the start of the engine, and the beginning of a new era for Hartford. For the first time, fresh pure drinking water would be no farther away than the hand pumps in people's kitchens and washrooms.

The Woodruff & Beach Engine.

Sadly, the *Times* had called the events of that Tuesday perfectly, as the Connecticut River water was introduced into the city almost without notice. Contemporary accounts mention no opening ceremony where a smiling mayor and overjoyed water commissioners might have shaken hands and made a few lofty remarks. Instead, the pumps were turned on in the pump house, peopled only with a few workers from the Woodruff & Beach Iron Works under the direction of a mechanic referred to as Mr. Smith. Reporters from the *Times* and the *Courant* stopped by to get their stories, and a few curiosity seekers watched as the final preparations were made and the pumps activated—but that was about it.

Absolutely no mention was made of any festivities and, perhaps, not without good reason. The city had been under a siege of excavation for the past two years as streets and sidewalks were torn up to bed pipes, and the tension between the council and the water board had lost its entertainment value. No longer was it fresh fodder for the gossip mills. Instead, it was just the byproduct of an unpleasant mésalliance. Adding to the general discontent was the overwhelming cost of the system. True, the water department would turn a profit in only six years, but in October 1855, the residents could not have known that and, at least for the foreseeable future, were in hock up to their collar buttons.

With a few mechanics looking on expectantly, the fourteen and a half ton flywheel slowly awakened. Necks craned as the mass of steel circled into motion. Thanks to the thrust generated by the 150 horsepower steam engine, the enormous flywheel quickly settled into a quiet, steady rhythm. A short time later, water from the Connecticut River could be heard pulsing through the chambers of the pumps en route to the Lord's Hill Reservoir. As the engine's flywheel spun with a reassuringly steady rhythm, the gurgle of the water quieted even further as the ascending main became full. For all its efforts to kill the water works, the *Hartford Daily Courant* delivered an exciting interpretation of the event for posterity—

> . . . The good news spread like wildfire through the city, Tuesday noon, that the engine was in motion; the pumps at work and water running into the Reservoir. We hurried to the spot and found the facts to be as stated. The stream flows continuously with no perceptible jerk or pulsation, in a uniform stream, into its receptacle on Asylum Hill . . . In a few days, we may expect to have the Connecticut flowing through and under our streets. . . .

The *Hartford Daily Times* was even more effusive in recording its reaction to the city's first successful attempt to impound drinking water—

> A Final Triumph
>
> At last the engine—that "Yankee Machine" which was introduced over the head of the Cornish engine, amid conflicting opinions, and angry discussions—has moved, and with complete success! Though not fully packed, and with only a part of its power in operation, on a small amount of steam, it carried the water straight up Lord's Hill, and poured

it into the Reservoir most successfully . . . we hail this triumph as a glorious day for Hartford.

As with every other water company in America at the time, the river water would not be filtered or treated in any way. Instead, it would be piped to people's homes and businesses in exactly the same condition it was when it lay in the channel at the big bend of the Connecticut River. Over the next few days, the engines were packed and the pumps began regular operation, delivering 100,000 gallons an hour to the Lord's Hill Reservoir which, to Hiram Bissell's relief, held water magnificently.

Chapter 4
The Quest For Better Water

Now that Hartford finally had a water works in place, the business of selling the Connecticut River water to the public became the *raison d'etre* of those who had championed the cause. Between October 23, 1855, when the water first flowed into the Lord's Hill Reservoir, and the beginning of December, when the ground was too frozen to install connections to homes and businesses, 154 service pipes were laid, giving the water department a grand total of about 200 customers. Putting this progress into perspective, Hiram Bissell noted in his annual report that the work ". . . gives general satisfaction."

While Bissell and his board busied themselves with the housekeeping chores of the water department and the Whigs plotted feverishly to kill it, the city changed little, except in population. While the decade before 1850 saw an increase in the city's residents of only 6 percent, in the decade immediately following mid-century, people—particularly the Irish—poured into the city, more than doubling the population to almost 30,000 souls. It was the only decade in Hartford's history—before or since—that the population more than doubled. The two biggest facilitators of this explosive growth were the railroad, which allowed men and their families to quickly flock to a city with good-paying jobs and unchecked immigration. This congestion did not go unnoticed as the newspapers reported—

> Few cities in the United States are so densely populated as Hartford, where the number of inhabitants is greater in proportion to the space occupied by the old city limits than in any other city in the country, except the three or four principal ones. . . . We have been informed of one house in the Sixth Ward where there were, at one time, no fewer than eighteen families and forty children!

Not surprisingly, there was a backlash to this wild expansion of the immigrant classes and the Know-Nothing party grew rapidly. This strange political party with its secret handshake and the "Have you seen Sam?" question, asking for the location of the next meeting, accounted for 75 of the 234 members of the U.S. House of Representatives and 11 of the 62 members of the U. S. Senate. In Connecticut—and in other Northeastern states packed with famine Irish—fears of the invading illiterates ran high, causing the ranks of Know-Nothings to reach a high water mark in the late 1850s.

Contributing to the decline of the Know-Nothing movement was the country's complete absorption with the issue of Southern secession and a reduction in Irish immigration during the years of the American Civil War. Times were marginally better in Ireland in the years after the potato famine of

1845-1851 and, quite naturally, the possibility of being forced to fight in America's domestic conflict was a great disincentive to emigration.

For Hartford's residents, the winter of 1855-1856—aside from the political tensions—was a time of bitter cold weather and lavish balls and other entertainments. The thermometer dipped below zero a total of forty-seven days and the ice on the Connecticut River could be transversed on foot until the first of April, but people were happily distracted by the relentless social whirl.

For years, the Firemen's Balls—which were one of the liveliest gatherings in town—were thrown to finance new equipment and this year it was the Neptune Company's turn to host the event. Dr. Wyatt's Lyceum and Lanergan's City Theater vied for Hartford's entertainment dollar along with the traditional homes of the lecture circuit—the Arts Hall and Union Hall.

For the men, racing their trotters on the ice of the Connecticut River in wintertime was a raucous pastime with the racecourse typically a straight run from a mile downriver up to the covered bridge and a $30 prize for the winner. It was generally believed that ". . . the ice makes a great trotting track." Sleighs were the preferred form of private transportation in the cold months, and young people skated on the Little and the Connecticut Rivers in great numbers.

One of Hiram Bissell's little annoyances was that, mixed in with the more practical customers of the water works, there were those who viewed the whole venture as a new toy. While he and his board wrestled with a Pandora's box of unforeseen problems, the council decided that a fountain on the lawn of the statehouse would be delightful. As winter turned to spring, the fountain materialized at the center of the legislative building's large east lawn. After the stone walls of the basin were laid, the water was tested and a jet shot sixty feet into the air. When it was finally finished, the *Times* gushed—

> The jets are so arranged as to form a fountain of spray or a lofty column of water. It is now in the form of rosette, the fine jets playing each a beautiful thin stream, the whole falling gracefully down somewhat in the shape of a willow tree. . . .

For Bissell though, the council's fascination with fountains was a time-consuming sideshow. By the time pipes were laid in all the streets and connections run to subscribers homes and businesses, the tab for the system would be nearly $300,000 and the interest payments would have to be made on the bonds even before the first water rents were collected in May of 1856. Thus, while the water works was already paying out about $18,000 annually in water bond interest, they would recoup the lordly sum of, perhaps, $2000 in water rents. Attracting new customers was a priority for Bissell and his board.

The *Times* tried to help, encouraging people to "try the Connecticut River water," while Bissell worked out deals with the owners of manufactories, hotels, livery stables, the city's street department and other big users. The water rates were established just after the water works came on line, with private homes paying just $5 annually for up to five people; additional family members were $1. Insofar as hotels, livery stables and the like, the board had discretion to set a reasonable rate according to usage. While entirely reasonable on paper, this put the department in a difficult spot. On the one hand, they wanted the rates to be low enough to lure customers, but with the interest debt mounting on the water bonds, they needed infusions of cash, with no pun intended, just to remain afloat.

An early flap arose when the city's street department wanted to fill their tank wagons from the fire hydrants, a much simpler process than making trips to the river to fill up. Therefore, it seemed axiomatic that the "expense of laying the dust [in the streets] ought to be less than formerly." The water commissioners set the rate at 10 cents a load, which the drivers refused to pay. After almost a month of haggling, the drivers accepted a flat annual rate of $700 to water certain streets. So it went as each shop and manufactory claimed special circumstances and protracted haggling became the rule rather than the exception.

The Fourth of July celebration was a fabulous opportunity for the water department to win over new customers. The Inauguration parades at election time in the nineteenth century were big, but they paled in comparison to the size and sensation of the celebrations held across the country on the Fourth of July. In Hartford, the post-office even cut its hours, opening for only an hour in the early morning and a similar period in the late afternoon. Since the streets would be packed with hot, thirsty revelers, it was a golden opportunity for Hiram Bissell to give everyone a taste of the Connecticut River water. Toward that end, he made ready for the merrymakers by erecting two water tubs in front of the statehouse, each sixteen feet long and containing the same number of stop cocks. Over these, he hoisted a banner with the inscription "Connecticut River Water" and topped off the whole display with an American flag. To increase the cooling effect of the water, he filled the tubs with ice—also from the Connecticut River. Thirty-two people at a time could drink from the watering trough as the water ran constantly into the tubs.

For sheer publicity value, Bissell also set up fountains in other parts of the city. In addition to the large permanent fountain in the east side of State House Square, three others were temporarily fitted up on the Main Street side of the statehouse and, to the delight of everyone, ". . . 15 or 20 fountains were playing in different parts of the city to celebrate the water works. Two or three of them played over 100 feet high."

On the morning of the Fourth, delegations from all of Hartford's fire departments met at seven o'clock to receive their marching orders for the parade. Bands from far and wide gathered at Captain Stratton's music store on Main Street for the same purpose—the Hartford Band, Manchester Band, Forestville Band and Colt's Armory Band, mentioning only the largest ones. Also, from among the Colt's machinists and willowware workers, there was the German Liederkranz (choral group) and the German Turnverein (gymnasts).

Dignitaries like the governor, the mayor and the full complement of elected officials met early in the morning at the United States Hotel in State House Square to get their assignments and learn of their positions in the oratorical pecking order and, more importantly, to steel themselves for the long parade. Every business, club, society, association and city department was represented in the parade. The Hartford Water Works was represented by a wagon ". . . drawn by four horses and elegantly trimmed. It contained a water tank with 12 handsome cocks and other fittings from Bidwell Pitkin & Co."

The parade itself was a long, tortuous affair that—among many other streets—traversed up the length of Main Street and, some time later, brought its sweaty, tired throngs down the same thoroughfare. A description of the entire parade route would leave little doubt that it was designed with the homebound in mind. As the parade gruelingly entered its third hour, the skies took on the nasty hues of Payne's gray and burnt umber, while the air became a broth of ozone. At one o'clock, a powerful thunderstorm broke loose, the wind whipping hats, flags and all other movable objects into the air. A driving rain followed as the procession disbanded and the crowds scattered for cover—

> The two . . . [carriages] . . . containing the ladies of 1776 and 1856 deposited their fair burdens in front of Union Hall in which the ladies ran in haste. The old long bonnets and quaint headdresses of the last century mingled with the Paris fashions of "young America" of 1856.

The stormed cleared in time for a regatta on the river at five o'clock. The boats started at Kilbourn's Wharf—a short distance south of the covered bridge—and sailed one and a quarter miles downriver, around a flag boat and back. More than 12,000 people watched the race from the wharfs, the embankments and the buildings along the shoreline, followed by leisurely picnic suppers on the riverbank before the fireworks began at sundown.

At dusk, about 8,000 people straggled to Colt's huge dyke along the river to watch the fireworks display, created by EDGE & Company of New York—said to be the very best makers of fireworks displays at the time. Thrilling the crowd, the most fascinating and diverse display of the pyrotechnic art was exhibited, including: the Scroll Wheel, True Lovers, Tribute of Ceres, Polka Dance, Indian Palmetto and Kaleidoscope. By tradition, the festivities were over by ten and everyone headed home with youngsters fast asleep in their parents' arms.

The Lord's Hill Reservoir erased some of the goodwill built up at the Fourth of July celebration by experiencing another slide in August. In a way, it was ironic—the members of the board had worried incessantly about the wisdom of choosing the Root engine, assuming that any problems with the system would probably be experienced at the pumping station. Instead the Root engine performed nobly while the simple earthen receptacle on Lord's Hill turned

Hiram Bissell's hair gray. Fortunately, the trouble was not with the sidewalls inside the catchment but the collar surrounding it, where rains had caused a small slide.

New Haven's death-grip competition with Hartford to become the state capital goaded its officials to lobby the Connecticut State Agricultural Society in favor of the Elm City for the State Fair of 1856. Though it was certainly less convenient for the farm families living in the remote regions of the state, the fair still drew a record crowd. The premier event was the women's horsemanship, with a Mrs. Langdon of Farmington winning in her division on a spirited horse. She sat on a man's saddle, yet she "appeared perfectly at her ease and rode [at] all great speed, displaying a marked degree of grace and skill that would master almost any horse."

The winter of 1856-1857 was a typical, hard New England winter, but the cold was broken by the fires burning within a most unusual visitor to Hartford—John Brown. With the divisiveness caused by slavery, Brown's appearance should have been about as welcome as snow in May, but he received a courteous reception. On February 26, 1857, John Brown—who had been born in Torrington, Connecticut—was back from Kansas, trying to convince Nutmeggers to emigrate to that territory. Speaking at the Odd Fellows Hall on Main Street —just north of State House Square—he told wild stories of his struggles with "border ruffians" in Kansas, where the Free Soilers and the pro-slavery Southerners had begun to square off. According to the *Courant*, "his purpose was to collect men and means for defense...he meant no offence by his appeal . . . The audience listened to him with interest as he spoke directly to their patriotism."

The Hartford Water Works had received permission from the council to issue still more water bonds and to complete the bedding of pipes throughout the city. The council was notoriously tight-fisted but, if the water works were to fulfill its mission of supplying all of the residents of the city, then bedding more pipes was the only way to make the dream a reality. So said, Bissell addressed the mounting economic problems thusly— " . . . A slight check to the increase of revenue has been experienced during the past six months, in common with all other departments of business . . ." At the same time, he noted that the number of connections to the street mains had increased to 1,103, or about a third of the buildings in the city. Less cheerfully, he noted that, after the second water rent payments were collected in November 1857, total revenues for the year were $16,340, while the total interest on the water bonds and other loans was $60,693—a loss of $43,000.

In the late 1850s, Bissell was a busy man. His company, H. & S. Bissell was building the new Methodist Church and he had committed himself to build a new church for the Universalist Society, the congregation to which he and his family belonged. The Methodist Church would be completed in the early months of 1860, while the new church for his fellow congregants would not be completed until July. The crush of his masonry business notwithstanding, he still worked tirelessly to win over subscribers and found time to sell more bonds, financing the conclusion of the piping network. All the while, he harbored an ugly little secret—after less than four years of operation and within a year or so of turning a profit, the new water works was already obsolete!

Actually, Bissell had reached this conclusion very early on for, in the report to the council detailing the activities of the water works for 1856, he noted that, ". . . The capacity of the Reservoir. . . is . . . entirely too small. . . ." Not so surprisingly then, Bissell was spending more and more of his time in the neighboring town of West Hartford during the spring and summer months of 1859, studying the hydrology of Trout Brook. This limpid stream had been the Waterloo of the Gleason and Cowles Aqueduct Company almost sixty years before, exerting some preternaturally magnetic power on the doomed water company in the first years of the nineteenth century. The Trout Brook waters—draining from Talcott Mountain's watershed and bubbling from a collection of natural springs in the area—was so pristine that it had an almost brilliant quality to it.

Hartford's complete dependence on the ten million gallon reservoir atop Lord's Hill became increasingly dicey considering how fast the city was growing. When the water system was first put to paper, ten million gallons—in the case of pump failure at the river—represented a three-week supply. But with the population closing in on the 30,000 mark, the same water would barely last a week. Worse, the water rent for the average family was only five dollars a year, and at those prices, it had lost its precious nature. Waste became common. In the winter months, and unrestrained by water meters, people typically left their taps open all night long to keep the pipes from freezing, causing the greatest water usage to occur during the night while the town slept. A final difficulty was that the existing reservoir was simply not high enough in elevation, causing distribution problems to the homes built in some of the higher sections of the city. Without sufficient head (pressure)—and depending on a few other conditions—the hill sections of Hartford were sometimes lucky to get a trickle.

Beyond all that, each year the pumps were running for longer periods of time, running up the coal bill, but, much more significantly, escalating the chances of engine failure. The boiler itself could be replaced easily enough but what if the Root engine gave up the ghost? Moreover, since the four pumps were running almost nonstop, what were the chances that they might give out? Of course, the real nightmare was that one or both of these components might fail during a drought, in which case wholesale misery would be the price for the city's improvidence.

As if this knowledge were not enough to give Bissell sleepless nights, there was a further complication that was reason alone to head for the West Hartford hills—the quality of the river water was deteriorating rapidly. This unhappy circumstance centered on the Little River, which wandered in a southeasterly direction through the heart of the city until it spilled into the Connecticut River at Dutch Point. The first intrusion on this small stream was during the days of the gristmills and the lumber mills, when waterpower was the driving force of the economy. There were so many mills along the banks of this creek that, for a time, it was called Mill River. Nevertheless, these businesses were not great polluters, and Baptist ministers still paraded new converts down Pearl Street to the Little River for "immersions" on Sundays.

Following close on the heels of these reasonably clean mills, were the much less healthful slaughterhouses, tanneries, soap factories, and dye works. As these businesses began dumping all of their waste products into the waters beside them, people began calling this watercourse the Hog River. Younger people dismissed it as the "Meandering Swine." Nonetheless, the assault on this once-beautiful waterway had only just begun.

The final insult was delivered—inadvertently—by the railroad. When the New Haven railroad reached Hartford in 1839, there probably wasn't a person in the whole city who could have anticipated the enormous changes that it would usher in. Owing to Hartford's centralized location, rather than becoming just another stop along the line, it became a hub. Tracks were laid in all directions—to Manchester, Willimantic, Putnam, Norwich, New London, and Springfield. In addition to an increase in the amount of freight passing through the city, simultaneously there was an influx of people, particularly immigrants. In fact, it was the construction of the railroad that brought the first huge waves of immigrants to Hartford. The same thing happened in every city, big and small, up and down the eastern seaboard during this period, particularly the great manufacturing centers.

Due in large part to the Great Hunger in Ireland, when a million and a half people died from famine and the fevers that it spawned, large numbers of Irish immigrants poured into Hartford. Despite their hard work building railroads and canals, they were not particularly welcome. Skilled workers cast a steely eye on them and the unskilled workers—especially the blacks—worried about the "micks" stealing their jobs. Most of these early Irish were single, young men who crowded into tenements and boarding houses on the northern banks of the Little River. Their wages were paltry and they were forced to accept living arrangements commensurate with their pay.

In the early 1850s, when Rev. Horace Bushnell of the Third Congregational Church approached the common council with the idea of setting aside a large piece of land at the center of the city for a park, the acreage that he had in mind was bisected by the meandering Little River. After the public voted to accept Bushnell's plan, the city went about purchasing the existing properties along the river for what would be called Bushnell Park—two decades later. The first business to be absorbed for the new park was the huge gristmill of William Imlay, situated on the eastern bank of the river. Clustered around the mill and, more or less in the middle of this forty-acre plot, were eight or ten tenements with as many pigsties. On the north side of the river—below Imlay's flouring operation was a garbage dump composed of "shavings, leather cuttings, cabbage stumps, rags, hats without tops, old saddles, [rusted out] stove pipes—everything, in short, that had no right to be anywhere else."

Adding to the general mess were "two old tanneries—one falling down to pieces, the other barely managing to stand upon a slant. . . ." Finally, there was a soap works and the backsides of a number of tenements on the south side of the river whose occupants had "projected their outhouses over it on brackets and piers—saying as it were. . . .'We give you such help as we can.'" Indeed, the residents along the Little River used it as a receptacle for every kind of waste imaginable. The sum total of the pollutants created a witch's brew of the most odious kind, contributing terribly to the pollution of the Connecticut River.

Unlike a high mountain stream, which by virtue of its acute descent was unlikely to become polluted by the waste of tenement dwellers and horse droppings, the Connecticut River was altogether different because it was a tidal river. It enjoyed a respectable flow at ebb tide, but when the ocean rose at the Connecticut shoreline, it slowed down considerably. This not only invited the commingling of the waters of the smaller Little River and its larger counterpart at their junction, but also caused a backwash effect, which despoiled the waters near the Connecticut River Pumping Station. A stone pier had been constructed out into the river to house the two-foot cast iron intake pipe, which sat six feet off of the riverbed in twelve feet of water. At the end of this pipe, there was an intake crib that had grates to keep out fish and other debris. From this intake crib to the well on shore was about 140 feet. The well was nothing more than a stone and masonry cylinder in the ground measuring six feet in diameter. The engine and pumps pulled the water the remaining twenty-five feet from the well to the pump house. The whole system looked good on paper, however, the location of the intake pipe in the river was a problem. This conduit, having been set just north of the business district, was adversely affected as the polluted muddle from the Little River found its way north.

So said, Bissell found the search for a new water source urgent. However, he was wary of the reception that such a proposal would receive at City Hall, especially so close to the introduction of the Connecticut River water into the city. Therefore, his search was a clandestine one for the better part of 1859, as he periodically drove his buckboard out to West Hartford. During the dog days of summer, he tested the quality and quantity of Trout Brook until he felt "assured not only of the perfect feasibility of the project, but of its real economy and indisputable advantages."

Nagging Bissell a bit was the idea of going into another town to grub out a reservoir and dam one of the residents' major streams. It had been done before, but it was fraught with problems. The Boston Water Works had gone into Natick and bought Lake Cochituate for a reservoir, building the Cochituate Aqueduct to transport water to downtown Boston, but the experience was far from a pleasant one. Naturally, Lake Cochituate had been tested thoroughly before the aqueduct was built and its waters were pure. After the project was completed though, the public complained bitterly of "a nauseous taste." Boston's preeminent chemist, Dr. Charles Jackson, examined the water extensively and found "nothing but vegetable matter . . . in it."

Not satisfied with the opinion of Dr. Jackson, the Boston water board hired a medical doctor named Mellon to dig a little deeper into the matter. About the middle of January, his team of dredgers unearthed Lake Cochituate's ugly secret. Among many things dredged up, they found ". . . a large Newfoundland dog, the hind legs and tail of a horse, two oxen, a bag containing a cat and thirteen kittens, the head and shoulders of a man (shockingly decomposed), one cow, four hogs, an immense quantity of dead eels and a rather large collection of the fragments of animals (undifferentiated)." Dr. Mellon attributed the detritus to vandalism because he reasoned that, ". . . people around the pond have a deep-rooted prejudice for the 'upstart city folks' as they call them."

How would the people of West Hartford react to a proposal by Hartford to dam Trout Brook? Difficult to say, but before Bissell could spend much time analyzing the relationship between the residents of the two cities, events elsewhere in the United States grabbed his attention.

On Monday, October 17 of that year, the *Times* received a series of telegrams that dumbfounded its editors. The first telegram announced—

> . . . that there was a slave insurrection in the vicinity of Harper's Ferry and that the Negroes and Abolitionists had taken possession of the government armory at that point and . . . distributing the arms among the insurgents . . . .

That telegraphic dispatch left everyone befuddled until a second dispatch recanted much of the earlier message, stating simply that the first communication was highly exaggerated. A short while later, a third dispatch arrived carrying the information that the matter was more serious than even the first message had indicated. It continued—

> . . . that the telephone wires had been cut—that the railroad trains had been stopped and that there was really an alarming trouble at Harper's Ferry. Harper's Ferry is in Jefferson County, Virginia at the confluence of the Shenandoah [and] the Potomac River[s].

The leader of the band of insurgents was John Brown, or as the press preferred to call him, "Osawatamie" Brown (after the town in Kansas where he and his family lived). For weeks, John Brown completely dominated newspapers and private conversation as people speculated what the raid meant and, more importantly, what should happen to Brown. The Abolitionists of the city, of course, remembered him well.

Apparently, on Sunday, October 14, 1859, he and his band of eighteen marauder—including several of his sons—stormed the arsenal at Harper's Ferry, Virginia (now West Virginia) and held the town captive until Marines, under the command of Col. Robert E. Lee, were dispatched to the scene the following day. In the ensuing skirmish, ten of Brown's men were killed—including two of his sons—and some escaped, only to be captured later. Wounded, Brown offered no resistance and was imprisoned in Charlestown, Virginia. Soon thereafter, he was tried for treason against the Commonwealth of Virginia, found guilty, and hanged on December 2, 1859.

Business had slackened enough that Hartford's dry goods merchants hatched a gentlemen's agreement to trim their store hours by closing at 7:30 each night. The merchants may have been experiencing lean times, but the manufacturers producing war related materials were running their plants flat out. Samuel Colt, for example, made pistols for the North and the South even after the advent of hostilities, labeling shipments to the Confederacy "hardware." Soon enough though, he was forced to restrict shipments of arms only to the Union army.

Getting about the city was soon to become easier, for in 1863, the Hartford & Wethersfield Horse Railroad Company was granted a charter by the legislature. Tracks were laid to Wethersfield, but steadily, lines were added until horse cars traveled all of the principal streets of Hartford and, by 1884, even ran over the covered bridge to East Hartford center.

The common council's requests for water devices throughout the city was an endless shopping list that Bissell was compelled to fill. In November, the water works took shipment of some stone watering troughs for horses to be located mostly around State House Square. They were long blocks of Portland stone, gouged out along the centerline and considered "not highly ornamental." Not much later, a written complaint reached the council that there were problems with the horse troughs in the square, saying that the "pipe doesn't connect because something has come 'agin it'."

The winter months of 1859-1860, were bitter cold and the iceman, J.L. Phillips, was able to cut "nice blocks of clear transparent ice from the Connecticut River as much as 15 inches thick." Travelers crossed the river on the ice below the bridge saving the fare, while children skated in great packs up and down the river. Newspapers kept skaters informed of conditions on the river almost daily, for example, noting—

> The river opposite Colt's factory and below and in spots further up gives tolerable and in some spots very good skating, but much of the surface is "hubbly" and rough, not at all suited for skaters. Two ice boats are on the river and are enjoying the lightning like sweep of these contrivances. . . .

The winter was hard times for the workers at the water department, the cold freezing up the new fire hydrants and bursting pipes all over the city. Sometimes a cracked hydrant leaked so profusely that water poured from it for a week, forming great ice sculptures in the streets. One freezing cold day in February, workmen busily tried to stop a leak in a pipe on Main Street that broke during the night ". . . and for twelve hours poured up a stream as big as a bushel basket in the middle of the street."

Toward the end of February, the *Courant* announced the imminent arrival of "The Hon. Abram Lincoln"[sic], who would be addressing the members of the new Republican Party at City Hall. On the appointed day, Lincoln's train was over two hours late, arriving at Hartford's Union Station just minutes before his address was to begin. Jumping into a carriage, he raced to City Hall where, when he took the podium, the "applause was almost deafening." While explaining his tardiness, he jokingly referred to himself as a "dirty shirt" exponent of Republicanism, as the crowd warmed to his presence. While he spoke, ". . . frequently his quaint allusions and similes brought out the laughter in the crowd," and when his remarks were concluded, there was thunderous applause. Lincoln was whisked away to the home of Mayor Timothy Allyn, where he and a dozen other guests sat down to dinner. When offered champagne, Lincoln "declined with a humorous smile."

The most peculiar part of Lincoln's visit to Hartford occurred the following day when, in spite of the raw and gusty weather, he left the Allyn House (hotel) for a walk about the city, winding up at the Main Street stationary store of Brown & Gross. While in the shop, he had a thought provoking two-hour conversation with Gideon Welles, one of the founders of the new Republican paper, the *Hartford Evening Press*. Although Welles was a delegate to the Republican convention in Chicago and supported Lincoln, the new president later stated that it was this chance meeting between the two in the stationary store that was the basis for his appointment of Welles as his secretary of the navy.

A further coincidence, though unrelated to Lincoln's visit, happened in September 1853 when President Franklin Pierce's secretary of war also visited Hartford, while touring New England. Jefferson Davis was given a fifteen-gun salute, a warm welcome by Mayor Hamersley and a dinner at the City Hotel.

Before leaving Hartford for New York, Davis, a man of impeccable manners, thanked all of the people of New England for the many kindnesses extended to him.

In April 1860, a little more than a month after Lincoln's visit, Mayor Deming addressed the common council with his annual report. Every member of the council was present and the room outside the bar was crowded with spectators. The mayor addressed the different components of city government, ending with the water department and offering—

> The Water Works ha[s] triumphed over the serious opposition which they encountered at the outset, and are now universally regarded as the wisest and most meritorious of our city's enterprises . . . A project will be shortly laid before you for a supplementary supply, which [is] . . . essential to the completeness of the Hartford Water Works.

Mayor Deming then went on to explain the precarious position in which the city would find itself if there were a failure of any kind at the Connecticut River Pumping Station and the large quantities of water needed to extinguish a sizable conflagration. Furthermore, as the city expanded in the higher elevations, more pressure was needed than the existing reservoir could supply. Warming to his subject, the mayor went on to outline the West Hartford option. He spoke of streams in the adjacent town that could deliver almost five million gallons of pure water in a twenty-four hour period, which was four times the present consumption. Then Mayor Deming shocked everyone by stating that the right to use these streams for this purpose, had already been negotiated and the whole system as designed and negotiated could be put in place for under $60,000.

Elected officials do have a tendency to keep their ears to the ground and Hiram Bissell's trips to West Hartford were no longer a secret, but when Mayor Deming presented the Trout Brook plan as a *fait accompli*, the council members were nonplussed. To a man, the members of the council had considered the waters of the Connecticut River to be nothing short of inexhaustible. Logically then, at least to them, the next step was to increase the size of the existing system as so many other cities had done. Surely a move to impound water in another town would entail more study than the water commissioners had given it and the Trout Brook option was problematic from several points of view.

Since West Hartford was now a completely separate town (incorporated in 1854), controlling one of its major streams was not going to be easy. Beyond that, what Hartford could have had a few years ago for the taking, would now be theirs only after they had been reduced to beggars and separated from a princely sum of money.

All the same, the most troubling part of the whole scheme had to do with the present system. The Lord's Hill Reservoir together with the Connecticut River Pumping Station had been delivering water for less than five years. With so many cities in America continuing to exploit the river on which their cities were built, why was Hartford even considering going to West Hartford? Philadelphia had never given up on the Schuylkill. Louisville and Cincinnati were happy with the Ohio. Baltimore had long used the Jones Falls River with satisfactory results. Nashville was committed to the Cumberland and Richmond to the James. Even Providence, the small mill town to the east, was still pumping water directly from the Pawtuxet River. Lastly, the cities along the Mississippi made a powerful argument for the use of river water all by themselves—Saint Paul, Minneapolis, St. Louis, Memphis and New Orleans. True, Boston and New York employed huge reservoirs in the hills and depended on long aqueducts for delivery, but they were the exceptions. If so many cities were sticking with their rivers, why was Hartford so anxious to exploit Trout Brook?

After only five years of operation, the common council—regardless of their personal feelings—could never have given the water department the green light to spend another $60,000 dollars to bring the waters of Trout Brook into the city without incurring the wrath of the voters. The make up of the council had changed some during the 1850s and, though the majority of the alderman remained Republicans (formerly Whigs), the lower chamber was now almost half Democrats. Under such circumstances, the protracted battles between the Whig-controlled council and the water board had subsided measurably. Unquestionably, the Republicans would still have preferred to own the water franchise, but the bitter wrangling at council meetings had vitiated. Quite apart from the political persuasions of the different alderman and councilmen was the always-present need to please the voters and, taking this into consideration, no one was anxious to act in haste.

By the end of May, the council produced some limited action. It authorized the mayor to approach the legislature seeking authority to float $100,000 worth of new water bonds. While this bill worked its way through the General Assembly, a committee—appointed by the council—would assemble a detailed study of the Trout Brook plan and the other options open to the city.

The following afternoon, a lovely, late spring Tuesday, a grand procession of carriages drove the Farmington road out to West Hartford for a first-hand look at Trout Brook. Along for the six-mile sojourn were the water commissioners, the members of the common council, some reporters and a handful of other guests. At the confluence of the smaller Mine Brook and the main body of Trout Brook—where the water board proposed to build its reservoir—the group disembarked. They were joined by the water commissioner of New Britain, Frederick Stanley, and by an eminent hydraulic engineer from Jersey City, MacRae Swift, whose assistance had been invaluable in the construction of New Britain's water works. For nearly three hours, the party examined a rickety, temporary dam that Hiram Bissell had constructed across the brook. A flume delivered the water from the dam to a tank, which was used to calibrate the amount of water that the brook could supply. After studying the stream and making some calculations, Swift had a number of conclusions for the group. In his opinion, the supply of water was ample for all the wants of the city for any conceivable increase of population and the quality of the water was exceptional. Beyond these crucially important Siamese twins of water systems, he said that impounding the water in a reservoir would not diminish its quality and, lastly, that once the citizens of Hartford tasted this water, they would eschew the Connecticut River water thereafter.

In spite of the laudatory opinions of MacRae Swift and Frederick Stanley, the one matter that had everyone completely baffled was the cost of the project. Estimating the cost of the land was child's play and the aqueduct under the Farmington road could be figured easily enough, but what did Bissell—or anyone else—know about building dams and compensating the downstream owners for the loss of their riparian rights? How much would all that cost? At this point, about the only thing that the Trout Brook plan did not lack was financial estimates. Everybody had one. Crude though they were, the estimates ranged from $60,000—Bissell's original guess in 1859—to $150,000—the guess of a cadre of naysayers.

Undeterred by the wildly vacillating cost estimates, two weeks later, the council voted to procure a supply of water from West Hartford and they authorized the water board to hire Professor Benjamin Silliman, an analytical chemist at Yale College to report on the purity of the waters of Trout Brook. At the same time that the Trout Brook plan seemed devoid of detractors, one voice arose. Never one to miss a business opportunity, Samuel Woodruff proposed that his company, Woodruff & Beach, double the capacity of the present pumps enabling them to throw 2,000,000 gallons every twelve hours into the Lord's Hill Reservoir, while keeping the same engine; the price? . . .only $5,000. Alternatively, his company could duplicate the present engine and pumps, doubling up the whole system and pump as much as 8,000,000 gallons in 24 hours for the sum of $30,000.

Possibly without even realizing it, Samuel Woodruff had introduced a skunk to a garden party. Woodruff's plan had a certain simpleminded logic to it and, with the addition of a standpipe—a tall water silo of sorts to increase the pressure—perhaps the city could get out of their current predicament on the cheap. Various configurations were tossed about, but the discussion always got back to the quantity of water at the reservoir, which would not increase at all just because the pumps at the river were doubled. This scotched the talk of bigger pumps for the moment.

By the end of June, when the city's electors should have been voting on the Trout Brook plan, the Republican majority among the aldermen reversed the decision of the councilmen and, effectively, killed the project. Just like that, the

West Hartford plan was dead. Though the Hartford Water Works was a firmly established and well-received department of the city, the Republicans were still opposed to it. From their standpoint, it was never too late to derail the department and secure the franchise for some worthy group in the private sector. The *Times* decried the aldermen's vote of June 25th—

> Some parties . . . seem to have been dictated by motives of personal pique or personal envy—motives entirely unworthy; men whose sworn duty is to act for the interest of the whole city whether certain persons reap the larger benefits or not.

By this time, the water works was supplying three-quarters of the 3,200 buildings in the city and was one year away from showing a profit but, while the Republicans might have thought that they had ended the new source of supply, they had only postponed it—for one simple reason. The city was still growing and it was only a question of time before every citizen knew the inherent danger of relying on the undersized Lord's Hill Reservoir. Aldermen come and go, but the public's need for water was constant.

Bissell was up to his ears in the Hartford Water Works, but his partnership in the masonry business with his brother Sylvester was still firing on all cylinders. H. & S. Bissell finished the work on the new Universalist church for their fellow parishioners and on Sunday, July 8, 1860 the cornerstone of the new "Church of the Redeemer" was laid with little fanfare. Due to some unfinished painting in the church, services were held for the first time in the building's basement that same day.

When the aldermen faced their constituents, they found that their vote to kill the Trout Brook project was not well-received at all. With the new water works now an established part of people's lives, residents were way ahead of the curve on the machinations within the department and had more faith in Hiram Bissell and his board than they did in their elected officials. When the aldermen next gathered, they displayed some truly astounding footwork by reversing their earlier decision in the time it takes to say "re-election." They then "asked the water commissioners to proceed in impounding the West Hartford Waters." Not that it necessarily changed any minds but, during their deliberations the proponents of the West Hartford plan served the aldermen water taken from Trout Brook. This, incidentally, was the same water that one alderman claimed two weeks earlier "he would not bathe in because he would come out dirtier than before."

For Hartford's young boys, out of school and looking for fun, the Connecticut River was their swimming hole. The only catch was that, in order to avoid accidents with steamboats, bathing was forbidden in the Connecticut River on the western side between the Little River and the Water Works, which was practically the whole waterfront. Easing the situation a bit, the city built a bathhouse just north of the water works where swimming was allowed. Boy's bathing suits came up to their chests and were only moderately confining but, for the young women, the suits were intolerable. Made of wool, they covered the whole body from ankle to neck and even had long sleeves. As a result, young women swam very little.

Baseball was the game for men, particularly the young mechanics in the manufactories about the city. Holding their contests on the "Base grounds" in City (Bushnell) Park, they always attracted a fair number of spectators. Under the New England Base Ball Rules, ten to fourteen players were allowed per team as the Independent Base Ball and the Mechanic's Clubs played for bragging rights. For young women, however, there was little in the way of sporting outlets. One of the most popular pastimes was buggy riding, but that "was a forbidden pleasure until you had selected your life companion when you might go with him." Still, one popular summer entertainment for everyone was to charter a steamboat, pack a picnic supper and cruise down to Middletown, coming back in the dark, when young people "sang and basked in the moonlight." The Maine Law—forbidding the sale of alcoholic beverages—was found to be faulty by the local courts in 1859 and so adults could once again quaff a beer or have a glass of rum without facing a $30 fine and a trip to the workhouse (jail). Taverns all over Hartford served a drink of whiskey for five cents or a whole bottle could be bought for eighty cents. Despite the Panic of 1857 and the tough times that followed, there was still enjoyment to be had for moneyed young people, but events in another part of the country were about to change people's lives forever.

During the presidential campaign of 1860, Southerners had threatened to secede should Lincoln be elected. His pledge to end secession with force if necessary could not be reconciled with their refusal to give up their slaves. On December 21, 1860, the *Times* reported gravely that—

> The drama begins. South Carolina has declared herself—by unanimous vote—no longer a member of the [Union]; and Commissioners are to be appointed to arrange with other states a new Union, and others to [deal] with . . . Washington for . . . her share of the public property.

The newspaper went on to remark that "no collision has occurred between the Federal and State forces at Charleston," and that it was hoped that none would for, such an incident would surely lead to "CIVIL WAR." People were stunned that matters had reached the point where one of the thirteen original states had decided to secede. By the time of Lincoln's Inaugural Address—

March 4, 1861—Mississippi, Florida, Alabama, Georgia, Louisiana and Texas had also left the Union. He pleaded with them to reconsider their actions but, by early April, it was clear that his words had fallen on deaf ears and he issued a directive for other states to send their militias to quell the insurrection. Rather than send troops to fight with other Southerners, four more Southern states chose to secede—Virginia, Arkansas, North Carolina and Tennessee. But before any of these states could act, events spiraled out of control as a shocked populace in Connecticut was to learn when they read the local papers on April 13, 1861—

> The blackest day ever seen by America dawned yesterday, when the *first clash of arms* commenced between the two Governments into which our wretched country is now divided. The approach of Lincoln's War Fleet precipitated hostilities and the thunder of cannon echoed from daylight to dark in Charleston Harbor—the Carolinian guns being directed upon Fort Sumter and Major Anderson pouring . . . fire upon the . . . secessionists.

Suddenly the Hartford Water Works quest for a new source of drinking water took a back seat to a rapidly failing economy. Boston's *Commercial Bulletin*, which tracked business failures and suspensions, counted eleven in New York, seven in Boston, five in Philadelphia, two in Baltimore, two in Detroit and nineteen in other places—forty-six in all, just for the week ending April 12, 1861. An economy that had already begun to show signs of stalling was now under great stress. Factories and workshops all over New England were reducing work or cutting their worker's wages. An exception was the arms business, which was at peak production. During the Civil War, Colt's Armory received government contracts for 112,500 arms, all of a type classified as the "Model 1861 Special Musket," but shipped only 75,000. Christian Sharps' Rifle manufacturing company produced 140,000 rifles for the Union Army.

Concurrently, war fever was turning friends into foes in the North as the anti-slavery *Hartford Evening Press* called for "a contest as will never be forgotten" while cooler heads rued the advent of hostilities. Meanwhile, the *Times* claimed that the expedition to Fort Sumter was undertaken against the advise of the general-in-chief of the army, Winfield Scott—who did not believe in the Lincoln-Greeley doctrine of holding the seceded states by force—thereby starting a Civil War for the sake of the Black Republican Party or the "Abolitionist-Disunionists."

Though business was contracting and the country had descended into the quagmire of war, Northerners were quick to appreciate how much it would affect them as men enlisted almost immediately. Hartford's 1st Regimental Infantry was organized in April 1861, just ten days after the shelling of Fort Sumter. Hartford's War Committee was paying a bounty of $125 to each private non-commissioned offer or musician, as well as an allotment for their families, while they were away fighting. By September, Hartford was only 415 volunteers short of its 1478 quota and a draft had to be organized. Unlike volunteers, draftees received no bounties. On September 10 and 11, a draft was held at City Hall to conscript the remaining 415 men, but all of them either disappeared or showed proof of a medical exemption, forcing another draft a month later. Despite the rapid mobilization of the forces in the North and the early onset of fighting, the first skirmishes of the war went almost completely unnoticed. Such was the case in the third week of July 1861, when Union and Confederate forces clashed at Bull Run; Hartford's newspapers were almost devoid of coverage.

As the dog days of summer descended on New England and the Union Army slowly set in place General Scott's "Anaconda plan"—whereby, like the snake of the same name, the Southern forces would be squeezed from all sides—Hiram Bissell received the long awaited report of Professor Silliman. Running twenty-five pages, the report compared the Trout Brook waters to those of the New and Thames Rivers in London, the Croton and Cochituate Aqueducts and the Schuylkill and Connecticut Rivers. Reduced to its essence, Silliman's treatise concluded that— ". . . [The] waters . . . proposed to be used for the supply of the city of Hartford are almost unequalled in purity and softness."

The next step—insisted on by the council— was to have a hydraulic engineer compare Hartford's two options: installing larger pumps at the Connecticut River Pumping Station together with another reservoir on a mightier mound, like Zion Hill or, conversely, to build the new Trout Brook system and allow gravity to deliver the city's water. MacRae Swift was the obvious choice for the assignment. To begin, he was a recognized authority in the field of hydraulic engineering and hailed from Jersey City, which had the same population as Hartford and a similar water works in place. Too, Swift had already studied Trout Brook and, in the process, met all of the principal players in the water drama at Hartford. Bissell engaged the engineer and received his analysis a few months later. McRee Swift's report—in addition to looking at Trout Brook's engineering requirements—also put the whole Connecticut River pumping alternative back under a microscope. Without regard for the purity of the water, he examined from an engineering standpoint the relative merits of the two disparate drinking water possibilities. In sum, MacRae Swift opined that the Trout Brook plan was the best of the two choices.

Still the council idled away precious time as the analysis of the two options slowly paralyzed them into inaction. When Bissell presented the report of the water commissioners to the council in March 1862, his frustration spilled over—

> The opinion which [we] have . . . expressed, in favor of . . . Trout Brook, so called, in West Hartford, was not a . . . speculative opinion, loosely formed, but . . . the result of patient and careful investigation of the whole subject—and neither a single member of the present nor any

of the past Board[s] . . . has ever . . . hesitated in giving this the preference over every other plan proposed.
    —Hiram Bissell, president, Board of Water Commissioners

A week later, the Confederate army attacked Union forces at Pittsburg, Tennessee, a battle that would later be called Shiloh (named after a meetinghouse three miles away). According to information contained in a communiqué sent to Secretary of War Stanton from Fort Henry on Tuesday evening (April 8), the *Times* reported—

> In overwhelming numbers, [the rebels] attacked our forces at Pittsburg Landing, Tennessee. The battle stood in the complete defeat of the rebels with heavy losses on both sides. General Grant is following up the enemy . . . A splendid federal victory; 18,000 federals and 30,000 rebels killed, wounded or missing. The greatest battle ever fought on this continent.

As Hartford's young men volunteered in large numbers, men and women at home mobilized to aid the war effort in any way that they could. The Hartford Soldiers' Aid Society organized during the first year of the war, with Samuel Colt's wife Elizabeth acting as the first president of the organization. Men, women, children and businesses gave either money or useful items for the cause. A few were able to donate $20 but the majority gave $5, $2 or $1. The variety of the items collected could have stocked a dry goods store—beeswax, sponges, flax lint, toilet soap, bandages, cotton and woolen hose, mutton tallow, linen shirts, old linens, bathing towels, tape, buttons, tin cups, dressing gowns, razors, brushes, pillows, books and magazines.

When sick and wounded soldier began passing through Hartford on their way home, the Hartford Soldiers' Relief Association was organized to tend to their needs. Men and women delivered food and other articles for the relief and comfort of the sick and wounded men and boys who traveled by train and steamboat. At regular intervals, the newspapers listed the dead and wounded from Connecticut.

In Hartford, with the reports of Benjamin Silliman and MacRae Swift in hand, Hiram Bissell and the other commissioners felt that the matter had been studied sufficiently, but try as they did, they could not bring the council around to their point of view. Employing everything short of explosives, they tried to coax some kind of action from the ruminating group. Still, the council was not entirely satisfied with the reports of the two experts. In response to the mounting pressure from the water board, they finally appointed a joint standing committee (of three men) to examine all of the material extant and reach a separate decision. Reflecting the make-up of the council, the committee was composed of

Andrew Euson, a Republican alderman; James Lockwood, a Republican councilman and Frederick Cady, a Democratic councilman.

Bissell may have been stymied by the council's inability to make timely decisions but, together with his brother, Sylvester, his masonry business never missed a beat. In October, H. & S. Bissell won the contract to build the car houses and stables for the new horse railroad line. The two red brick buildings were to be built near the City Gardens on Wethersfield Avenue, about three-quarters of a mile south of State House Square. The project would require 400,000 bricks and be completed in three months.

For all of America, 1863 began with an event that had been generally expected since Abraham Lincoln was elected president—the abolition of slavery. Lincoln had planned to free the slaves in September, but was persuaded by his advisors to wait for a sizable Union army victory before he went public with his decision. The defeat of the rebels at Antietam gave Lincoln that victory. Therefore, as enunciated in his Emancipation Proclamation of January 1, 1863, ". . . all persons held slaves within any State or designated part of a State . . . shall be . . . forever free . . . and the executive government of the United States . . . will recognize and maintain the freedom of such persons. . . ."

Two months after the Emancipation Proclamation was issued and almost a year after the joint standing committee on the water works was appointed, they delivered a report to the council that outlined all of the preceding reports and came to the conclusion that, ". . . your committee [members] express themselves unqualifiedly in favor of the introduction of water from Trout Brook, West Hartford." Moreover, they suggested that the mayor call a city meeting to allow the residents of the city to vote on the West Hartford plan. Accepting the findings of its own committee, the council made plans for a citywide vote on whether or not to bring the waters of Trout Brook into the Hartford. Accordingly, in early April 1863, residents of the city were asked to vote either for "gravitation" or "pumping." Gravitation had come to mean allowing gravity to deliver the waters of Trout Brook to their homes, while pumping simply meant continuing with the Connecticut River Pumping Station, albeit on a much larger scale.

Bissell and his board had made a good case to the people, selling the idea door-to-door, while the newspapers groused over the finer points of the choices line by line. With the *Courant* and its subscriber firmly against the Trout Brook plan and the *Times* and its patrons allied with the experts who had studied the watercourse in great detail, the six wards of the city voted in three separate fire houses on the prescribed day. The opposition had tried to damage the water works at every opportunity while Bissell and his board struggled to build the system, but the Republicans remained quiet for the moment. The water franchise had been a coveted asset even before it was built, but after it began to produce a profit in 1861, it became the irresistible grail. If it could be demonstrated that the city was incapable of managing the water works, then it would have to be given over to a private group. Should such an opportunity materialize, the system could probably be had for fifty cents on the dollar and once again returned to a profitable venture.

As expected—considering that Silliman, Swift and the joint standing committee had all shown a marked preference for the Trout Brook plan—the voters chose the West Hartford waters by a 3-1 vote. Nevertheless, the vote immediately came under attack.

As Trout Brook meandered past the site chosen by Hiram Bissell for the new reservoir, it headed to the northeast until, about three miles hence, it ballooned out into a three-acre pond before continuing on its way. This pond was part of a gristmill operation, which was the oldest in West Hartford. Originally built by Thomas Morgan, the Goodman family purchased the gristmill in 1778 and Childs Goodman assumed control of the operation in 1842. Together with his wife, Sarah, and their four children, he ran the gristmill and farmed the acreage to the north of the millpond. At one time in his life, Goodman was the collector for the Northern District of the town, which made perfect sense because people had to visit his gristmill to have their corn ground into cornmeal anyway, so why not have them drop off their tax money at the same time?

The term "downstream owner" was used incessantly and generically in discussions of the Trout Brook project but, in fact, Childs Goodman was the real article. By 1864, all of the Goodman's four children were grown and had left the farmstead while the seventy-two-year-old miller and his sixty-eight-year-old wife, Sarah, continued the gristmill operation. Goodman was careful with money and, by 1864, had managed to squirrel away more than $11,000. Now the new reservoir project threatened to dry up Trout Brook and bring his gristmill operation to a halt.

His dander up, in early December 1864, Goodman hired an attorney and secured an injunction against Hartford's water commissioners, restraining them from "stopping or interfering with the natural flow of the waters of Trout Brook." Moreover, the injunction also forbade the water board from "any prosecution of the preparatory works." Although Goodman was right in the sense that the water board had made no effort yet to compensate him for his riparian rights, it was the usual David and Goliath story with just one small mill owner pitted against the whole General Assembly—that had chartered the Hartford Water Works in the first place.

The legislature stepped on Goodman like a bug, redrafting the wording of Hartford's charter, allowing for the Trout Brook waters to be taken. The only hitch was that the water commissioners could not act until Hartford's electors voted on the matter in a citywide ballot on July 7, 1863. Childs Goodman was left with nothing but lawyer's bills and wounded pride. As a lifelong Republican though, he had inadvertently done his party members a favor by showing that the water commissioners could be stymied by court action. Even if Childs Goodman had not acted, the Republicans in Hartford had plans of their own. The only difference was that their sense of timing was much better. What could not be accomplished at the beginning of the Trout Brook project might have a far better chance of succeeding at the end.

Hartford's Republicans had three reasons to oppose the new source. To begin, many of these men had been behind the private water company that was subsequently rejected by the voters. If, for any reason, the department should fail—and it well might if it were forced to keep pumping dirty river water into an undersized reservoir—then the entrepreneurs would have another chance to gain control of the water works. The ever-increasing revenues from water rents made it abundantly clear that the franchise was a real money-maker.

The second reason for the Republicans to be completely disenamored of a city-owned water works sprung from the simple belief that business should be conducted by businessmen not politicians. Sure, the city ran the fire department, but only because no sane man would want such a messy and uncertain franchise. Similarly, the city maintained the roads. Again, who would want a business whose principal activity was cleaning up tons of horse manure and watering the dusty thoroughfares? Conversely, the gas company, formed in 1849, was a private for-profit company and the horse railroad company—incorporated in 1859—was privately owned as well. Even the bridge crossing the Connecticut River to East Hartford was a toll bridge, whose profits—abundant in the worst of times—went into private pockets.

The Republicans final disputation with the concept of a city-owned water company was one that would go unuttered, even in the privacy of the exclusive clubs where these men gathered. The newly minted Republicans, descended from the city's earliest founders—the Hookers, Morgans, Bulkeleys, Wadsworths, Trumbulls and so forth—would consider it bad form to even discuss the matter. These men, who each had a reliable private well on his own property, were opposed to a municipal drinking water system, whose financial shortcomings would be papered over with their tax money. Why should they subsidize the drinking water of itinerant workers and immigrants—particularly Irish Catholics—who lived in the run-down tenements in the Fifth and Sixth Wards and along the Little River? Why shouldn't this canaille take care of their own drinking water needs? Republicans harbored all the exclusionary sentiments of their forebears.

Leading up to the second vote, the Republicans and their followers spoke out against the Trout Brook plan wherever and whenever they could. In their battle, they had the help of the most formidable ally of all—indifference. Bissell and his commissioners were almost completely lulled to sleep by the outcome of the first election. Reasoning that a three-to-one majority was unassailable, they spent little time re-selling the issue. Conversely, the Republicans whipped their followers into a frenzy and descended on the polls hungry for victory.

The weekend before the July 7 ballot was one of mixed emotions for Hartfordites. Throughout the country, Fourth of July celebrations followed the bloodiest fighting of the war at Gettysburg in the rolling fields of western Pennsylvania. Between July 1 and 3, General Robert E. Lee made his second attempt to invade the North, hoping that by doing so, the carnage would sour Unionists on the war. In the wake of the fighting—he hoped—Southerners would be allowed to secede without further bloodshed. The rout of the Confederate army at Gettysburg was the turning point of the war, although no one knew it at the time. On the rainy night of Saturday, July 4—with a third of his 75,000 troops killed, wounded or missing—Lee began his retreat to Virginia. Of General Meade's 85,000 Union troops, casualties were almost as high, including some of Hartford's native sons.

Against this backdrop, the city celebrated the Fourth of July quietly and returned to the polls the following Tuesday to decide the water question. As the direct result of a shameless campaign of misinformation—particularly with regard to the costs of the Trout Brook plan—the Republicans were able to hand defeat to those in favor of the new water source. In the July 1863 vote, "pumping" carried the day. The Republicans undoubtedly celebrated, but too soon; this vote would not stand either.

When Hiram Bissell issued his report to the council covering 1863, he offered the good news that once again the water department had turned a profit, but addressed another matter in an angry tone. Some newspaper editorial writers at the *Courant*, who were opposed to the West Hartford plan, were using their columns to sabotage the Trout Brook initiative. This incensed Bissell, who wrote that—

> . . . It is much to be regretted, that in so . . . important a matter as an additional supply of pure . . . water . . . attempts should be made to bias the . . . popular judgment . . . by . . . irresponsible writers. Unless the voting class will have the wisdom to discard...all representations made . . . by anonymous . . . parties, and base their actions . . . on the authenticated results of . . . responsible engineers, of known integrity and ability, we shall . . . fall into . . . grave mistakes. . . .

The council was in an incredible snarl now. All the experts—as well as their own joint standing committee—were pointing in the direction of West Hartford and the voters had just chosen the Connecticut River. All of the problems inherent in an expanded Connecticut River operation were out in the open now, but somehow the council had to reconcile this madness. Bowing to the superior knowledge of the common man, they hired another consultant. This time, they chose William Worthen, an engineer from New York who, it was hoped, would render order out of chaos. The situation at the reservoir dictated that Worthen design a whole new system and, of equal importance, estimate the costs of bringing it on line. When his report finally arrived, Worthen advised against the use of another engine of local manufacture, explaining—

> . . . I would not recommend the construction of another machine like the present . . . the moving parts are too many, the stroke of the pumps too short, and their construction unnecessarily complicated. [I suggest] a crank type engine [able to pump] 4 million gallons . . . in a twenty-four hour period . . . the boiler . . . to be a duplicate of the present one . . . a new reservoir on Zion Hill . . . [holding] 35 million gallons. . . .

Everyone connected to the proud—but struggling—water department must have done a slow burn as William Worthen practically described the Woodruff & Beach engine as a piece of junk. They had been so proud of the machine, not to mention their own business acumen in substituting it for the Cornish engine. Presumably, William Worthen had the good sense not to deliver the report in person.

Social gaffes aside, Worthen's report was about as welcome as warts, because it outlined a pumping system that was inordinately expensive. The most reckless estimates of the Trout Brook plan pegged its cost at $150,000, but the estimates forwarded by Worthen called for an expenditure of $230,000. This was too much for even the harshest critiques of the West Hartford option to stomach. With the help of Worthen's cold-water bath, the members of the council were numbed into inaction once again. Hartford's electors had chosen, for the moment, to continue pumping from the Connecticut River, but the exorbitant cost, essentially, negated that vote.

After months of wandering about in a daze, the council's water discussions now degenerated into a wilderness of prattle, with conferences and motions, votes and vetoes. Their every move was wrapped in the most confusing morass of verbiage and parliamentary bogs ever seen anywhere, as a newly elected council stepped into the void. Full of vim and vigor, the new council did the only logical thing it could; it ordered a third ballot on the issue, which would take place in October 1864.

Impounding the waters of a stream in a neighboring town and then running an aqueduct under one of that town's main highways was a matter that required a certain delicacy. Ultimately, the authority would come from the legislature but, before that body would dare make a move, there would have to be some meeting of the minds at the local level.

While Mayor Deming had declared that the negotiations with the officials of West Hartford were already completed, in truth, he had gotten a little ahead of himself. Representatives of the two towns had talked, but no concrete agreement had been reached. Since the city had not even decided exactly where the reservoir would be located, how could any firm commitments be made? Getting the elected officials of West Hartford to sign off on such a project at the General Assembly level would be a little more difficult than the mayor had intimated and the outcome was, to put it mildly, unclear.

Since the original boundaries of Hartford, as granted by the Sukiaug Indians, ran from the "whole bredth from Connecticut river on the east six large miles into the wilderness on the west," West Hartford had indeed originally been a part of Hartford. It was, however, always a separate parish— referred to as the West District—and too far away from the city for any meaningful interaction between residents of the two communities. After 1854, things were quite different with the West District incorporated as a separate entity. The 1,300 inhabitants of this new town looked down their noses at the big city and its immigrant masses. The West District was a rural, agrarian and almost inbred group of families descended from colonial stock and averse to the congestion of the city. By the 1860s, the sheer size of the immigrant population had diminished Hartford in their eyes; yearly, the city to the east became of less interest to them.

It should come as no surprise that the negotiations over the Trout Brook waters required a great deal of horse-trading. A proposal of this sort, at least on the surface, would seem innocuous enough except that the history of lakes and reservoirs in the United States up until that time was an ugly one. They were treated as receptacles for trash and waste of every sort, including the disposal of dead animals—as the people of Boston had found out the hard way at Lake Cochituate. With the heightened awareness of contaminants and associated diseases, a town might welcome a small reservoir today, but such was not the case in the 1860s. Add to this the loss of riparian rights for the downstream farmers and mill owners and the whole enterprise became a very tough sell indeed.

The water board was up against it. They had two options: they could buy the necessary rights or they could bargain away some of their newfound water, the second option far more palatable than the first. Another source could still be found elsewhere but, lest it be forgotten, the supplies to the west had one overarching advantage—their elevation. Assuming the aqueduct was properly bedded, gravity would deliver the water to all points in the city. Since all of the towns along the Connecticut River were at the lowest point in the valley, a water supply located in West Hartford would flow downhill through an aqueduct to Hartford without the need for pumps of any kind. This point was not lost on the elected officials of West Hartford as they held the water commissioners' feet to the fire.

From West Hartford's point of view, any money received would probably be used at a later time to build a water works of their own. In the same vein, since the Farmington road—the intended route of the city's proposed aqueduct—ran right through the center of West Hartford, when the time came to construct their own water system, they would most likely be laying their pipes right alongside Hartford's conduit. Such redundancy was lunacy. The residents of West Hartford, obviously, could benefit by connecting to Hartford's water system. Until that time, they would continue relying on private wells for drinking water and, unfortunately, their ability to fight fires would remain negligible.

Even though it was clear from the start that water distribution in West Hartford from the new reservoir was in the best interest of both communities, the negotiations unfolded in a painstakingly slow manner. The water board, of course, wanted to part with as little water as possible and the elected officials of West Hartford had dreams of clean, safe water piped into every building in town. Accordingly, the talks bogged down.

The Civil War was taking a toll on the residents of Hartford as the exigencies of war were forcibly driven home. Lincoln's suspension of habeas corpus angered Democrats who were strict constitutionalists and, for the same reason, considered the Emancipation Proclamation an abomination. For the average citizen, the litters of sick and wounded soldiers returning home and the lingering effects of the carnage at Gettysburg were gruesome reminders of the waste and suffering of war. Others people's kin were captured and imprisoned at Andersonville in Georgia—or other hellholes—where poor food, overcrowding and filth led to deaths from exposure, dysentery, scurvy and typhus.

Adding to the unrest and weariness were the draft riots in New York in July. Violently protesting against the ability of the upper classes to pay for substitutes, young men rioted in the streets, causing $1.5 million damage in a day's time. Several buildings were burned, including the Third Avenue draft hall. New York's police force was unable to quell the rioting and the state militia was off at war.

For the most part, Hartford's entertainment halls fell on hard times during the Civil War, perhaps because potential patrons either would not allow themselves a night of pleasure while men and boys were dying on distant battlefields or were engaged in relief work for the soldiers. As a result, Touro Hall was for sale and the American Theater was barely making it. That said, the city's population did support Allyn Hall, which was owned by former Mayor Timothy Allyn who began his business career selling the "family encyclopedia" for Oliver D. Cooke & Sons, one of the twenty or so publishing houses in Hartford. His theater catered to the upper classes by serving up a steady fare of Shakespearean plays and other highbrow productions. A fashionably appointed theater, with well-timed facelifts, it managed to remain in business long after the Civil War ended, while competitors foundered. In October 1863, it was announced in the *Courant* that, "J. Wilkes Booth and Mrs. Barrow will appear at Allyn Hall on Tuesday Evening next, accompanied by a full company of the best artists in the profession. The play will be "Richard III" with Mr. Booth as the Duke of Gloster [sic] . . . ."

Critiquing the first night's performance, the *Times* opined—

> Mr. Booth is one of the few who succeed in commanding the admiration of the audience in the many difficult parts of the character of "Richard," . . . But of all the absurdities . . . half of the audience rush[ed] from the hall before the close of the last act . . . scarcely had "Richard" received his death blow, than up sprang half of the audience and were, no doubt, at home and in bed before the close of the play.

In March of the following year, 1864, General William Tecumseh Sherman entered Georgia and, beginning with the battle of Kennesaw Mountain, started his now-legendary march to the sea. By September, Sherman's troops had sacked Atlanta. The press noted, "Atlanta is the great rail center for the South . . . and the key to the central states of the Confederacy . . . ."

Bissell and his water commissioners—determined not to be beaten in what they thought would be the third and final vote—visited their supporters around the city and sold the Trout Brook system anew. Up to his ears with the work of re-selling the upland water source and running the masonry business with Sylvester, Bissell's days were full. He worked long hours while his wife, Nancy, ran the household and tended to the needs of their two daughters. Tragically though, on September 10, 1864, Nancy Bissell died. Her physician diagnosed "gastric fever" as the cause of death, which, in truth, could have been anything from appendicitis to peritonitis. On the day following her passing, a Sunday, it rained hard all day long and that Monday, a chilly and cloudy day, a 2:30 P.M. service was held for family and friends at the new Universalist Church on Main Street. After the ceremony, she was interred at the Spring Grove Cemetery on the northern end of the city, within a half-mile of where she was born, forty-five years earlier.

Bissell was a self-possessed man who was used to commanding the events of his life but, after twenty-one years of marriage, things would, of course, be very difficult. His daughters were a concern—Belle was now a seventeen-year-old high school student and Ella was only nine and went to school diagonally across the street at the South School House. Fortunately, he had amassed some money and his wife had hired an Irish domestic servant, Catherine, who ran the household. Also, Nancy's forty-four-year-old sister, Sarah, lived with the Bissells and she would help ease the loss for her nieces. Lastly, Bissell's brother, Martin, was there. He worked all day, six days a week, but he, undoubtedly, helped where he could. With so many people living under his roof, Bissell was able to continue his work with the knowledge that his daughters would be cared for adequately and not left alone after their mother's passing.

A month later, the day of the water vote arrived. The balloting returned another three-to-one majority in favor of the Trout Brook project. Nevertheless, the balloting alerted Bissell to a change in public sentiment. A total ballot count of 2018—as against 3332 at the first vote—suggested that the voters, perhaps dispirited by the Civil War or the ham-fisted leadership at City Hall, were losing interest. It was true that many men were off fighting in the war, but the drop in the total number of ballots was still worrisome.

A month after this third vote on the West Hartford supply, the 1864 presidential elections were held. Gen. George McClellan proved not to be President Lincoln's type of military leader, stalling attacks until he had an overpowering advantage, but the Democrats believed in the general and embraced him as their candidate for president. With the war going badly and the mood of the country dour, Lincoln did not expect to be re-elected. However, the Democratic Party was split between the Peace Democrats—called Copperheads—and the War Democrats, who Lincoln wooed by running on what he called the National Union ticket. For insurance, Lincoln chose as his running mate a Tennessee Democrat, Andrew Johnson, who had stayed loyal to the union even as his home state seceded in June 1861. Lincoln's strategy worked as he bested McClellan by 400,000 votes and won a second term as president.

Wasting little time after the third Trout Brook vote, Bissell decided to buy the necessary land in West Hartford for the new reservoir. When Professor Silliman had studied the stream, he pronounced the waters of its northern tributary, Mine Brook, to be the purest. Bissell and his board, therefore, decided to build a dam just below the confluence of this tributary and the main body of Trout Brook. One of the principal considerations, of course, was the availability of land on the two brooks.

They swiftly cobbled together five adjacent parcels of land, the purchases beginning in October 1864, when a 15-acre piece of pastureland was acquired. The last four tracts of 20, 25, 10 and 8 acres, respectively, were bought in the following two months. The final site added up to 78 acres, for which they paid a total of $5,525. Even before the final 8 acres were added, they began grubbing out the reservoir. On the edge of this rapidly expanding crater, they began building an earthen dam—facing Hartford and right next to the Farmington road—whose spillway would be 250 feet above the riffling surface of the Connecticut River, six miles to the east. A whole year had been lost to the political wrangling and very little was accomplished at the site before winter. The foundation for the dam was prepared with its waste pipes and gates before the cold weather shut down the project for the winter.

The year 1865 brought a flurry of events. Much to the chagrin of Bissell and his fellow water commissioners, the tenacious Republicans hatched a truly inspired and devious three-pronged attack that was, to put it mildly, troubling. Critics like the *Times* cursed them for their black hearts but, in spite of their treachery, it could not be denied that their timing was impeccable.

Lucifer himself could not have scripted a more underhanded plan, which would be a combination of an attack on some questionable wording in the charter of the water works, a petition for another private water company charter at the state legislature and another court injunction against the Board of Water Commissioners introduced at exactly the right moment. The ringleaders of this plot to derail the water works—just before the Trout Brook system could come to fruition—were a pair of Hartford lawyers—Eliphalet Bulkeley and William Hungerford. Their names did not surface until March 1865 when the court injunction was secured against the water commissioners (the names of the twelve conspirators were listed on the petition). Almost all of the men behind the injunction were Republicans and some, like Eliphalet Bulkeley, were even original incorporators of the private water company of 1851.

Bulkeley was sixty-two and still hurting from the loss of his firstborn son and fellow attorney, Charles, during the Civil War. Probably from a lifetime of reading law books and later poring over the fine print of insurance policies, he was also nearly blind.

It is important to understand that Bulkeley was not an evil man. He, like the rest of the Republicans, was simply dead set against a city-owned water works, feeling that mercantile businesses of every stripe should b e in the hands of private businessmen like him. He was from a long line of brilliant, if eccentric, clergymen and physicians, who traced their roots in America back to Rev. Peter Bulkeley who landed at Boston in 1634 and founded the town of Concord, Massachusetts the following year.

Eliphalet Bulkeley

Eliphalet Bulkeley was born in Colchester, graduated from Yale College in 1824 and practiced law in different places before settling in Hartford in 1847. A judge in East Haddam since 1832, he then served in the state legislature almost continuously from 1838 on, eventually landing the position of Speaker of the House. In middle age, Bulkeley began to take a more active interest in business and spent less and less time at the law. Shortly after moving his wife and children to Hartford, he became the first president of Connecticut Mutual Life Insurance Company and then later Aetna Life.

Highlighting Bulkeley's enormous brainpower, contemporary accounts note that his memory was so acute he could "give with surprising accuracy many genealogical facts relating to families whose own members were in ignorance." In state politics, Bulkeley knew his way around the capitol better than most.

Teamed with this brilliant pied piper was the learned, but reticent, William Hungerford, who graduated from Yale College in 1809. At his eulogy in 1873, Atty. Richard Hubbard— a future Connecticut Governor—said these words about his good friend. "His manner, though not awkward, was not graceful. His temperament was not magnetic, his mind was not imaginative or brilliant, and he rarely rose into eloquence. His voice was somewhat harsh and untrained . . . [and] his style was not free from mannerisms . . . [yet] he was a profound attorney . . . possessed [of] a vigorous common sense. . . ." In spite of the fact that Hungerford did not possess even the bare minimum requirements for political life, he served many terms in the General Assembly. So said, William Hungerford playing Brutus to Eliphalet Bulkeley's Cassius. The pair recruited ten fellow travelers, hoisted their burgee and sailed confidently into the storm.

Their plan was a masterful symphony of three distinct movements. First, they played their hole card—the General Assembly. By plying selected members of the state's highest legislative body with "champagne suppers and other persuasive influences," all the right arms were twisted in unison. Moreover, the *Times* reported, ". . . they have already succeeded in securing the nomination of a state Senator, the Reverend Mr. Rockwell, who will cooperate with them in their plan to defeat the decision of the people of this city. . . ." The trick for Bulkeley and Hungerford was to have the legislature demand another vote on the Trout Brook plan and—of paramount importance—insist on a *three-fifths majority* for the new water source to pass muster. Given the controversy surrounding the matter, three-fifths was a high hurdle indeed. Still, Bulkeley and Hungerford kept their powder dry for the moment, allowing no hint of their progress at the statehouse to surface.

Secondly, they employed the courts. Exactly a week before the council was to give Hiram Bissell permission to spend $120,000 for 24,000 feet of cast-iron aqueduct material from the Patent Water & Gas Pipe Company of Jersey City, the fiery, irritating former-councilman, Lawson Ives—acting as front man for the Republicans—obtained a court injunction against the city and the water department. It forbade Bissell or anyone else from "purchasing any pipe or land or other materials, or making any contract, or doing any other act for the purpose of bringing the water from Trout Brook to the city, or taking the same from any other place but the Connecticut River."

Once the injunction was in place, Bissell could dig reservoirs in West Hartford to his heart's content but, without the aqueduct, he would never be able to get the water to Hartford. This injunction would have gone the same route of Childs Goodman's effort, except that Bulkeley and Hungerford were seasoned advocates who knew how to use the courts as well as the legislature, having acquired friends at each institution over the years.

The reason that the injunction was so devious was that it exploited a small technicality in the city's water charter at the worst possible time. Hartford's original charter for a water works made no mention of taking water from anywhere except the Connecticut River. Thus, Trout Brook was beyond the scope of the charter. By filing this injunction when they did, the Republicans forced the council to withhold the authority to purchase the aqueduct pipe. How could the city possibly spend $120,000 for cast iron pipe before the injunction was lifted? Further complicating matters, the council had no way of knowing what the legislature would do.

Still, the real genius of the Republican plot was that it preyed on the frailty of human nature. By sowing seeds of doubt about the viability of the Trout Brook plan, when it came time to vote again, almost inevitably, the turnout would be light, reflecting voter uncertainty. Logically, this would increase the chances that the water works would fall short of the legislature's *three-fifths majority,* which of course no one knew about yet except for Bulkeley, Hungerford and their Republican friends. For the next four months, all eyes darted anxiously toward the statehouse as the work at the Trout Brook site in West Hartford came to a halt.

As a final twist, Buckley and Hungerford ginned up a sideshow to try to muddy the waters further. On April 4, fellow Republican Charles Beach, a foundry owner, gave notice that he was petitioning the General Assembly for an act of incorporation which would also allow him "to build a dam and reservoir on the same stream (Trout Brook) for a water power, and to supply a distribution for family use. . . . " Obviously, such a petition was problematic because if mill owners and the Hartford Water Works had the right to exploit Trout Brook, how could the legislature deny Beach? His petition, though, was clearly antithetical to the goals of the water works. With its three-pronged attack firmly in place, the Republicans sat back in anticipation of victory at the polls.

Less than one week after the Republicans put the last piece of their campaign against the water company in place, a far more important struggle came to a conclusion. On Sunday, April 9, General Robert E. Lee of the Army of Virginia surrendered to General Ulysses S. Grant of the Army of the Potomac at a private home in the tiny town of Appomattox Court House, Virginia. The Civil War was over. It had cost the lives of more than 620,000 of the country's most able young people. Connecticut alone lost 5,354, two-thirds of them from disease; Hartford lost 400.

News of the surrender reached Hartford late in the day by telegraph. Messengers were sent to notify the police so that the bell atop the state house could be rung. The fire department responded first, mistaking the wildly clanging bell for an alarm. Shortly after, church bells began to peal and ". . . thousands of people . . . appeared on the streets, and such a scene of rejoicing has never been witnessed in Hartford before." Bonfires were lit, Christy's Minstrel band was engaged and a procession spontaneously formed. With flags flying and led by the steamers and hose carriages, the crowd paraded down Main Street, around the South Green and back. At nightfall, the noise and mayhem continued with lights burning brightly all over the city. The *Times* noted, ". . . At 2 o'clock in the morning, bonfires were still blazing, pistols firing, and there was every prospect that the Union men could keep up their enthusiasm until daylight."

The joyous mood turned to abject horror five days later when the actor, John Wilkes Booth, snuck into the presidential box at Ford's Theater and shot Abraham Lincoln. The president, Mary Todd Lincoln and another couple were watching a Friday night performance of *Our American Cousin*, when Booth struck. Lincoln was carried to a private home across the street from the theater where he lingered through the night, finally succumbing at 7:20 A.M. He was 56 years old.

Lincoln's assassin, John Wilkes Booth, jumped from the box to the stage—breaking his leg in the leap—and shouted the now-familiar words "Sic Semper Tyrannus," the Virginia state motto meaning, "Thus Ever To Tyrants." Twelve days later, the 27-year-old Booth was cornered in a barn in Bowling Green, Virginia and shot to death by government troops.

West Hartford was in an enviable bargaining position because not only was it in no rush to reach an agreement with Hartford, but town leaders had the luxury of doing absolutely nothing, if they chose. Be that as it may, before the fourth—and final—vote on the Trout Brook supply, a bargain was struck and three-fourths of the voters of West Hartford ratified it. In exchange for allowing the Hartford Water Works to build a reservoir and extend their aqueduct across the east-west axis of West Hartford—under the Farmington road—the water board agreed to supply water to homes and businesses "within a reasonable distance of the aqueduct." (This wording fomented an endless succession of court cases until the legislature amended the private act in 1913, thereafter requiring Hartford to supply the whole town of West Hartford.) Under the original agreement though, while the Hartford Water Works might lay fifty feet of pipe to a new home in the city, they could conceivably be forced to run a water pipe ten times that length—or more—to a farm in West Hartford. The consumer would pay for the connection, but the process of costing out individual connections, each with special circumstances, was both burdensome and time-consuming.

The Republicans' friends in the statehouse, in a craven attempt to permanently injure the water department by stopping the work at Trout Brook and ending the city's quest for an additional supply, withheld their resolution of the water board's legal woes until the end of their spring session. The governor signed the bill on July 21, 1865 and the *three-fifths majority* made its public debut that same day. It was at this point that the chicanery of the Republicans came to light. In the last paragraph of the Private Law, the mayor was required to assemble the electors of Hartford to re-vote the issue and, instead of settling for a simple majority that was the norm in all city matters, the legislature insisted on a *three-fifths majority* in favor of the Trout Brook plan. Only by meeting the higher standard would the injunction be lifted and the water commissioners be allowed to bring the waters of Trout Brook into the city.

When the full import of the legislation registered with Hartford's citizens, there was at first stunned silence and then anger. The *Times* ran long articles railing against the *three-fifths majority* when all other matters in Hartford were settled with a simple majority vote. They concluded by stating that, ". . . it is not a sound principle that a minority [two-fifths] shall be authorized to defeat so important a question."

It got worse. The legislature enacted the law on a Friday and, at the meeting of the council on Monday night, a vote was passed directing the mayor to call a meeting of the city's electors to vote on the West Hartford water question on Saturday, July 29th, only six days hence. The *Post* reported the following day that, "The resolution, which was offered by Alderman [George] Sill, gave rise to a spicy debate between him and Alderman [Samuel] Woodruff, who said that the council had no authority to direct the mayor in the matter, the legislature having already authorized him what to do." Sill, reading directly from the statute to prove that he was right, after which Woodruff asked him to rescind his resolution, guaranteeing ". . . that the mayor would call a meeting before long." Both men were Republicans, but Samuel Woodruff had a longstanding and cordial relationship with Hiram Bissell and the water works, his firm having built the original Root engine for the Pumping Station at the river. However, Sill refused to withdraw his resolution and it passed. The Republican mayor, Allyn Stillman, could have vetoed the vote but did not. Though not necessarily conspiring with the Republicans, the mayor simply allowed the resolution to pass and the vote was scheduled for the last Saturday in July.

This gave the Democrats almost no time at all to re-sell the Trout Brook plan door-to-door as they had done in the past. By compressing the time frame so radically and setting the bar so high, there was every chance that the Republicans would defeat the West Hartford plan. In that sense, Bulkeley, Hungerford and their friends had played their hand masterfully.

Hiram Bissell knew that the *three-fifths majority* was problematic for a number of reasons. First, people were sick to death of the additional water supply question and, given their druthers, would beg off. Secondly, the war— like all wars—cut more deeply into the ranks of poor Democratic voters than it did those of wealthy Republicans who could afford to pay for substitutes to take their places at the front. Of the 400 Hartford men killed in the Civil War, it was entirely reasonable to assume that more were Democrats than Republicans. Lastly, the lack of time was crippling. The additional supply of water was a complicated issue and winning and maintaining support required time, an item which, thanks to the perfidy of the Republicans, was now in short supply.

Racing against time, on Tuesday the 25th, Bissell placed the following advertisement in the city's newspapers—

> At the request of several gentlemen, a meeting of those favorable to the introduction of an additional supply of water from Trout Brook, West Hartford, will be held at Room #7, Marble Block, Central Row on Tuesday evening, July 25, at 8 o'clock, to make provision for calling out a full vote at the city meeting to be held upon that subject. Your attendance is especially desired.
>
> —Hiram Bissell

At the meeting, held at Central Hall, "ward committees and committees on printing [leaflets, etc.] and other business were appointed." The following day, the *Post* wrote, "The project was well talked up, and there is no doubt but that the favorers of the Trout Brook project will employ all possible means to carry out their plans on Saturday. . . ."

On the afternoon of the 25th, the *Times* printed a letter from a subscriber claiming that, " . . . the clique who are fighting Trout Brook were today busy in certain quarters using money freely to buy votes . . . One prominent opponent, whose pocket as well as his pride, is said to be interested in the defeat of Trout Brook, said he would use $5,000 to carry his point . . . " Along with letters from readers, the *Times* ran long articles outlining the history of the West Hartford plan as well as the city's desperate need for an additional supply of water. Their articles ended with the caveat that, ". . . the examinations [were] made by such practical men as Hiram Bissell and others of admitted capability to judge accurately, developed the fact that Trout Brook would afford an ample supply by gravitation."

The *Courant*, showing its partisan stripes in regal fashion, coordinated its scabrous attacks in perfect concert with its Republican subscribers. They labeled the Trout Brook system a Democratic plan simply because their competitor, the *Times*, favored it. Two days before the vote, and in order to convince the populace that opposition to the West Hartford source was widespread among citizens of all social stations, they printed a lopsided recitation of their beliefs and signed the piece—A Mechanic (factory worker). The anonymous "Mechanic" even hinted at corruption—

> . . . Depend upon it, there is a "cat in the meal" somewhere. It is strongly advocated by some who need watching. Speculation may and

may not have something to do with this thing . . . .No "frog pond" for me, thank you.

The *Courant's* readers continually described the Trout Brook water as poor while offering reassurances regarding the quality of the Connecticut River water. This was utter nonsense, though, for the water in the river had deteriorated a great deal in the decade since pumping first began. Moreover, analytical chemists and eminent hydraulic engineers alike had attested to the purity of the West Hartford water. The *Courant*, however, saved its most powerful salvo for the day of the crucial vote. As a disingenuous gesture of fairness, on the morning of the vote the paper printed two articles, which purported to give a reasoned examination of both sides of the issue—the opposition to the Trout Brook plan received a generous 2,000 words, while the proponents got a paltry 300.

Using their 300 words wisely, the advocates of the West Hartford plan offered a simple balance sheet highlighting the great economies guaranteed by the new source. By their calculations, the new source would cost $161,000. With regard to the riparian rights of the downstream owners and the possibility that the citizens of Hartford might have to pay annual damages to farmers and mill owners downstream, the matter was addressed thusly. An annual amount of $20,000 was allocated for "land damages," with an explanation at the bottom of the article. The footnote explained that this money presupposed that no "compensating reservoirs" were to be built. In the event that the water board decided, at a later time, to build such a catchment to compensate the downstream owners [with water], then no annual land damages would accrue.

This scenario threatened to cheat the bondholders and taxpayers of all the monies invested in the new source to date, and also to doom Hartford's residents to the rapidly deteriorating Connecticut River waters forever. On the other hand, if they were to beat the *three-fifths majority* hurdle, the Democrats had to make sure that every favorable vote was cast on Saturday and pray that, after that date, the Republicans would have no cards left to play.

By the day of the big vote, Hiram Bissell had done all that he could. It was up to the voters now. As expected, the Republicans blanketed the ballot boxes like pigeon droppings on public statuary. Thankfully, so did the proponents of the Trout Brook plan, but because six different venues were used for the balloting—mostly firehouses in the city's different wards—the outcome was in doubt until late Saturday night. At five in the afternoon, the polls were closed and the ballot boxes whisked off to City Hall, where the council met in the evening as a board of canvassers, Mayor Stillman presiding. Painstakingly the 3,236 votes were counted. The First Ward—the largest—came in with only 41 votes over the *three-fifths* barrier. The Second Ward was worse, delivering only 17 votes over the number required. The downward trend continued as the Third Ward only cleared the hurdle by 10 votes and the Fourth Ward actually fell 7 votes short. Fortunately for Bissell and his water commissioners, the tide turned as the Fifth Ward beat the *three-fifths* obstacle by 21 votes, with only the Sixth Ward left to count.

It was always difficult to count noses in the Sixth Ward because, although it was crowded with potential voters, only a small percentage of the newcomers had become naturalized Americans and were thus eligible to vote. Also, the people of the Sixth Ward lived so close to the Connecticut River that spending enormous sums of money on fancy water projects did not sit well with a group who thought soda bread was caviar. Nevertheless, the Sixth Ward cleared the *three-fifths* hurdle by 50 votes.

With the members of the council, the water commissioners and some interested citizens watching from behind the rail, Mayor Stillman made it official—the Trout Brook ballots exceeded the required *three-fifths majority* by a slim 132 votes. It was settled. The West Hartford water would be Hartford's new source of supply. The Republicans had lost and the common folks of the city had won. (In time, the final piece of the Republican's gambit failed when Charles Beach's petition to damn the Trout Brook for his own purposes was denied by the legislature.)

What none of the men voting that day could possibly have foreseen was that the initial reservoir in West Hartford was the all-important first step in building the huge and efficient water system enjoyed by the cities of central Connecticut today. While the waters of the Connecticut River—along with all of the other rivers in America—deteriorated further each year, Hartford's water department was able to impound ever-larger bodies of pure water in the hills to the west of the city. Initially the source was Trout Brook and its tributaries, but later the different branches of another unspoiled watercourse were exploited—the Farmington River. With all of this in mind, it is hard to underestimate the value of those 132 votes on a hot July day in 1865.

Chapter 5
The Dam Collapse of 1867

On the Tuesday following the decisive water vote on the additional supply from Trout Brook, Judge Elisha Carpenter of Hartford's Superior Court withdrew the injunction won by Eliphalet Bulkeley and William Hungerford. The newspapers hinted that the pair would file another injunction but, in truth, they had had enough; there simply was no fight left in them. Moreover, it was believed that such a move "would be universally regarded as purely factious and mischievous."

With the injunction lifted, the water consumers in Hartford could breath a sigh of relief, but Hiram Bissell had no time to waste. Not a single shovelful of dirt or length of pipe had been touched since the end of March and there was much to do before winter. Quickly, he placed an advertisement in the newspapers soliciting bids for the remainder of the Trout Brook work—laying the pipes, grubbing the reservoir, piling up embankments and building the gatehouse. The companies doing the bidding were none other than the companies who were working on the project before the injunctions, so the process moved at lightning speed. In three weeks, the contracts were awarded, giving the false impression that the lost time would be quickly recovered. For completing the excavation of the reservoir and the building of the dam, Milton Clyde of Springfield—the original contractor on the new reservoir—was chosen. Clyde specialized in contracting out to the railroads, employing large gangs of laborers to lay track, but he was also a director of the Springfield Aqueduct Company, which left him well versed in the exigencies of water works projects.

The laying of the pipes was more complicated because different sections of the aqueduct required different types of conduit material. In the segments of the aqueduct closest to the population centers of Hartford and West Hartford, cast iron had to be used so that lateral connections could be affixed but, for the longest section of the aqueduct, wrought iron and cement pipe was the choice. Supplying and bedding the four miles of expensive wrought iron and cement pipe went to the manufacturer of that product—Patent Water & Gas Pipe Company of Jersey City, New Jersey, while the laying of the other two sections went to Camden Iron Works (later J.W. & J. F. Starr), also of New Jersey, and James Walker of Hartford. (Walker was, ultimately, unable to perform the work, and his contract was assigned to Isaiah Wadleigh & Son of Brooklyn, New York.) Henry Tryon, Bissell's cousin, won the contract to build the gatehouse and do some other masonry work at the reservoir.

The last item on Bissell's checklist was the hiring of a full time engineer to oversee the work at Trout Brook. It would have been impossible for Bissell to oversee the work in West Hartford while managing the water works in Hartford and helping his brother, Sylvester, with the masonry work connected with H. & S. Bissell. The easiest solution was to have a full time engineer supervise the work in West Hartford at Reservoir No. 1 (as it was designated). The remoteness of the new works made this decision an easy one; a two-hour buckboard ride to and from the West Hartford site was a poor use of his time. Bissell chose a well-respected city surveyor and engineer, George Marsh, to be his eyes and ears at Reservoir No. 1. Marsh was by nature and training an exacting man, meticulous about his work and that of those under him, but he was also a terrible worrywart, making the whole project an ordeal for him.

The awarding of the contracts appeared to put things right back on track, but this was illusory; through no fault of their own, the contractors held up the work. Unsure whether Hartford would ever end its contentious squabbling and balloting, the contractors had no choice but to accept other work. As a result, only about a mile of the six-mile long aqueduct was bedded before the cold weather shut the project down for the year.

On the brighter side, Milton Clyde brought in 100 men and worked energetically on the reservoir, removing more than 4,000 stumps over the thirty-two acre basin. Using wooden scoops pulled by a team of mules to skim out the soil, most of Clyde's work was completed by the end of the year. His construction of the dam was also well along, leaving little to finish in the spring. Henry Tryon and his masons worked steadily on the gatehouse all through the fall and it too was near completion by the end of 1865.

The dam was a simple earthen structure with a core of riprapped stonework. It very much resembled the sloping embankment at any other point around the reservoir, except, of course, that its opposing face was a sloping surface—of perhaps forty-five degrees—and fifty-five feet tall. No one on the board had any experience with dams but the principles involved were not exactly new.

As early as 1631 a dam was built near Boston to harness waterpower along Mill Creek. The first dams in America were fairly crude and built in connection with tidal power schemes. Almost always, the dams' water faces were long, sloped affairs covered with a layer of earth and gravel. More than anything, they resembled a wood-splitting wedge laid down flat. The water exerted a downward pressure that, it was hoped, would keep the structure in place. Excess water—the result of rains or snowmelt—would exit the reservoir through a spillway off to the side, which would absorb the erosive effect of constantly moving water instead of the top surface of the dam. These spillways were cut into solid rock and located some distance from the dam itself. The face of the dam, away from the reservoir, was normally just a vertical drop—or near so—to a rock apron. This classic earthen dam described the structure at Trout Brook well. Two differences were that the earliest dams did not have waste pipes laid underneath them, allowing a second avenue to discharge water, and the dam at Reservoir No. 1 in West Hartford had a more gently sloping face on its downstream side.

While the contractors had been slowly assembling their crews at Reservoir No. 1 toward the end of summer, Hiram Bissell took time to rearrange his life by remarrying. After more than two decades as a married man, he was no longer content to live without a mate. On a warm Thursday in September 1865, only four days past the traditional one-year mourning period, he married Elizabeth Barnard, the widow of a farmer, Dorus Barnard, who died of "confluent smallpox," leaving her with three young children. By weight of the evidence, their marriage was beneficial for all concerned. Raising three small children alone in 1865 would have been difficult for Elizabeth, affording her nothing but hardship and struggle. Bissell would have had it little better. Still, working twelve-hour days, six days a week—and with political and business meetings at night—he would have found life hard and lonely. He had too much on his plate to fulfill his obligations without a helpmate and his daughters had needs that he could not hope to fill. His older girl, Belle, now out of high school, could take care of herself—to a point—but the real concern was the now-ten-year-old, Ella, who needed a woman's guidance to get over the difficulties of the early teen years that all adolescents find awkward.

For Hiram and Elizabeth Bissell, post-Civil War Hartford was different in subtle ways from the place they knew before the bloody conflict engulfed the country. While theaters had begun to proliferate in the early 1850s, most of them had been driven out of business during the war. The American Hall still hosted Masquerade Balls, the Fenians and other, less-expensive forms of entertainment, while Allyn Hall catering to almost every conceivable segment of the community. Due to the inflation both during and after the war, the cost of putting on a legitimate play had skyrocketed. The *Times* estimated that to rent Allyn Hall for one night, purchase a license and pay for the travel expenses, hotel bills and salaries for a troupe of eighteen, it would cost a traveling company $256 for one show. At that time, a $300 house was rare, so very few traveling shows could make a go of it. Allyn Hall was in the best position of the two houses because it booked everything short of animal acts. The Connecticut State Billiards Championship—which began right after the war—was held at Allyn Hall. The theater was also host to the Beethoven Society, which staged symphonic events, choral arrangements and socials throughout the year. Lastly, the hall put on Shakespearean plays and even Italian operas, like *Fra Diavolo*.

Besides these halls, there were new and growing pastimes—some familiar and others strange and exotic. For the gamblers, the Hartford Trotting Park ran regular contests for the state's fastest horses ("to harness") with purses as high as $1000—a fantastic sum in 1865. More mundane but infinitely more popular was Base Ball, which attracted more fans and participants every year. Almost every day at three o'clock on the Ball Grounds in the Park, mechanics from different manufactories played Base Ball until dark. The better clubs—like the Charter Oaks—challenged clubs from around the state to contests and, when the talent was unevenly distributed, the score could get astonishingly high. In the summer of 1866, the Charter Oaks played the Uncas Club of Norwich, with a final score of 51-1.

On the more exotic side were the balloon ascensions that were sweeping the country as hydrogen and helium were found to have unexpected uses—

> . . . Mr. Bassett will make a balloon ascent . . . at 3 PM in his "Stars and Stripes," and at the height of a mile he will renew his feat once before successfully performed of letting down a dog safely to the earth attached to a parachute. . . .

Counterfeiting of currency was rampant after the war, demanding increased vigilance by police officials and merchants alike. Barely a week went by without an arrest for passing bad money, a direct result of a major shift in the financial framework of the nation. Up to the time of the Civil War, printing and circulating banknotes fell predominantly to the states as financial institutions each circulated their own notes, creating more than 7,000 different bank notes—plus 4,000 spurious ones—and a wide latitude in the exchange rates from state to state. For example, since branch banks were illegal, a Yankee peddler selling his wares before the war in, say, the Carolinas, could expect to have his Connecticut paper notes discounted according to their perceived worth.

During the Civil War, however, regional control of banknotes ended as the printing and distributing functions became the province of the federal government. Counterfeiters saw great opportunity in the confusion caused by this shift. The first issues circulated by the government—owing to the color of the ink on the reverse of these notes—were dubbed "greenbacks" and, since the public was unfamiliar with them, spotting a forgery was nigh unto impossible. Worse, the issuance of fractional paper currencies, like the twenty-five-cent bill, only compounded the confusion.

Incidentally, the conversion to federal control of the nation's currency was an effort to curb the inflation attendant with all periods of turmoil, but the unrestricted printing of greenbacks during and after the Civil War had the opposite effect, driving inflation to the highest levels seen since the American Revolution.

Postal money orders made their first appearance right after the war, with the nation's post-offices acting as clearinghouses for this new method of sending money over long distances. Ten dollars could be sent to any post office in the United States for a commission of ten cents. The largest amount allowed under this new system was $30, which could be sent for twenty cents.

Beyond the burst in counterfeiting, the police blotter in Hartford resembled that of the pre-war years with a plethora of assault-and-battery charges, a fairly constant amount of arrests for drunkenness and an increased number of infractions for prostitution and running houses of ill repute. The miscreants paid fines and court costs, and did anywhere from ten to forty days in the workhouse.

Ascending still higher on the criminal ladder, the state prison at Wethersfield saw a large drop in its population during and shortly after the war because "the demands of the war saved . . . many a police court customer from becoming a Wethersfield [prison] boarder by taking him into the army instead."

Women's fashion even took a welcome turn as the devilishly clever mavens of high fashion introduced the "Bon-Ton" Hoop Skirt. This miraculous garment proffered, what one baffled newspaper called, "a new invention 'that entirely dispenses of the old and imperfect manner of fastening with gum or glue and spangles' and offers various other inducements that will be appreciated by those who are better versed in the mystery of the female toilet than we are." For all the innovative fashions offered in the better shops, there were infinitely more stores selling sewing machines, with no fewer than five companies competing with Singer for the amateur seamstress's dollar.

As Reservoir No. 1 came together in the late fall months of 1865, Bissell began to experiment with the new Trout Brook catchment. However, the rate at which water collected in the basin and, more importantly, how fast it could be released troubled him. Soon after a moderate rainstorm, with Trout Brook—and Mine Brook—swollen and filling the reservoir exactly as planned, he let the water rise to within six feet of the breast of the dam on the east, while water rushed out of the sluiceway, which faced northeast a little ways around the perimeter of the reservoir. Then he cranked open the waste gate under the dam until water gushed from this large cast iron pipe in explosive bursts. With the sluiceway dumping water at peak capacity and the waste gate wide open, he waited. A reporter explained the subsequent drama this way—

> The struggle now became fearful. The water rushed through the pipe with a terrible velocity and the water flowed into the reservoir with equal force. With all this outlet, the water did not fall *but slowly rose* in the reservoir . . . .(Italics added)

Unfortunately, the *Times* completely missed the import of the rising supply in the reservoir. Heralding the accumulation of water as a *welcome* outcome—since inadequate supply had been an oft-repeated criticism of the Trout Brook plan—the newspaper overlooked a significant point. Water cresting over the top of an earthen dam—thus scouring away the soil—was a long-appreciated formula for disaster. The sluiceway, made of masonry, if constructed of sufficient size, would protect the dam itself.

Whether Bissell recognized this inability to control the amount of water in the reservoir for the problem that it was cannot be known. There were two cast iron pipes laid under the dam—one was the waste pipe with which he was experimenting, and the other was the aqueduct to the city. Since no water was flowing through the aqueduct, Bissell may have reasoned that without this added outflow, the water almost had to rise in the reservoir. Whatever the case, before anything could be done, the cold weather arrived and, at the beginning of December, the project was shut down for the winter.

The following April, the spring rains and the snowmelt raised the water level in the reservoir to within eight feet of the top of the dam and, this time, Bissell lowered the level by opening both the waste and aqueduct pipes. Even with both of these twenty-two inch pipes wide open, it took all day for the water to drop four inches. By building the reservoir right at the nexus of Trout Brook and its northern tributary, Mine Brook, the inflow was even more abundant than first calculated. Nevertheless, during drier spells, the reservoir was emptied and refilled a number of times because "drawing it off and letting it fill again . . . would render [the water] still more pure . . . ."

The water works suffered another set back at the end of April when the engineer George Marsh suddenly died. He had had a bout of typhus, but it was thought that he was past the worst of it and would recover. Instead, he began to hemorrhage internally and soon passed away. The *Times* linked Marsh's premature death to his work at Reservoir No. 1—

> . . . it is said that he became sick because of care and anxiety about the filling up, by the rising water, of the entrance to the waste pipe, at the large dam . . .

After the Governor's Foot Guard laid George Marsh to rest, Samuel Gray— the first man at the water works to officially use the title of "chief engineer"— was hired to complete the project in West Hartford. Gray was fairly young man for such an important job, only thirty-three, and consequently did not have the years of experience that George Marsh had. Nonetheless, he did a creditable job overseeing the work at Trout Brook.

June was the month of graduation ceremonies and class trips and the ten graduates of the Hartford Female Seminary, the finishing school founded in 1823 by Catherine Beecher, chose a riverboat excursion for their final fling. Harriet Beecher Stowe—eleven years younger than her sister Catherine—had attended the school in 1824 and later, in 1829, taught composition and rhetoric there. For their class trip of 1866, the ten graduating students—from as far away as Illinois—and their families and guests chartered a steamboat to take them downriver to Goodspeed's in East Haddam, where "three hours were spent enjoying the collations and picnicking at the side hill grove in that place and also in dancing." Following an afternoon of fun, the steamboat headed back upriver, reaching the city wharf at the bottom of State Street at 6 P.M., where its passengers disembarked and headed home.

Reservoir No. 1 only covered thirty-two of the seventy-eight-acre parcel purchased for it, but it still promised to hold what was then a fantastic amount of water—165 million gallons—a three-month supply for Hartford.

Throughout the year 1866, Milton Clyde's laborers continued the nasty work of grubbing out the new reservoir. It was a slow process inasmuch as each scoop skimmed from the bottom of the basin tore away only about a yard of soil. Clyde's workers would drive their teams along the bottom of the reservoir until their scoops were full and then steer them up the embankment to the disposal area. All day long, a dozen teams marched in and out of the growing pit, removing a yard at a time from the crater. At the end of the project, it was estimated that the contractors had made almost a million passes through the deepening pit, removing more than 800,000 yards of soil, rocks and stumps.

Concurrent with this work, another team piled up earth on the upstream side of the rip-rapped stone corewall of the new dam, which was thirty-five feet through at the base and narrowing to eighteen feet at the summit. The top six feet of the dam was just soil but, since the water in the reservoir was never supposed to come in contact with this part of the dam, the cap material was thought to be inconsequential. It extended the full length of the two hundred foot structure. Eventually, the long sloping mound assumed a wedge shape. Meanwhile, Henry Tryon completed the gatehouse and some other small projects around the site.

As the men of the Hartford Water Works brought the new supply slowly to fruition, the city addressed one of the problems that had convinced Bissell and others to abandon the Connecticut River water. In August 1866, Hartford's Sanitary Board made the initial moves that would eventually transfer all of the slaughterhouses beyond the city limits. At first, they tried to evict the whole industry by fiat, but settled for some stringent regulations regarding the disposal of blood, offal and manure until all of the businesses could be relocated by January 1867. Along the same lines, the Sanitary Board took control of the Little River, keeping it full year-round thus reducing the awful stench—and errant pathogens—arising from the dry river bed during the hot summer months.

At the end of October—with the connection to the city's pipes and the Lord's Hill Reservoir made—Bissell was, at long last, able to tell the newspapers that the aqueduct from Reservoir No. 1 at Trout Brook to Hartford was completed. Since all of the supply lines to homes and businesses originated at the old reservoir, the simplest way to bring the additional supply into the system was to dump it into the Lord's Hill Reservoir. The long term plan, however, was to eliminate any connection at all to Connecticut River water by eliminating the old Lord's Hill receptacle from the system.

Before the aqueduct could be used, however, it had to be tested for leaks, which was wise, because there turned out to be many. The aqueduct lifted an enormous burden from the shoulders of Hiram Bissell and the other water commissioners because if, for any reason, the pumps should fail at the river, the Trout Brook water could be coursing throughout the system in the time it took to open the gate valve at Reservoir No. 1. While the contractors from Patent Gas & Water Pipe Company, one by one, unearthed and repaired the leaks in the aqueduct, Bissell attended to another matter.

From the very beginning of the Trout Brook project, he knew that four downstream owners of sawmills and gristmills would have to be compensated for the loss of their riparian rights. If the water works were removing two million gallons a day from Trout Brook, then obviously these water-powered mills would be adversely affected. As a not-so-gentle reminder, Bissell had only to remember the injunction secured against the water board by the gristmill owner, Childs Goodman, immediately after Hartford first voted to impound the waters of Trout Brook. Try as they did, however, the board could not reach a settlement with any of these four mill owners who, given their druthers, would still like to see the project halted. In order to break up the logjam, Judge Elisha Carpenter of the Superior Court in Hartford named three disinterested citizens—from towns unaffected by Hartford's water works—to settle the matter of damages. In one case, the water board actually took possession of the Stanley sawmill for $8,000 and hired the young miller, Giles London, to run the operation for them. In the second instance, Seth Gilbert, whose mill was located near West Hartford Center—where Trout Brook flowed south under the Farmington road—was awarded $2,000, but allowed to keep his mill. The third miller claimed $17,000 damages, but was awarded only $2,000, leaving only the damages to Child's Goodman's gristmill with which to contend.

Sadly, Childs Goodman did not live to see the matter brought to a conclusion. He died in September 1866 at the age of seventy-five, a month before the awards were announced. Without implying any connection with the court awards, Childs Goodman's wife, Sarah, died in November, a few weeks after the Goodmans received their compensation from the water works. The award was $1,500. (The gristmill was taken over by Childs Goodman's son, Chester, who continued the operation for some years thereafter.)

The leaks in the aqueduct turned out to be more numerous than earlier imagined and the most reasonable estimate for the completion of the repair work was the end of the year. When the gate to the aqueduct was closed so that the workmen could fix the leaks in the joints, Reservoir No. 1 inadvertently filled to overflowing, holding what was roughly calculated at 212 million gallons of water. An amazing fact was that in rainy weather, the Talcott Mountain watershed usually sloughed off a startling 100 million gallons a day. This embarrassment of riches encouraged Bissell and others to talk of gouging out a second reservoir just as soon as was practicable. As the *Times* put it so succinctly—

The great merit of the West Hartford Water Works is the remarkable facilities they afford for storing water. A reservoir can be built there for $50,000 while it would cost upwards of $500,000 in some other places.

Hiram Bissell wanted to do away with the pumps at the Connecticut River forever and a second reservoir was a good step in that direction. With the city still growing, he could foresee the day when Hartford would need to store a billion gallons. The common council, however, was not so easily won over on this point. Not at first, anyway.

After the Republicans lost the final vote on the Trout Brook plan, the council showed a new respect for Bissell and his water commissioners. Before that time, the regular Monday night council meetings were mean-spirited verbal donnybrooks with the air at City Hall thick with insulting barbs and accusations. Now, weeks went by with nary a mention of the water department, almost as if the city did not have one. The voters had made it clear that they respected Bissell's judgment and would side with him when push came to shove. Instinctively the members of the council adopted a hands-off policy toward him and his water board. Of equal importance was the changing make-up of the council. The city elections of April 1866, for the first time, delivered a perfectly divided common council; three of the six aldermen were Democrats as were twelve of the twenty-four councilmen. Charles R. Chapman, the newly elected Democratic mayor of the city, would break any deadlocks. As a bonus for the water works, some Republican aldermen with longstanding, congenial dealings with the water works, like Samuel Woodruff, would also side with Bissell in a pinch. The Democrats were riding high and so was Hiram Bissell. Not surprisingly, he was re-elected president of the Board of Water Commissioners for a twelfth term.

When the question of a second reservoir in West Hartford arose, the councilmen acquiesced immediately, but the aldermen held out—for one week. The following Monday night, they quickly boarded the bandwagon and voted to appropriate the $50,000 for the second catchment. There simply was no percentage in opposing the water works any longer. Moreover, as the dependability of its service and the quality of its product increased each year, the voting public became more enamored of the water department in general and Hiram Bissell in particular. Accordingly, they became less interested in the opinions of men like Eliphalet Bulkeley and William Hungerford—at least when it came to drinking water.

In the long fight over the Trout Brook plan, Bissell had learned a valuable lesson about planning. He had first mentioned the need for a new source of supply in early 1860 and the new source did not come on line until 1867. Could he afford to wait until the situation was again desperate before adding to the system? He thought not.

Just as soon as the council authorized the bonding for the second reservoir, Bissell sent Samuel Gray and a platoon of surveyors into the woods north of Reservoir No. 1 to begin laying out more basins. Accordingly, the crew platted three additional facilities, two of which were located farther up Mine Brook. The proposed site for Reservoir No. 2 was about 2000 feet to the north of the original reservoir. It covered an area of thirty-nine acres and would have a capacity of 144 million gallons, but could be increased, at a later date, to 200 million. Another impounded source, Reservoir No. 3 (as it was first designated), was located a little over one mile in a northerly direction from the original works and sat on a forty-nine-acre site. Projected yields put this reservoir at 248 million gallons, with the possibility of expanding it later to impound upwards of 400 million gallons. Since Reservoir No. 3 on Mine Brook offered the greatest storage potential, Bissell decided to develop it ahead of any work on the second site. Feeling that there was no time to lose, he had his water board begin purchasing the necessary acreage for this second catchment and solicited bids for the excavation and dam construction.

Bissell may have had an easier time with the water works in 1866, but he experienced trouble in his masonry business. The newly organized Masons and Plasterers Association sent Bissell a letter stating that, in the future, its members would not work for any boss who hired more than three apprentices at a time. Also, newcomers would be required to serve a three-year apprenticeship after which time, their boss would furnish them with a "written discharge" that would serve as their license from that time forward. Speaking for himself and his brother, Bissell's response was to the point. He wrote curtly that, ". . . we beg leave to give notice that we shall hire whoever we choose... [and] propose to pay each man according to his worth." The union movement was needed in many quarters to curb the hellish working conditions of flint-hearted employers across America, but the masonry operation that Hiram and Sylvester Bissell were running did not even remotely resemble such a misuse or abuse of workers. As such, the new Bricklayers and Plasterers Association had chosen a poor and unreceptive target when they decided to force their opinions on Hiram Bissell. As one would expect, they had very little luck over the years telling him how to run his business.

In January of 1867, almost four years after the first vote on the matter, Reservoir No. 1 began to supply the 35,000 residents of Hartford with drinking water. With the pristine waters of Trout Brook flowing steadily into the city, the Woodruff & Beach pumps at the Connecticut River Pumping Station were at last shut down. They had performed admirably and long past their anticipated useful life. While it was the expectation that the residents of the capital region would never again be forced to pump their drinking water from the river, the massive pumps and the dignified brick pump house remained in place—though silent. Prudence dictated that, although at rest, they should be kept in tip-top condition lest the future deliver an unpleasant surprise. The West Hartford Reservoir, at least initially, looked like a resounding success, but for the piece of mind that they offered, the Connecticut River Pumping Station and the Lord's Hill Reservoir were left intact.

Curiously enough, the entry into the city of the Trout Brook water went completely unnoticed. There was no mention in any of the city's newspapers and water customers were completely oblivious to the changeover. Nonetheless, as the residents of Hartford continued the wasteful and illegal habit of leaving their taps running during the cold months to prevent freezing, consumption remained inordinately high.

In February, Bissell ran an experiment. Filling the old Lord's Hill Reservoir to brimming with waters of Trout Brook, he then closed the main valve—located at West Hartford center—so that he could accurately measure the consumption by the hour as the water level in the Lord's Hill Reservoir dropped. The results confirmed his suspicions precisely. Peak consumption was from eight to nine o'clock in the morning when almost 100,000 gallons was used but, almost beyond belief, between one and two o'clock in the morning, when almost everyone in the city was sound asleep, an astounding 50,000 gallons was used, indicating clearly that people were still leaving their taps open at night.

Not surprisingly, in Hiram Bissell's next annual report to the council, water meters were mentioned for the first time. Actually, by the late 1860s, meters had been introduced in a number of larger cities with enviable results, not the least of which was higher overall water revenues. One confounding problem for all of the early water companies, that decided to adopt meters, was how to locate the meters so that they would not freeze in the winter months. In the end, at least at the Hartford Water Works, the subject of metering always ended the same—with procrastination. The quandary with meters was simple. While they could pay for themselves quickly at a hotel, livery stable or beer hall, they were too expensive to install on private residences. The water works would go broke putting $25 meters on the homes of customers whose annual water rents were only $5. Considering that Hartford's system was not completely metered until 1902, this discussion during the 1860s was premature indeed.

Unfortunately, the water company would have to live with the waste, at least for a time because, while they still had one final option, it was not a very agreeable one. Somehow, fining their own customers was an unappetizing choice. Accordingly, on cold nights, the taps stayed open. Waste aside, the water company had come a long way since its beginnings in late 1855. From less than ten miles of pipes when the water system was first built, that number had exploded to more than forty miles of pipes in 1867. The water works now serviced almost 3,000 connections to homes and businesses and maintained approximately 175 fire hydrants.

One rather immediate consequence of the creation of a new water works—coupled with the creation of a gas company in 1849—was the emergence of the plumber. Men who were essentially steam fitters found a whole new use for their skills as the residential market awakened. In one decade, there sprung to life seven plumbing companies—Kelsey Brothers, Jones & Winslow and Pitkin Brothers—as well as four other men who chose to work alone. The plumber became a constant visitor in people's homes.

There was a larger problem simmering, however, that few people, including Hiram Bissell, recognized. While luxuriating in the wondrous supply from Trout Brook, the water works tended to the usual problems of frozen fire hydrants and towering fountains as water pipes burst in the cold. The increased head from the new aqueduct turned what had been mild curiosities into dangerous geysers. Even as the city consumed 2 million gallons a day, the *Times* reported—

> . . . a large stream is running through the raceway [at Reservoir No. 1] all the time; enough . . . to supply two more such cities as Hartford . . . There is danger when this great body of snow melts away that the raceway will not carry the surplus water and that the *overflow may wash away the dam*. (Italics added)

As the cold and confining winter slowly gave way to spring, Clara Barton, who would found the Red Cross in 1881, gave a lecture in Hartford. Just after the Civil War, she became the first woman to head a government bureau when she accepted the responsibility for locating thousands of missing soldiers. With Congressional backing, the Missing Soldiers Office managed to collect information concerning the fate of approximately 22,000 soldiers by 1868.

By early April, another citywide election gave the Democrats complete control on the common council. Not only did they manage to fill seventeen of the twenty-four council seats, they also won four of the six seats on the board of aldermen. The re-election of Mayor Charles R. Chapman gave them control of Hartford, which they had never enjoyed before. When Bissell was re-elected to the presidency of the Board of Water Commissioners—for the thirteenth time— he had the great pleasure of looking forward to a year of harmony between the council and the water board.

Even as the city chose its leaders for 1867, the water flowing from West Hartford continued to astonish even the severest critics of the Trout Brook plan. The gate at the reservoir's supply aqueduct was raised only 1/20th of its full height and provided enough water for the entire city from January through April. Nevertheless, by the time the good weather arrived in 1867, a new contracting firm, Lobdell & Company, was in West Hartford with a huge crew, excavating for Reservoir No. 2 (as it was renamed), a mile up Mine Brook. As they cut down trees and grubbed out the soil and stumps, a second dam rose at the downstream (southern) end of the new catchment.

On May 1, the regular election parade was held in Hartford and for the first time in memory, it rained with a vengeance. The streets were so wet and muddy that all outdoor activities were cancelled. If the first four months of 1867 were any indication of what was to be expected of the last eight, it would be one of the wettest years on record.

In June, President Andrew Johnson visited Hartford, which created some humorous moments at the council meeting as members of both parties tried with equal zeal to disown the unpopular politician. The debate actually centered on the city's usual welcoming fund—$500—earmarked for exactly what it sounded like. The Democrats refused to accept Johnson as one of their own, stating with adamantine rhetoric that he had run with Lincoln as a Republican. The members of the council—on the other side of the aisle—abandoned Johnson on two counts: first, because he was a lifelong Democrat and, secondly, because he was too accommodating to his fellow Southerners after the war.

When Tennessee had seceded in 1861, Johnson had remained loyal to the Union, but his actions then were winning him little respect now. After Lincoln's assassination, he catered endlessly to the former Confederates, angering the Republican Congress, which was controlled by right wing reactionaries. In effect, Congress grabbed Reconstruction from Johnson by overriding his vetoes time and again until, finally, they tried to remove him from office with a bill of impeachment. Even before his nasty skirmishes with the Congress escalated into pitched battles—which were in full swing by the fall of 1867—he was not a popular president. In the one article mentioning his visit to Hartford, the *Times*— that great bastion of Democratic sentiment—ran a story about the president's visit and never mentioned him by name once!

Now that the war was over, steamboat traffic on the river was picking up as Hartford's business community sought to reestablish lucrative trade links with foreign ports and the owners of the steamboat lines continued to slug it out with the railroads. Half a dozen steamboat lines ran on the river and, one of the newest and most comfortable boats, the *Granite State*, slashed the cost of passage to New York to only fifty cents. The *Granite State* sailed at 3:00 P.M. every Tuesday, Thursday and Saturday, while the *State of New York*—still one of the most elegantly outfitted steamboats ever to cruise the Connecticut River— sailed at 4:00 P.M. every Monday, Wednesday and Friday. Completing the schedule, the *City of Hartford* left for New York on Sunday afternoons. The steamboat lines had lost a great deal of their business to the railroads, but were still handling about 600,000 tons of cargo and 28,000 passengers annually.

Communications between metropolitan centers was expanding greatly in the aftermath of the war as telegraph lines were strung along railroad rights of way throughout the eastern Unites States and Canada. The Franklin Telegraph Company, by August 1867, had already extended lines to Pittsburgh and the oil fields around Titusville, Pennsylvania, followed closely by service to Albany,

Rochester, Cincinnati, Buffalo and St. Louis. By late 1867, they had extended their lines to Concord, Nashua, Montreal and St. Johns, New Brunswick.

The weather, however, continued wet. By the middle of August, the Connecticut River was more than sixteen feet above the mean low water mark. No sooner would it begin to recede but the skies would open up again. The *Times* reported on August 23—

> The rain has beat with a steady ceaseless patter upon the streets all day and bids fair to continue over Sunday. Business, which has been dull for the past two months, is improving and a short spell of pleasant weather would make it better.

The years during and after the construction of Reservoir No. 1 had been busy ones for Hiram Bissell. True, George Marsh and later Samuel Gray oversaw the construction in West Hartford but, ultimately, the responsibility was Bissell's. Additionally, he had an unending array of tasks in running the day-to-day operations of the water company, from supervising the old pumping station (and then later mothballing it) to the laying of new pipes within the city proper. As with all relatively new enterprises, there was a long litany of problems constantly demanding his attention.

So said, Bissell spent a great deal of time shuttling between his home on Wadsworth Street and the West Hartford site. Reservoir No. 1 had been located snug up against the north side of the Farmington road on the far margins of West Hartford in the shadow of Talcott Mountain. From his home on Wadsworth Street, it was exactly six miles to the new reservoir. In his buckboard, he would head west along the dirt pack of the Farmington road. During good weather, it was not a difficult trek but, when things turned nasty, the road quickly turned into a muddy and rutted slough. Under such circumstances, it was a punishing journey.

When the Trout Brook system finally came on line, initially it was considered by those closest to the project as an unqualified success. There were the initial problems, like the leaks in the aqueduct, but these had all been worked out by the time the water entered the city for the first time in January 1867. Later however, the city's two major newspapers were quick to point out that the dam had some serious problems. The *Times*, ordinarily a booster of the water works, reported that, ". . . The main dam, a sort of earthwork, a shoddy structure, never safe—never properly built—a failure from the start—always leaking and always weak—this thing was found to be porous . . ." The *Courant*, never a fan of the water works was subtler but still quick to find fault averring that, "For some time now water has been oozing through the lower portion of the dam, and many of the people in the vicinity have predicted that it could not long stand the heavy pressure to which it was constantly subjected . . ."

Despite what appeared to be a very rainy year, including a summer freshet at the Connecticut River (very unusual), amateurs—who made it a hobby to chart the rainfall from year to year with crude homemade rain gauges—insisted that the rainfall for this period varied only slightly from previous years. Reservoir No. 1 held more than an eighty-day supply for the city and calculations showed that just the water running down the main branch of Trout Brook each day would have been enough to satisfy Hartford's needs. This presupposed that the level of rainfall and snowmelt held steady, which was presupposing a great deal. It was anybody's guess what Trout Brook would deliver in the case of a drought.

In the first part of September 1867, Lobdell & Company had completed about one-half of the work on the dam at the second reservoir, building it up to a height of seven feet. Concurrently, they had grubbed out about one-third of the soil from the new forty-nine-acre catchment. At the pace they were going, Reservoir No. 2 would be completed before the end of 1867.

On September 5, a Thursday, a black cloud rack poured from the west over Talcott Mountain, casting an eerie gloom over the site of the two reservoirs. At first, Lobdell & Company's laborers paid no attention to the ominous storm front rushing in and continued to excavate the reservoir site with their mules and scoops. Just as they finished for the day, ozone filled the air like a noxious gas, the precursor of a succession of the most violent thunderstorms. Almost immediately, the skies opened up and the workers scrambled for shelter. The rain began in the late afternoon and was accompanied by the most frightening thunder and lightning, the black clouds disgorging colossal sheets of rain on the Talcott Mountain watershed for the better part of the next six hours (some said longer).

The gentle streams of the Talcott Mountain watershed swelled almost instantly into wild torrents that resembled mad rivers, capable of great damage. In the first few hours of the storm, the water in Reservoir No. 1 rose an astounding five feet. By mid-evening, the enormous quantities of water cascading "down the hillside from the Farmington road, to the foot of the lower slope of the dam . . . joined with the drainage of the outer . . . slope [and] cut rapidly into its outer edge at the foot, [causing] an extensive landslide from the lower slope, thus weakening the embankment. . . . "

The waters of the Talcott Mountain watershed were draining into Reservoir No. 1 so fast that Samuel Gray, the water works' chief engineer at the West Hartford project, sensed that the dam would soon be in grave danger. Uncertain what to do, he dispatched a messenger to Hiram Bissell's home on Wadsworth Street.

When the messenger finally got to Bissell's house and advised him of the rapidly deteriorating conditions at Reservoir No. 1, it was 10:30 at night. Bissell donned a rain slicker, hitched a horse to his buckboard and left the city in the pouring rain, traveling by way of the Farmington road. Despite the driving sheets of rain, jouncing along the muddy streets within the city limits was easy duty compared to what lay ahead. Gas streetlights, spaced a good fifty yards apart, illuminated his way and the city's street department groomed the roads, reducing muddy potholes to a minimum. The last enclave of people within the city limits was comprised of the families who lived at Nook Farm, including Harriett Beecher Stowe. The Nook Farm community was built on a densely wooded tract purchased by John Hooker and his brother-in-law, Francis Gillette and had become the most exclusive address in the city.

Nook Farm was the last cluster of houses in the city, but they were nestled so deeply in the dense foliage of the area that the only house that could be made out was Attorney Franklin Chamberlin's large brick house at the corner of Forest Street and the Farmington road. Nook Farm was considered so far from the rest of the city that the Hartford & Wethersfield Horse Railroad Company did not even lay tracks out there. If Harriet Beecher Stowe, her sisters or their families had business in the city, they could use their own horses and carriages.

Whether the horse railroad tracks extended to Nook Farm or not was of no moment to Hiram Bissell, but the fact that the gaslights stopped there was another matter. Thanks to the steady rain and the absence of gaslights, the last four miles of the journey out to Reservoir No.1 would be traversed in almost total darkness. He still had about a half mile to go before crossing into West Hartford and then more than three miles out to the reservoir. Once he got beyond the amber glow of the city's gaslights, the darkness closed in forebodingly. With nothing but an oil lantern to light the way for his horse, Bissell's buckboard slowly juddered along. Even so, with the muddy, puddled road, it was a long, wet ride. If it had been earlier in the evening or if it were not raining, he might have caught the light of a whale oil lamp from a farmhouse along his route, but nothing was in his favor that night.

When he crossed city line into West Hartford, he knew that he only had a little more than three miles left to go. First, he would pass through a long stretch of slight peaks and troughs in the road where there were a dozen small houses. When he reached the center of West Hartford, he had a little less than two miles remaining to the reservoir.

This last stretch was the worst part of the journey because there were only a dozen farmhouses spread out over the whole distance and the hour was late. From previous trips, he knew that when J. W. Griswold's farm appeared, he had only a mile remaining. Griswold's place was on the north side of the Farmington road along with most of the other farms. There were only two small houses on the south side all the way out to the reservoir.

The journey was wearying but the situation at the reservoir was even more troublesome. What would he find? Would the dam still be standing when he got there? If so, would he be able to reduce the pressure on it? Such foreboding thoughts were all this night had to offer as the driving rain drowned Bissell's usually optimistic spirit.

As he shuttled along the Farmington road, there was one thing he could not possibly have known. The laborers at the upper reservoir had made enough progress on the new dam at Reservoir No. 2 to hold back a massive quantity of water there—35 million gallons. What Bissell did not know, as he tried to imagine his first course of action when he reached the stressed dam at Reservoir No. 1, was that the seven-foot-tall dam at the upper reservoir had already breached, sending 35 million gallons cascading down Mine Brook and into the already overburdened Reservoir No. 1. This unexpected turn of events raised the water level in the lower reservoir to within two feet of the top of the dam and—of infinitely more importance—onto the six-foot section of berm at the summit that had no inner core of rip-rapped stone. This berm—made of a gravely soil and covered over with sod—was not designed to hold back any water at all. In fact, ". . . the water began...soaking through the upper portion of the dam, until it had formed a very small but free passage across the top of the dam. . . . " This rivulet connected to a landslide that was in process on the downstream face of the dam. The situation was rapidly escalating out of control.

After a maddening hour and a half on the Farmington road, Bissell arrived at the dam just before midnight. Scrambling with his lantern along the saturated grass on the crest of the stressed dam, he instructed the engineer, Samuel Gray, to get to the gatehouse quickly and open both the waste and the aqueduct supply pipes as wide as possible. Then Bissell raced for the sluiceway. Opening the gate on the sluiceway as wide as he could, he watched as the water roared past him out of the reservoir.

With every available pipe and sluiceway wide open, Bissell and Gray waited anxiously. Because of the recent rainfall, the Talcott Mountain watershed, rather than acting like a sponge and soaking up all the new rains, simply sloughed off the water and sent it down the watershed where it added to the burden of the network of streams that made up Trout Brook. Consequently, the water was running into the feeder streams of Trout Brook at an astonishing rate.

Ever so slowly, the water began to abate. Over the next hour and a half, the water level dropped three feet. At 1:30 in the morning, feeling that the danger had passed, Bissell got back in his buckboard and started for home. Disinclined to trust the weather, he left the sluiceway and waste pipes wide open. The rains continued though and, during the night, the water level in the reservoir did not decline any further.

By 9:00 the following morning, all five members of the water board were at the site, sullenly inspecting the dam at Reservoir No. 1. They watched helplessly as the waters of the Talcott Mountain watershed continued to fill the reservoir and unremittingly placed an undue burden on the crippled dam. Of particular concern was the water that poured freely through the widening rivulet at the top of the dam. As this channel of water scoured the earth from the peak of the dam, clod by chunk, it continued to weaken the structure.

Simultaneously, water leaked fiercely out of the bottom of the dam. At the time, it was estimated that the whole seven mile long Talcott Mountain watershed was throwing off almost twenty million gallons an hour—and it all seemed to be collecting at Reservoir No. 1. The commissioners were powerless to stop this unwanted flow of water. As they stood in their gummed rain slickers watching the situation worsen, the pressure mounted on the now buckling earth and stone embankment.

At 9:30, the dam let go. While all eyes were on the rivulet of water slowly scrubbing away the earth at the top of the dam, an immense plug of water exploded out of the bottom near the waste and aqueduct pipes. Water began to pour out of the reservoir at an ever-increasing speed as large stones and massive amounts of dirt and sod were catapulted into the air by the thunderous power of the water. Only minutes later, the earthen berm at the top of the dam collapsed into the growing flume shooting freely down the Trout Brook valley. In twenty-two minutes, the water tore a yawning, 125-foot wide chasm through the middle of the dam, leaving two forty-foot hunks of stone and earth on either side of the great cavity. All the while, the reservoir disgorged its 200 million gallon load down the Trout Brook valley. All that remained was a small trickle wandering through the center of the basin. The brick gatehouse now showed seventy-foot tall in the empty basin.

Down the valley of the Trout Brook roared the great wall of water, destroying everything in its path. With it traveled all of the counterparts of the once mighty dam. About forty tons of earth used to build the dam were now mixed with the raging flood waters and, pushing along the valley with tons of stones, which once formed the inner core of the dam. Topping off this muddy, roiling mess was the sod that once covered the exposed surfaces of the dam. The noise was deafening; bystanders comparing it to an earthquake, for it shook the very ground on which they stood as it blasted through the breached dam and muscled its way down the valley—an angry, destructive obscenity.

The surging wall of water was "two or three hundred feet wide and deeper than the height of some of the surrounding trees . . . " The great iron pipes that had been the waste and aqueduct floated along on top of the crest of this churning cataract like long tubular corks. Huge trees were uprooted and pushed ahead of this wall of water in a collection of debris that shot down the Trout Brook valley.

The first mill flattened by this mountain of water was the Stanley saw mill along with a gristmill on the same property. The water works had purchased these twin mills earlier in the project for $8,000. The dam at the millpond was "a solid structure and was six or seven years old" and was operated for the benefit of the city since the purchase. The thunderous waters crushed the sturdy milldam and swept away the sawmill as if it were a child's toy. Along with it went 5,000 to 6,000 feet of newly sawn lumber. The gristmill remained, but its foundation was so badly cut asunder that it was expected to topple over in the aftermath of the devastation. The gristmill contained half a ton of meal, which was completely ruined. The waterwheel and machinery was "jammed in a mass under the mill—that portion of it, at least, which was not swept along [with the flood]."

The first farms devastated were that of George Brace and Edwin Belden at "Belden's Corners," the crossroads where the Farmington road intersected West Road (present day Mountain Road). As the cataract exploded down the valley, it entered into the outbuildings of George Brace and cluttered his fields with rubble. Simultaneously, it lapped into the barns of Edwin Belden and mowed down his cornfields. His meadowlands, said to be worth $300 an acre, were "covered with dirt, rocks and rubbish of all sorts." Included in his losses were thousands of fence posts and rails.

Still moving at a frightening pace, the perilous wave reached the farms of Deacon Josiah Griswold and his brother, John. Both of their farms were left covered by a collection of sand, soil and wreckage that destroyed their corn crops and tore out miles of fence posts. Five of John Griswold's dairy cows were swept away in the flood, only to be discovered some time later in a wood lot miles away, unharmed, but unlikely to produce milk for a time.

The high water rushed toward the farm of Moses Griswold near the Farmington road. He and his family were certain that the destructive waters would carry off their home. They described the oncoming mass as "a vast tumbling, boiling wave, the crest rolling over and over, bearing trees, mills, and everything before it, and the whole lifted high in the air—as [a] solid wall of water."

As the thunderous wave reached the northernmost part of the Trout Brook valley, it swept over the mill pond of the late Childs Goodman, just to the west of Bishop's Road (present day North Main Street). In a way, it was a blessing that Goodman did not live to see his property destroyed. He had tried to protect his mill through the courts, but had been rebuffed. In the end, the destructive mass swept away his millpond and, of course, deprived the mill of the waterpower that it needed to function. The *Times* wrote in its Friday afternoon edition that the Goodman gristmill was left standing, but stated flatly that, "not one stone [was] left upon another of what was once the solid and high dam at [the millpond] . . . "

Not more than fifty yards from the Goodman gristmill sat "Bishop's Bridge," which crossed Trout Brook on Bishop's Road. After the wave destroyed the dam at the Goodman millpond, it completely swept away this bridge and all traces of the structure's substantial abutments. Again the *Times* reported, ". . . It was a good solid bridge; and its loss, at a point so near West Hartford center, puts the people to much inconvenience."

As the surging, foaming water—now heading due south—crossed the Farmington road near West Hartford center, it took out another gristmill belonging to Seth Gilbert. The bridge at "Gilbert's Corner" was the most substantial bridge in all of West Hartford—recently built of stone from the Portland quarry—was left sinking in the muck and tilting badly towards the north. Horses and carriages were allowed to cross in the coming days, but at the traveler's own peril.

After passing "Gilbert's Corner" the still menacing barrier of water entered the sparsely populated southern section of West Hartford, where it eventually entered the south branch of the Little River. Later in the day, there was a tremendous surge of water in Hartford that swept away two footbridges near the Sharp's Rifle factory and the bridge at Daniel's Mill. Soon thereafter, the contents of the reservoir in West Hartford—now more than eight miles from the skeleton of the dam at Trout Brook—emptied its collection of muddy waste and rubble into the Connecticut River.

The one bright spot in the collapse of the dam at Trout Brook was that no one was hurt. In the first accounts of the breach, there was an unconfirmed report that one of the laborers at the upper reservoir had been drowned. The newspaper held that the man "walked into the stream in the dark, not knowing that the bridge was gone." (Presumably, this was a construction bridge somewhere on Mine Brook up above Reservoir No. 1.) A few days later, however, the paper wrote, "The man who was supposed to have been drowned at the West Hartford water works last Thursday, had turned up all right after three days wanderings." For all of the devastation that day, luck was with the Hartford Water Works, for loss of life has always been the difference between an embarrassing mishap and a never-to-be-forgotten catastrophe.

Chapter 6
The Drought of the 1870s

In the days following the devastation at Reservoir No. 1, many hundreds of people visited the site of the Trout Brook dam to see the mess for themselves. On Sunday following the breach, there was a steady stream of curiosity seekers straggling west along the Farmington road. People ". . . in buggies, on horseback and on foot formed a continual procession along the West Hartford road."

The *Times*, the only newspaper to support the Trout Brook plan, felt in an exposed position. They calculated that if the dam were not rebuilt immediately, the whole following year would be consumed with "plans, red tape and fuss," and that it would most likely be ten months before the project was completed. The paper expressed further annoyance when Bissell announced that the dam would not be rebuilt straight away even though the city was again pumping from the Connecticut River—at an annual cost of more than $15,000. Trying to goad him into action, the paper retorted—

> In some cities, they would whistle such a job as this into completion in a jiffy. Look at Chicago, where [boring] a hole under the lake for two miles to get pure water is [a] pastime for them. The work was about done when we heard it was commenced. And what [is] our puny Trout Brook dam when compared to that work?

Newspaper editorials aside, Bissell's first move was to make restitution with mill owners and farmers downstream of the dam, and to compensate West Hartford for the bridges and roads that were either washed away completely or severely damaged by the roiling, devastating cataract. Topping that list was the new stone bridge at Gilbert's Corner, which had to "removed entirely and replaced with a more substantial structure." Toward this end, Bissell hired two men to handle the claims. One of the men was Nathan Starkweather, the first engineer of the water works. As a surveyor, Starkweather had a good understanding of property and its worth. Teamed with him was a Hartford farmer and former selectman, Jonathan Goodwin, who could accurately judge the value of the crops lost. The losses to the farmers, mill owners and West Hartford came to $18,000. This was paid as soon as the council released the funds.

As Starkweather and Goodwin set to work assessing the damages, Bissell began the search for a talented engineer to help with the rebuilding. He did not have the luxury of "whistling" the work to a rapid conclusion, as the *Times* had suggested, and left unsaid was the obvious caveat that the new structures had to be able to withstand the wrath of God. Bissell's choice to help with the reconstruction of the dam at Reservoir No. 1 was the well-respected civil engineer, William McAlpine, from Stockbridge, Massachusetts. However, no sooner had McAlpine set to work than the weather soured and the project had to be shut down for the winter.

During October, November and December, no water at all flowed through the aqueduct from Trout Brook. Instead, the Connecticut River Pumping Station was placed back in service until January, when the waters of Trout Brook were allowed to flow directly into the aqueduct—and thus to Hartford—solving part of the supply problem and taking some of the pressure off the tired pumps at the river. Bissell was able to keep the Lord's Hill Reservoir full, even though it now only represented a four-day supply for the city.

In the professional opinion of McAlpine, the wisest course of action was to complete the new reservoir on the upper reaches of Mine Brook as soon as possible and then concentrate on the mess of rubble that lay by the side of the Farmington road. Since Reservoir No. 1 would require much more work than Reservoir No. 2—and held 60 percent less water—the new reservoir on Mine Brook represented the water board's best chance to bring the Trout Brook system back on line in the shortest amount of time.

The original contractor of the upper reservoir, Lobdell & Co., was not responsible for the collapse and, since their work was not seen as shoddy or deficient, they were allowed to resume construction on Reservoir No. 2. Meanwhile, Bissell, with the guidance of McAlpine, tackled the ugly job of stripping down the rubble at Reservoir No. 1 and beginning the dam building process from scratch.

In discussing the pumps at the Connecticut River, Bissell wrote, ". . . spring, they will again be put into action while the repairs of the dam of the lower reservoir are progressing." The original builder of the pumps, Woodruff & Beach, had graduated to larger projects, including the "cylinders and other parts of machinery for the Brooklyn Water Works," and the smaller firm of Hunter & Sanford was hired to maintain the machinery at the river.

Hartford, like so many other cities, had daily reminders of the Civil War and its heavy personal cost. Former soldiers, with missing limbs, were reduced to organ grinders in State House Square, cranking out monotonous tunes for a few coins dropped into a cigar box by some charitable matron. Drunkenness rose to levels not seen before the war accompanied by a high number of arrests for assault and breach of the peace. In time, temperance societies proliferated as the men sobered up—Good Samaritans, South End Temperance Society, Saint Peter's Temperance Society and many others.

Post war, the population of the city grew by 30 percent to almost 38,000. Though nothing like the spurt of the 1850s, the city was still growing at a phenomenal clip, reaching a peak as a manufacturing center where 17,000 workers fabricated a stunning array of peacetime goods in Hartford's 200 manufactories.

Growing pains continued though. For example, during the war, the Hartford & Wethersfield Horse Railroad Company had laid tracks up the center of Main Street and immediately became a valuable asset to the community. There were a great many city dwellers, who had neither the means nor the desire to keep horses and carriages, and the horse cars were a great benefit to them, shortening long commutes about the city and making travel in bad weather possible. The winter snows presented a dilemma though. In order to protect the rights of the sleighing public, the council passed an ordinance forbidding the removal of snow from the company's tracks (sleigh runners scraped badly on the rusty iron rails). Eventually, the mayor issued a permit so that the horse car tracks could be cleared, providing that the displaced snow was spread evenly on both sides of the tracks. Once the horse cars were free to run, the public had another complaint—that the cars did not run on the Sabbath, particularly vexing those with long hikes to church. This problem was eventually solved by a group of well-to-do businessmen who subsidized the line by purchasing enough tickets to defray the cost of running the horse cars on Sunday. Their only condition? That the cars be shut down immediately following the last church service at midday.

The greatest amusement after the war was the velocipede, the improbable looking bicycle with the huge wheel in front and the tiny wheel at the rear. The subject of bicycles is an important one because their effect on life in the United States was huge but almost completely overshadowed by the later invention of a much more efficient means of travel—the automobile.

When Col. Albert Pope introduced the Columbia—the first bicycle mass-produced in the Untied States—to the public in 1878, it revolutionized transportation and life in general for millions. After organizing the Pope Manufacturing Company that year at the old Weed Sewing Machine Company, the Col. Pope began selling 60" Columbia Hi-Wheeler velocipedes for $125. (To put this in prospective, Weed had been selling sewing machines for $13.) Not only did Pope's bicycles allow people to roam more freely and widely about the city, it enabled factory mechanics to go home for a hot meal at lunchtime.

Velocipeding was an unstoppable craze, creating some difficulties as young men chose to ride them on the stone sidewalks as opposed to the dusty—and usually manure-filled—streets. Finally, a city ordinance forbade the use of velocipedes on the sidewalks but, owing to poor wording, baby carriages came under the same strictures. To maintain domestic peace, the members of the common council quickly exempted baby carriages, thus allowing women and children free reign over the cleanest outdoor surfaces in the city. This change forced the velocipedes into the streets, which spooked the horses no end and caused the number of runaways to climb exponentially. To restore order and protect life and limb, still another ordinance was passed barring velocipedists from the streets and forcing the vehicle's growing ranks of enthusiasts to repair to specially designed riding halls. The newspapers were quick to note—

. . . hundreds of young men . . . find in it a pleasant and exhilarating sport, cheaper and more agreeable than billiards, and in every way preferable to . . . amusements . . . of a questionable character. Among the spectators of this new pastime are many of the fair sex . . . .

When Col. Pope introduced the women's safety bicycle about 1890, it freed a whole generation of young women to travel about unescorted and introduced them to the pleasures of Sunday drives. At its height, the Pope manufactory was selling over a million Columbia bicycles annually at $200 apiece in every civilized country in the world. Bicycling peaked just before the beginning of the twentieth century as electric—and later gasoline-powered— automobiles exploded onto the scene.

Though temporarily distracted by the new velocipedes, the ranks of Base Ball fans continued to grow, with the sophistication of the teams and leagues and the level of the competition increasing markedly. The games were contested by a wide cross-section of teams from colleges and clubs around the country. Mentioned every few days in the newspapers were outings between the Red stockings of Cincinnati, the White stockings of Chicago, the Atlantics of Philadelphia and the Yale, Harvard and Princeton teams.

On the home front, life was getting more expensive by the day. The ice business was a dicey affair and, more by attrition than ruthless business practices, the Hartford Ice Company had achieved a virtual monopoly. They put up 15,000 tons in January 1870 and, when the hot weather arrived, bumped the price from forty-two to fifty cents, leaving the consuming public no recourse but to accept the increase or go without. In time, the company's lucrative corner on the ice business was cracked as entrepreneurs saw an inviting opportunity and stepped into the breech.

For heating and cooking people still depended on coal as the seventeen coal companies in the city attested to quite convincingly. The alternative was gas, but a gas stove did not throw off the heat of a cast iron coal stove and could not warm a whole apartment. The Hartford Gas Light Company had fifty miles of pipes buried beneath the streets by 1870, but these pipes supplied mostly streetlights, making the city its biggest customer. In the main, people still depended on oil lamps for light after nightfall, as gaslights in homes remained mostly the province of the wealthy.

The one final change in city life since the war was the result of a peculiar mindset. Many people still thought of Hartford as a small town while the number of tenements and manufactories—and hence the population—burgeoned around them. Strangely enough, horses were the most sensitive barometers of this change. Before the Civil War, there were few runaway horses but, in the ensuing decade, they became a constant—and dangerous—nuisance. The crush of pedestrian traffic, the velocipedes in the streets, the bells and commotion of the horse cars and the general elevation in the noise level of the city spooked horses endlessly. Yet people were still not accustomed to tying up their horses. One man wrote that while riding the length of Main Street, "he counted on one side of the street twenty horses at the curb and only four were fastened." Accordingly, it was common to read in the paper that, "There were two runaways yesterday, but nothing serious," or as a livelier account stated—

> The runaway today was a milkman's horse attached to a sleigh full of milk cans. At the rate the horse went down Main Street, either butter or cream must have been made in the cans by the time he stopped . . . .

As one might expect, the different entertainment halls came to life after the war. Music Hall, China Hall, Harbison's Hall and a number of other smaller venues began to book lectures, traveling minstrel shows, circus acts, magic shows and even performances by trained dogs. One young Hartfordite had earlier complained that, ". . .for many years, Allyn Hall was the only theater." The tired condition of the best hall in Hartford just after the war can be gleaned from a revue of Balfe's opera, *The Bohemian Girl*—

> . . . the opera [was] spoiled for want of proper scenery. Imagine a stone barn used for a hotel, the scenery representing an Irish cottage down in a glen, . . . a street in Venice to be seen on one side and half a bedroom on the other . . . It has been over 7 years since a new scene was painted on that stage and the public has gotten . . . tired of seeing the same old scenery.

Coincident with this grousing, the construction of Robert's Opera House was announced and billed as the finest showcase of its kind in all of New England. Slated to be built on Main Street—diagonally opposite State House Square—it was designed to seat twice as many people as Allyn Hall. In an effort to stay competitive—Allyn Hall dropped its booking fee from $55 to $40 a night, which of course did nothing to improve the general ambiance of the theater. After Robert's Opera House opened, ex-mayor Timothy Allyn had no choice but to pay for an expensive facelift of the moribund theater.

The grandeur of Robert's Opera House created a bit of unpleasantness for its new owner. While women did not dress up for an evening at Allyn Hall, the *trompe l'oeil* appointments and general grandeur of the new Opera House demanded high fashion. English and Italian Operas occasioned the biggest hoop skirts and tallest hats, which unhappily obscured the view of those seated directly behind. At length, management was forced to put drab signs on the walls which read, "Patrons will please remove their hats."

Though the Opera House showcased all sorts of sophisticated as well as common entertainments, Hartford also had a well-deserved reputation as a center for fine arts and high culture. In part, this could be traced back to 1842 when

Daniel Wadsworth established the first public art museum in America—the Wadsworth Atheneum. Actually begun as a library and natural history museum with a few paintings on the walls, it blossomed into one of the finest art museums in the country. This emphasis on culture spilled over into business as the city boasted almost twenty publishing houses in the years immediately following the war.

Charles Dickens had come to Hartford on a speaking tour in 1842 and returned twice in 1868. He was not considered a good speaker, but he was well-received nonetheless. A month before Dickens last appearance at Allyn Hall, one line appeared in the newspaper, stating casually that, "Mark Twain was in town yesterday." Samuel Clemens visited his publisher in Hartford that January to make final arrangements for the release of his first book *Innocents Abroad*.

Clemens's life in Hartford has been written about extensively but, besides the fact that his publisher was in Hartford, it was the town itself that enticed him to move his family to the city. More to the point, it was the small Nook Farm enclave, on the west side of town that particularly attracted Clemens. Nook Farm took wing in June 1853, when John Hooker, an attorney and real estate speculator, teamed up with his brother-in-law, Francis Gillette, to buy a 140-acre parcel of woodland from the once-wealthy—but now bankrupt—William Imlay. The land sat in a "nook" of the Woods River (the northern branch of the Little River).

After the purchase, John and his wife, Isabella Beecher Hooker, hired Hartford's sole architect, Octavius Jordan, to design a home for them on Forest Street. (Since Hiram Bissell had a business relationship with Jordan, it is possible that he did the masonry work on the house.) Meanwhile, Francis Gillette moved his family into the old Imlay farmhouse on the opposite side of the street.

Since John Hooker was a prominent attorney—and sixth in descent from the founder of Hartford, Rev. Thomas Hooker—and his brother-in-law, Francis Gillette, had been a member of the Connecticut General Assembly and was a U. S. Senator from 1854 to 1855, Nook Farm became a magnet for prominent and influential families. Although Hooker initially tried to sell the lots to anyone who had the money, he eventually sold them to family members and close friends. In time, Nook Farm became a diverse group of wealthy, church and family-oriented intellectuals from many different parts of the country.

Samuel Clemens's first visit to Nook Farm was brought about by a happy coincidence. On a gorgeous June day in 1869, he returned to Hartford in the company of Olivia Langdon of Elmira, New York, who was to be a bridesmaid in the wedding of her friend, Alice Hooker. The bride was the daughter of John and Isabella Beecher Hooker and remained a lifelong friend of Olivia Langdon Clemens. Alice Hooker's wedding ceremony took place on a Thursday afternoon, the newspapers carrying the announcement the following day—

Mr. John C. Day, son of Calvin Day, Esq. was united in marriage yesterday to Alice B., daughter of John Hooker, Esq. The ceremony took place at the residence of the bride's parents on Forest Street and was performed by Henry Ward Beecher, an uncle of the bride. A large and elegantly dressed party was present and the affair was one of the most brilliant to have ever taken place in this city.

Calvin Day, the father of the groom, was the same man who joined with the Whigs in their effort to snatch the city's water franchise in 1851. At that time, he was a Democrat but, in the mid-1850s, he joined the new Republican Party. Day spent all of his adult life rubbing elbows with the descendents of the city's founders and his desire to be one of them was not exactly a secret. That Thursday in June 1869, when his son married a descendant of Thomas Hooker, must have been the happiest day of his life.

Calvin Day's experience in Hartford is worthy of mention here because it mirrors Samuel Clemens's experience so well. One can imagine the powerful impression that these affluent, intellectual Republicans had on a Missouri roustabout when he visited Nook Farm. Alice Hooker's neighbors and relatives included Harriet Beecher Stowe, former U.S. Senator Francis Gillette and the prominent newspaper editor Charles Dudley Warner. Also present was the publisher of the *Courant* and former governor, Gen. Joseph Hawley—whose wife was Harriet Beecher Stowe's cousin—and educator Catherine Beecher of the Hartford Female Seminary. Rounding out this heady collection of notables was the witty and fun-loving Joseph Twichell, pastor of the Asylum Hill Congregational Church, who became Samuel Clemens's closest friend in Hartford. (Twichell's daughter, Harmony, later married composer Charles Ives.)

Samuel Clemens held many different jobs in his life, giving him a reputation as a dreamer and a wanderer but, the following year, his future would finally be secured, as *Innocents Abroad* became one of the fastest selling books of the age. Nevertheless, when he accompanied Olivia Langdon to Hartford in 1869, he was actually a dim star among such an aurora borealis of wealth and achievement.

Sam Clemens married his "Livy" the following year and, in 1871, the couple was back in Hartford, renting the home of John and Isabella Hooker. The Hartford of Clemens's time, the one that he loved so much, was—on a per capita basis—the wealthiest city in America with manufacturing the key to its enviable affluence. It had an extensive park system—some of which was designed by Frederick Law Olmstead—and the common council annually expended $400 for free concerts in Bushnell Park, filling the warm summer evenings with the pleasant sound of popular melodies. By the fall of 1874, a new home was completed for the Clemens family fronting the Farmington road in Nook Farm, where they lived for the next two decades.

While Clemens was still enjoying the social whirl and squiring Olivia Langdon about, Hiram Bissell was putting in long days overseeing the reconstruction of the beleaguered Trout Brook system. Reservoir No. 2, the crucial first step in restoring the much cleaner Trout Brook water to the city, was completed in 1869 thanks to the steady labors of Lobdell & Co. Work on the original reservoir was dogged by chronic labor shortages. Hiram Bissell was paying laborers $2 a day—fifty cents more than the going rate—to wrestle the mountain of stones for the rip-rapped corewall back into place, but the work was so extensive and backbreaking that he was always fifty workers short. Improvements to the dam included an enlarged sluiceway and a waste pipe that was double the size of the original pipe. Despite the changes and the manpower shortages, Bissell was able to fill the reservoir in 1869 and return it to service the following year, once again idling the pumps at the Connecticut River.

Having completed the dirty job of rebuilding the two reservoirs in West Hartford, the most pressing concerns were reduced to the everyday concerns of any water company—maintenance, personnel, payroll, connections for new customers, fire hydrants and the continuing problem of waste. Contributing to this last category was the sudden popularity of the lawn mower. These, of course, were manually operated reel-type mowers which, at first blush, have nothing to do with water, but they scalped the grass badly and made watering a necessity. Placing such burdens on the water system was not Bissell's idea of providence in the face of great demand and limited supplies, but he was powerless to change the habits of the whole city.

Fire hydrants created their own special problems because a fixture that drained below the frost line had not yet been invented. Not surprisingly, the cold weather froze their cast iron housings with great regularity, splitting them wide open and filling the streets with great pools of water. Packing the hydrants in hay for the winter was the only workable solution.

For all the unusual and sometimes humorous stories in the newspapers of Hartford, some articles were not quite so sanguine. In the spring of 1870, information began arriving in newsrooms across the country of a tremendous drought in the heartland of America, which enveloped large sections of the southwest as well. In April and May, Kansas had been "cracked and warped by drought." In the small town of Humboldt, over 100 immigrant wagons filled with weeping women and children were left neglected, while others returned eastward. New Mexico was suffering terribly with "a remarkable scarcity of water." The hydrologic cycle was acting in an uncharacteristic fashion but, except for the obvious lack of water in America's heartland, there were no precipitating signs to indicate that serious trouble lay ahead for New England.

The April elections of 1870 represented the beginning of a whole new era for the Democratic Party in Hartford, as they locked up a majority on the board of aldermen and the common council; Democratic Mayor Charles R. Chapman was also elected to a third term. With the Fifth and Sixth Wards completely engorged with immigrants who voted Democratic and this tide spilling out into nearby wards, the future looked bright for the Democrats. Predictably, the ever-increasing masses of poor and uneducated residents—Irish, Germans and Jews—concerned the city's old guard.

Still smarting from their losses at the polls, Republican members of the council tried to shore up their power base by loading up the different committees with their own members. One of the biggest troublemakers was a man who, heretofore, had been a friend to the water works—Samuel Woodruff. His engine manufactory, it will be remembered, had built the first engine for the Connecticut River Pumping Station. At the time of the original contract, he had received extra compensation for the installation of the engine at the pumping station, but this was a simple business misunderstanding and antagonized no one.

However, the year before the Democratic landslide at the polls, as president of the Putnam Fire Insurance Company, Woodruff was caught selling more stock than the company's charter allowed and he was forced to resign. The repercussions of this imbroglio spilled over into his steam engine company and orders lagged in an otherwise prosperous economic period. (His company was finally acquired by Hunter & Sanford in 1871.) Although Woodruff was still a wealthy man, these financial reverses may have unhinged him a bit and his erratic behavior became copy for newsmen.

Woodruff became a terror as he sought to redress the Republican losses at the polls with his own brand of political legerdemain. First, in the gubernatorial election of 1870, he changed parties so that he could make a huge display of tearing his ticket in half and refusing to vote the top half for the Democratic candidate and odds-on favorite, James English. It should be noted that English's opponent was ex-governor Marshall Jewell, who stood by Woodruff during his troubles at the Putnam Fire Insurance Co.

After this pointless scene—English was elected governor as expected in 1870—Woodruff began throwing around his weight as an alderman, trying to replace Hiram Bissell as president of the Board of Water Commissioners with a Republican. Richard Lawrence—who was caught in the middle of Woodruff's maneuverings—was a native of Vermont, who had come to Hartford as a master armorer at Christian Sharps Rifle manufactory. In response to Woodruff's nomination of Lawrence, the Democratic council simply refused to ratify his choice, which was its right. Hiram Bissell had built up such an unassailable reputation as president of the water board that if push came to shove, it would be Woodruff who would be turned out—a fact lost on the aging boilermaker.

During Woodruff's little power play, the *Times*, taking the popular position that Bissell had become indispensable to the water works, quoted a reader as saying that, ". . . On one occasion when Mr. Hiram Bissell ordered some of the men . . . [to clear] . . . a large pipe that was stopped up, he found no one willing to take the job. Mr. Bissell himself went through the pipe and when he came out, no muddier looking man ever appeared in our streets . . . ."

Elevating this little political comedy to farce, at the council meeting the following week, Lawrence—also a water commissioner—claimed that, ". . . the presidency was not sought by him, and he did not want it." This, in spite of the embarrassing fact that, with Bissell abstaining, all of the other water commissioners—including Lawrence—had been coerced by Woodruff to vote for the change. The sheer lunacy of Alderman Lawrence's stance may have struck Hiram Bissell as comical at the time but, on the other hand, seventeen years of this folderol was wearying. Not surprisingly, Bissell began to plan for his retirement from the water board.

In July 1870, President Grant and his wife, Julia, paid a visit to Hartford. They stayed with ex-Governor Marshall Jewell, heir to the Jewell Belting fortune, who lived with his wife in an elegant mansion on the north side of Farmington Avenue. Later in the day, the presidential party repaired to the Allyn House—on the corner of Asylum and Trumbull Streets—where a public reception was held. At six o'clock, Grant appeared on a balcony where the throngs in the street cheered him. He offered the crowd a long presidential wave, but never uttered a word. Back at the Jewell property, a big party extended into the night, accompanied by enough fireworks to thrill the most demanding potentate.

The following afternoon, the President and Mrs. Grant were driven to Farmington where they called on Sarah Porter, the founder and headmistress of Miss Porter's School. The Grants' daughter Ellen (Nellie) was to matriculate at Miss Porter's in October. Early Monday morning, the President and Mrs. Grant left on the first train out of Hartford. (Later, when Nellie Grant arrived at the school, she hated it, wiring home, " I shall die if I must stay here." Sarah Porter subsequently wrote to her brother that, "Miss N. Grant went away last week . . . she is a nice child—although greatly behind many girls in study.")

Unfortunately for President and Mrs. Grant, the summer of 1870 was not one of those balmy, halcyon New England summers; instead, it was a scorcher. Though no one knew it at the time—it was the beginning of a fifteen-year long drought that would test the mettle of water commissioners and consumers alike. Newspapers chimed in, "This is an unparalleled summer . . . three months already we have had an unbroken succession of hot days. July has kept the Mercury up in the 90s right along. Today, the mark was 95°."

On a brighter note, the water works, despite the increased usage because of the dire weather, was able to stay ahead of demand. Throughout the hot months, the upper reservoir on Mine Brook remained about half full and Reservoir No. 1 was almost brimming. Hiram Bissell advised the newspapers that it was, "enough to last until the first or second week in September without any rain."

Because of the blistering temperatures experienced in 1870, Hartford's inhabitants drew heavily on the supplies in West Hartford. In fact, consumers used two a half times the amount that they had used the year before. Unlike the previous year, however, rainfall for the entire year was only about 5 percent below the average but *a full 35 percent below the average amount that fell in the 1850s and 60s*. Consequently, the public was accustomed to vast supplies and behaved accordingly while, in reality, the hydrologic cycle had turned sour. The people of Hartford could not have known it at the time, but their wasteful habits—acquired during times of plenty—were about to catch up with them.

To the untrained observer, the behavior of the Trout Brook network of streams was almost as regular as clockwork, their ebb and flow coinciding beautifully with the seasons. As a result of the winter snowmelt and the spring rains, the two new reservoirs were burgeoning by early May each year, and slowly surrendered their supply throughout the hot months. If the water supply could be extended until the November rains, then the foul river water would be a thing of the past.

The bête noire of the water works was autumn. Typically, the supply in the two reservoirs would last until late September, when the water works would be forced to crank up the pumps at the Connecticut River, the very last thing anyone wanted. By the 1870s, the water around the intake crib at the river was positively repugnant, and it was especially bad during the fall months when it was needed most.

Simply put, population growth and rampant waste had left the water works one reservoir short. As obvious as the need for a third reservoir was to the water board, the council, faced with the recent expense of rebuilding the first two reservoirs at Trout Brook, was slow to accept this position.

As if limited supply was not trouble enough for the system, occasionally the water took on an "ancient and fish-like" smell, with Bissell and everyone else scrambling to remedy this predicament. The smell in the water lingered like the stink in the streets, until people began to abandon the city water in favor of their old wells. Even "one-armed Billy" at the northwest corner of State House Square, whose waters were falsely praised as, "plenty pure and sweet" was resurrected to slake the thirst of families living in the area.

As the complaints of the "fishy water" grew, Bissell found himself in an awkward position. After fighting so hard for the Trout Brook system, he was determined to find the cause of the smell and restore confidence in the upland sources. Opening stopcocks all over town, he had the pipes "blown off" several times but, at least initially, to no end. After repeated—and futile attempts—to rid the system of the awful smell, Bissell was forced to shut off the water from the West Hartford reservoirs and supply the city again from the Connecticut River Pumping Station. Quite apart from the knowledge that the Trout Brook waters were infinitely cleaner than that from the river, his decision was tantamount to admitting that his belief in the upland sources was misplaced. As the streams of

Trout Brook and its tributaries alternated between a gentle trickle and nothing at all—and the supply got smelly—he simply had no choice.

In an age when disinfectants were unknown, "blowing off" the system was about the only tool available to a water works. Men continued to flush the system until, by the third week of September, the smell in the water departed. News of similar problems with other water works appeared regularly in the newspapers and members of the water board who traveled to other cities found the same problems there, but that offered little comfort for those entrusted with delivering potable water to the residents of Hartford. The real dilemma was that it took huge quantities of water to "blow off" the system at a time when critically short supplies grew more precious each day.

But something even more pressing became apparent at the old pumping station. Designed to satisfy the needs of a population half the present size, unnoticed, the engine and pumps had slipped into obsolescence. When powered up, the engines ran at full bore but still could not meet demand. To augment the river water, Trout Brook water—what little there was—had to be added back into the mix. Recognizing for the first time that the Connecticut River Pumping Station was not the reassuring backup that it was thought to be was unnerving. Bissell now had to make one of the most difficult decisions of his tenure. He had no interest at all in expanding the capacity of the Connecticut River Pumping Station when he had worked so hard for the upland sources, but he was up against it. Caught between his own pride and the exigencies of an expanding populace, he petitioned the council in November for the funds to install new and larger pumps at the Connecticut River Pumping Station. It was a bitter pill to swallow.

By the spring of the following year, the cycle at the Trout Brook reservoirs had begun again. The two reservoirs in West Hartford—by the middle of May—were burgeoning with the runoff of snowmelt and spring rains, and Trout Brook was flowing like some mythological fountainhead, promising the city, as always, that wholesome drinking water was not a concern. However, the droughts of the Midwest were descending upon New England accompanied by blistering hot weather. By May 30, the temperatures up and down the eastern seaboard were in the mid-90s, leaving people to wonder what was in store for them when summer truly arrived.

While the mercury climbed, there was some excitement of a different kind. At the beginning of the summer, on the order of Captain Charles Nott, a raid was made of the most notorious houses of ill-fame in the city. The police descended on "Joe Week's" and "Hanna Corgan's" on Market Street; "Toot's" on Temple Street; "Andrews's," "Pratt's" and "Durant's" on State Street; and "Atherton's" on Ferry Street. Nineteen girls were taken to the station house, the proprietors allowed to remain on their premises under written promise to appear at police court in the morning. These arrests illustrated the shifting patterns of vice within the city. When Hiram Bissell arrived in Hartford, such vice was centered in

Hotel Row (Gold Street), which one resident described as, ". . . a menace to the town. It was filled with gambling dens, lottery shops, saloons, pawn shops, and all sorts of entrances led therefrom literally to sinks of iniquity." Now, Hotel Row was simply a filthy alley, the vice having drifted to the areas around City Hall and the flophouses and flag taverns by the river.

Hiram Bissell, by virtue of the great demands on his time and due to his training as a builder, was a man who planned meticulously. Accordingly, he would handle his retirement from the water board no differently than any other change in his life—with care. Since he had expended so much energy in the building of the water works, the problem of succession was important to him. One fool at the helm could undo all of his hard work in no time.

There are a number of points to consider when examining Bissell's decision to retire from the water board. To begin, Bissell was a builder and as such, was accustomed to bringing projects to fruition. In point of fact, his training and subsequent work made him temperamentally unsuited for a job without end. With the city's water coming from the upland sources for at least ten months of the year—and sometimes longer—he certainly could have viewed the system as a completed project, but that was really not the case. As the population grew, more reservoirs would have to be dug and more aqueducts bedded. The water works, at least for Bissell, amounted to a job without end.

The second point—perhaps a little more subtle—was that Bissell was a man who liked challenges. But the great challenges of the water works were at the beginning when a reliable network had to be created from scratch, not when the next giant leap forward was to grub out another crater in the ground. For a man like Hiram Bissell, the water works had reached an important stage—where new catchments were definitely required—but also where ennui was sure to set in.

A third consideration was H. & S. Bissell, his masonry partnership with his brother. Sylvester had been doing the lion's share of the work at the business for the past seventeen years. Even while Hiram spread himself so thin between the two ventures, the brothers had begun to manufacture drain and sewer pipe, which they sold from a small storefront on Pearl Street. Could Sylvester be expected to continue this way forever? Hiram's high profile undoubtedly led to important building contracts for the pair, but at some point, Sylvester needed him at the firm. (As it turned out, the two brothers went their separate ways five years later, when Sylvester left the masonry business to superintend the West Hartford Ice Company.)

The last concern lay with the politics of the water department. While the city-owned system was the only reasonable choice as far as Bissell was concerned, it effectively made the system a Democratic enterprise. This exposed the water commissioners to a never-ending series of skirmishes with the city's old guard. While he had weathered all of the storms with surprising resilience, no one can stomach relentless criticism forever. At 53-years-old, it was time to let someone else to take the reins.

As Hiram Bissell prepared to step down as president of the water board, his choice for a successor became apparent. It was Ezra Clark. One would think that Clark's treatment at the hands of the Whigs in 1854 would have made him wary of any dealings with the common council, but it did not. He had a special affinity for the water department, having served on the first board of water commissioners and—though a Whig—championed the principle of the city-owned water system from the start. Bissell and Clark had gotten along well back in 1854 and, when it came to the practical business of supplying Hartford's residents with pure drinking water, they spoke the same language. That said, they were vastly different men in other ways.

Ezra Clark was born in Brattleboro, Vermont in 1813 and moved to Hartford six years later when his father, Ezra Clark, Sr. became a partner in the iron store of David Watkinson & Co. in 1819. Watkinson began, like so many of Hartford's wealthiest citizens dealing in a diverse collection of West Indies goods, but soon specialized in just iron and steel products. By the time that Ezra Clark, Sr. bought into the State Street store, Watkinson sold ". . . bar, bolt, hoop, sheet and band iron; steel of all kinds; carriage springs, anvils vices, axletrees, shoe shapes, horse nail rods, horse nails and shoes, Taunton cut nails, iron wire, &c."

When the Clarks left Vermont in 1819, Ezra, Sr. and his wife, Laura, already had five children and would have three more in Hartford. Ezra, Jr., who was the youngest of the five existing children had two brothers and two sisters. The Clarks were a close-knit family who, after 1833, lived in a three-story brick home on the east side of Main Street, about four blocks south of State House Square. As faithful communicants at the first Congregational Church and loyal members of the Whig Party, they had exactly the right amalgam of beliefs to fit in comfortably. Given these facts, it is not surprising that the large and talented Clark family did well in their new-found home.

Although there were too many mouths to feed in the Clark household for any of the Clark children to attend college, the girls went to private finishing schools in New York and the boys learned business at their father's knee. Upon reaching the age of 21, first George, then Morton, and then Ezra, Jr. entered the iron business. When David Watkinson retired, another Hartford merchant, Albert Gill, bought into the store and the name was changed to Clark, Gill & Co. Finally when Gill retired in 1840, the shop became simply Ezra Clark & Co.

Now owned solely by the four Clarks—father and three sons—they took stock. The original iron store on State Street, sold a considerable line of iron and steel goods, but was not large enough to engage in the lucrative business of wagon and carriage repair. The repair business would require more space, which could never be found on State Street, at least not at a price that they could afford.

Ezra Clark

For the next seven years, they paid attention to business and banked their money, waiting for the right piece of property to become available.

Meanwhile, when he was 28, Ezra, Jr. fell in love with and married a 19-year-old girl, Mary Hopkins, from one of Hartford's oldest families. At the time, Ezra was living on North Prospect Street about a block from the shop, but the couple soon purchased a more fashionable home on the newly developed Winthrop Street, a small side lane on the north end of Main Street. Over the next decade, the couple had three children. The oldest, Frances, nicknamed Fanny, was born in 1843 and later married Albert Butler, a reticent—some said misanthropic—man who was a dealer in art supplies and photographic goods with a small shop on Main Street. The second child, Charles Hopkins Clark, came along in 1848 and, after graduating from Yale College, worked his way up to editor-in-chief of the *Courant*. The youngest, Howard M. Clark, born in 1850, entered the banking business and eventually became a cashier (principal) of the United States Bank in State House Square.

As the Clark home filled up with babies and domestic servants, Ezra, put in long hours at the iron store and developed an interest in politics. Actually, considering the limited entertainments available to young men in the early 1840s, politics filled the void nicely and it would have been more noteworthy if he had shown no interest at all in city government. In due course, he was elected councilman, alderman and judge of the city court. (Much later in life, he also served as city auditor.)

In 1847, Ezra Clark, his father and two brothers bought a 50 by 100-foot lot on the corner of Front and Ferry Streets for $3,050 and built a squat brick building with a low-pitched gable roof that would give them all the space they needed for wagon and carriage repairs. Just a few steps off of State Street—in the heart of the business district—the location proved invaluable as the three men added new products and expanded their lines far beyond what David Watkinson ever envisioned. In no time, besides bar stock of iron and steel, the Clarks sold axles, rims, hubs, spokes, shafts, wheels, chains and bolts, and repaired wagons and carriages. As sidelines, they dealt in firebrick for stoves and a complete assortment of blacksmithing tools—hammers, anvils and bellows. Just about anything made of iron or steel, or closely related to it, could be purchased at the new Ezra Clark & Co.

As the venture expanded, including the sales and installation of central heating furnaces, Ezra Jr. financed another store in New York, run by his brother

Morton and a partner, E. M. Coleman. The new shop of Clark & Coleman was located at 35 Bank Street, between Union Square and the Hudson River. Ezra Clark got along famously with his brother Morton and even tried to interest him in business ventures as his letter of June 18, 1850 indicates—

> Dear Brother,
> Received C & C [Clack & Coleman] letter today . . . I do not know how you intend arranging details between yourself and me, but I am sure that we will have no disagreement.
> What do you think of trying to buy some corn in Ohio? Can't you buy this through some of your correspondents . . . [in the] West? . . . I am told [it] costs about $6.50 for mess at some point on the Ohio River. Is that not money?

To understand the young Ezra Clark, it is important to remember that the wealthiest men in Hartford at mid-century had all made their money in speculation of one sort or another. The wealthiest man in the city before 1804, Jeremiah Wadsworth, had invested heavily in the West Indies trade and built a fabulous fortune in the process. Hartford's most affluent citizen from Wadsworth's time until about 1850 was William Imlay, who was involved locally in flouring mills and land speculation, but also had lumbering operations in Michigan and owned Atlantic Drydock Company in Brooklyn, N.Y. With these examples, it was natural that Clark would enter into speculative ventures.

However, the 1850s was not a particularly good time to speculate as business slumped badly on the eve of the Civil War. For Ezra Clark, what might have been reasonable speculations a decade earlier snowballed into a collection of financial millstones around his neck. He invested in a gold mine in Virginia, a flourmill on the Farmington River in Simsbury and the furnace business in Hartford and New York. All of these speculations were in addition to his interest in Ezra Clark & Company. But even with all of these far-flung business ventures, Clark may not have gotten into trouble had he not fallen under the spell of a charismatic oddball, Richard Bacon, who talked him into mining copper at the New-Gate Copper Mine in Simsbury.

Around the time that the citizens of Hartford voted to build a city-owned waterworks in 1853, Ezra Clark began preliminary negotiations with Bacon in forming a partnership to exploit the copper of the old prison property. One of Simsbury's most peculiar personalities, Bacon was a farmer who, like an old prospector, was inexorably drawn to copper mining, albeit with increasingly calamitous results.

The New-Gate Copper Mine was a legendary property with a rich and storied history. The mine was the result of a lucky discovery in the sandstone hills on the east side of Simsbury early in the eighteenth century. Sixty-four of Simsbury's property owners became the shareholders of the claim which, in

1707, was formalized as the first commercial corporation in America. In the ensuing sixty years, the proprietors worked the mines, either themselves, or by leasing to other parties. By 1714, the mines were under contract to a Massachusetts group who mined "Copper Hill" for about twenty-five years, after which time the land comprising the claim was divided among the original owners. A blacksmith, John Higley, used the copper from his mine to strike "an interesting series of threepence pieces during the period from 1737 to 1739." These Connecticut Coppers were the first copper coins struck in America. Although the easily accessible high-grade ore had been exhausted by this time, mining continued for the next thirty years by free labor, slave labor and private enterprises.

In 1773, Connecticut began to use the principal mine as a prison—named New-Gate after its English counterpart—first for Tories and prisoners of war during the Revolution and, later, for burglars, horse thieves, robbers and counterfeiters. As the need for prison's outstripped the space available, still more hardened criminals were added to the mix, including arsonists, rapists and those found guilty of manslaughter. New-Gate's inmates were initially forced to mine copper, which was infinitely more humane than branding and mutilation which were common then. But copper mining by inmates proved unmanageable and they were later made to produce nails and shoes, retiring into the subterranean shafts at night. The state pursued other efforts to make the prison self-supporting, including cabinet making and cooperage; they even installed a human treadmill for grinding grain, on which a dozen inmates at once would supply the power for the huge millstones. Not surprisingly, the place earned a well-deserved reputation as a hellhole and was abandoned in 1827 when a new state prison at Wethersfield was completed.

After this time, several independent mining operators tried unsuccessfully to make a go of the played-out mine until Richard Bacon took an option on the property in the 1840s. He was an innovative miner, introducing steam engines—to speed up the work—and safety fuses, invented by William Bickford of England, to reduce the human carnage during blasting. But Bacon could not stay with anything long enough to achieve success. While working at New-Gate, the easily distracted Bacon had an epiphany—never mind the copper mining business—the manufacture and sale of safety fuses could make him rich. Chasing his latest dream, Bacon obtained a charter from Bickford-Smith & Company of England and became the U.S. manufacturer of these remarkable fuses. Among his other flaws, Bacon was guilty of careless business practices and sloppy bookkeeping, and these shortcomings eventually forced him out of the business.

In 1846, Bacon paid John Viets $200 for the right to take another crack at the old claim on "Copper Hill." As Bacon worked the mine, he went through a number of frustrated partners including his brother, George, and John Pettibone, another Simsbury resident. By the time he approached Ezra Clark, Bacon was working the mine alone and was deeply in debt to Pettibone. With his childish enthusiasm and his natural gift of salesmanship in overdrive, Bacon convinced Clark to form a partnership.

Strictly from a personal standpoint, there probably was not a worse time for Ezra Clark to form a partnership in a Connecticut mining operation than the mid-1850s. In 1854, he was running for the U.S. House of Representatives and, if elected, he would be spending large blocks of time in Washington. Typically, in the years before the Civil War, a Congressman spent about 270 days in session, which would leave him tethered to his desk in the U.S. Capitol with little or no time to oversee a copper mine back home. Beyond that, Clark had very mixed felling about Bacon. In letters to his brother Morton, he constantly contradicted himself such as in the following two excerpts from letters written in late 1854 and early 1855—

> . . . I don't believe there was ever such a man. [Bacon] is a distinct class by himself and, when he dies, the world will lose an original . . . .
> . . . I wish I had a "common sense man" to deal with out there [at New-Gate]. If I had, I would fix that thing so that no creditor could touch it, but I dare not trust Bacon . . . .

When Bacon and Clark formally organized Connecticut Copper Company in November 1855, the property was a junkyard of "boilers, furnaces, engines, hoists, screw shafts, pulleys, file benches, separators, bottles, acids and . . . tools, fixtures [and] machinery of every kind . . . " By then the copper content of the ore had slipped considerably, but was still double that of the copper content of the Cornish mines in England and, accordingly, the two men were upbeat about their prospects for success. One thing that the New-Gate mine badly needed was more power and, in exchange for ninety-eight shares of stock in the company, Clark convinced the principals of Woodruff & Beach to fabricate a new steam engine for the mine house. (Samuel Woodruff thought so little of the New-Gate mine that he immediately fobbed off his shares on Elisha Colt at the Exchange Bank.)

Eighteen months after the formation of the partnership, the Panic of 1857—which was ignited by the collapse of the New York branch of the Ohio Life Insurance and Trust Company—devastated businesses throughout the country. When John Pettibone called his notes, Bacon was unable to return the money, dumping the matter into Ezra Clark's lap. Unhappily for Pettibone, Clark was in no position to repay the notes either. While Pettibone vigorously pursued the options available to him—and, at the same time, the Clark family's one-time partner in the iron business, Alfred Gill, attached all the Ezra Clark's furniture to settle a $2,000 debt—the young congressman had no choice but to seek bankruptcy protection.

The aftermath of this fiasco is noteworthy. Over the ensuing years and, although he was not required to do so, Clark repaid Pettibone and all of his other creditors the complete amount of his debts and with interest. By dint of rectitude and an ingrained sense of propriety, Clark always chose the high road. It was unthinkable to him that he would not repay John Pettibone or Alfred Gill because the business climate had changed and left the Connecticut Copper Company high and dry. (When Richard Bacon died in 1871, Ezra Clark was awarded all of Bacon's property and mineral rights at New-Gate.)

After the New-Gate mining shambles and the completion of two terms representing Connecticut's first district in Washington, Clark settled his family in New York in 1859, and became active in the fertilizer business. In 1864, after almost a decade in Washington and New York, Clark purchased a home in Hartford and prepared to return. The new house—at 5 Collins Street off Myrtle—was, coincidentally, within spitting distance of the Lord's Hill Reservoir. The Clark family took up residence at the home in June 1865 after Ezra and Mary's children finished the school year in New York.

As an interesting sidebar, Ezra Clark got his older brother, Morton, a position at the Printing Bureau while in Washington and, during the Civil War, Morton Clark invented much of the machinery used in the production of government greenbacks and fractional currencies introduced in 1863. In a very real sense, the intricate engravings of Spencer Morton Clark were the inspiration for the legions of counterfeiters who bilked thousands of unsuspecting shopkeepers and customers during and after the war.

It was during the mid-1860s that Gen. Joseph Hawley of the *Courant* spearheaded the drive to build a church in the western side of the city and Ezra Clark and his wife, Mary, were generous contributors to the building fund. Rev. Joseph Twichell's Asylum Hill Congregational Church, dedicated in 1866, was the eventual result. (This is the same institution that Mark Twain humorously dubbed the "Church of the Holy Speculators.") Sadly, Mary Clark did not live to enjoy the new church. She passed away in May 1866 at the age of 44. She was laid to rest at the Grove Hill Cemetery on the north end of Main Street, and Ezra Clark, 53-years-old at the time, never remarried.

Later in life Clark managed to build a considerable estate, but during this period, he needed to work. By his lights though, that did not mean returning to the family iron and steel business. In truth, Clark & Co. was a grimy business, whose biggest single source of revenue came from wagon and carriage repairs. As a result, the yard around the building was always strewn with wagon wheels, axles and a gloomy assortment of rusted iron refuse. The building was a filthy brick and mortar affair with a large set of barn doors front and center, and a couple of small windows, opaque with grime, to the right and left. For Clark, who once spent his days in the polished halls of the United States Capitol, it was a déclassé workplace that he chose to avoid. Toward that end, he bought into the

National Screw Co. on Sheldon Street—about four blocks south of Clark & Co.—and served as the firm's president.

Four years after Mary's death, in January 1870, Clark's father died. Ezra's older brother, George, continued in the business although he had to buy out the interests of his remaining siblings, which was accomplished by allowing a new partner, Lester L. Ensworth, to buy in. For the next eleven years, the company's letterheads read simply—Clark & Co. When George Clark died in 1881, Lester Ensworth began to buy out George Clark's interest and was the sole owner by 1892. (When a new sign went up on the building at that time, it read: L.L. Ensworth & Son.)

The screw manufacturing business was exactly what Ezra Clark had been looking for, except that he was entering the business at a time of rapid mechanization. The screw industry, very much like the horse nail business, was undergoing huge changes. Up until the Civil War, screws were imported from distant cities, but that never sat right with the industrialists of Hartford—some of the most capable manufacturers in America.

In the two decades after the war, a number of screw companies sprouted in the city—National Screw, American Screw, Connecticut Screw, Hartford Machine Screw and a few smaller shops. Just as a simple example of the efficient mechanization within the industry, consider that typically a screw company employed one boy to attend a dozen machines, each capable of producing 2000 screws a day from bar stock. This was miraculous by the standards of the day, but all this was accomplished only with enormous capital expenditures. As a 59-year-old man, Clark was reluctant to invest the huge sums of money needed to make National Screw competitive, so he negotiated a sale to the American Screw Co. of Providence instead.

In 1871, Ezra Clark was re-elected to the water board, acting as Hiram Bissell's right hand man. While serving as a commissioner, he studied the new Trout Brook system and a host of other changes put into place while he was living and working in New York. A decade and a half earlier, when he left Hartford, the Connecticut River Pumping Station had not even been completed and now the water works was structured on an entirely different principal— upland reservoirs. There was a lot to learn.

Since it is clear that Hiram Bissell wanted Clark to succeed him as president of the water board, Clark had to decide if he could live on the reduced salary that a city position would pay him. Dividing his time between jobs, the way Hiram Bissell had done, was out of the question. The workload had simply become too big. As president of the water board, Clark would draw a salary of $2,000 a year plus a horse allowance of $600. With his children grown and his earlier interest in speculation gone, he felt it was enough.

Clark's interest in the water works was mesmerizing considering the drubbing that he received in 1854 by members of his own party but, as he perceived correctly, the inroads that the Democrats had made on the council over the intervening years had lowered the level of acrimony considerably. Notwithstanding Samuel Woodruff's odd behavior, the sophisticated machinations of the water works, to some degree, insulated it from the oversight of newly elected aldermen and councilmen. Even a man like Woodruff, who had been around engines and boilers all of his life, was not quick to appreciate some of the more esoteric points concerning watersheds, soil filtration rates, sluiceways and waste weirs. While every little detail of the water system was discussed in great detail in the 1850s when the original works was under construction, by the 1870s, months of council meetings went by with nary a mention of the water department. True, a committee was assigned to oversee the water board, but without an intimate knowledge of the system, they were slow to interfere.

As Hiram Bissell served out his last year at the helm of the water works, and the weather heated up in Hartford, events half a continent away added to local business concerns. On a Sunday night at the beginning of October 1871, a fire broke out in Chicago. When Chicago's fire and police departments assessed the situation later, they found that the blaze originated in a two-story barn in the rear of 137 DeKoven Street, the premises of Patrick and Catherine O'Leary, who ran a neighborhood milk business. The fire was first spotted at about 9:30 in the evening by a drayman, who noticed the flames while sitting on the curb opposite the O'Leary's home. When the damage was finally tallied, 18,000 homes and business were destroyed and almost 300 lives were lost.

The Chicago fire decimated the insurance industry in America, as only 25 percent were able to meet their obligations. The rest folded. Eleven of Hartford's insurance companies had exposure to the conflagration in Chicago. Aetna, Hartford, Phoenix and National had limited exposure while other companies— among them Merchants, Connecticut, North American, Putnam, Charter Oak and City Fire were not so fortunate, some insuring life and property in excess of a million dollars, which was way beyond their resources. After the Chicago fire, only the first four companies mentioned—Aetna, Hartford, Phoenix and National—remained in business.

In 1872, Hiram Bissell persuaded the other water commissioners to elect Ezra Clark president. Given Bissell's forceful personality and the enormous respect that he had earned over almost two decades with the water works, no one challenged his decision. If Bissell wanted Clark to follow him, then even Samuel Woodruff—with his unpredictable disposition—would have had a hard time preventing it.

Clark could not have known it, but he was stepping into the top job at a most inauspicious time. Like some evil, wayward pendulum, the fortunes of the water works never seemed to reach equilibrium. Instead, they swung wildly from feast to famine and back again. No sooner had the water department finished rebuilding Reservoirs No.1 and No.2—and hopefully had lived down the embarrassment associated with the disastrous collapse of the dam in 1867—than Mother Nature proceeded to give the whole country a good parching.

According to the old records—which it must be pointed out are slightly at odds with precipitation rates calculated with modern instrumentation—the Trout Brook valley got a little more than 50 inches of precipitation each year. (It is accepted now that the precipitation in central Connecticut averages about 44 inches annually.) But in 1869, "the rainfall during the year [had] at certain times been the largest ever known in [that] locality." Unfathomably, during a June shower that year, 4.14 inches of rain fell in an hour and a half. Likewise, a downpour in October delivered an astounding 8.7 inches of rain in about thirty hours. Rainfall and snowmelt, like so many other things in nature, tend to even out over the long run, but that provided no solace to those who depended on a steady amount of both. Very often wet years came in strings as did dry ones.

The amount of rainfall measured in the 1860s must have delighted the farmers of the Connecticut River valley, but for those who understood the annoying regularity of cycles, it must have been unsettling. In 1865, the area recorded more than 54 inches of precipitation, which was four inches above the norm. That was nothing compared to the rest of the 1860s when the annual precipitation amounted to 71, 69, 74 and 75 inches, respectively. Judging by these years that were way beyond bountiful, it was little wonder that the dam at Reservoir No. 1 breached. Unhappily for everyone though, the abundant rains of the 1860s would not be seen again for a decade and a half.

The drought of the 1870s was considerably more than a ten-year long dry spell. At least in the Northeast—it was actually a period of fifteen years, from 1870 until 1884 inclusively, when below average precipitation dogged farmers and water companies alike. The only two exceptions were 1871 and 1878 when the precipitation was just slightly above average. During this time of extreme drought, the precipitation recorded at Reservoir No. 1 in West Hartford ranged anywhere from just slightly above average to almost 25 percent below the norm for any given year.

The waters of the Connecticut River got so low sometimes that steamboats were unable to maneuver into their slips along the wharfs. Smaller boats like the *Silver Star* offloaded cargo from larger steamers like the *State of New York* and the *Granite State* as they lay out in the deepest part of the channel, buoying them just enough to effect a landing at their regular berths.

Such a long drought inevitably racked up wholesale misery on rural farming communities, but the potential for a real litany of sorrows lay with congested cities like Hartford. The council was slow to perceive the severity of the drought and the need for future reservoirs, but Ezra Clark was not. Thanks to his efforts, disaster was barely averted even as the public wasted water at a shocking rate.

Owing to the public's foolishness, before the drought had even begun in earnest, the city had a truly sobering brush with disaster.

Ezra Clark inherited a decision of Hiram Bissell's that would give him more heartache than any other matter in his long tenure with the water works. One of Bissell's final acts as the president of the water board was to commission Hunter & Sanford, a local engine works, ". . . to take out the greater portion of the pumping machinery (which was so worn as to unfit it for use) and replace it with new pumps of larger size and greater capacity." Upon accepting the contract, John Hunter, a tall, good-looking and charismatic man—and also a member of the water board—assured his fellow commissioners that the work would be completed in four months.

But it was not. Instead, it dragged on for a frustrating amount of time because of unexpected changes at Hunter & Sanford. In 1871, John Hunter and his partner, Edwin Sanford, acquired the complete operations of Woodruff & Beach. At that time, the name of the firm was changed to Hartford Foundry and Machine Company, with a whole new slate of administrators. The president—figurehead actually—of the new entity was Jonathan Bunce and his vice-president was John Hunter. Apparently Hunter, although trained as a machinist, had no interest in the dirty business of grinding machine parts when he could be in the administrative end of the business. The superintendent of the company, the man who actually ran the production department was Edwin Sanford, who was quite content as a machinist. The future looked bright for this company since they inherited the mantle of the finest machine and steam boiler manufactory in the city and, at least by appearances, had gathered together a large collection of talented workers. Sad to say, the appearance of great competence was an illusion.

Because of the difficulties of combining two businesses and the attendant problems with works in progress, Hunter's promises turned out to be worthless. No sooner had the two firms been merged, than John Hunter announced to the water board that the pumps could not be completed within the original schedule.

This wasn't particularly unsettling at the time because the city was sitting on about 550 million gallons of water, more than 60 times what the old Lord's Hill Reservoir held. Sadly, with the lack of metering and such an enormous supply, water customers did not even give conservation lip service. Such a fabulous stockpile of water caused John Hunter and Ezra Clark to view the city's supply in entirely different ways. Hunter did not consider the new pumps a top priority, while Clark, ever a cautious man, most assuredly did.

Hartford Foundry's workshop was located on Commerce Street, only two blocks from City Hall and, in the course of many trips to the manufactory, Clark was assuaged by Hunter with ever more reassuring promises of performance. Still nothing. Finally in June 1872, seven months after the contract was originally let, Ezra Clark and Mayor Timothy Allyn visited John Hunter at his foundry loaded for bear. In his most courteous and soothing manner, Hunter bought himself still more time by assuring the pair that the pumps would be completed by October 1 of that year and throwing water a month later. Despite this latest round of reassurances, Hunter did not have the pumps installed or working by November 1872 or anytime soon thereafter.

Clark conducted himself with civility, but he was fast running out of wiggle room. Instead of the dry spell breaking and Hartford returning to the days of plenty, the drought bore down. The early months of 1872 had given no reason to expect that the hydrologic cycle would right itself and, taken as a whole, the drought continued unabated, with the city receiving 6 percent less rain than normal that year. Even with this deficit, the water board was not forced to go to the Connecticut River for water at any time during the year. As a bonus, the quality of the water was excellent.

Under Ezra Clark's leadership, the small works continued to grow with the water mains increasing to a total of fifty-four miles. The board also decided that the time had come to add another twenty-inch main from the reservoirs in West Hartford. With the single main, it was becoming more difficult to maintain water pressure in the higher sections of the city or the top floors of some of the commercial buildings.

The number and diversity of the problems experienced by a growing city were demonstrated by the fact that when the streets were graded and curbstones set, very often the dirt was scraped right down to the water pipes, either breaking them or, at the very least, leaving them exposed. Apparently, the communication between the different departments was almost nonexistent. Consequently, in some cases the water pipes had to be laid and bedded two and three times. Clark implored the council to allow the water department to set their pipes only after the roads department set the final grade of the streets, but his plea fell on deaf ears. As a last resort, and to avoid waste until things were settled, he ordered his workers to stop laying new mains until better coordination could be achieved.

Beyond these irksome housekeeping chores, the water works finished 1872 with the largest financial surplus in its history—$20,814, not including two unpaid water bills amounting to $17 (out of 4,250 customers). Still, Clark was concerned. Weighing on his mind, like the remnants of a bad dream, was the question of supply. The public was using eight million gallons a day, which was *three times* the consumption that one would expect from 40,000 people in the early 1870s. Waste had gone beyond rampant to profligate and Ezra Clark realized that the water works was barely making it with the supplies they had. If the level of precipitation should continue to worsen or any other problems arise with the Trout Brook system, Hartford would be in serious trouble. Accordingly, he began to agitate for a third reservoir.

Ezra Clark was an erudite man and knew that the southwestern United States had continuous problems of supply, but the possibility of a water famine in Hartford was unsettling. Concern building now, Clark began to make regular pilgrimages to John Hunter's shop. Perhaps if he stopped by often enough,

Hunter would fulfill his contract just to get rid of him. Clark tried to impress upon Hunter that unless a substantial amount of rain should fall—and soon— there was every reason to believe that there could be a catastrophic breakdown in supply. This period of delay lasted so long and caused so much concern that, once again, Clark tried to effect some sort of performance by enlisting the help of the mayor. Through the fall months, Mayor Timothy Allyn repeatedly visited the workshops of John Hunter and Edwin Sanford, and ". . . personally and officially urged upon them the necessity to the city of the fulfillment of their promises."

The year came to a conclusion with the contract still uncompleted. Ezra Clark, his water board, Mayor Timothy Allyn and everyone else connected to the department were beside themselves, unsure whether to cancel the contract and look elsewhere for a new builder or to stick it out with Hunter. It was the most perplexing of situations. Later Clark summarized his feelings when he wrote that the, ". . . delay in the work has not been satisfactorily explained to this board."

When Clark was reappointed in 1873, the council spoke very highly of him, stating that it was—

> . . . in favor of confirming him [Clark] at this time. As he had during the past year, given us not bad-smelling, fishy water. He was an efficient man, and a good one for the place. It would be difficult to get as good a one.

The only thing on Clark's mind as his new term began was the problem of supply. No one could make heads or tails of the unconcerned John Hunter, Edwin Sanford or the other men at Hartford Foundry. Their management was so unprofessional and their reckless disregard for the looming water crisis so appalling that everyone connected with the water works was dumbfounded and out of ideas when it came to coazing the work out of the firm. (Although Hartford Foundry and Machine Company did a fantastic business, including the elaborate castings for the St. Louis Water Works in 1875, it surprised no one connected with the Hartford Water Works when the company folded in 1881.) By the end of the summer, the supply in the West Hartford Reservoirs was dwindling fast and, consequently, things were at a flash point between the water board, John Hunter and Edwin Sanford, for the company's machinists were still nowhere near completion of the new pumps.

While the Hartford Foundry dawdled, the blistering hot weather made conditions almost unbearable for Hartfordites, and the battle to maintain some semblance of cleanliness was a losing one. Recognizing this dilemma the council appropriated $4,500 for the erection of free public bathhouses by the river. To expedite matters, they dispensed with competitive bidding and gave the contract to a local builder, insisting, of course, that the houses be ". . . strong, safe and...with one division containing rooms for gentlemen and another for rooms for ladies." Even during the early summer, the papers could only report that, ". . . The dry time holds. Rain is much needed."

During June, July and August of 1873, the amount of rainfall was less than half of what it had been the year before. Under these conditions, the ground was so dry that, even if it did rain, little if any of the water that fell in the Talcott Mountain watershed would make it to the reservoirs; instead, the ground would hungrily soak up the water. As the summer faded, the water levels in the reservoirs dropped rapidly. The most obvious culprit was the unforgivable waste of the inhabitants of the city, who remained oblivious to the mounting crisis.

Since the original engine at the pump house, running at full bore, could not even supply one-third of the water needed, an enormous rainfall was the only thing that could stave off disaster, and that was not in the cards. Adding further to the crisis, the Lord's Hill Reservoir—which would inevitably be pressed back into service—now had the capacity to store only a one-day supply. Reverting to the river water was a detestable option and Ezra Clark would delay such a switchover until the very last minute.

On Friday evening, September 26, with the reservoirs running perilously low, the *Times* admonished its readers to be provident with their water use, while using the looming crisis to lobby for a third reservoir in the Talcott Mountain watershed. In the same story, the paper also referred to "pumps just set," implying that the new units sat at the ready, but, having close ties with the water board, the publisher clearly knew that this was not true. In point of fact, the new pumps were not yet installed and, therefore, were ready to do absolutely nothing. At the same time, the reservoirs in West Hartford had, at most, a twenty-four hour supply of water remaining. As if matters could not get worse, the skies were without a cloud; rain was not expected.

Goaded into action by the rising level of alarm from the water commissioners and the mayor, the mechanics from Hartford Foundry finally began to install the new pumps at the Connecticut River Pumping Station. And when they realized that the reservoirs at Trout Brook were almost exhausted, their work escalated to fever pitch.

Around suppertime on Saturday, September 27—and much earlier than expected—the West Hartford reservoirs gave up the last of their water, sending Ezra Clark and the other water commissioners racing for the Connecticut River Pumping Station. The aqueduct to the city went dry except for a tiny trickle from the streams leading into it at Reservoir No. 1 and the new pumps were still not ready to raise water up to the Lord's Hill Reservoir. The city was completely without drinking water. The only thing separating 40,000 people from a complete water famine was a one-day supply at the Lord's Hill Reservoir, which had to be kept in reserve for fire fighting.

The pressure to complete the work on the new pumps at the river became intense. Men who had suffered through eighteen months of promises from John Hunter were now second-guessing themselves. Should they have fired him a year ago? Should they have vacated the contract before it came to this? More important, how long would it be before the water famine began to really affect people? There were the old wells of course, but even those had their limits and, during such a drought, many of them would run dry.

Ezra Clark and the entire water board stood there watching as the work progressed. An hour ticked by and then two, with the connections to the rising main still not completed. Another hour dragged by and still the mechanics offered no indication of a time of completion.

As the installation of the new pumps progressed, the spigots and taps in people's homes throughout the city ran dry—first in the neighborhoods at higher elevations and, finally, even in the more low-lying areas.

After four tense hours, the installation of the new pumps was completed. In the late evening hours, after the city had been completely without water for four hours, the engine was started and the pumps engaged. Since it was a race against the clock now, there was no time for a shakedown run of any kind. Water rushing into the pumps was forced through the long ascending main up the gradual grade to the old reservoir atop Lord's Hill. In the higher elevations, the lack of water continued over the following weeks.

The original pumps in the engine house moved only two million gallons a day while the new ones were able to raise twice that amount. With the new units running around the clock, a total of four million gallons a day could be raised to the Lord's Hill Reservoir. The springs that fed the Trout Brook network might, with any luck, be able to deliver another million gallons a day. Still, that was only five million gallons for a city that had previously been consuming eight million a day. Clearly, until the area experienced a substantial rainfall, the city's residents would have to trim their usage sharply.

Since news coverage was scant on weekends, many of the city's residents whose homes were in the lower lying areas were blissfully unaware of the city's close brush with disaster. On Monday morning, however, they awakened to read the following news in their morning paper—

> . . . We had a taste of Connecticut River water this morning. The [new] pumps moved, and the water flowed slowly; but very soon we had no taste, for the supply was exhausted. The washerwoman was in distress, every family was in trouble, for Lord's Hill is not much higher than many of the parts of the city . . . After the use of water for years from a reservoir 260 feet above the Connecticut River [in West Hartford] . . . our citizens felt the weakness and inadequacy of the pumping power as soon as it was tested.

To manage the crisis, the city had to depend on a combination of supplies. The limited amount coming from Trout Brook was diverted to the homes and business in the higher elevations of the city, while the pumped water from the Connecticut River serviced everyone else. The *Courant* was quick to point out what the water board already knew—

> . . . the amount flowing in a day [from Trout Brook], although utterly insufficient for the whole city's demands, is not altogether inconsiderable. The supply from both sources is not adequate to furnish the amount usually consumed by the city. It is necessary, therefore, that everybody should be careful . . . There can be no complete relief until rain comes. . . .

Hartford struggled through the winter with this inefficient system, while the council continued to debate the wisdom of building another reservoir, an option which had been first placed before them by Hiram Bissell three years earlier.

The water crisis of September 1873 had Ezra Clark dispatching runners back and forth between the reservoirs in West Hartford and the Connecticut River Pumping Station almost continuously and the inability to know what was happening moment-to-moment was frustrating. To remedy this inefficiency, the following year, a contract was initiated with the Farmington Stage, calling for its driver to stop at the reservoir in the morning and pick up Henry Ayres's report of the condition of the reservoirs. This report was delivered to Clark's office at City Hall. On the return run to Farmington, the driver would forward any messages from Ezra Clark to the engineer at the Trout Brook site.

By 1877, a telegraph line was strung to the reservoirs and was used until telephone service was initiated almost a decade later. The little flaw in this otherwise ingenious plan was that Henry Ayres was not anywhere near the telegraph key during the day. He spent all of his time out at the reservoirs, not in his cottage next to the dam at Reservoir No. 1. But the engineer fashioned an ingenious solution. Ayres taught his thirteen-year-old daughter, Sarah, to use the telegraph key and this young girl tapped out her father's communiqués to Ezra Clark for many years thereafter, becoming the youngest person to ever work for the Hartford Water Department.

***

At this juncture, the water works went a little astray. Perhaps more accurately, it could be said that it came face to face with a problem that all water companies eventually had to grapple with—the exact role of engineers within the bureaucracy. When there were big projects afoot, engineers were given almost complete control, but when water supplies were abundant, they were gently nudged back behind their drafting tables.

Since there were relatively few American-educated engineers before the Civil War, cities and towns hired either foreign-educated or self-taught engineers who usually—but not always—received their training working as surveyors for the railroads or canal companies. The standards of engineering work in this country during the nineteenth century varied widely as the self-taught engineers, the foreign educated men and, finally, their American-schooled counterparts vied for the design work connected with water systems. Surprisingly enough, the systems designed by this obviously uneven pool of talent were very often reliable and enduring.

For its first upland water supply, the Croton Reservoir and Aqueduct, New York hired a Long Island native, John Jervis, who received no formal education beyond the age of fifteen. The Erie Canal was Jervis' big break, giving him seven years of engineering training in the field, from whence he graduated to platting railroads. A true innovative genius with many inventions to his name, including air brakes for trains, Jervis was, fortunately for New York, blessed with astounding perseverance and he needed every bit of it while working on the Croton Aqueduct. With the patience of Job, he dealt with a plethora of labor and materials problems that daily threatened to derail the ambitious project.

When Boston needed a hydraulic engineer, they hired Ellis S. Chesbrough, a Maryland native, who left school at the age of thirteen and received his engineering training while working for the Baltimore & Ohio Railroad. He designed Boston's Brookline Reservoir and its Cochituate Aqueduct before leaving for Chicago to build a water works there. Later he designed systems for New York, Toronto, Memphis and Milwaukee.

In California, the chief engineer of Los Angeles Water & Power was a tough-as-nails, self-taught Irishman. William Mulholland began as a ditch-digger for the water works, studying engineering texts every chance he got and eventually this diamond in the rough rose to the position of chief engineer.

The second great pool of talent was the foreign-educated engineer, who became the mainstay of water works throughout the nineteenth century. Lured to America by the rapidly expanding railroads, many of these engineers found the principles and practice of hydraulic engineering more rewarding and drifted into that discipline, traveling from town to city while designing aqueducts and drinking water systems.

When Philadelphia built its first water works in 1799, it hired an architect-engineer, Benjamin Latrobe, who was trained in Moravian schools at Fulneck, England and later at Nieski in German Silesia. His received his engineering training under the tutelage of England's renowned John Smeaton. Architecture was Latrobe first love, but his engineering projects were more remunerative. In addition to Philadelphia's Centre Square Water Works, he also designed a system for New Orleans, which he was still working on when he died of yellow fever in 1820.

A German engineer, Albert Stein, designed a reservoir and distribution system for Nashville in 1833, another system for New Orleans in 1835 and still others in Cincinnati, Lynchburg and Mobile.

Sometimes it was the chief engineer of the city who either designed or oversaw the construction of water projects while not actually working for the water company. When the pugnacious M.M. O'Shaughnessy, who received his engineering degree from the Royal University of Dublin, completed the Hetch Hetchy Reservoir in 1923, he was the chief engineer for the City of San Francisco, not the water company. The city's water was delivered by the Spring Valley Water Company, a private concern.

Finally, the engineering graduates of American Colleges took the lead in the field of drinking water. Sometimes they stayed in one city, but often they worked on a consulting basis, as had the foreign-born engineers a half-century or more before them.

In the decade leading up to the Civil War, an engineering graduate of West Point, Capt. Montgomery Meigs, developed a plan and supervised the construction of the Washington Aqueduct, providing the nation's capital with its first clean and reliable drinking water supply. (When Meigs entered West Point in 1832, it was the only engineering school in the United States.) Shepherding the work to within months of completion in October 1861, Meigs was reassigned by President Lincoln to the post of quartermaster general at the outbreak of hostilities. As a trusted advisor and close friend of the President, Meigs gave sound advice to Lincoln during the war and was even at his bedside in the Peterson home on 10th Street—opposite Ford's Theatre—when the president died. Capt. Montgomery Meigs, who worked later with the Army Corps of Engineers, spent more than forty years attending to matters concerning the Washington Aqueduct.

***

Up until this time, the water board at Hartford had engaged engineers from the private sector on an ad hoc basis. Their services were crucial to the toddling water works and they were generally paid between $2,000 and $3,000 for each reservoir project. However, the complexity of the operations of the system had grown to the point where full-time engineering talent was imperative. All the same, up until the mid-1870s, when push came to shove, the board instinctively chose a businessman as president.

Still, they were paying out huge sums of money to engineers on a contractual basis and since a third reservoir was badly needed in West Hartford, appointing an engineer to run the water department seemed like a logical step. With all of this in mind, the man who was elected president of the Board of Water

Commissioners in 1874 was a local engineer, Seth Marsh. He was not a college trained engineer, but was considered a man of "practical good sense and judgment," who had come to Hartford just before mid-century to help lay out the Hartford, Providence and Fishkill railroad.

That spring, when Marsh began his first term as the head of the water board, both reservoirs in West Hartford were recharged to overflowing by the usual snowmelt and rainfall. As the weather heated up though, the supplies at Trout Brook vanished by the first of August and the city was back to pumping from the Connecticut River. This water was unacceptable to everyone and spurred the council into action. Without its usual cautious—even snail-like—deliberations, it gave the necessary permission for the board to start building a third reservoir in the Trout Brook watershed. Reservoir No. 3, built between the two existing catchments, was completed in the fall of 1875.

This third reservoir offered some relief but, with the drought bearing down hard, plans for a fourth followed quickly. The stakes had increased though. There were now more than 40,000 people living in the city and the drought was beginning to look like a permanent fixture. Adding another reservoir with the same general storage capacity as the others generated little enthusiasm. Marsh had his eye on something much bigger.

Two miles to the south of Reservoir No. 1—in the Town of Farmington—was a piece of land belonging to a farmer, John Cadwell, that looked promising. The principal watershed for this new reservoir, Farmington Mountain, could be viewed as the southern tip of the long Talcott Mountain—had the two mountain ridges been connected. The real draw of the Cadwell land was the fact that the proposed reservoir would have a larger capacity than all of the other three—combined.

Excited by such a grand project, Marsh began his work in high spirits but did not live to see it completed. He caught pneumonia and died in September 1878 at the age of 57. Henry Ayres, the engineer at the Farmington road reservoirs, completed the project the following year.

Inexplicably, Edward Murphy—who was the secretary and treasurer of the Hartford Foundry—was appointed head of the water board for the next few years until Ezra Clark was again available in 1882. Murphy's election to the post of water commissioner in the first place speaks volumes about the ability of Clark and his water board to keep silent about the Hartford Foundry's miserable performance in 1873. Had the public known how close that firm had come to subjecting them to a crippling water famine, undoubtedly they would have shunned Murphy.

Though the choice of Seth Marsh as chief engineer and general manager of the department showed some forward thinking on the part of the council and the water board, the move was premature. Combining the posts of head of the water board and chief engineer—or chief engineer and general manager—eventually became the configuration at the top of most water companies during the golden age of hydraulic engineering in the United States, but that time would not come for another quarter of a century.

Before the huge Reservoir No. 4 could be completed, the city faced another crisis as a result of the terrible drought. At a special meeting of the water board, two representatives of the state board of health, Drs. Fuller and Chamberlain, informed those present that ". . . sickness [typhoid fever] was occurring in the city on account of the bad quality of the Connecticut River water now in use . . ." With this information, the board had no choice but to shut down the pumps at the river and open the gates at the reservoirs in West Hartford, regardless of the pathetic supply. All horse troughs and city fountains were shut off and the board requested, ". . . all good citizens to be as economical in the use of water as possible . . . " They also warned that, ". . . if there be waste, the pumps must soon be started again." After studying the matter thoroughly, it was discovered that a tiny brook, North Meadow Creek, was depositing sewage from the crowded tenements of the Sixth Ward into the Connecticut River just 75 feet from the pump house intake crib. Immediately, the water board had the creek diverted to dispel its effluent farther downstream. After the two doctors were satisfied that the water was now unaffected by the waste from North Meadow Creek, the pumps at the river were reactivated.

In the mid-1870s, the long competition between Hartford and New Haven for sole capital of Connecticut came to a head. Each city offered the legislature inducements to set up shop permanently in its bosom, but Hartford emerged the winner. Offering a beautiful site overlooking Bushnell Park in the center of the city and $500,000 to build the capitol building itself, constituted an offer the General Assembly couldn't refuse. There was only one small obstacle—Trinity College was already located on the site. By offering still more inducements to the administrators of the college, the land was purchased and Trinity College relocated to the South End. In 1879, the new Connecticut State Capitol building was completed and, while the legislators set up in the cavernous new capitol, the common council moved into the old capitol building in State House Square, which would now serve as City Hall. (The old City Hall on the corner of Market and Temple Streets became the police headquarters.)

For a decade and a half after the Civil War, as immigrants bloated the ranks of the Democratic Party, Hartford politics—like that of so many other cities in America—was controlled by the Democrats. In 1880, however, the city went Republican again as the popular president of Aetna Life Insurance Company, Morgan Bulkeley, won the mayoralty race and the seats on the council were overwhelmingly filled with members of his party. Bulkeley was one of the most versatile politicians the city ever produced, serving as mayor, governor and U. S. senator. He was a whirlwind of activity, generally centered on efforts to better the City of Hartford. A genial man, but also an astute politician, Bulkeley was not to be taken lightly. Political careers began and ended on his say-so and his uncanny ability to maintain lasting friendships kept the Republican legislators in the General Assembly firmly in his pocket.

The introduction of electricity into Hartford shortly before Morgan Bulkeley took office in 1880 offers a wonderful look at City Hall run Bulkeley-style. Unlike his father, Eliphalet Bulkeley, who was unable to wrest the water company from the city's Democrats, Morgan Bulkeley gathered together the heads of the three competing electric companies and explained to them his vision of the future. That vision was built on one electric company in which he would be a major shareholder. (Conflict of interest was not much of an issue in the 1880s.) As a peace gesture, they would each be allowed to take shares in the Hartford Electric Light Company but, from that moment forward, it was the only game in town. Once Morgan Bulkeley and his Republican cronies had the electric franchise in hand, they did nothing. The Hartford Electric Light Company charter was carefully placed in a safe deposit box at the Connecticut Trust and Safe Deposit Company on Main Street, where it lay undisturbed for nine months. During this period, no manufacturer of electrical equipment was allowed a franchise. Finally, one company broke ranks. Rumor of American Electric Company's plans to enter the city was the catalyst needed to spur the incorporators of the Hartford Electric Light Company to enter the production phase. Soon Helco introduced electric streetlamps and incandescent lighting in stores and manufactories. Would it have been any different if they had managed to snatch the water franchise back in 1851? One can only wonder.

While the water works had flirted with the concept of engineer as administrator, Ezra Clark kept busy. He was the president of the Connecticut Screw Co. on Pearl Street for five years and then served as city auditor for another two. Once again though, he was drawn to the city's water works. He was re-elected to the water board in 1882 and appointed president the same year. This time, however, his tenure would be substantially longer than in the past, as he held the post for the next fourteen years.

Actually, up until this time, Ezra Clark had turned up so regularly in the affairs of the city's water works, it appeared that the ubiquitous liquid had some heretofore undocumented—but powerful—magnetic quality. As a result of his long years of public service, he was a revered figure in Hartford and he was appointed to the head of the water board so many times that it was obvious he had a stalwart following among voters. Clark was 69 years old by this time and, thanks to the completion of Reservoirs No. 3 and No. 4, he would not go to an early grave worrying about supply problems, instead enjoying a relatively soft term. With the four reservoirs brimming in the spring, the city generally entered the hot months of the year sitting on a supply of more than a billion gallons of water. With that kind of storage, the ongoing drought was no longer the concern that it had been in the early 1870s.

Now the water works could get down to some nagging issues that had been let go for some time. The number of service connections in Hartford had risen to over 5,000 and, after twenty-eight years of operations, some of the earliest ones were failing, victims of rust and corrosion. In 1882, more than 100 of the original connections had to be replaced. In a way, this was a shock because, leakage aside, the earliest wooden log pipes very often lasted much longer than 28 years. However, as time went by, better and better materials were employed in the underground pipes and, eventually, cast iron pipes became so strong as to last more than a century.

More importantly, in the late 1870s, the water company had begun to install meters. The first meters were expensive but crude contrivances of such questionable reliability that the water company tested six different models on the first 148 businesses. Ninety-six of the units were homegrown, made by the Hartford Water Meter Company. All but two of the city's thirty livery stables were metered as were the biggest beer halls and manufactories. Clark added another 21 of the "Undine" units from the Hartford Meter Company in 1882, but that still left more than 4,800 connections unmetered. In these early years of the 1880s, even the relatively cheap meter made by the Hartford Meter Company was still uneconomical to install on residences but, in time, the situation improved and instead of installing about seventy-five meters a year on the largest customers, the number of annual installations increased dramatically.

Even as Ezra Clark set about streamlining the operations of the water works, the people of Hartford pursued their usual pastimes. Baseball had blossomed into a full-blown mania, with teams traveling widely for the chance to play. Before his four terms as mayor, Morgan Bulkeley served as president of the Hartford Dark Blues of the National Association and in 1876, when the National League was formed, he was elected unanimously as its first president. In the league's initial season, Bulkeley polished baseball's image by reducing gambling and drinking among the spectators and players alike. Ultimately, Bulkeley was forced to sell the team to William Cammeyer, owner of the New York Mutuals (Brooklyn).

At this time, the ball was pitched underhand but that changed to sidearm and then overhand in the 1880s. Baseball, for all of its supporters, did not capture the fancy of everyone though. Some subscribers wrote into the daily newspapers complaining about the space given the news of these athletic contests (there were no sports sections then). One reader complained, "I can't find anyone who isn't playing or talking 'base ball.' It may be an improvement on the old game of wicket—though I can't quite see it; and I suppose the next national game will be marbles." A less rigorous pastime was the board game of chess, which was also sweeping the country. Typically, newspapers gave the whole front page of the paper over to advertisers, but now illustrations of chessboards and discussions of gambits took up some of that valuable space.

As the city street department now employed steamrollers to pack down the dirt avenues, horses had one more reason to be discomfited. The number of incidents of horses bolting—damaging carriages and human cargo in the process—continued to mount. By far the biggest annoyances for the horses were the bicyclists who wondered about the streets in packs, causing many runaways and thrown passengers. Another concern for horse owners was the number of nails that were carelessly discarded in the streets. Horses died of lockjaw or were permanently maimed when these nails were run into their hooves. Horse thieves were common, very often stealing horses and wagons right out of the livery stables and selling them in New Haven or other distant cities. They were not the only crooks out and about. Hotel thieves plied their trade in the city's five largest hotels and countless smaller establishments. When the horse racing was in full swing at Charter Oak Park, the chief of police was forced to remind homeowners—

> . . . the races always bring to our city a crowd of roughs and others, and would call their especial attention to persons who may visit residences in Hartford this week on the pretense of selling small articles or begging for food or clothing.

Iceboxes were difficult to keep provisioned because of the hot weather and the ice companies typically ran out of product earlier in the season if the temperatures soared. For the table, both fish and game were plentiful. Two local men brought home 341 trout on a single day, while on another day, a food market displayed a sixty pound bass caught in the Connecticut River. As for wild game, the newspaper kept their readers abreast of conditions in the field—

> . . . This morning we noticed a handsome string of game in front of Langdon's general store on the corner of Park and Main Street. There were twenty-two gray squirrels, half a dozen partridge, a number of pigeons and other kinds of game.

Amusements at the American Theater, Robert's Opera House and Allyn's Theater changed little over the years, but other entertainments slowly crept into the mix. Hartford now had nine pool halls and two bowling alleys, and, in 1873, P.T. Barnum assembled his traveling circus, which visited Hartford thereafter as regularly as the seasons. Barnum loved to say that Hartford was a great circus town. His great traveling museum and menagerie annually grabbed people's attention—and their wallets—bringing young boys to the train station early in the morning to greet the animals as they disembarked and assembled for the raucous parade down Main Street. Billed as "100,000 rare, novel and interesting curiosities," Barnum's inimitable shows began, in the early 1870s, to make the annual trip from Bridgeport to Hartford, usually only the first stop on a long itinerary. Barnum mounted five shows in two days and cleared the spectacular sum of $10,800 in profit.

At Robert's Opera House, Buffalo Bill thrilled western enthusiasts with a play featuring his Indian company—and of course himself—re-enacting his scouting days on the prairies of the American West. His little play was a hit, but the showman did not get out of town cleanly. His mule kicked a little girl on Main Street and he had to pay $35 in doctor's bills.

The riverboats were doing a thriving business in the sweltering weather as overheated city dwellers booked excursions to New London, Sag Harbor, Coney Island, Block Island, Newport, Martha's Vineyard and Nantucket. The low water in the river continued to be a problem though as, sometimes, passengers had to disembark at towns downriver and take a smaller steamer, like the *Silver Star*, the rest of the way to Hartford.

For Ezra Clark and the water works, a seemingly insoluble problem—the poor quality drinking water—persisted in Hartford. As he reported to the council, the fishy-tasting water was caused along the distribution lines, not at the reservoirs. It was caused by the decomposition of vegetable matter in the mains. Flushing the mains took on an added importance as the drought refused to let up. In an effort to keep debris out of the pipes, Henry Ayers drained and cleaned one of the reservoirs each year. Repairs to dams, gatehouses and pipes were made while the catchments were empty.

In 1884, the water works completed a smaller reservoir (No. 5). It was designed as a catch-pond to collect water from Reservoirs No. 2 and No. 3, which would otherwise be lost during the spring runoff. It was capable of holding only 100 million gallons of water, but reduced waste in the whole system a great deal. Henry Ayres oversaw the grubbing of the new reservoir. Construction of this facility was completed in a relatively short period of time and at a cost significantly below that of the other reservoirs.

As the autumn leaves dropped throughout Hartford at the end of 1884, Ezra Clark and his water board had no indication that the long drought was about to end. On the drawing board was still another reservoir in the Talcott Mountain watershed, and residential and commercial construction in the city continued unabated. The growth in the number of residents of Hartford—then almost 48,000 strong—showed no signs of slowing and the water needs of the city's inhabitants grew relentlessly. However, on November 23, the Sunday before Thanksgiving the weather was cloudy and unsettled. The barometric pressure dropped all day long. By six o'clock, a sou'easter had descended on the city turning the sky a deep sepia color and stirring up vicious storm winds. Along with this combination of terrors, the clouds opened up and delivered a deluge of water that lasted for more than six hours. It was thought to be a simple rainstorm—welcome and sorely needed—but it was considerably more than that. This sou'easter was the harbinger of a more generous turn of the hydrologic cycle and it was the first of many abundant downpours as nature reverted to a period of plenty. Only after the city had met all of the demands of the relentless dry spell, and increased water storage to meet the most outsized needs, did nature yield. The drought of the 1870s was over.

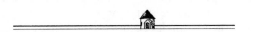

Chapter 7
Completion of the Trout Brook System

From the standpoint of inventions with the potential to change the way people live, the last decade and a half of the nineteenth century was one of the most important periods in American history. Electricity improved life in the manufactories as prosperous owners embraced the new technology for the increased production it would deliver. The average family still used kerosene lamps at home while their wealthier counterparts preferred gaslights, but brighter electric streetlights made Hartford a safer place for everyone. Along with this mysterious new form of energy came the telephone. By the mid-1880s, there were a great number of telephones in the city, revolutionizing the way people communicated with one another.

Hartford was a sophisticated city during the Victorian age, its stores boasting of almost every product and service extant and stood ready to meet the needs of a wide spectrum of customers from the country and the city alike. In addition to a large collection of haberdashers, milliners, dress shops and department stores, there were sixteen publishing houses, seventy boot & shoemakers, thirty blacksmiths, twenty private schools and a hundred and fifty saloons.

The dirt streets continued to create a dusty atmosphere even though steamrollers packed them down to a rock-hard surface and the city's street department watered them four times a day with horse-drawn tank wagons. The city's street crews, called "bluebirds"—because of the color of their uniforms— even hand-swept the main thoroughfares.

Children walked the railroad tracks to school rather than dirty their shoes in mud puddles or piles of manure. The horse cars shuttled people along the major avenues to work, doctor's appointments, shopping, or just visiting friends. It was these horse cars that were primarily responsible for Hartford's lofty perch as the last word in shopping excellence. Brown, Thomson & Co. and G. Fox & Co., sitting side by side on Main Street, battled it out for the retail dollar by catering to customers from all over the state. It was the ability of the horse cars to deliver shoppers from nearby towns that allowed Hartford stores to prosper mightily.

When the young German immigrant, Gershon Fox, began in the retail trade just before mid-century, he operated out of a seven- by nine-foot basement hole-in-the-wall at 126½ Main Street, selling silks, cravats, vests, and collars. With the steady flow of customers from greater Hartford arriving by horsecar and an awe-inspiring amount of raw energy on his part, within a few decades he was able to open a full department store. From his days as a marginal merchant, Fox learned that price was the single most important ingredient in the retail business and prided himself on his ability to offer goods at the cheapest price. As he upgraded the quality of the merchandise, his ever-growing department store— the mighty G. Fox & Co.—became the gold standard in style and elegance.

Not long after Gershon Fox began his retailing career in Hartford, a Scottish immigrant, James Thomson—together with two partners—opened Brown, Thomson & Co. Even at the beginning of his career, when his dry goods store took up only a portion of the first floor of the Cheney Brothers building on Main Street, Thomson was preoccupied with growth. His advertisements always trumpetted "The Big Store," and, sure enough, his lines quickly expanded until he was renting the whole, enormous first floor of the building. Thomson had no interest in Fox's preoccupation with cheap merchandise, instead focusing on the high end of the retail market. His store—"Hartford's Great Shopping Center"— favoring the most fashionable collection of goods money could buy. By the late 1800s, Brown, Thomson & Co. was the largest department store in Connecticut.

Goods arrived at these great stores mostly by railroad and, to a lesser degree, by steamship. The railroad was still the chief mover of freight, mail and passengers while the steamboats continued to haul cargo and passengers to and from coastal ports along the Eastern seaboard. The steamship business was, however, still constricted by its slow speed and the weather, the whole waterfront at Hartford closing down for the entire winter each year. In the 1880s, more than a hundred sea and river captains made their home in the city and 796 vessels visited Hartford's wharfs annually. A number of vessels, like the *Granite State* and the *City of Hartford*, continued to offer luxurious, but inexpensive, overnight accommodations to New York. First class fare was only $1.25.

In an effort to beautify the city, people took it upon themselves to enlarge the city's park system. Building on the work of Rev. Horace Bushnell, who lobbied for the large park in the center of town, Rev. Francis Goodwin began to assemble a ring of parks around the city. Salivating over the large landholdings of elderly industrialists, he was successful in persuading a few of them to leave their estates to the city as public parks. Perhaps, the most notable of these was Charles Pond's 106-acre Prospect Hill Farm, a gorgeous estate gifted to the city with one unwritten request—that the subsequent park be named after his late wife, Elizabeth.

Bicycles were still the rage with a new model emerging from Col. Pope's huge Capital Avenue plant every year—three wheelers for women, tandem bikes for couples and safety bikes with chain drive for the masses. Prices ranged from $75 to $225.

For young men, baseball was bigger than ever. By 1884, Mayor Morgan Bulkeley's Hartford Dark Blues who were actually a bunch of "ringers" recruited from Brooklyn, New York, were supplanted by the Hartford Orioles. Both teams played their games at a park next to Colt's Armory in the south meadows. It was during the 1880s that pitchers changed from underhand to sidearm and, finally, to overhand pitching. Because of the increased speed of the pitches, chest protectors for catchers—originally of the pneumatic variety— made their appearance. However, since baseball was a rough game then, played by tough men without the benefit of gloves, chest protectors never really caught on—at least not in the nineteenth century.

Twenty years after the guns went silent in the greatest conflict ever fought on American soil, Hartford completed the first Civil War memorial in the United States—the massive Soldiers and Sailors Memorial Arch in Bushnell Park. Drawn by the architect George Keller—brought over from Ireland by James G. Batterson, the president of Travelers Insurance Company—the stone and masonry work was contracted to Hiram Bissell. (A little known fact is that Keller was terrified of cemeteries and his ashes, along with those of his wife, are entombed in the eastern column of the arch.)

The Hartford Water Works was finding the last half of the 1880s an enjoyable time to be running a public utility. The great drought of the '70s and early '80s slowly became a distant memory and new concerns energized Ezra Clark and his water board. Clark frequently addressed the topic of metering water use, a subject that had been mentioned in almost every report of the commission since water first flowed into Hartford in 1855. However, at the end of Ezra Clark tenure in 1895, there were still only 464 water meters in the city.

The water meter discussions never seemed to end with the members of the water board, but with the price of the meters. Technology was on the side of the water department though, for the cost of meters was falling and water rents were rising. (The appropriate combination of these two elements did not materialize until just after the new century arrived.)

Homing in on the continuing waste, Ezra Clark wrote in one of his annual report—

> . . . The principal sources of waste (in addition to a large quantity wasted in cold weather to prevent pipes from freezing) are the livery stables, where hose[s] for washing are left running most of the day, beer saloons, where one or more faucets are kept constantly running . . . and through the 5,828 [water] closets in use, at least 3,000 of which are the hopper species . . . which are left running twenty-four hours per day. . . .

These forerunners of the modern day toilet were vexing for Clark and with good reason. During each twenty-four hour period, they wasted 10,000 gallons of water. Even at the residential rate, the water used in just one water closet was $2 a day. On a brighter note, by the late 1880's, all of the principal wastrels— except private households—had been metered. This included thirty-seven public stables, seventy manufactories and all the city's barrooms and beer saloons.

Up to this time, the total cost of the Hartford Water Works was $1.6 million and the upland reservoir system was working admirably. The one sour note was that the Connecticut River Pumping Station still had to be activated in November and December each year—for anywhere from a few days to six weeks. The engines and pumps had been completely overhauled for the second time and were as reliable as ever. For thirty-six years, since 1855, these pumps had been used to augment the Trout Brook supply and they had always responded to the call. Originally, they could lift only 2 million gallons a day. That was doubled after they were rebuilt by Hartford Foundry and Machine Company in 1873, and increased again to almost six million gallons-a-day in 1884.

The constant reversion to the Connecticut River Pumping Station irked the board because it gave the lie to the superiority of the whole upland reservoir system. How could the water works continue to brag about the waters of Trout Brook when they had to resort to contaminated river water at the end of each year? If they were not fooled by the caprice of nature, then they were blindsided by the ever-expanding population of the city, now fast approaching 50,000 souls.

The only answer to the supply problem was to do what they knew best—build another reservoir. As early as 1890, Ezra Clark began looking for a suitable site to excavate still another basin near Trout Brook. Just as he undertook his search, the nasty side of the hydrologic cycle re-emerged and total precipitation for the early 1890s dropped alarmingly. Even with the existing five reservoirs, the Connecticut River Pumping Station was pressed into service more than normal over the next few years.

This new catchment would be the final one in the shadow of Talcott Mountain because no river system can be tapped forever. For such a small watershed, it was really something just this side of miraculous that the board was able to impound the quantities of water they did. When planning this final reservoir, Clark turned to yet another tributary of Trout Brook. It was a robust stream, running into West Hartford from Bloomfield, its neighbor to the north. The Tumbledown Brook Reservoir would impound a billion gallons of water. Since the five existing basins collectively held a billion gallons, the new facility would double the supply.

In 1892, repeating a now familiar cycle, the five Trout Brook reservoirs were filled to overflowing in the spring, but by Halloween, Clark was back at the Connecticut River, pumping water up into the old Lord's Hill Reservoir. Only when a series of drenching rainstorms recharged the reservoirs just before Thanksgiving was he able to idle the pumps once more.

That same year, there were 200 men and sixty horses guiding scoops through the rocky soil of West Hartford and Bloomfield, grubbing out a fantastic hole in the ground at the future site of the Tumbledown Brook Reservoir. To speed up the work, in the spring of 1893 the workforce was increased to 500 men and 160 horses. In spite of the added men and horseflesh, the work continued at a snail's pace. The following spring, the men were back at the huge cavity, making their endless back-and-forth passes with cumbersome wooden scoops for another season until finally, in October of 1895, it was completed. To the uninitiated, the time spent grubbing out the Tumbledown Brook Reservoir seems interminable, but it is important to remember that, since Reservoir No. 1 was first dug at the end of the Civil War, excavating equipment for this type of work had not improved at all. Employing the same methods used at Reservoir No. 1 meant that it took more than five million passes with horses and scoops through the growing crater to complete the job. Obviously, it was not a project for the impatient.

When the last reservoir in West Hartford was coming on line, life in Hartford became both more crowded and more hurried. Even while the number and variety of amusements increased, factory workers still worked long hours six days a week. But from the lowest of the workers to the hard-driven superintendents of the city's huge manufactories, Sunday was the day of rest. Merchants shuttered their stores and everything was closed except Houses of Worship, the Wadsworth Atheneum and the Hartford Public Library, which was organized when the Hartford Library Association— housed at the Atheneum— opened to the public.

Sunday was a day for quiet family pastimes and, very often in good weather, it called for a drive in the country. Toward this end, Ezra Clark envisioned a beautiful bridle path through the maze of reservoirs on the water works' West Hartford property. Far more than a series of simple winding roads through a collection of amorphous basins, it was a fabulous parkland with exotic trees and shrubs for the public to enjoy. Clark completed work on his beatific dream just before he retired from the water board in 1895.

Making these drives through the West Hartford reservoirs even more enjoyable, modes of transportation took a series of lunges forward. The last horsecar was retired from service in 1895, turning the trolley system into an all-electric line, complete with an implausible grid of overhead wires and—wonder of wonders—heaters in the cars. That same year, Hiram Maxim, an engineer at Pope's Manufacturing Company, ran a gasoline car along Park Street. Col. Pope's interest, however, lay more with the electric car because of a proposition made to him by a group of New York businessmen, headed by William Whitney. The New Yorkers joined forces with Col. Pope's Hartford manufactory to build electrically propelled cabs for Manhattan. Unhappily for the consortium, no sooner were they up and running but an obstacle emerged.

The snag was a patent on the automobile held by a Rochester attorney, George Seldon. After protracted negotiations, Selden agreed to license the patent to their newly formed firm, The Colombia and Electric Vehicle Company. Shortly thereafter, royalties poured into the coffers of Columbia with forty percent of the proceeds going to a new entity, the Association of Licensed Automobile Manufacturers. Selden received a lump sum of $10,000 and twenty percent of the proceeds. It was claimed that this netted him more than $200,000 over the next eight years.

A year later, and quite apart from his venture with the New Yorkers, Pope added gasoline models, including a four-wheel vehicle with a two cylinder air-cooled gas engine that was able to go from Hartford to Boston, with repeated stops for spooked horses and impassable roads. Year by year, Pope expanded his offerings to the public, including the Pope-Waverly Electric, the low-priced Pope-Tribune and the luxurious and powerful Pope-Hartford, cherished for its speed, ruggedness and reliability.

When Henry Ford balked at paying royalties to Columbia, a prolonged legal battle ensued. A decade later, in an appeals court, Ford emerged victorious. By then, Col. Pope was dead and, despite the quality of his firm's cars, sales nosedived. When the last Pope-Hartford automobile left the plant on Capitol Avenue in 1915, Hartford's future as a great auto-manufacturing center dissolved.

Ezra Clark's final report to the common council summed up the status of the Hartford Water Works succinctly. He noted that, by the close of business in March 1895, the water works had cost the City of Hartford $2.4 million. This included The Connecticut River Pumping Station, the Lord's Hill Reservoir, over ninety-two miles of mains and the six reservoirs of the Trout Brook system. Collectively the water works was sitting on 2 billion gallons of water, amounting to a year's supply (with no supplement from snowmelt or rainstorms).

He further emphasized that, such a huge quantity of water ensured that the city should not ever have to resort to the waters of the Connecticut River again, a source that each year was contaminated more by the filth of growing communities farther upstream. However, he cautioned—

> . . . The purity of the water supply is even more important than its amount and, . . . to protect our watershed . . . [Hartford should] purchase large areas of land . . . .

After stepping down from the water board at the end of his term in March 1895, Ezra Clark checked out of the United States Hotel in City Hall Square (which was demolished a year later) and then went to live with his son on Prospect Street. Charles Hopkins Clark's first wife, Ellen—who was the daughter of Elisha Root—had died the year before. Ezra Clark's daughter, Fanny, lived with her husband and children only a few doors away. Fanny was an eccentric, obsessed with fires, and when the alarm rang, she frequently beat the fire engines to the blaze. In spite of this fairly common obsession, she was a dutiful daughter and checked in on her father regularly.

Unfathomably, the man who succeeded Ezra Clark as the president of the water board was the man who almost single-handedly thrust Hartford into the worst water famine imaginable in 1873—John Hunter. This must have galled Clark who spent eighteen months listening to Hunter's excuses, unable to exact a performance from the man or his company, Hartford Foundry. But Hunter had been elected as a water commissioner in 1894, sitting on the six-man board throughout the year—Clark's last in office—and was appointed to the top job by the council. The outgoing president's advice was not sought.

Ezra Clark continued to live with his son on Prospect Street and was frequently seen walking about town during the next year. Then in the early fall of 1896, after a brief bout with "cystitis," he passed away at four o'clock in the morning on Saturday, September 26. He was eighty-three years old.

**

In the fourteen years following the death of Ezra Clark—from 1896 until 1910—Hartford's water department, for the first time, enjoyed a period of relative unconcern over supply. Despite Ezra Clark's cautionary comments in his final report to the common council, the two billion gallons of water stored in the six reservoirs of the Talcott Mountain watershed remained pure, and offered the illusion of inexhaustible reserves. As a result, Hartford's inhabitants continued in their wasteful ways.

Nevertheless, some small progress was made when, as the streets were paved, the amount of water used by the city to damp the dust plummeted. State Street was paved in 1895 and, a year later, the street department tackled Main Street. New macadam surfaces made an enormous difference in the cleanliness of the city. Clouds of dust had been a mainstay for two and a half centuries and now people could walk about the city in all weather without concern for their clothing. Asphalt created such a clean, smooth surface for wagons and automobiles alike, that in just a few years, the first speed limits had to be enacted.

In the last years of the nineteenth century, people seeking to fill their free time with a bit of fun were deluged with a steady stream of new venues and concepts. While a group of entrepreneurs built a "casino" on Sigourney Street, featuring bowling alleys and rooms for billiards, smoking, reading and music, the Parson's Theater opened up in the southeast corner of City Hall Square. This theater featured the complete gamut of stage acts from magicians to plays, music to lectures. The Hartford Opera House went Parson's one better by offering their usual highbrow entertainments plus—on slower nights—the Metropolitan Burlesque Company, featuring comedians and "twelve of the handsomest women to be found among the chorus girls of New York."

Perhaps the greatest amusement of all—judging by audience size—were the horse races at Charter Oak Park, just over the line in the Parkville section of West Hartford. (This horse racing track was so far removed from the center of West Hartford that a special act of the legislature mandated that the grounds be patrolled by Hartford's police department.) On race days, sometimes 5,000 people rode the Park Street trolley out to Charter Oak Park to enjoy the harness racing. In the 1890s, the premier event in all of harness racing—the "Charter Oak"—offered the munificent reward of $10,000 and a cup valued at $500.

Although some young men headed for Alaska when the word "Klondike" was first uttered, most were content to stay behind and continue making money in the manner of their forebears. Insurance companies added new lines of auto and health insurance, generally not missing a trick when it came to the business of personal protection. As larger and larger commercial buildings sprung up and new streets opened up each year for more upscale private homes, banks prospered.

Women and children drank "Moxie Nerve Food," sold in bottles at the grocers and by the glass at drugstores. Most men drank beer in saloons and smoked cigars, as national consumption of the dark stogies climbed to almost twelve million a day.

By 1898, Hartford's 80,000 inhabitants consumed 28,000 quarts of milk per day, all supplied by local dairies. When the automobiles sputtered onto the scene just before the turn of the century, dairymen shunned the noisy contraptions, preferring to make their pre-dawn deliveries of milk and cream using the time-honored—and quieter—horse and wagon.

In 1899, Francis "Frank" Goodwin managed to talk his first cousin, J. P. Morgan, into donating $150,000 to the Wadsworth Atheneum. This was only the first of many bequests by the well-known financier, who later gave more money to the Atheneum for a memorial to his father, Junius. After the dedication of the Morgan wing a decade later, James Goodwin threw a lavish luncheon for Morgan at his sprawling estate on Woodland Street. Though happy to be back in his hometown, Morgan did register a complaint about the slums along the Park (Little) River, which were an eyesore so close to the new monument to his father. Quietly over the next few months, the financier bought the tenements, tore them down and donated the land to the city. (Hartford's Municipal Building sits on some of this land today.)

Meetings of the common council were still held on Monday evenings and politics was still as lively as ever. Members addressed matters related to the streets, the fire department, hack stands, city liens, the cemeteries, charities and a host of other issues, but news of the water department was conspicuously absent. The water works had become such a huge and complex affair that its internal affairs were left to the water committee. Generally speaking, its business was no longer discussed among members of the entire council. Only a decade before, newspapers kept a daily tally of the water in the reservoirs in West Hartford. Now, the business of the water department seldom appeared in print with the exception of the occasional three-line advertisement informing the public that the water would be turned off in a certain section of the city for repairs of the mains. Strangely enough, the water works—once the all-consuming obsession of every businessman and property owner in the city—now slipped from sight.

In the decade and a half after the death of Ezra Clark, the water board had five different presidents—John Hunter, the foundry owner; George Fairfield, the manufacturing magnate; Edward H. Judd, a wool merchant; Joseph H. Birmingham, a businessman; and Henry Roberts, a former Connecticut governor. They served, from one to five years, during a period of abundant water supplies and a generally pleasant phase of the hydrologic cycle. In short, when weighed against the tenures of Hiram Bissell and Ezra Clark, they had it easy.

The Hartford Water Works' six reservoirs in West Hartford were all connected to one another and flowed finally into the original Reservoir No. 1, which acted as a distribution hub. Fortunately for the residents of Hartford, the water contained within these six reservoirs was enough to supply the city for the next twenty-seven years. The single biggest reason why the Trout Brook system was able to supply the city for so long was the lowly water meter. With the addition of the Tumbledown Brook Reservoir, the cost of meters had finally fallen to the point where universal metering was practicable. From a modest 464 meters in 1895, the water works installed thousands of the devices over the next few years, completing the project in 1902.

The combination of the new supplies and, more importantly, universal metering, created an almost inexhaustible surplus for the first time in memory. As rising water bills taught customers to curb their usage, consumption fell almost a million gallons a day. This was extraordinary considering that the biggest wastrels, the manufactories, livery stables, and beer halls, had been metered two decades before. This huge reduction in demand bought the water commissioners precious time before new stores were required.

Realizing full well that eventually they would have to secure a new watershed for the residents of Hartford, the men at the head of the water works did what all commissioners do—they began scouting the countryside for the next reserve for the city. As early as 1897, the board approached the state legislature with the idea of impounding the waters of Salmon Brook in Granby, a small farming town about ten miles north of Hartford. The legislature was receptive to this idea but imposed a set of conditions that were extreme. To begin, they insisted that the people of the Town of Granby be supplied with drinking water under the same terms that the people of West Hartford. That meant, of course, that the people of Granby would actually receive their water under the same conditions as the people of Hartford. This stricture alone would cost the city dearly if they chose to take Salmon Brook.

It got worse. Very much in keeping with the New York law that forced the city to supply everyone in the area of their reservoirs and aqueducts with drinking water, the General Assembly insisted that Hartford supply water to all inhabitants within a half-mile of the aqueduct—no matter what town they lived in. The cost suddenly got prohibitive.

It got worse still. In a final section of the resolution, the legislature specified the exact section of Salmon Brook that could be impounded and, added that, *"...no authority is hereby given to take water from the Farmington River or any of the ponds and streams tributary thereto..."* In one quick session, the legislature had made the water board's interest in Granby completely unappetizing and forbade it from impounding any section of the Farmington River. This was a huge setback.

The final section of this disastrous bill was, of course, the handiwork of the mill owners on the Farmington River, who depended on waterpower to run their manufactories. Any attempts to interfere with the flow of the Farmington would be contested bitterly. For the water board, this resolution by the General Assembly was completely unworkable and, distracted by an unexpectedly large amount of rain at the turn of the century, the water commissioners shelved the Salmon Brook project—for what turned out to be forever.

As contradictory as it may sound, once the legislature forbade the water works from taking the waters of the Farmington, naturally that body of water emerged as the most attractive of all the options available. The logic is less complicated than it sounds because, if the right section of the Farmington was taken, the aqueduct would run right through West Hartford where the water works was already supplying the inhabitants. That left only a sparsely populated area to the west of the neighboring town with which to deal. From that standpoint, the Farmington River was an ideal choice.

Oddly enough, when Hartford had studied supply options before construction of the original water system was even begun, their choices had come down to three—the Connecticut River, Trout Brook or the Farmington River, farther to the west. In the space of about a half-century, the water company had used the first source until it became too contaminated, had exploited the second to the point of exhaustion and now were eyeballing the last one covetously.

The Farmington was an eighty-mile long tributary of the Connecticut river, whose headwaters were at Mount Becket in the Berkshire Hills of western Massachusetts. In the nineteenth century, the waters of the Farmington powered hundreds of machines in small manufacturing towns along its banks as it snaked it way southeasterly toward the Connecticut River. Large and small businesses like Sawyer's Cotton Mill in Colebrook River, Lambert Hitchcock's Chair Factory at Hitchcocksville, the Union Hardware Co. in Unionville and the Collins Axe Company at Collinsville relied on the waterpower of the Farmington River to run their manufactories. Collectively these communities employed the largest workforce in the state during the nineteenth century. In fact, Connecticut had 200 of these manufacturing settlements before steam power brought men and machines together in the cities.

By 1907, thanks to the great centralization of manufacturing, which supplanted—for the most part—these industrial hamlets, the population of Hartford was closing in fast on the 100,000 mark. It seemed almost incomprehensible that only sixty years before a tiny collection of people—18,000 to be more precise—lived in an unhurried manner in this same city with oil lamps for streetlights, no plumbing of any kind and power sources like horses, mules and oxen. It was a miracle they survived at all.

A resident from just a half-century ago would not recognize the city in the first decade of the twentieth century. With the gas company using every bit of political muscle it could muster against it, the Hartford Electric Light Company won the contract to convert all of the streetlights to this mysterious new power source. By 1888, more than a thousand streetlights were converted from the Welsbach gas mantle to the new Nernst electric filament. Electric lights were retrofitted into older buildings and added routinely to new construction as people embraced this invisible wonder. Telephones were everywhere, albeit mostly party lines, where a maddening number of families shared the same wire.

In addition to the streetlights, the roads themselves underwent an extraordinary overhaul. Of the 130 miles of streets within the city, fully 108 were either "macadamized or paved with block or sheet asphalt." The water company's pipes—and the city's sewers—still ran beneath these streets but no longer alone. Joining them, and congesting the area under the small roads now, were the pipes and wires of the gas, transit, telephone and electric companies. Believed by all to be uncharted territory, it was unclear if so many different conduits could peacefully coexist.

This congestion of power lines led to a heretofore-unknown phenomenon—electrolysis. The word began to appear in the annual reports of the water board at the end of the nineteenth century. The word was used, in a vague way, to describe a condition that might be the beginning of serious problems or might be nothing at all. The Hartford Electric Light Company had sheaths of cables running under the streets, as did the Electric Railway Lines and the telephone company. At engineering conferences across the country, great discussions ensued regarding the damage that stray current could do to a water company's pipes. However, no one understood the phenomenon fully and, at least in Hartford, the whole issue unfortunately wound up on a back burner for many years. As a result, lengths of pipe in some sections of the city were eaten away by the stray current while the issue was first ignored and then studied to death.

The different commissioners of the water department ran the day-to-day activities in an efficient manner but, to a man, put off the difficult decision of the new supply for as long as they could. Finally, convinced that they could change the minds of the state's elected officials, they ignored the old prohibitions against taking the waters of the Farmington River and began to scout its many tributaries. Like a man holding a divining rod, they were drawn to a particularly promising area of the watershed—the Nepaug River. With gravity as an ally, this stream could deliver the finest quality of water at the cheapest cost. Western Connecticut was sparsely populated, which ensured that the water would be free of contaminants. Thanks to gravity, Mother Nature would dump an enormous supply at their feet with but one new aqueduct—though it would have to be bored through the base of Talcott Mountain.

In early 1908, the water board hired an engineer, Allen Hazen of New York, to investigate the many branches of the Farmington. As the leaves returned to the trees of western Connecticut, Hazen, along with members of the water board, visited seven streams above the Town of Unionville. Soon thereafter, Hazen completed a preliminary report, indicating that three of the streams held great promise—the East Branch of the Farmington River, the Nepaug River and Phelps Brook. In his final report though, the sites that Hazen singled out for special attention were the Nepaug River and Phelps Brook.

Though undoubtedly happy to have Hazen's report in hand, the water commissioners were still not anxious to begin the design work necessary to impound the waters of the Farmington River. This was understandable because any project on the Nepaug River promised to be complex. Even after a decision was made as to which waters would be impounded, the on-site survey work, engineering drawings and actual construction would clearly take the better part of a decade. A meatier matter was that any attempt to secure the waters of the Farmington would take a special act of the General Assembly. With the reception that the board received when they had attempted to take Salmon Brook in Granby, a return trip to the capital was filled with a sense of doom.

In the interim, another completely different source was explored— groundwater. Very little was known about aquifers in 1909, but these mysterious underground reservoirs might have been Hartford's salvation. Accordingly, the water works began a series of test borings to explore for a groundwater source. These experiments had all the geological uncertainty of "wildcatting" for oil in Texas. In the final analysis, the digging crews at the water company were reduced to gut feelings and speculation, as they bored test holes willy-nilly around the city. Was it possible that central Connecticut sat atop a limitless aquifer?

Possibly. Groundwater is the most important source of water in the United States. It accounts for 40 percent of all public water supplies, 53 percent of all of the drinking water for the total population and 97 percent of the drinking water for the rural population. Throughout the world, it is the largest reserve of potable water located where humans actually live. It is estimated that about half of all the water needs of the United States come from groundwater sources. This is especially true when one considers the massive irrigation needs of the farms in the heartland of America that are met almost entirely by wellfields.

Some states sit atop huge aquifers, other states do not. While it is possible to drill a well almost anywhere in the United States and find a source that will produce 50 gallons per hour, it is an altogether different proposition to assemble a wellfield that will deliver 50 million gallons per day. But just exactly what was the case in the Connecticut River valley?

For the Hartford Water Works, there was, alas, only one way to find out whether or not they were sitting atop a bountiful aquifer. Sending teams into the field to drill test wells, they soon had their answer. A total of eighteen wells were drilled in the area of the Connecticut River—with some of them actually punched into a sandbar in the middle of the river just north of the old pumping station. They ranged in depth from about five to fifty feet, with the best results coming from the wells that were fifteen feet deep. However, the most water that any of the wells could deliver was forty-five gallons a minute, which was woefully short of the city's needs.

Early well-drillers for the Hartford Water Works circa 1910.

The constant worry about supply in the first forty years of the water works' history obscured a far more fundamental concern—reservoir failure. The prolonged drought of the 1870s had imprinted on the collective brain of the water board a permanent fear of a water famine. As has been mentioned before, the water commissioners wanted desperately to bid *adieu* to the Connecticut River Pumping Station, but for no other reason than simple insurance, they could not. As if pouring salt in a wound, they had to lay out huge sums of money to keep the aging facility in tiptop condition. Two Worthington pumps, which had been purchased at the turn of the century but never used, were now installed permanently and the whole intake pier in the river was completely rebuilt. A consulting chemist had also been retained to advise on the treatment of the water should the city be forced to use it. Making the water clear was out of the question, but eliminating harmful bacteria was not. The Connecticut River water had deteriorated so much by that time, it was hoped that by adding bleaching powder, it might still be a viable back up source. The board stated—

> . . . bleaching powder . . . Within two or three years this chemical has come into prominence as a germicide in the purification of water . .

. experiments showed that when one part per million of available chlorine was used, the removal of bacteria was always greater than 99.5% . . . .

Actually, chlorine had a much longer history than the members of the water board indicated in their report of 1910. Typhoid fever epidemics had become so deadly in Louisville, Kentucky that the city was roundly called the "Graveyard of the West." In desperation, they began to treat their drinking water, which came from the Ohio River, in 1896. In the years following the first experiments with chlorine, many cities began to use it in their water, most notably Chicago, Cleveland and Cincinnati, all around 1911. Hartford began universal chlorination of its water in 1913. It should be noted though that some cities did nothing to their water until much later. Portland, Oregon, for example, did not chlorinate until 1929.

Discussion among the water commissioners about chlorinating the repulsive Connecticut River water highlighted an obvious truth—the time to do something about an additional water supply was upon them. Therefore in 1909, a proposal was introduced at the General Assembly for the authority to develop the watershed surrounding the Nepaug River. This tributary of the Farmington wandered gently for about ten miles between the rolling hills of western Connecticut until it joined up with the main branch of the river just above Collinsville. At this point, its waters were just fifteen miles from Hartford.

The sticking point, and the reason that the bill was defeated, was that such a move would markedly reduce the flow of water in the Farmington River. The water board's proposal would obviously trample on the riparian rights of the downstream mill owners. Until some kind of a solution was found that addressed these riparian rights, all such resolutions would be dead on arrival at the capital.

The board approached the General Assembly again in 1910 submitting much the same bill except that this time the project included a dam and reservoir on the East Branch of the Farmington, which was called a "compensating reservoir." In addition to damming the Nepaug River to create a huge reservoir for drinking water, this extra reservoir on the East Branch of the Farmington would give the water department almost complete control of the flow down the river. While constructing the three dams necessary to impound the Nepaug River, the waters of the East Branch of the Farmington would be slowly held up as well. This new basin, located principally in the Town of Barkhamsted, would catch the snowmelt that ordinarily was lost, and could be used at any time to augment the supply of water along the river. This insured that the riparian rights of the downstream owners would not be violated. It was a fairly simple idea—at least on paper—but still the bill died on the floor of the legislature. At the last minute, it dawned on the elected officials of other nearby towns that by building the

Nepaug Reservoir, Hartford would be encroaching on a valuable watershed that was partially in their towns.

To sum up, there were three major obstacles to the Nepaug Project. First, and most problematic, the damming of the Nepaug River would inevitably violate the riparian rights of the mill owners and farmers along the Farmington River. Secondly, a reservoir that contained such a large watershed would, in point of fact, be stealing water from other cities and towns. Lastly, it would require three dams to impound a large enough body of water to make it worthwhile, not to mention a fourth dam at the compensating reservoir on the East Branch of the Farmington River.

The complexities of the three sticking points took time to resolve. Addressing the problems in the order presented, item one was infinitely the most complex because, taken as a whole, the factory owners along the Farmington River were a force to be reckoned with. They were all familiar with the legalities involved and every one of them could count a number of politicians among his friends. Beyond that, they were seasoned businessmen and any promises made to them would have to be ironclad. The principal of the "compensating reservoir" sounded fine, but they would need assurances. After months of education and persuasion, the mill owners finally acquiesced.

The second item was easier to address. By simply forging an alliance with the municipalities who would be losing water as a result of the project, the principals of the affected towns signed on. The biggest of these towns was New Britain, a manufacturing city, whose largest employer was Stanley Tool Company. By promising them access to the water, at the same rates being charged Hartford residents, that particular problem was solved.

Once the twin problems of compensating the downstream mill owners and pacifying the nearby towns were settled, that left only the enormity of the project. With the aforementioned solutions spelled out in excruciating detail, the bill finally passed the legislature in 1911 and allowed for the building of the Nepaug Dam and Reservoir in the towns of Canton, Burlington, and New Hartford with a compensating reservoir in Barkhamsted.

The third problem was of a slightly different nature—an internal matter for the water company, one might say. The concept of the compensating reservoir solved all of the problems with the mill owners quite nicely, except that it created a new one of its own. At the very inception of the Nepaug Project, it was accepted by everyone that three dams would have to be built at the site of the new reservoir to plug the missing pieces of the saddle of the catchment. Now, in order to satisfy the rights of the riparian owners, a fourth dam had been added at the "compensating reservoir." Up to this point, the Hartford Water Works had built only squat earthen dams on small bodies of water and one of those had breached in 1867 during an unusually heavy rainstorm. The Hartford Water Works' experience with dams—even viewed in the most charitable light—was spotty. In order to impound the waters of the Nepaug River, they needed the services of a professional engineer.

More to the point, they needed a dam expert. Perhaps it would be even more succinct to say that they needed a hydraulic engineer with a wealth of experience in the construction and maintenance of dams. Moreover, since the dams would be impounding huge bodies of water with almost incalculable effects on the areas surrounding them, they would need a man who also had a considerable knowledge of two relatively new water sciences—hydrography and hydrology.

In hindsight, the water works was blessed with men who were, at the very least, able guardians and, at the most, true geniuses of incalculable industry and foresight. Hiram Bissell and Ezra Clark were straightforward men dealing with rudimentary problems the best way they knew how. Still, for all of their diligence and hard work, men like Bissell and Clark, along with the thousands of supporting characters in the unfolding drama of the water system at Hartford, were not highly educated men. Unfortunately, due to the escalating technical intricacies of these systems, common men at the helm of water departments had become an anachronism. More complex every year, the water works was constantly buffeted by the advance of new technologies and the need for scientific understanding that men like Bissell and Clark did not possess. Water companies across the United States increasingly turned to highly educated professional engineers to manage their affairs, and this was now the case for the water works at Hartford. The time for amateurs, despite the best of intentions, was over.

Chapter 8
The Nepaug Dam & Reservoir

If ever there was a case of the right man being in the right place at the right time, it was the appearance of Caleb Mills Saville at the offices of the Board of Water Commissioners at Hartford in 1911. He was a forty-six-year-old engineer, who had graduated *cum laude* from Harvard College in 1889. After earning his B. A., he continued with postgraduate work at the Lawrence Scientific School (now affiliated with Harvard), was employed by the Boston Water Works and spent the last five years working for the Isthmian Canal Commission in Panama. His job on the canal? Engineering work connected with the Gatun Dam—one of the largest in the world. Additionally, he did hydrographic work connected with the canal's water supply. Made to order? Wait, it gets better.

Caleb Mills Saville

Before leaving for the Canal Zone in 1906, Saville had worked for the Metropolitan Water District in Boston for twelve years under two of the most widely respected hydraulic engineers in the country. The first man was Frederic P. Stearns, chief engineer for the district. The second engineer was Stearns's right hand man and a member of the water board, John R. Freeman. Stearns had been president of the American Society of Civil Engineers in 1906 and Freeman would assume the same role in 1922. Beyond their duties in Boston, both were hired to do consulting work for the Isthmian Canal Commission in Panama. It was on the basis of Stearns's report that President Theodore Roosevelt approved the "lock canal" against the strong objections of the other consulting engineers who proposed a sea level canal.

Moreover, it was during Saville's time in Boston, under the watchful eye of Frederic Stearns, that the Wachusett Reservoir was built. This project impounded the waters of the Nashua River above the town of Clinton. Designed as a rubble masonry structure (large chunks of aggregate in the mix), the Wachusett Dam was a quarter of a mile long at the spillway and 185 feet high, requiring over a quarter of a million cubic yards of concrete. It created a reservoir, which had a surface area that was staggering—six and a half square miles, sprawling into the towns of Sterling, Clinton, Boylston and East Boylston. Its spillway was 365 feet above sea level, an important consideration since the original idea was to pipe water into Boston by gravity alone. The water from the Wachusett Reservoir was so pure that it required no filtration of any kind.

Begun in 1897, the project was completed in 1905 when the filling of the reservoir began. This was the devilish part of any reservoir project, because most of the water in the river had to be allowed to flow downstream while enough was kept back to allow the valley to fill up. Depending on the amount of rainfall and the overall temperature and wind conditions (which taken together control evaporation), even a small reservoir—say, 20 billion gallons—could take as much as a half-decade to fill. The Wachusett Reservoir held over 65 billion gallons.

Naturally enough, there probably isn't a more frustrating experience than watching a reservoir's water level slowly rise. It is little wonder that after the completion of the Wachusett project, Saville asked Stearns and Freeman to recommend him for a post with the Isthmian Canal Commission. The prospect of sitting around watching a reservoir fill up with water could not possibly have been appealing to Caleb Saville. Any highly educated hydraulic engineer would have been anxious for a new challenge and he was no different. Besides, the magnitude of the Panama Canal must have given every talented engineer in America "itchy feet." It was the largest engineering project in the world at the time and riddled with the kinds of problems that truly great engineers hunger for.

A brief description of the canal and its fascinating lock systems is instructive in understanding the importance of the work that the 3rd Division of the Office of the Chief Engineer did under Saville's command. Even a cursory study of the canal leads one to the inescapable conclusion that the single most important asset in the functioning of the canal is Gatun Dam.

By damming the Chagres River, thereby creating one of the largest man-made lakes in the world, two things were accomplished. First, a shipping lane almost halfway across the Isthmus was created. Second, and far more important, was the impounded water itself, which was used in the locks. By allowing the water to flow into the Gatun Locks, ships were raised the eighty-five feet necessary to transverse the nine-mile long Culebra Cut through the Continental Divide. Without any pumps at all, the water from Gatun Lake simply gushed through the huge conduits into the locks, thereby magically raising the ships. The lake, of course, would be depleted in short order if it were not for the rain forests, which surround the canal. Rainwater draining out of the forests into the lake, replenished the water that was lost as vessels descended the eighty-five feet to sea level through the two southernmost locks (Pedro Miguel and Miraflores).

In effect, the engineers working on the canal conceived and constructed their own eco-system. It took an almost incalculable amount of data and study to determine that all of the parts of the canal would work in harmony once the project was completed.

Two relatively new sciences were employed in the complex calculations of the water supply for the canal. The first discipline was the study of rivers and their flows—hydrography. The second science, hydrology, was the study of the properties, distribution and circulation of water on the surface of the land, in the soil, the underlying rocks and in the atmosphere. A thorough understanding of these twin sciences would be essential to the success of the Panama Canal. When Saville left for the canal, his wife, Elizabeth, accompanied him. The Saville's fourteen-year-old son, Thorndike, remained in Malden with Elizabeth's sister, Anna, and joined his parents during his summer vacations.

By August 1907, when the Saville's arrived on the Isthmus, the *Stegomyia fasciata* mosquitoes carrying the yellow fever virus and the *Anopheles* mosquitoes, whose bite introduced the parasite that caused malaria, had been eradicated. Furthermore, due to the efforts of the well-liked chief engineer, John Stevens, living conditions had become rather comfortable.

Saville's salary was about $350 a month, which was slightly more than he would have been making in the states. Housing and medical benefits were free and he got forty-two paid vacation days annually. In addition to this, he was allowed thirty sick days a year—with pay. Meals cost half of what they did in Boston and the engineers enjoyed a lifestyle significantly more luxurious than the Caribbean blacks who did the actual digging. For the upper echelon workers, there was bowling, billiards, books, magazines, chess along with other board games and a gymnasium. For a paltry $10 a year, a man could join one of the Y.M.C.A. clubhouses. In the town of Culebra, a young couple could have a nice meal, go to a dance or even catch a silent movie at the cinema. By all accounts, Caleb Saville's time spent on the Isthmus was enjoyable, stimulating and rewarding.

Only six months before the Savilles arrived on the Isthmus, the whole company was shocked beyond belief when it was learned in January 1907 that John Stevens had abruptly resigned. There must have been a considerable amount of anxiety as the engineers tried to continue their work amidst the uncertainty. Speculation ran rampant as to the reason for his unexpected departure from the Isthmus. It is generally accepted now that he was simply overworked and broke down from exhaustion. For the workers left behind, however, the question of the hour was—who would take the popular man's place?

Regardless of the reason for Stevens' departure, President Theodore Roosevelt had a problem. If one counted the French efforts in the Canal Zone toward the end of the nineteenth century, Stevens was just the latest in a procession of capable men to abandon the task. In typical Teddy Roosevelt fashion, he handled the problem in a most unique way. He replaced John Stevens with a man who couldn't quit. By assigning the job to Col. George Washington Goethals, a career army officer—who was the man under which Saville actually worked during his time on the Isthmus—the work continued.

Once all of the engineering work was done, the nine-mile long Culebra Cut remained the only obstacle to a functioning canal. It would take seven long years to blast through "the Cut." Day after day, men drilled 100-foot deep holes into the sidewalls of the canal, filled them with dynamite, and exploded away sections of earth at Culebra. It was extremely dangerous work with premature explosions killing men almost daily. Watching workmen get blown to bits trying to plant charges in the walls of "the Cut," must have been infinitely less agreeable to Saville than sitting on his hands watching the waters rise in the Wachusett Reservoir in Boston.

Herein lay one of the great paradoxes of hydraulic engineering work. While the great bulk of the work was done before a construction crew even arrived on site, engineers were usually required to remain on the job and oversee the building process, which must have been pure boredom for them. Quite obviously in their minds, they had not studied engineering in order to be construction managers. So could anyone blame an ambitious man for looking elsewhere once his principal assignment was completed?

Caleb and Elizabeth Saville's son, Thorndike, was in his sophomore year at Harvard studying engineering, and with the engineering work completed on the canal, it was probably a good time to think about pulling up stakes. The years in the Canal Zone could not have been particularly pleasant for Elizabeth Saville. While Caleb put in long days, completely absorbed with the fascinating work of such a huge enterprise, she was left at home with little to do. She would have had to have been less than human not to be homesick for New England, her son, and the affluent, upper-class life that she had known in Massachusetts.

All of Caleb Saville's life, he kept a running correspondence with selected engineering colleagues around the country and, at first blush, it would be a reasonable assumption that he heard about the job at Hartford either from Frederic Stearns or John Freeman. But such was not the case.

The man responsible for bringing Saville to Hartford was John Dower, the president of the Board of Water Commissioners in 1911. Dower was an even-tempered, forty-four-year-old bachelor, who was originally from Massachusetts. Educated in Worcester schools, he came to Hartford with his parents as a young man. He was first employed by E.J. Mulcahy where, for a decade, he learned the retail clothing trade. After this apprenticeship, he and a friend opened Dower & Cosgrove, a haberdashery shop on Asylum Street. Meanwhile, Dower lived with his widowed mother on Farmington Avenue. The Panic of 1907 was particularly hard on small retail businesses and it was in its aftermath that Dower's partner left for greener pastures. The business continued as the John L. Dower Co., but the hours were punishing in a one-man clothing business, so he turned to politics.

John Dower

The serious-minded Irish Democrat ran a taut ship at the water works and earned the praise of his fellow citizens irrespective of their politics and, as proof of this endorsement, he was kept on as president even when the Republicans returned to power in 1912.

Dower was first made aware of Saville by the head of Boston's public works department, Louis Rourke, who had been in the Canal Zone and knew the engineer. On Rourke's recommendation, Dower then contacted the chief engineer of Boston's Water and Sewerage Board, Dexter Brackett. Knowing Saville from earlier days in Boston, Brackett considered Saville the ideal man for the Nepaug project. Furthermore, he opined that Saville combined "splendid expertise with his technical knowledge and was an authority on seepage," an important incidental problem connected with the construction of all dams. Covering all his bases, Dower then queried Frederic Stearns who had nothing but the highest praise for the "technical abilities and the character" of his former assistant. The last call Dower made was to John Freeman. As if to emblazon proof marks on the engineer in Panama, the older man said that he was "willing to stake his reputation on Caleb Saville." With the quality of these recommendations, John Dower was confident that after one quick interview— just a formality really—Saville would have the job. He could not have been more mistaken.

John Dower's subsequent difficulty rose from the changing political tides in Hartford. Connecticut's "rotten boroughs" system of representation—whereby each town, regardless of size, received the same two representatives at the state capital—tilted the balance of power to the Republicans. Indeed, when the state had the chance in 1902 at a statewide constitutional convention to correct this shameful political system, it was former Republican Governor Morgan Bulkeley who sabotaged the process by fashioning a fix that voters found unacceptable.

In 1912—and for the two and a half decades following— the undisputed "Boss" of the Republican Party in Connecticut was J. Henry Roraback of North Canaan. He played puppet master with political candidates and electors alike. But the Republican Party's dominance caused great tension between the state's old guard and the burgeoning masses of immigrants in the river wards of the city—the Fifth and Sixth Wards. It was in this environment that Dower, an Irish-American and a Democrat had to wrestle a favorable outcome from a divided board.

Dower wired an invitation to Saville to interview for the post, and the engineer responded favorably. In late December 1911, Caleb and Elizabeth Saville returned to Boston on a government boat for the Christmas holidays. They stayed in the Brookline area, visiting with their son, Thorndike. While there, Saville took the train to Hartford and registered at the stately, Victorian Heublein Hotel, which bragged of "a window and an oriental rug in every room." For $1.50 a night, Saville would be only two blocks from the water commissioners' offices at City Hall. (Strangely enough, forty-one years later— and after his wife Elizabeth died—Saville sold his home on North Beacon Street and went to live in the Heublein Hotel. He told fellow workers that he was given the exact same room in which he stayed on his first trip to Hartford.)

The interview was in the early evening and lasted about an hour, with Saville explaining his experience to the board. He was not an especially imposing figure. He stood only five-foot-six, with black hair parted high on the right, piercing dark eyes, and a thick brush of a mustache trimmed just below the corners of his mouth. Balanced against this, he dressed impeccably, preferring the rounded collars of the day, a solid colored silk tie with a gold stickpin. His muscular frame completely filled out his custom-tailored three-piece suit. Lastly, his black shoes were polished to the blinding glint of chromium.

After Saville left the interview, the board entered into a private session that lasted until midnight. For all the discussion and the lateness of the hour, they came to no agreement. In truth, there were three engineers in the running. Besides Saville, there was a local man, Frederick L. Ford, for many years Hartford's chief engineer, and Ebert Lockridge, the head engineer for the water works at Springfield. Saville's fellow applicants were a vastly different pair in that Ebert Lockridge had many years of experience with water systems while Frederick Ford, though possessed of estimable engineering skills, had done no work with water systems at all. In fairness, Lockridge and Ford ran a distant second and third to Saville. In fact, neither of the two was ever interviewed. When asked about Saville's appearance, John Dower praised Saville highly saying, "He made a very strong impression. He is a high grade man, and I think Friday night the matter will be settled." Sensing that the deliberations might take on a life of their own, Saville took the train back to Boston.

One of the problems in reaching a decision went all the way back to 1868, when the common council decided—because the city had six wards— to add a sixth member to the water board. Previously, stalemates were unheard of, since an odd number of voters guaranteed a majority, for good or ill. With six members, the board often split right down the middle, as was the case with Caleb Saville.

However, the nub of the matter lay in the contentious relationship between John Dower, the Democratic president of the board, and a stubborn, provincial Republican, Shiras Morris. The men could not have been more different. Dower was an affable, appeasing Irish Democrat, who in his decision-making invariably put the city and the water works ahead of politics.

Conversely, Shiras Morris was from a long line of Whig-Republican partisans and reveled in the rough and tumble world of take-no-prisoners politics. Morris was the secretary and treasurer of Hart & Hegeman, a firm that produced electrical switches. During the course of the discussions concerning the new chief engineer, it became increasingly apparent that Morris had a dual agenda. First, since the water board was top heavy with Democrats, he viewed the business now before the board as a chance to even the balance. John Dower's term as president would end in three months and by stalemating the hiring process, Morris could discredit the Democrats and cast doubt on their ability to manage the water works. Accordingly, the common council would appoint a Republican to take Dower's place and Morris would have an evenly split board.

Secondly, Shiras Morris was also a decidedly parochial man. From his point of view, the board shouldn't even be considering engineers from Springfield or Panama when they had an eminently qualified man living right in their midst—Frederick Ford. Showing just how pigheaded he could be in the matter, Morris even went so far as tell local reporters that, ". . . he did not regard Mr. Ford's inexperience in water works construction as an insuperable matter." Although Morris was the only water commissioner who favored Frederick Ford, citywide the engineer

was well-liked and had many friends and supporters.

Shiras Morris

Dower's enthusiasm for Saville was shared by two other board members—Thomas Shannon, the assistant secretary of the Fidelity Trust Company and Arthur J. McManus, of J. C. McManus & Sons, a firm that sold plumbing services, ranges and stoves. The last two men on the board— Judson Root, a wool merchant, and Edward Hatch, president of the Johns-Pratt Company, which produced electrical insulators—favored Ebert Lockridge of Springfield.

The board's meeting on the Friday before Christmas was a disaster with heels dug in around the room. After a number of hours of talk, with none of the three camps giving an inch, they disbanded. In an effort to let tempers cool and

hopefully fashion a solution at the next meeting, John Dower suggested that they meet again on Tuesday, the day after Christmas. Pushing the matter off for three days was dicey because Caleb and Elizabeth Saville were scheduled to be on the government boat steaming their way back to Panama on the Wednesday after Christmas.

As agreed, the board met on Tuesday shortly after noon and the meeting was over in less than a half hour. Unbeknownst to the other commissioners, Dower had privately struck a deal with his fellow Democrat, Edward Hatch. If Hatch would support Saville, then he could join Dower on the official welcoming committee and receive the attention—and

Edward Hatch

press coverage—attendant with the honor. Judson Root, the other man in favor of Lockridge might have been persuaded, but Hatch's personality was the more conciliatory of the two. The thought of approaching Shiras Morris was not even an option. Anyone who was so adamantine as to contend that hydraulic engineering experience was not a prerequisite for the building of four dams was beyond his reach. Dower had chosen his swing vote wisely and the matter was settled. Later, Hatch and Dower showed Saville around the city and helped get his wife settled into a home in one of the more fashionable neighborhoods of Hartford.

There has always been a persistent rumor at the water works that someone, at about the time that Saville was hired, referred to him as the "Panama lemon"— unfairly, of course. Smarting from his defeat at the hands of the craftier John Dower, and with his unusual opinions about engineers, it was undoubtedly Shiras Morris.

On Wednesday, December 27, Saville—now back in Boston—was offered the job by telephone. He then cabled Col. Goethals in Panama requesting that he be relieved of his duties with the Isthmian Canal Commission. Later in the day, Goethals wired back to say that he encouraged Saville to accept the job in Hartford and that the affairs of his lieutenant on the Isthmus could be concluded without undue hardship. Having been honorably relieved of his duties in Panama, Saville returned to Hartford on Thursday, December 28 on the 2:55 P.M. train. Upon his arrival, he went directly to the office of the water commissioners, where John Dower offered his congratulations and welcomed him to Hartford. In the late afternoon, Edward Hatch joined the two men for dinner at the Heublein Hotel. During the meal, the three men decided that the water company's new chief engineer would begin his duties the following Tuesday—January 2, 1912. After a good night's sleep, Saville returned to Boston to collect Elizabeth and their few belongings, and to arrange for their household goods to be forwarded from Panama.

In his first few months, Caleb Saville showed the board exactly why they needed an experienced engineer. In less than sixty days, he offered the board a plan of organization whereby six different engineering divisions would revolve around him and he would answer only to the water board. It is interesting that while he was working in Panama, he headed one of only two non-military engineering units. However, his organizational chart showed that he had adopted the U. S. Army's rigid methods with alacrity. In time, this chart would get even more complex resembling twenty small blocks dangling on strings from a headpiece, which of course represented Caleb Saville.

Beginning with the March 1912 annual report, the new chief engineer's writings vaulted the information to such a technical level that it was almost certainly beyond the understanding of the men on the board. Saville's reports included maps, graphs and surveys that were impossible for a layman to understand. At long last, addressing the question of "electrolysis," Saville hired Professor Albert F. Ganz of Hoboken, New Jersey, an electrical engineer, to examine every street in the city for stray current. While Ganz's final report was more reassuring than alarming, it did have its moments. One graph showed the results of a test where the stray current actually topped 135 amperes, on one of the city's tonier boulevards. However, the wattage was so low, that the voltage generated was not a hazard. Happily though, the report put to bed the board's concerns about "electrolysis." After more than a year of study, Ganz concluded—

> . . . The investigation which I have made shows that the only source of substantial stray current affecting the water piping system is the electric trolley railway system of the Connecticut Company, which is supplied with direct current power from the electric power station of the Connecticut Company in Commerce Street, Hartford. . . .

Beyond the tedious chore of reorganizing the water works, Saville used his early days with the company to hire the men who would help him construct the Nepaug Project. These men represented every discipline imaginable. There were eminent university professors specializing in geological investigations and forestry work as well as chemists who were experts in bacteriological and chemical analysis. Since the Connecticut River Pumping Station would function as a backup facility while the Nepaug Reservoir was built, still more engineers with river pumping backgrounds were brought on board. Lastly, there were even experts in landscape design.

The level of organization and the complexity of the work being done was undoubtedly far beyond even the wildest dreams of the water board. What might have been hard for them to fathom was that the small water company that Hiram Bissell nursed along sixty years before was gone forever. A tectonic shift had occurred and only now were they beginning to realize it. Their small city was about to impound vast quantities of water the same as Boston, New York and Baltimore had done. What's more, the very heart and soul of this new water company would be well educated and highly experienced hydraulic engineers. Essentially, the water board was along for the ride.

The putative reason for hiring Caleb Mills Saville was the water company's need for an expert to take control of the Nepaug Project and see it to completion perhaps a decade later. However, Saville's job also included the engineering maintenance work of a water company that now included more than 150 miles of cast iron pipe, over 12,000 service laterals, 2,400 stop gates, 1,220 fire hydrants and almost 12,000 water meters. Add to this the work of maintaining the aging Lord's Hill Reservoir, the six reservoirs in West Hartford and the two long aqueducts running under Farmington Avenue and the job seemed staggering.

Not surprisingly, the magnitude of the job brought out the genius in Saville. With his tremendous organizational skills, he had talented engineers running six disparate departments within the company. For the next decade, the company would be run out of this matrix—Headquarters (chief of office), Reservoir (existing reservoirs), Distribution (existing infrastructure), Designing (new work), Nepaug-Farmington River (new work) and East Branch-Farmington River (new work).

This seems like an obvious delegation of responsibilities, but in fairness to Caleb Saville, nothing of the kind existed before his arrival. Realistically, it was a critical adjustment that would allow him to concentrate on the Nepaug Project.

In the way of assembling talent, Saville made another move that must have given him great pleasure—he hired as consultants two of the greatest hydraulic engineers in the country. The first was his old boss Frederic Stearns from Boston and the second man was another old friend from the Boston water board, John Freeman. As a favor to his former mentor, he even hired Stearns' son, Ralph, to head the new Design Division, which was an incredibly important job for the thirty-three year old man. At the time, Frederic Stearns and John Freeman were close in age—the former was almost sixty and the latter, fifty-eight, but their backgrounds were quite different.

Frederic Stearns

Frederic Stearns was born in Calais, Maine in 1851 and made his way to Boston where he apprenticed to a surveyor. After considerable study on his own, in 1872 he went to work for the Boston Water Works. In 1875, he was appointed head of the team responsible for the construction of the Sudbury Aqueduct. Twenty years later, he became the chief engineer for the Metropolitan Water Board and immediately began the designs for the Wachusett Reservoir, which was completed in 1905. Along with John Freeman, he was on the thirteen member consulting board for the Panama Canal (1905-6). Later, he consulted to municipalities all over the United States even teaming up with Freeman again on the design of the Los Angeles Aqueduct in 1906. (Rounding out the design triumvirate of the aqueduct for the "city of the angels" was James D. Schuyler of New York.) In a fitting testament to Stearns's love for and satisfaction in his work, both of his sons, Ralph and Herbert, became engineers as well.

John Freeman was also from Maine but, after attending public schools in Portland, he received his degree from M.I.T. in 1876. For many years, Freeman had two diverse interests—working for insurance companies devising fire-extinguishing systems to reduce their losses in large industrial conflagrations, and drawing and developing waterpower systems for industry. In 1899, he consulted for New York City on the Catskill Water System and, between 1909 and 1912, he did consulting work for Baltimore, San Francisco, San Diego, Nashua, Denver, Seattle and many other municipalities. When Saville asked him to consult on the Nepaug project, he was living in Providence, Rhode Island where he and his wife were busy raising their seven children. The most fascinating aspect of John Freeman's life though was that, even though he worked on all of the largest and most interesting water projects in the country, he only spent half of his time in the field of hydraulic engineering. The other six months of the year, he was the president of Manufacturers Mutual Fire Insurance Company of Providence, Rhode Island.

John R. Freeman

The important thing about these two men was that, irrespective of their other talents, they were both dam builders of enormous experience. Caleb Saville could rely on his own instincts but having the talents of such engineering giants at his disposal was the rough equivalent of wearing a belt and suspenders too. Very reassuring indeed.

Caleb Saville was born on May 27, 1865 to George W. and Helen Mills Saville of Melrose, Massachusetts. The elder Saville was a special sheriff of Middlesex County, was active in Masonic affairs and could trace his ancestors back to Mayflower passengers, John Alden and Priscilla Mullins. Young Caleb was an only child and attended the public schools of neighboring Medford. Before entering Harvard, he studied for a year at Stone's School in Boston. Very little is known about his college years except that as a lifelong non-smoker and teetotaler, with an overdeveloped desire to succeed, there was precious little playtime. After his postgraduate work, he accepted a job with M. M. Tidd, a firm specializing in water supply and waterpower. A year later, he joined the engineering department of nearby Malden, only a few miles south of his hometown. Shortly thereafter, he married a young woman, Elizabeth A. Thorndike. She was the daughter of Edward Thorndike, a financier, and his wife, Hannah, of Beverly, twelve miles to the northeast.

Caleb Saville's wife, Elizabeth, was also a direct descendant of a Mayflower passenger—Myles Standish. The Savilles were proud of their lineage and were lifelong members of the Mayflower Descendants and the Society of Colonial Wars. Beyond that, Caleb Saville maintained a membership in the Royal Meteorological Society and corresponded frequently with a number of other British technical organizations. At one time, he even sent money to Westminster Abbey to have a brass plaque mounted on the wall adjacent to the grave of Herbert Thorndike, a distant relative of Elizabeth Saville. Oddly enough, he requested that there be a Latin inscription of some kind on the marker, although he seemed completely indifferent as to the exact wording.

Following his work with the Boston Water Works and the excitement of working on the Panama Canal, a good question might be: Why Hartford? It is easy to see that the city needed him, but more to the point, what made the Savilles think that after all their travels they would be happy in a small city in central Connecticut? Their thoughts on the matter, if ever articulated, were never recorded. Nonetheless, with the benefit of hindsight, certain considerations are obvious.

First of all, Hartford was a stone's throw from Beverly and Melrose, Massachusetts so that the opportunity to spend time with family was ever present. Perhaps after five years in Panama, this had greater weight than anything else. Also, for Saville, Boston offered no great challenges at the time. The Wachusett Reservoir had almost filled by this time, but still had not been on line for more than three years. Saville could probably glance at the population trends, look at the available water and calculate the start date of the next big reservoir in his head. (Work on the Quabbin—Boston's huge reservoir in central Massachusetts—did not start for another twenty-five years.) Hartford, on the other hand, had a least one great reservoir project ready to go.

The job and the location seemed like a good fit for both of the Savilles but, given the peripatetic nature of hydraulic engineering, it is not terribly surprising that they did not purchase a home right away. Initially, they rented a home at 53 North Beacon Street in the fashionable West End of Hartford. It was a *fin de siècle* ark of a house with overhanging roofs going in several directions seemingly held in place by rich cornices, dormers, bay windows and a wide front porch running the width of the house. The structure and the two car detached garage combined to dominate the fifty-nine by one hundred and ten foot lot, leaving very little room for grass or flowerbeds.

At first the Savilles depended on vehicles from the water works, but since Caleb worked such long hours and Elizabeth had to hold home and hearth together alone, they soon bought their own transportation. In 1914, Caleb bought his wife a small electric car.

One of the ugly little annoyances of the early gas-powered automobiles was the hand-crank starting mechanism, notorious for kicking back and breaking fingers and forearms. Since Elizabeth Saville was not an especially hearty woman, her husband bought her a Rauch Lang Coach Electric car. It wasn't exactly cheap though. Gas-powered automobiles could be purchased for $500, but the Rauch Lang cost $3,000. Nevertheless, the engineering was first rate. (Thomas Edison owned a 1912 Rauch Lang Electric Town Car.) Achieving a top speed of 20 miles per hour, Elizabeth Saville was able to get about the city in all weather for whatever errands demanded her attention.

When the Savilles finally decided to purchase the big house on North Beacon Street in September of 1915, they talked former owner Bertha Pembrook—now living in Boston—into taking back a mortgage in the form of a 6 percent promissory note for almost the complete sale price of the house, payments to be made semi-annually. The Saville's paid off the $5,750 note in 1924, a little over nine years later.

When one considers that Saville was paid more than he could have made in the states for the previous five years, while he and his wife were in the Canal Zone, and that lodging and medical care were free, one wonders why he needed a mortgage at all. Since income taxes were non-existent at his income level, Saville was probably able to bank most of his weekly paycheck. The most logical explanation is that he did not want to touch the couple's savings while their son, Thorndike, was still at Harvard. Perhaps they anticipated his interest in pursuing further engineering studies, which turned out to be the case. Thorndike Saville went on to receive several masters degrees and a doctorate in civil engineering. (Thorndike Saville's son, Thorndike Jr., earned his engineering degree from Harvard as well and had a long and successful career with the Army Corps of Engineers.)

One of Saville's idiosyncrasies was privacy. He resented drivers parking their cars in front of his house. At one point, he painted the curb yellow to dissuade drivers from leaving their vehicles there. Ultimately he settled on a five-foot tall, heavy-duty wrought iron fence with a small gate at the front sidewalk and an elaborate double gate at the driveway. Whether the fence gave him and his wife the privacy they craved is anyone's guess.

The Nepaug project, which was given wing when the legislature approved the water board's 1911 petition, allowed for work to commence along the Nepaug River in the Farmington Valley. As might be expected the bill was a masterfully complex piece of legislation that spelled out exactly what was required of the water company in order to build the Nepaug Reservoir. To begin with, the water commissioners were given the necessary permission to "take and hold . . . the Nepaug River . . . above the village of Collinsville . . . and also . . . Phelps Brook, one mile below that hamlet." Secondly, the water board was allowed to build the necessary dams, reservoirs and aqueducts to complete the project.

The third part of this legislation is where the bill really got interesting. One of the little penalties associated with the project was the demand that the city supply water to inhabitants of the cities and towns through which the aqueduct ran. Moreover, water was to be supplied on the same terms that the citizens of West Hartford enjoyed.

At this time, the board was only obligated to supply the inhabitants of West Hartford who lived within a "reasonable distance from the line of main pipes . . . upon the same terms and conditions that the inhabitants of . . . Hartford . . . are . . . supplied." However, two years later, the legislature passed another law called " An Act Concerning A Supply Of Water Within The Town Of West Hartford." Suddenly, things were quite different. The "reasonable distance from the line of main pipes. . . ." clause had been removed from the law, which, in effect, meant that now the water company would be required to supply the whole town of West Hartford with water. A good case could be made that, taking this new legislation into consideration, the water company might be required to supply water to all of the inhabitants in any of the towns where it builds reservoirs or aqueducts—at any time in the future. The 1913 law was in effect a full employment act for lawyers inasmuch as, the cities and towns involved wrangled over the meaning of the new legislation for decades.

Returning to the third part of the Nepaug legislation of 1911, there was another passage that bound the water works' hands in a way that they came to regret later. Specifically, the water commissioners were *strictly prohibited from selling water in competition with any other water system in any other city or town*. In effect, no matter how large the capacity of the water works became, they were enjoined from entering into competition with other water companies—public or private.

The final section of the bill addressed the compensating reservoir in Barkhamsted, specifying that it would be built ". . . on the East Branch of the Farmington River . . . near 'Richard's Corner' . . . for the purpose of returning . . . water . . . [to the] Farmington River. . . ." Once the principal of the "compensating reservoir," which had been the sticking point of the whole project, had been thus spelled out, the mill owners along the Farmington River were protected. With such concrete guarantees written right into the law, they could run their businesses unaffected by the water department's new Nepaug Reservoir.

In light of the water company's future projects, it is fascinating to note that the 1911 law, allowing them to develop the Nepaug watershed, does not give them the powers of either condemnation or eminent domain. In fact, in one of the later sections of the law, a long and irksome process was laid out for the water company to acquire the properties it needed to complete the project. However, this process ultimately boiled down to a variant of collective bargaining with the superior court acting as the final arbiter. If the presiding judge failed to settle the issue, the final compensation due the property owner was to be calculated by three disinterested freeholders. Eventually, the judge reviewed the estimates and made a final assessment of the amount of compensation due.

On a slightly lighter note, in 1913 the General Assembly also authorized the water company to "manufacture, buy, house and sell ice from any reservoir controlled by (the) board." This is humorous because there were ice companies doing business in Hartford for about seventy-five years by that time and, since the city now had electricity—and would very shortly have refrigerators—the water company was a little late to the feast.

Caleb Saville's first full year as chief engineer could be considered inordinately productive on many different counts. The maintenance of the existing West Hartford reservoir property required little more than the harvesting of forty tons of hay, used through the coming year by the water department's horses. Pigsties were a small problem though. Twice in 1912, the local health department had to be called because of potential contamination risks posed by pig farmers in the area of Reservoir No. 4 in Farmington. This was a continuing problem but, because the Nepaug project would obviate the need for the West Hartford-Farmington reservoirs, it was decided not to acquire more land to protect the watershed, but to live with the nuisance instead.

Serving as a constant reminder of the seriousness of their work, in 1912, Saville was startled to learn of a new outbreak of typhoid fever in the Town of Torrington, just nine miles to the west of the proposed new reservoir. As a precaution, when the West Hartford reservoirs were drained down during the course of the summer—at which time they were most susceptible to contamination—he had their waters treated with hypochlorite of lime. Fortunately for all concerned with the water supply, the residents of the city were of one mind on the Connecticut River water—they never wanted to taste it again. In spite of this clear preference concerning the city's water source, he had the engine, boilers and pumps at the Connecticut River Pumping Station maintained religiously.

Before the passage of the Nepaug Reservoir legislation and a few years before Caleb Saville's arrival in Hartford, some survey work had been done on the Nepaug project. During the good months of 1912, considerably more accurate surveys were made, not only to plat the watershed, but also to pin the boundaries of the properties that would have to be acquired to clear the watershed. In the path of the principal aqueduct, thirty-eight separate parcels had been surveyed. For the Nepaug Reservoir itself, forty-one parcels had been surveyed and another forty-seven in the locale of the compensating reservoir.

In the end, the board purchased forty-two farms in the vicinity of the Nepaug Reservoir, thirty-eight around the compensating reservoir and removed a total of 105 houses, barns and principal buildings. Additionally, they relocated ten miles of highways. A grisly item on the board's punch list was the removal of bodies and monuments from two cemeteries—Southwest Canton and St. John's. All together 372 bodies were reinterred in a new cemetery and 124 monuments were reset. In order to assure clean drinking water, all dwellings, outbuildings, fences, trees, shrubs and anything else that would float was removed from the reservoir's upper limits.

The actual purchase of properties was not begun until the final surveys and design work was completed. The drawing of the specifications for four dams, together with the accompanying geological and hydrological work, consumed more than a year. In 1913, everything was ready. All around the Nepaug project and in the area of the compensating reservoir, the board began buying up property. In Barkhamsted, by the end of three years, they had purchased about 35 farms and homesteads. The purchase of properties in the Nepaug watershed followed along the same lines and, by 1917, all of the needed acreage had been acquired.

In Saville's report to the board in March of 1913, he capsulizes succinctly the dam building aspect of the work—

. . . To make the Nepaug Reservoir it is necessary to construct two dams of considerable size to close the gorges in which the present streams run and to construct a dike along a low saddle in the dividing ridge between the Nepaug and Farmington River basins.

The Nepaug Dam was classified as a high masonry dam, 110 feet tall and 650 feet across the roadway that traversed the top of the structure. The specific type of construction, cyclopean masonry, employed large rocks embedded in the poured concrete. Arched upstream, the finished dam had enormous strength and was elevated by its handsome lines to something of an architectural masterwork.

The Nepaug Dam.

Of the dams that Saville would build for the board over the years, the Nepaug Dam was the only one that left the concrete exposed. The other two dams at the Nepaug Reservoir were of the earthen variety with a concrete core wall, as was the one built at the southern end of the compensating reservoir in Barkhamsted.

In 1912, the area of the Nepaug watershed was a sparsely populated part of the state and heavily wooded with thousands of acres of virgin pine forests. All the same, every inch of it had to be surveyed before work could begin on the reservoir and dams. A story, perhaps apocryphal, explains better than anything else the great chasm between the new chief engineer, fresh from the jungles of Panama, and his fellow engineers and surveyors in the land of steady habits.

For many years, the fire department had been passing their worn-out horses down to the water company as younger animals were purchased. (Under a heavy burden, a work horse's hooves and ankles were only good for a few years on cobblestone or dirt streets.) The water company kept about six of these horses in their Union Street Barn in Hartford to pull maintenance wagons but also kept some of the oldest of their collection at a farm they owned in Avon. Relatively few people rode horses for pleasure back in 1912 and the huge Belgian draft horses used by the fire company were not especially suited for riding. Usually they were of enormous girth, weighing over 1,200 pounds, and they had thick necks and over-muscled stifles. However, they had the distinctive plumed fetlocks, close-cropped manes and quiet dispositions—probably because their whole lives were spent behind blinkers—so with management's blessings, the employees of the Hartford Water Works did occasionally use the animals for recreational purposes. As one of the small perquisites of his new post of chief engineer, Saville was given his own horse.

Naturally enough, from the chief engineer's point of view, a close inspection of the whole watershed would offer him an invaluable pool of knowledge. So with his plans known only to the manager of the water company, he took his horse from the Avon stables and rode into the Nepaug valley for an indeterminate stay. After a week, a rumor began making the rounds within the department to the effect that the company's new chief engineer was lost somewhere in the wilds of Connecticut. Believing that it couldn't take more than a few days to inspect the land, a search party was organized. Into the woods they rode, undoubtedly expecting to find the lifeless body of Caleb Saville on the side of some long-forgotten logging trail. Instead, they found nothing more than a string of cold campfires. After a few days of searching, they gave up. When Caleb Saville had assembled the appropriate information, he emerged from the forest and went directly to his drafting table to transform his rough field notes into precise drawings. The search party—and attendant hand-wringing—was never mentioned to him.

For Saville, the easiest part of the Nepaug project was the Nepaug Dam itself, even though it consumed 81,000 cubic yards of concrete. Bear in mind that this is less than a third of the concrete used to build the Wachusett Dam, and accordingly, at 600 feet in length along the spillway and 112 feet in height, it was a much smaller dam than the one he helped build a decade before. Furthermore, the Gatun Dam in Panama was more than ten times the size of the Nepaug, and for sheer size, would dwarf anything that Caleb Saville would work on for the rest of his life. That said, it must be pointed out that he was not the chief engineer of the two previous projects, and the responsibility for the whole Nepaug Project was now his to bear.

The other two dams at the Nepaug site were much smaller affairs. The Phelps Brook Dam was the largest of the two earthen structures at 1250 feet long and reaching a height of 67 feet. What later became known as the East Dike was a much smaller, though essential, part of the puzzle. It merely beefed up a low spot in the saddle of the reservoir. Again, it was built exactly the same way as the Phelps Brook dam.

Straddling the boundary between Barkhamsted and New Hartford, the fourth and final dam—the Richards Corner Dam—was built. This impoundment held the waters that, at least for a time, were called the compensating reservoir (later, Lake McDonough). This last dam, constructed in the same manner as the earthen structures at the Nepaug Reservoir site was about two-thirds the size of the earthen dam at Phelps Brook.

As implausible as it sounds, Saville's encyclopedic knowledge in the fields of hydraulic engineering, hydrology, and hydrography proved inadequate on the Nepaug Project. In addition, he had to acquire an academician's understanding of the frustrating complexities of riparian law and practice. When it came to research and analysis though, he was a draft horse. Night after night, he devoured volumes on the subject, amassing his own private library in the process. As was his way, he wrote papers continually on the application of his newfound knowledge and its relevance to hydraulic engineering. With his peers, Saville was extremely generous with information. Apparently, he understood the old chestnut that "teaching is just another form of learning."

The reason for Saville's obsession with riparian law was that, on average, the water company would be diverting about 6 percent of the water from the Nepaug River and Phelps Brook. As a consequence, they would have to find a way to release the same amount from the compensating reservoir in order to satisfy the riparian rights of the downstream mill owners. Since the waters collected in the compensating reservoir were the result of snow melt and spring flooding, which up to this time had been wasted, the levels of water in the Farmington River could be maintained without stealing water from any of the other branches of the river.

All well and good but, in actual practice, coordinating the movements of large amounts of water in four different streams and rivers and two augmenting reservoirs was easier said than done. In short, it was an extremely problematic balancing act.

Compounding and confusing the execution of this plan was the natural variable of rainfall. In a wet year, there may be little need for the waters of the compensating reservoir at all, while in a dry one, the 3 billion gallons of water in the reservoir might not be enough. In theory, the design of the system took into account the worst possible scenario, but nothing could be taken for granted when dealing with Mother Nature. In Caleb Saville's writings was this fascinating dictum, which apparently was the lodestar of his work—"It is axiomatic in hydraulic engineering that the worst flood and the most severe drought will someday be surpassed."

Toward a better understanding of the rainfall in the region and the exact flows in the rivers and streams, Saville established "gauging stations" to measure the flows in the rivers and "rainfall stations" to measure the exact amount of precipitation that fell in the watershed each year. Up to this time, the water company had relied on the data collected by a Canton resident named G. J. Case. Without impugning the work of Mr. Case, it seems obvious that a public utility embarking on a water project as complex as the proposed Nepaug Reservoir had reached the point where they would have to measure precipitation themselves.

By the end of 1913, the water company had a total work force of ninety-eight people, thirty of whom were engineers. While these engineers drew the plans for the proposed four dams, about eight miles to the west a truly gargantuan task was underway. Besides the building of the dams, one of the most laborious jobs connected with the Nepaug project was the tunneling under Talcott Mountain to clear a path for the aqueduct. Thanks to a mild winter the men were able to tunnel almost all year long. The path under the mountain was dug as a simple trench for as long as possible with work progressing from both the east and the west. The laborers' machinery was crude. There were small steam shovels, but simple farm wagons and horses did all of the carting of earth and rock. Spring was the toughest time as the heavily laden wagons sunk into the muddy roadbeds up to their axles.

This work progressed until the middle of 1914 when the concrete conduit through the tunnel was complete. It would house a water pipe that was almost four feet in diameter. Also by the end of the same year, the dams at the Nepaug Reservoir were partially completed. In 1915, Saville estimated that about 25 percent of the project had been completed. He also felt that about 90 percent of the land in the Nepaug watershed had been purchased as well as the greater portion of that required for the compensating reservoir—all, without extended litigation.

While the work progressed on the Nepaug Dam and its smaller siblings, the existing utility within the city continued to deliver water to about 120,000 people with some great improvements. In 1913, the complete water supply to the city was chlorinated for the first time. This was accomplished using both hypochlorite of lime and chloride gas, each at different times. (The water company's hand was forced by the pigs and other farm animals in the vicinity of the West Hartford reservoirs.)

Showing its frugal side, the board had the fields around the reservoirs reaped once a year and the resultant forty tons of hay was stored in barns on their West Hartford property or brought to their Union Street yard. It was enough hay to feed all of their horses for a year. Additionally, a 12 by 20 foot addition was added to the blacksmith shop for the shoeing of horses. From that time forward, the department would shoe all of its own horses. This addition was actually ill timed because horses were fast losing ground to automobiles. The water works itself already owned three auto trucks, one touring car (used by Caleb Saville) and a small emergency automobile.

Beginning in late 1916, the waters of Phelps Brook were held back and, by the end of the winter, 300 million gallons had been collected. Also, two days before Christmas, the lower waste gate at the Nepaug Dam was closed and water began to collect from the Nepaug River. Because the dam at the compensating reservoir was nowhere near completion, the amount of water that could be held back was small and determined in large part by the amount of rainfall. Fortunately, there was slightly more precipitation than usual and in no time at all there was 600 million gallons in the new reservoir.

The Nepaug Dam was dedicated in July, 1917 and three weeks later the common council changed Saville's official title to "Manager and Chief Engineer," a job title that he would enjoy for the next thirty years. The plaque on the dam reads—

NEPAUG DAM AND RESERVOIR
CALEB MILLS SAVILLE, CHIEF ENGINEER
FREDERIC P. STEARNS AND JOHN R. FREEMAN
CONSULTING ENGINEERS
FRED T. LEY & CO. INC., CONTRACTORS

The Richard's Corner Dam at the compensating reservoir was held up because of manpower and material shortages caused by the First World War. The work had begun in the late summer of 1915 under a contract scheduling completion in January 1918, but wasn't finished until a year later.

As an unwelcome reminder of the deadly potential of drinking water, in September of 1918, there was an outbreak of B. Coli bacteria in Hartford. It was traced to a well in the center of the city, which the health board was forced to cap. Saville was angered to have gone to so much trouble chlorinating the whole water supply only to have B. Coli introduced to the population by a resident who blithely continued to use an outdated private well.

Another item of interest was the apparent stealing of water by some citizens. By its own tally, the board came up with a figure of about 18 to 22 percent as the amount of water that they classified as "unaccounted for." At the time, there were almost 16,000 metered water customers in the city and, while there certainly could have been theft, such a large amount begged further examination. Metering of the largest users—livery stables and beer saloons—had begun in 1878 with the installation of 19 meters. Another 206 were installed by 1884 and the whole system was metered by the end of 1902. One fifth of the water supply unaccounted for? Not likely.

What the board—and even Caleb Saville—may not have realized at the time was that the amount of water for which they could not account was suspiciously close to the average amount of water lost by all water companies due to leakage and other maintenance chores, such as back-flushing filters. Since this was a hot topic one year and never mentioned again, one suspects Saville came to the correct conclusion on his own.

The fall of 1919 was a time of loss. In October, the Lord's Hill Reservoir was sold to the Hartford Fire Insurance Company. Conjoining the land with other parcels, the firm built its corporate headquarters on the site, erasing any trace of the little reservoir that started it all. The total water storage capacity of the system now—not including the compensating reservoir—was almost eleven billion gallons, more than a thousand times that of the old Lord's Hill Reservoir. The population of the city increased sevenfold since that day back in 1855 when the Woodruff & Beach pumps filled the tiny reservoir with Connecticut River water for the first time. This reservoir, which held an appallingly small ten million gallons of water, had served the city for almost sixty-five years. Even after its size made it useless for drinking water storage, it was used for firefighting. When the Trout Brook valley dried up in 1873, it was the only thing between the residents of Hartford and a devastating water famine. With the Nepaug Reservoir on line, it was reduced to a memory.

With the Lord's Hill Reservoir gone, the Connecticut River Pumping Station was on borrowed time. Where would it pump water to now? Toward the end of the year, the old horizontal boiler was removed and the space temporarily used for storage. The building itself received a short reprieve, but was razed in 1922.

Also in 1919, with the largest chunk of the new reservoir project nearing completion, Saville lost his mentor, Frederic Stearns. The older man had consulted from the earliest stages to the completion of the dams, helping his old friend bring in his first big municipal water supply project. Frederic Pike Stearns died in December 1919 at the age of sixty-eight.

The final bit of engineering on this long project consisted of building a slow sand filtration plant at the West Hartford Reservoir site. Once again, the principal was so simple but the actual implementation was quite involved. Recognizing that engineering drawings could only carry them so far, a series of experiments were conducted to determine the best type of filters and media. Consider the following—

> . . . Six second-hand...hot water tanks were obtained from local plumbers...[and] set up on end with outlet pipes in the bottom of each tank. Over this was placed about two feet of sand, a different sand in each of the six tanks. Rates of flow were controlled by stopcocks [which] measured the loss of head . . . From the result, . . . it is expected that a decision as to the [best] sand . . . can be determined . . . .

In reality, the water company's engineers had been conducting experiments with slow and rapid sand filters at Reservoir No. 1 in West Hartford as early as 1915. They built a fifteen-foot cube out of cypress, which they used as a slow sand filtration unit. The water then moved to an eight-foot tall box (three-foot square), which acted as a rapid sand filter, and finally the water went thru a cypress coagulating basin.

In today's world of high technology, this little experiment seems eerily reminiscent of a junior high school science project, but necessary at the time. Saville, as a result of these experiments decided on a sand that was bought from a pit in Plainville, Connecticut. Over time though, the water company moved toward a finer sand that could not be purchased locally. In the end, they settled on a special quartz sand brought in from New Jersey and Rhode Island.

In 1922, eight huge sand filter beds—each about half of an acre—were built to purify twenty million gallons of water a day. After filtration, the water was stored in covered concrete reservoirs before it moved into the aqueduct headed for the city. Simply put, sand filtration plants are really only an effort to repeat what occurs naturally as water slowly makes its way down into aquifers beneath the earth's surface. Not surprisingly, gravel and sand have been the media used in these filters for more than a century and a half.

After completing the slow sand filters in West Hartford, the mammoth Nepaug Reservoir project was finished. It was early 1922 and even the most pessimistic person in the area would have believed that Hartford's water supply was assured into the distant future. What was never revealed to the public was that the Nepaug Reservoir was not quite yielding what the original calculations had promised. There were a number of different variables that contributed to this shortfall, not the least of which was the unpredictability of the precipitation in the Nepaug watershed. Still, who would have guessed that only seven short years after the completion of such a huge reservoir, the water board would be asking the state legislature for permission to impound even more water on the East Branch of the Farmington River? Probably no one—except Caleb Saville.

Chapter 9
Graduation to Regional Supplier

After the completion of the Nepaug project in 1922, Caleb Saville still spent his afternoons in the northwestern hills of Connecticut. He had his driver, Marty Cannon, bring him out there to inspect the small fits and finishes on the Nepaug and compensating reservoirs and the new sand filtration system in West Hartford. In an effort to secure the watershed, he pushed constantly to increase the city's land holdings around the new catchments. True, the compensating reservoir was not technically for drinking water purposes, but Saville had plans for the East Branch valley and, one might say, he was just keeping things at the ready. High on his list of concerns were the feeder streams that emptied directly into the reservoirs. On one visit to Nepaug, Saville caught a man urinating into one of the streams and almost strangled him to death with his bare hands. When it came to protecting the purity of the water supply, Caleb Saville took a back seat to no one. Word of the chief's zeal traveled quickly in the sparsely populated environs of the Nepaug and there were no further incidents of this kind—at least none that anyone lived to tell about.

Saville had a deep interest in the natural world as it pertained to drinking water systems, but otherwise he was completely oblivious to the beauties of nature. He did not fish or hunt, nor did he collect duck decoys or any other outdoor sporting art, and he had no interest whatever in birds or butterflies. Neither were golf or tennis part of his weekly exercise routine, and he and his wife did not socialize. (This was in sharp contrast to their time in Panama when they entertained the engineers under Saville's command regularly—particularly the ones without families.) The chief was a man completely devoid of hobbies, preferring to spend all of his time engrossed in the finer points of hydraulic engineering.

Saville was an early riser, reading the morning *Courant* (he read the *Boston Sunday Herald* on the weekend) and gathering together the notes and letters that he composed while working late the night before. He then showered, shaved and slapped on some bay rum—the only aftershave he ever used—before dressing in a clean, starched shirt, a plain tie and dark colored suit that he had custom made by Peter Johnson, a tailor with a small shop on Asylum Street. Though Saville paid less and less attention to style as the years progressed, his clothes were always immaculately clean and neatly pressed.

His breakfasts were Spartan, usually just eggs, toast and coffee. (At one point, he purchased eggs from an employee of the water department, who saved all the "double yokers" for Saville, even going to the trouble of penning the chief's initials on the shells—C.M.S.) At precisely 7:45, his driver, Marty Cannon, pulled into his driveway to collect him for the drive to his rented office in the Pilgard Building, at the corner of Main and Morgan Streets. (John Pilgard ran the Union Grocery on the first floor of his building.) Saville arrived at work every day at eight o'clock, preferring to walk up the stairs instead of using the elevators, in the belief that the exercise would do him good. Ordinarily he spent the morning dictating letters, internal memos, and writing recommendations to the water board. He also composed notes and correspondence regarding construction contracts and so forth from the rough scribblings he had made the night before. Lastly, he reviewed the drawings done by the engineers in the different offices of the water department. Saville never did any drawings himself, leaving all of this work to his staff. For these professionals, the discipline of the drafting rooms could be severe. Engineers were required to wear drafting aprons, white shirts and ties, and their workstations had to be kept immaculate. Supplies were strictly controlled, including the turning in of pencil stubs for replacements.

Strangely enough, for an engineer, Saville had very poor handwriting. To remedy this little flaw, he purchased a rubber stamp and had all the department's drawings and surveys stamped with an India ink facsimile of his signature. In a further refinement of this routine, Saville worked out a system with his secretary, Gerry d'Avignon, whereby he would affix a tiny red "s" in the lower corner of any correspondence that he wanted stamped with his signature, whereupon d'Avignon dutifully stamped the documents and sent them on their way.

Between this tedious paperwork, Saville met with the heads of his six different divisions, spending the lion's share of his time with those working on the initial rough survey work for the East Branch valley of the Farmington River. The drawings were as detailed as they were voluminous. No matter what the subject, each was rendered from every elevation with corresponding cross sections and exploded views. Saville was absolutely unrelenting when it came to perfect drawings, tolerating neither shoddy work nor shortcuts.

Barring something unusual, every day he ate lunch—either with his driver or a member of the water board—at Honiss's Oyster House, where he arrived at exactly noon and was given his usual table. Honiss's was a quirky place, located in the basement of the United States Hotel, on the north side of City Hall Square. The management always claimed in their advertising that it was the oldest Oyster House in the United States, having been established in 1845. This wasn't quite true.

Oystering was one of Connecticut's oldest industries and because the shelled favorite was so plentiful, even families of mean estate ate them regularly. So much so in fact, that by the beginning of the nineteenth century, oystermen were forced to embark on an extended cultivation program. Not long into this program, almost 100,000 acres of Connecticut's shoreline was tied up in oyster cultivation. The demand never slackened though and many merchants made a good living selling only oysters.

In the mid-nineteenth century, a succession of fishmongers used the basement of the United States Hotel to sell oysters and clams while Thomas

Honiss, just like his father before him, made a living as a gunsmith. But competing with Colt's Patent Fire-Arms was foolhardy and by 1878, Honiss was hawking oysters on State Street. Eventually, his little venture increased to the point where it needed a permanent home and he rented a part of the basement of the United States Hotel. Soon thereafter, he opened a restaurant that was enormously popular from the get-go. He died in 1903 and a tall, barrel-chested man, Edwin Tolhurst, continued the business. Two years after Saville arrived in Hartford, three men bought out Tolhurst and they were the chief's hosts for the rest of his career. Undoubtedly, Saville gravitated to the place because of its history, reminding him of Boston's Union Oyster House. Too, he may just have been lured by the restaurant's boast—"Where the best stews in the country can be had."

Tucking a linen napkin into his shirt collar, as was his habit, Saville ordered the same thing every day—a big bowl of oyster chowder with a cup of coffee. On the way out of the restaurant, he grabbed a bag of peanuts at the cashier's station. By 12:30 P.M., he was en route to the reservoir sites for his daily inspections. His habits were about as flexible as the concrete in the Nepaug Dam.

On occasion, he would ask Marty Cannon, to run into Hartford National Bank on Farmington Avenue to cash a check for him and, it was understood, he was always to get crisp, new bills. There was one teller at the bank who knew the drill by heart, keeping a ready supply of pristine bills in his cash drawer, which he dispensed without discussion. When it came to Saville's compensation at the water department, he was paid twice what the highest paid engineer in the place received. When a top-flight engineer with a B.S. degree from M.I.T was earning $5000 a year, Saville got $10,000, and through the years, his pay increased accordingly. The Cadillac and driver were additional perquisites of the office. (Saville also received a check every month from the Isthmian Canal Commission, a pension of sorts for working on the Panama Canal.)

He was a difficult—some would say impossible—taskmaster, demanding the best out of every worker, regardless of his or her position at the water works. During his long years as manager and chief engineer, he was described as an autocrat and a demanding bastard but, in fairness, he drove himself much harder than he drove anyone else. There was not a worker in the place who put in the kind of hours that he did. Nonetheless, there was no getting around the fact that he was overbearing. His longtime secretary, Gerry d'Avignon summed it up this way, "Some guys couldn't take it. But I went to Catholic schools and was used to tough discipline, so it never bothered me."

Ironically, Saville was probably the simplest man to understand and, at the same time, the most complex. His life was simple because his only interest was the water company, his total immersion in the department bordering on monomania. As his secretary averred, "Everything Mr. Saville did was for the water system . . . He lived it and breathed it."

He was complex though because, while he could and did terrorize the workers under him, alternately, he was capable of extraordinary kindnesses. It has been said by more than one retired employee that he was such an intimidating man that competent, seasoned engineers used to "shake like leaves" when they were summoned to his office. Tony Fornabi—Saville's last driver—was quoted as saying, "You kind of came to attention . . . You made sure that you said 'Good morning, Mr. Saville'. . . . There was just an aura about him . . . He was a legend in his time." Of the legions of men and women who worked at the water company, not a single one called him Caleb. He was "Mr. Saville" from the janitorial staff to the most highly paid engineers. Only the water commissioners called him by his first name.

Past workers of the water department—who knew Saville—each have their favorite story of the chief's gruff side. Reportedly, one cold winter's day, he saw a surveyor's "rod man" with his hands in his pockets and the chief tried to get him fired. In another instance, he saw a member of the water department standing on a street corner smoking a cigarette and tried to have him fired as well. The only flaw with these tales is that if Saville wanted the men dismissed, they would have been gone immediately. He had that much power. Since these two men were not actually fired, this calls into question the veracity of much of the Caleb Saville lore. True, he was a driven man and hard to work for, but Saville was not a nasty or vindictive man. Judged in the full light of day, such pettiness seems beneath him.

On the other hand, when Saville's son Thorndike—who in 1921 was an associate professor of engineering at the University of North Carolina at Chapel Hill—picked a southern belle for his bride, Caleb Saville was bitterly opposed to the union. So steeped was he in the Boston Brahman tradition, that he refused to accept that a southern girl could be a suitable mate for his son. One former water department employee insists that Saville did not attend the marriage ceremony in Chapel Hill. The newspaper articles from Raleigh, reporting the wedding, make no mention of Saville's attendance either, but the truth of this matter is certainly open to question at this late date.

Actually, for every unpleasant anecdote about Saville, there are a number of stories illustrating a whole different side of the man. He was capable of great acts of kindness toward those who worked closest to him at the water department. During his years in Hartford, Saville had three drivers—Marty Cannon, Malcolm "Mac" McInnes and Anthony "Tony" Fornabi. Since these men were required to put in longer hours than the typical water department employee, Saville made it a point to tip each of them in cash each week; a little something beyond their usual paychecks to thank them for the extra effort. At Thanksgiving and Christmas, he always bought turkeys and candy for the people who worked closest to him—his driver, his secretary and others in the executive offices of the water company. When he asked a man to work extra hours to help him with something of a personal nature, he always stopped to buy a box of candy or some flowers for the man's wife. Later in life, when his own wife, Elizabeth, was confined to Sloan's Convalescent Home in Hartford's West End, he took a bus out to see her nightly and always brought a bouquet of fresh flowers for her pleasure. When he put his mind to it, he could be especially solicitous of the needs of others. Sadly, since so few people saw this side of Saville, the stories of the driven, impossible taskmaster assumed greater weight in the lore of Saville's stewardship at the water company.

The chief spent afternoons examining the continuing refinements out at the dams, usually concluding the day's fieldwork at the compensating reservoir. It was natural for Saville to take an inordinate interest in the East Branch valley since surveys and drawings done by engineers more than a decade before made it clear that the topography of that area made it the most logical choice for the site of a future reservoir. In hindsight, it is breathtaking to consider that even while Saville was shepherding home the immensely complex Nepaug reservoir project, he was mapping out in his head—and in physical surveys—another project that was more than three times the size of Nepaug. The enormity of even one of these projects would have overwhelmed the average man.

As Marty Cannon guided the chief's huge black Cadillac along the winding country roads that Saville enjoyed like a little child, the chief had plenty of time to think about the future of the water works. With ten billion gallons of water impounded at Nepaug and another two billion in the basins on the West Hartford property, it would be a long time before the city would need further supplies. Not a particularly happy thought for a man like Saville who craved massive engineering projects. Would he be reduced to an engineer who only maintained a small city water works, when he was just hitting his stride? He was only fifty-eight years old, in perfect health and without any thoughts whatsoever of retirement. But how would he justify another huge reservoir for a city of only 150,000 people?

Of course, the idea of the regional supplier did not just pop into Saville's head one day while he was counting cows in Connecticut's northwestern hills. It is worth remembering that when Saville helped bring in the Wachusett Reservoir project in 1905, Boston was already a regional supplier, whose duties expanded greatly with the new supply. Therefore, Saville understood the pros and cons of the regional supplier concept perfectly. It is fair to say in retrospect that when he first came to Hartford in 1912, he had in mind that Connecticut's capital city would follow the lead of Boston, New York, Philadelphia and every other city of importance in the United States by becoming a supplier to the neighboring towns. When one considered that Hartford had been meeting the water needs of parts of West Hartford since the Civil War, it was not exactly uncharted territory. Thus, the question for Saville was not if but how. How would he get the people of all the small towns around Hartford to embrace the concept of a large regional supplier? More important still, how would he get the residents of Hartford to want to share their water works—paid for dearly over seven decades—with the surrounding communities? Since Saville was the furthest thing from a salesman or politician, this was a dilemma indeed.

As the verdant forests of rural Connecticut whizzed by his window, Saville sat in the back seat of the Cadillac studying drawings, reading correspondence and making notes, which would be transformed into letters once he got back to the office. The chief's car never had any kind of a telephone or two-way radio, as Saville did not like his schedule interrupted. Immersing himself in census data and population shifts, he realized that something unusual had been happening in the small towns surrounding Hartford, and it provided just the opening that he was looking for.

In addition to the city providing water for West Hartford, a number of other communities around the city had approached the water board inquiring about buying water from the city. There was nothing terribly surprising about this, what with all the waterborne diseases about. What could be more logical than towns looking for pure drinking water?

But the towns had no interest in drinking water. The residents of these smaller towns around the city were quite content with their private wells, but knew that they could not fight fires effectively with such a limited source of water. Therefore, their initial entreaties were an effort to secure water for firefighting, not for domestic use.

In 1919, a pipe was laid for the Wolcott Hill Fire District in the small farm town of Wethersfield to the south of the city. Though fire hydrants were—and still are—never metered, this conduit had a rare meter on it at the city line. Actually, this was not the first Hartford water pipe run into Wethersfield. In 1909, The Wethersfield Fire District was incorporated by an act of the state legislature, but at that time, the fire district only served the oldest part of the town—John Oldham's original settlement near the Connecticut River. When the first pipe was laid, slightly more than three thousand people lived in this quiet, agrarian village. This figure does not include the two or three hundred inmates at the Connecticut State Prison at Wethersfield, the state's only penitentiary. By a special act of the General Assembly, a water pipe was run to the prison in the late 1800s.

Several other towns surrounding the city also had fire districts— Newington had two; Windsor and Bloomfield each had one. These fire districts purchased most, if not all, of their water from Hartford.

The need for water for fire districts was only a small part of the equation though. In truth, the very best argument that the district commission had going for it sprung more from the problems associated with water after it had been used than before. Almost all towns in central Connecticut were using the Connecticut River as the basin for their collective waste. But things had reached the point where even people with no olfactory function at all noticed the problem. That said,, the small towns along the river simply did not have the resources to deal with sewage and so the concept of a regional commission to handle the problem, at least at first blush, seemed attractive.

As a direct result of the horrendous pollution, the state legislature issued a charter for a State Water Commission, which would study and hopefully control pollution in the waters of the state. After spending a couple of years assembling a huge file of complaints from around the state, the committee concluded that, ". . . a complete remedy requires that all sewage from the various communities be treated before discharge into the Connecticut [River]." So, in effect—and perhaps for the first time—the twin problems of water and wastewater were bundled together. Up until this time they were viewed separately, to the point where the water company had nothing to do with sewerage. People working at the water company did not even know anyone who worked for the city sewer department (or were smart enough not to admit it). Suddenly, it dawned on people that these were the Siamese twins of the water industry—one presented you with the other. Just as drinking water was part of the majestic hydrologic cycle, so too was wastewater a part of that cycle—just not a very pleasant part.

In addition to the firefighting and sewerage needs of the small towns, population shifts were a concern for Saville as well. Due largely to the popularity of the automobile, during the 1920s an astounding number of people left the city for the suburbs. The figures of the national census for 1920 and 1930 bear this out. What amazed everyone was that, while Hartford's population advanced marginally, all of the surrounding towns grew by close to 50 percent. One town—West Hartford—almost tripled in size. Some of the city's first families remained in Hartford, but it was clear that as the immigrant population of the city grew to one-third of the total, many of the old guard up and left. West Hartford was the town of choice for most of these people. One of the pleasant amenities offered by this town was a ready water supply—they were already connected to the city's water system and they were guaranteed reasonable rates as a matter of law.

In much the same ham-fisted way that the city tried to annex West Hartford twice in the 1860s, it tried three more times in the 1920s. (Bills were introduced into the state legislature in 1923, 1925, and 1927). By annexing the smaller town, the city felt that West Hartford could be forced to shoulder some of the costs of maintaining the roads and providing parking in the city, which were two big problems that resulted from the new commuter lifestyle. All of the bills, however, were defeated.

But as more and more families left the city, the need to expand the water department became a non-issue. Again, Saville was confronted with a strong argument against the regional supplier concept—how could he justify another reservoir project with a constant—or God forefend, slumping—demand? Without a huge increase in the customer base of the water works, he couldn't. Once again, Saville could see the solution to his problem in the district commission, but the whole issue was a political minefield.

Still, as early as 1925, Saville was agitating for additional water supplies in his reports to the water board and he had his eye on the East Branch valley of the Farmington River. He spelled out in detail for the commissioners his feelings on impounding more water—and the sooner the better—

> . . . Sources adequate for greater Hartford for at least the end of the present century are now available, and immediate steps should be taken to acquire control of them. The urgency of such procedure is attested not only by Hartford's own experience, but by the experience of every large city in the country having a municipally controlled water supply . . . Not only do prices of land increase tremendously as time goes by, but difficulties with other interests take on serious aspects and cause delays that, while not insurmountable, are nevertheless a cause of unnecessary expense. . . .

The answer to Saville's little dilemma of selling the regional supplier concept to the state legislature—as well as the residents of the surrounding towns—came in the form of a prominent Hartford attorney, Charles Goodwin, whose forebears were among the city's original founders. In the mid-1920s, when he took up Saville's cause, he was forty-eight years old and a senior partner in one of the city's most influential law firms—Shipman and Goodwin—and also the president of the State Savings Bank. Goodwin sat on the boards of a dozen companies and public institutions and was widely respected on both sides of the political aisle. Without question, he was the perfect point man for Caleb Saville's new water project.

It is unclear at what point Caleb Saville met Charles Goodwin, or better stated, at what point Saville decided that Goodwin was the man he needed to push his new project. Since both men were graduates of Harvard and both were members of the local chapter of the alumni club as well as the University Club on Lewis Street, they may very possibly have known each other since 1912 when the engineer first came to Hartford.

Saville's personal political beliefs were clearly the same as his Yankee ancestors, who were right out of the

Charles Goodwin   Federalist-Whig-Republican mold. But it would have been a mistake for Saville to maintain such a rigid political affiliation when the publicly elected water commissioners came from both parties and foretelling the politics of the president of the water board was about as predictable as forecasting the weather. Wisely, Saville registered as an Independent. With regard to religious affiliation, Saville was equally cagey. Again, his forebears were almost assuredly Congregationalists, but Saville and his wife attended the Unitarian Church until later in life when they moved over to the Episcopal Church where, among the other congregants, were Charles Goodwin and his family.

Saville was eleven years older than Charles Goodwin, but, by virtue of the Goodwin family's prominence and the attorney's own reputation as an able guardian of the city's many institutions and well being, he was the perfect person to breathe life into Saville's plans both at the state capital and in the small surrounding towns. Saville had a first-rate intellect and many other fine qualities, but he was adrift in the world of politics. Buying drinks for strangers, kissing babies and counting noses were all exercises completely lost on him. For the concept of the district commission to take wing, he needed Charles Goodwin.

Unless particularly well informed, most people in the nearby towns had never heard of Charles Goodwin. The son of Reverend Francis and Mary Alsop Goodwin, he had done his undergraduate work at Yale and earned his law degree from Harvard in 1901. A short time after leaving law school, he teamed up with a classmate to form the law firm of Bennett and Goodwin. Four years later, he served as a councilman from Hartford's Fourth Ward and in 1906 became an alderman. He was asked to run for mayor of Hartford, but demurred. In the first decade of the twentieth century, the city's Democrats were coming into their own. As such, Goodwin correctly adjudged his chances at the polls as poor to dismal. Instead, from 1909 to 1911, he served as executive secretary to Governors George Lilley and Frank Weeks. Seizing a rare—albeit regrettable—opportunity, Goodwin then threw his hat in the gubernatorial ring. Although only in his early thirties at the time, Goodwin had all the qualifications to be an excellent governor, as the *Courant* was quick to note—

> . . . Charles A. Goodwin is a candidate of whom no one can say a single ill word. He is a gentleman of the highest character, in politics from a sense of public duty and not as a game or as a means of support. His public and private life are irreproachable in every respect. A clean, high-minded, honorably ambitious young man, he will grow daily with the people of the state. . . .

Between his brilliant legal mind, family contacts and a life completely devoid of scandal, Goodwin was the perfect candidate for the Republicans in 1910. Or so they thought.

What no one could have known during the State Republican Convention was that an ugly bit of family warfare dating back more than a half-century would rob the promising young lawyer of the highest office in the state and end his political career.

The other family involved in this unfinished business was the Bulkeley clan, represented in 1910 by U.S. Senator Morgan Gardner Bulkeley. Back in 1846, just before the city's water works was built, the Yale-educated attorney, Eliphalet Bulkeley—Morgan's father—accepted the job as president of the Connecticut Mutual Life Insurance Company and brought his family to Hartford from East Haddam. This firm was the brainchild of a young attorney, Edwin O. Goodwin and Dr. Guy Phelps. Unfortunately, Bulkeley had a serious disagreement about the structure of the company with many of the principals within the firm. This disagreement centered on Bulkeley's preference for a stock company, where the profit flowed directly to the shareholders. Goodwin, Phelps and the other incorporators wanted Connecticut Mutual to be a true mutual company with the profit going back to the policyholders. It should be noted that their motives were not the least bit altruistic. They expected to make more money for themselves by charging inflated premiums and then returning small amounts to the real owners of the firm—the policyholders. Nevertheless, the mutual company had all the financial patina of a non-profit firm, benefiting greatly anyone who bought a life insurance policy. The upshot of this difference of opinions was a proxy battle that led to the untidy ouster of Eliphalet Bulkeley in favor of James M. Goodwin (J.P. Morgan's uncle).

Ordinarily, such a messy piece of business would be forgotten over time or the aggrieved party would never be in a position to even the score, but this was more like a painful boil that desperately needed to be lanced. The final act of this little Greek tragedy played itself out during the gubernatorial campaign of 1910.

Across the years, Eliphalet Bulkeley's middle son, Morgan Bulkeley, had become one of the most powerful Republican politicians in Connecticut and was presently serving as a United States Senator. Moreover, he had learned his politics in the rough-and-tumble wards of Brooklyn, New York, where the politics was considered *rank*. This would not be quite so meaningful except that back in the late 1840s, when Judge Bulkeley had been so badly humiliated, Morgan was a twelve-year-old boy who idolized his father. Now, at least to Morgan Bulkeley's way of thinking, the time had come for the Goodwin family to pay for their scabrous treatment of his father.

Senator Bulkeley, who had a million friends around the state and the country, put out the word that he was throwing all of his political muscle behind Judge Simeon Baldwin, the Yale law professor and Democrat from New Haven. Out of loyalty to Senator Bulkeley, his friends did likewise. Just as Morgan Bulkeley intended, Charles Goodwin lost his bid for the governorship.

The Goodwin Family was bitter about this, feeling of course that Charles Goodwin should not have had to pay for the hardnosed business dealings of others. So deep was the wound that the Goodwin family rented out their summer cottage at Fenwick—the summer barony of Morgan Bulkeley—and vacationed at Cataumet, Massachusetts and Fisher's Island, New York for the next thirty-five years. Only after World War II, with Morgan Bulkeley cold in his grave the better part of three decades, did Charles Goodwin return to Fenwick.

As for the Hartford Water Works, there are some fascinating historical ties involving these two families that are worth mentioning. It will be remembered that James M. Goodwin was the one who secured the court injunction against the sale of water bonds by the original Board of Water Commissioners in 1854, accusing Ezra Clark of malfeasance and trashing his good name before construction of the water system even began. James Goodwin did all he could to kill the water works and now his grandson envisioned a vastly expanded system including all of the towns of the capital region. A bright historical spotlight on the city's past makes Charles Goodwin's interest in the Hartford Water Department a tad implausible. But how many of Hartford's residents were in a position to remember James M. Goodwin's efforts to derail the water works a half century before?

Not to be outdone by the mischief of the Goodwin family, it was Eliphalet Bulkeley—by 1853 the president of the nascent Aetna Life Insurance Company—who had acted as secretary during Dr. Hunt's dissertation on Hartford's options for drinking water supplies. And it was the same Eliphalet Bulkeley who, with his friend William Hungerford, obtained a court injunction barring the water works from impounding the waters of Trout Brook in 1865. Without the ability of time to wash the slate clean, none of the Republicans at the top of the political infrastructure at the water department in the first half of the twentieth century—and particularly Charles Goodwin—would have been especially welcome. The confluence of their great talents and the growing needs of the citizens of central Connecticut made their presence desirable, if not necessary.

Two years after his defeat in the gubernatorial election of 1910, Charles Goodwin finally married, and when he did, he chose a woman, Ruth Cheney, from another of the area's oldest families. She was a descendent of the Cheney brothers, famous for their silk mills in nineteenth century Manchester. Charles and Ruth Goodwin had five children—Charles, Jonathan, Benjamin, Dorothy and Nancy. They lived in a palatial home that Charles' father, Francis Goodwin, built for them at the southeastern end of Scarborough Street—a small chunk of the hundreds of acres of land the older man owned in Hartford. When Charles Goodwin's father died in 1923, he left an estate worth $6.6 million, lest anyone think money problems should ever be a concern for the Goodwin brood.

In the mid-1920s, the state legislature was studying a host of problems faced by the city and all of its neighbors. In the process, many of these lawmakers slowly became sympathetic to a district commission that might manage a number of different resources. They, of course, were not living in a vacuum and could not help but notice what other cities in the country were doing to address the same problems.

It could be argued that New York was the first city to become a regional supplier when it annexed the four outer boroughs in 1898, but Boston's wholesale annexation of separately incorporated towns on a huge scale was more akin to the example Hartford would follow. Both cities water histories were the result of events an ocean away. The potato famine in Ireland in the middle of the nineteenth century caused a wave of immigration through the two cities that continued for almost a century. Owing in great part to the throngs of impoverished Irish pouring in through Boston Harbor, that city's population crested the 200,000 mark in the late 1860s.

When the engineer Ellis Chesbrough completed the Cochituate Aqueduct in 1848, he envisioned the city drawing on Lake Cochituate forever. Unfortunately, the immigrant masses made his hard work look shortsighted, as new sources were needed by 1870. In that year, Boston annexed the town of Charlestown, along with its Mystic Lakes water system in Winchester, Medford and Arlington. In sum, Boston's history as a regional supplier had begun. By the time that Frederic P. Stearns—with the help of Caleb Saville—completed the Wachusett Reservoir in 1905, the city was serving twenty-nine municipalities within a ten-mile radius of Boston Common.

Boston wasn't alone. As a direct result of a devastating typhoid fever epidemic in Philadelphia in 1793, New York City grew to be the largest city in the United States by 1810. Nevertheless, as mentioned earlier, the real giant step came in 1898 when the four outer boroughs were absorbed by Manhattan. Instantly, the population doubled to 3.5 million. While the annexation may have been greeted as a happy event by some, it must have given the engineers at the city's water works nightmares, because even though a second aqueduct had been added to the Croton System, the watersheds in Westchester County could not supply enough water for such a huge population. Immediately the search for additional water sources was afoot. The solution was the damming of Esopus Creek in the Catskills, whose first waters were delivered into New York in 1916.

Chicago has always been described as a city of neighborhoods. Indeed, even a quick look at a map of the city emphasizes this truth. From its very inception, Ellis Chesbrough's water system of 1867, featuring a two-mile tunnel under the bed of Lake Michigan to an intake crib, pumped water to many of the same towns that Chicago supplies to this day.

When discussing regional suppliers though, Los Angeles is interesting for a surprising reason. From the beginning, the city did not have the water resources to be a supplier of any kind. Wedged between a desert and the Pacific Ocean, Los Angeles could not have been settled in a less desirable spot, at least from a drinking water standpoint. In truth, it would never have grown to be the second largest city in the United States without the self-taught engineer William Mulholland.

In the nineteenth century, Los Angelinos drew their drinking water directly from the Los Angeles River, which was a limpid little stream with willow trees crowding its banks. It wasn't long before this river proved inadequate and the search was on for a better source. The solution to their dilemma was the Los Angeles Aqueduct. The credit for this marvel of hydraulic engineering has always been given to Mulholland, but a triumvirate of eastern engineers—Frederick Stearns, John R. Freeman and James Shuyler—actually designed it. The 233-mile-long aqueduct was completed in 1913 and, with this new source, the city was able to become a supplier to many of the smaller towns in Los Angeles County.

The story is much the same in San Francisco, St. Louis, Detroit, Pittsburgh, Phoenix, Houston and Miami. However, the most impressive example of a regional wholesaler in the United States is Providence Water. True, Rhode Island is our smallest state, but still Providence Water supplies 60 percent of all the people in the state with drinking water. A quick look at a map of the state and one cannot help but be taken aback by the size, proportionally, of the Scituate Reservoir. Subtracting for inland waters, the state is barely 1000 square miles and the total watershed area of Providence Water's six reservoirs is almost 10 percent of the state's whole landmass.

While Connecticut's legislators listened to overtures from the proponents of the district commission concept, the water company still had a business to run. In the early part of 1926, the engineers drew a set of plans for a new garage at their Union Street property. This yard had been in use for almost seventy years and the repair and maintenance crew always called it the "pogeys." It stabled a half-dozen old draft horses and maintenance buckboards loaded with pipes and fitting for the system. (In Canadian slang, the word *pogey* refers to an institution, maintained by private charities for the housing of the aged, sick, orphaned, or feeble-minded. Since the water company's horses were the worn-out hand-me-downs of the fire department, the term "pogey" makes sense, after a fashion.)

The new plans for the yard called for the demolition of the old blacksmith shop along with the stalls for the horses. In its place would rise a new garage capable of housing ten motorized vehicles. The water company's entire fleet was composed of twenty-seven motor vehicles—mostly trucks of all sizes—but also four Cadillacs, for Caleb Saville and members of the water board. At least for the water department, the day of the horse and wagon was over.

The General Assembly kicked around the idea of a regional commission for some time, paying particular attention to a few guiding principals. Recognizing the sensitivity of the annexation issue, they decided that if a regional commission were to be created, the possibility of the city absorbing other towns had to be off the table. Furthermore, each town would become a member of the proposed regional body only by a vote of its residents. Beyond that, they decided to leave the details in the hands of a study committee. In 1928, they appointed a draft committee of thirty-five members to look at the issue and, to chair the panel, they appointed none other than Charles Goodwin.

Goodwin was the natural choice for chairman of the legislature's study committee because—with the obvious prodding of Caleb Saville—he became the strongest proponent of regional solutions to problems. He believed that the water, sewage, health, street paving, building inspections and zoning functions for the people of the capital area could be much better handled on a regional basis. Such a super agency would take a good deal of selling, particularly among the people of West Hartford who had good reason to distrust Hartford's politicians. They believed that inclusion in such a regional district would be the first step in their demise as an independent town. Goodwin was a patient man though and had the enthusiasm to convince others of the efficacy of the plan.

He lobbied hard for the idea, even holding meetings in the proposed member towns. Unfortunately, though the plan may have been sound as a dollar, it was just too big for the average person to accept. Additionally, the components of the huge agency were so diverse and complex that each town wanted the final package custom tailored to meet its own needs. This would be fine if the towns were very similar but such was not the case. Just one example—Hartford already had paved roads while the smaller towns did not. Why should the residents of the city pay to pave the roads in the suburbs? Conversely, the towns had their own building and zoning regulations. Why should the city dictate new standards to the smaller towns? In the end, the disagreements outnumbered the points of accord.

For the city, the biggest bone of contention was that they had built a large and reliable water works, which by 1920 had cost $10 million. Why on earth should they share it with the surrounding towns who collectively had not spent a dime on the system? As one newspaper noted—

> . . . we doubt seriously if Hartford can accept such a proposal. It is highly doubtful if the property of the people of Hartford, as represented by their water system which they own and manage can with any propriety be transferred to a body in which they do not have a controlling voice.

When Goodwin, who was generally the coolest of heads, read this, he responded angrily. He fired off a pointed letter to the newspaper in question, stating that—

> . . . as for the people of Hartford owning the water system, of course they do not. The corporation called Hartford holds it as trustee . . . Does Hartford realize that . . . [these smaller] towns will come to the district with an additional grand list of more than $100,000,000? We are not giving away our water system by sharing its benefits and burdens.

This is a movement, which is inevitable and irresistible for a greater community. Hartford must not discourage her own development by a narrow and selfish viewpoint. . . .

No matter how hard he sold the idea at the state capital, little by little the legislators whittled down the areas over which the new commission would have control. By the end of March 1929, the only things left were water supply, sewerage, highways (to a small degree) and regional planning. The health work would not be taken from the towns, nor would zoning issues. Permission to sell electricity was ruled out (undoubtedly by lobbyists for Morgan Bulkeley's Hartford Electric Light Company) and the commission's financial freedom was curtailed. The lawmakers feared that bundling too many services into one super agency might be unwise. In the end, they decided instead to include in the new commission's charter only such powers as related to water supply and sewerage.

In early May 1929, the state Senate authorized the establishment of the Metropolitan District Commission (MDC). The bill, *"An Act Creating A Metropolitan District Within The County Of Hartford"* was approved later in the year. The bill itself is a most tedious affair consisting of ninety-six separate sections. Once again, the MDC was forbidden to sell water in towns that already had water systems in place.

The only remaining hurdle was an October vote in the towns of West Hartford, Windsor, Bloomfield, Newington, and Wethersfield. (East Hartford, which was expected to be one of the original member towns opted out even before the vote.) For a bill with such sweeping authority, oddly enough, only one third of the 44,000 eligible voters cast a ballot. Nonetheless, four of the five towns accepted the new regional water authority. West Hartford, not surprisingly, voted it down.

Actually, West Hartford had two good reasons to reject the proposal. To begin with, the town had been granted all of the drinking water that it needed as a result of the reservoir negotiations of the early 1860s, and further clarified by laws enacted by the state legislature in 1878 and 1913. How would the new commission benefit them? On that score, it would not. Secondly, West Hartford had originally been a part of Hartford and the five attempts by Hartford to annex the town had alienated the residents. The annexation bills may have failed, but the memories of the people of West Hartford had not. The townspeople were justifiably wary of any agency that would meld the services of the two municipalities. For more than a half-century, they avoided membership in the agency, fearing it as a possible first step toward the absorption of their town into the City of Hartford. (In 1984, they finally joined the MDC.)

The new Metropolitan District Commission, was given their charter and Governor John Trumbull set about appointing the first slate of commissioners. At the first meeting of the MDC, Charles Goodwin was chosen as the agency's first chairman. In his acceptance speech, Charles Goodwin mentioned a "gigantic" new reservoir on the East Branch of the Farmington River upstream of the compensating reservoir. By now, the Barkhamsted Reservoir project was common knowledge, but Goodwin's comments were a trifle premature, inasmuch as the agency would not begin operations until July 1930.

What few people knew was that in 1927, 1928 and 1929, before the legislature even approved the charter of the MDC, the water company had been purchasing landholdings in the East Branch valley. Their first acquisition was the 53-acre Robert Stewart Farm in October of 1927. The farm sat in the northern end of the valley in the small town of Hartland Hollow. It was a sleepy little hamlet almost completely forgotten by time. The number of people in Hartford who had ever been to Hartland Hollow could probably have been counted on one hand.

Fewer people still knew that in October 1927, the water department paid Fairchild Aerial Survey of New York $1,250 to photograph the whole East Branch valley.

Fairchild Aerial Survey was the brainchild of Sherman Fairchild, an engineering *wunderkind* of importance in the field of aerial mapping. About 1920, he invented a camera with a shutter inside a pair of lenses, allowing photographs to be taken inside a vibrating airplane. Fairchild's first camera ship was a Fokker bi-plane. The copilot—in the second seat—lay on his belly and shot pictures through a hole cut in the bottom of the fuselage. Naturally, Fairchild's photographers were less than pleased with this arrangement and not a bit bashful in airing their complaints. The solution was a high-wing monoplane designed specifically for aerial photography, featuring an electrically controlled shutter on a camera mounted permanently in the belly of the plane. The FC-2 had a cruising range of 700 miles at high altitudes, owing to its enclosed, heated cabin. Between 1927 and 1929, Fairchild Aerial Survey received 133 aerial mapping contracts, six of which were in Connecticut, including two for the Hartford Water Works—one in the East Branch valley and the other in the valley of the West Branch of the Farmington River.

Flying at about 1000 feet—and just above stall speed—the cameras mounted underneath the plane clicked a picture of the valley floor every fifteen seconds. Saville's engineers made their original surveys, extremely rough ones, from these aerial shots. On these photographs, the water company's engineers even drew the boundary lines of every piece of property in the valley that would have to be purchased over the next decade.

The aerial photography was heartrendingly poignant. Charles Lindbergh had flown the Atlantic just five months before and there was great excitement and romanticism attached to flight. When the little plane sputtered noisily along the river, high above the valley floor, the people of Barkhamsted and Hartland Hollows, waved wildly at the small plane. Little did the farmers and their families know it, but they were waving madly at the demise of life as they knew it. Completely oblivious to all of the excitement was an infant who was born to a young couple in the valley that year—Charles Lindbergh Emerick.

During 1928, the water company acquired still more farms and acreage and by the time Hartford's neighbors voted on the district commission—near the end of 1929—3,300 acres had been acquired for the new reservoir and surrounding watershed. The water company was buying up property so fast that Saville decided to lease some of the farms back to the original owners—or other families—to reduce the maintenance costs on the houses, barns and outbuildings until they could be demolished.

Caleb Saville did not participate in any of the land negotiations. The process of buying out the farmers and inhabitants of the hollows fell to a special land committee within the water department. Saville's report to the water board in 1928 designates the new catchment as the Barkhamsted Reservoir for the first time—

> . . . preliminary study on the proposed Barkhamsted Reservoir Project, rough estimates of the cost of a dam, a pipe line from the proposed reservoir to the present Nepaug Reservoir . . . were made; a rough estimate of the power available at the Bills Brook Dam site [Barkhamsted Reservoir] and at the Richard's Corner Dam site [compensating reservoir] were made . . . .

Casting a long look backwards, it is fascinating to recognize that Saville's attention to the principal of the district commission was principally for the hydraulic engineering work that it would offer him. Naturally, clean drinking water would be a boon to every man, woman and child in the area of the new MDC, but the end users were of little interest to him. His dream was to impound more Connecticut water than anyone had ever put in storage before. While politicians split hairs in MDC hearings, Saville was merrily buying up land and making increasingly more sophisticated surveys in the East Branch valley, fully intent on building the next great receptacle for the system. His hopes and dreams would come to fruition two decades later with a nine-mile long catchment holding thirty-two billion gallons of water—the Barkhamsted Reservoir.

Chapter 10
The East Branch Valley

A few short weeks after the October vote on the new Metropolitan District Commission, the people of Hartford experienced the first shock waves of a market crash that would change their lives forever. Yet few realized the hardships that lay ahead because by that time, the United States had weathered dozens of rough economic spells. When the Treaty of Paris was signed in 1783, establishing America's independence, it ushered in hard times for all the former colonists. As a major supplier to the continental army, Hartford had exhausted itself trying to keep the soldiers in provisions, leaving the city virtually bankrupt by the end of the fighting. Only after long years of thrift and industry was the city able to rebuild its West Indies trade, the key to its steady pre-war growth.

Perhaps because of this country's four-year election cycle, all of the serious panics in the history of the United States have erupted during odd calendar years. For example, the Panic of 1819 was a direct result of bad banking practices during James Monroe's administration coupled with the crippling aftermath of the War of 1812. In this case, the country was lucky and the hard times lasted only a few years. Banking was the catalyst for the Panic of 1837 as the nation's wealthiest merchant bankers reeled in the wake of Andrew Jackson's refusal to renew the charter of the Bank of the United States in favor of a new national bank. Twenty years later, in 1857, the collapse of the New York office of the Ohio Life Insurance and Trust Company brought on another period of dire instability for businesses throughout the United States. Since the Civil War followed so closely on the heels of that collapse, it remains difficult to assess accurately the lean years that followed.

The Panic of 1873 was triggered by the failure of the banking firm of Jay Cooke & Co. of Philadelphia, the financiers of the Northern Pacific Railroad. The disastrous downturn that followed lasted into the 1880s. When the U.S. Cordage Company failed in 1893, it set off a depression that lasted for much of the inappropriately named "gay 90s."

In the twentieth century, history continued to repeat itself. The 1907 collapse of the Knickerbocker Trust Company in New York unleashed a vicious—but short-lived—financial panic that was brought to heel by an amalgam of investment bankers led by J.P. Morgan. While this list is woefully inadequate in summing up all of the business slowdowns in the first 150 years of the republic, it does suggest that seasoned businessmen with good memories could point to any number of previous periods of business contraction before 1929 and declare confidently that this was nothing new. Or was it?

The crash of 1929 was different in one fundamental way. While previous market gyrations were essentially triggered by mistakes made by once-prosperous firms and tended to affect wealthy investors the most, margin buying of securities—sometimes with as little as 10 percent down—had brought a much wider swath of the population into the game. More importantly, for the millions of laborers, teamsters, cordwainers, bootblacks, and newspaper peddlers, it was never considered investing. It was speculation of the wildest kind for anyone honest enough to admit it. The effects of the crash were felt quickly in businesses all over America. From October 1929 until the market bottomed in July 1932, 75 percent of the value of the nation's total listed securities—representing some $90 billion—vanished.

In Hartford, insurance companies cushioned the blow a bit because this particular sector of the economy has always been noted for entering recessions later than most industries. Other companies suffered along with all of the other businesses across the nation. Hartford was a highly industrialized city at the beginning of the Great Depression, and the panic affected the city's manufacturing base terribly. Rather than laying off employees though, "spread the work" became an industry standard. Not surprisingly under this regimen, the Manufacturers Association of Hartford reported in 1931 that eighty-one factories—which employed 36,250 persons—had 8,873 persons on their payroll in excess of their production demands.

The city's water department was not immune from the devastating financial crisis. When delinquent water rents threatened to reduce payrolls, Caleb Saville had his secretary, Gerry d'Avignon, put together a questionnaire that would help him determine the size of a man's family and whether he had any special responsibilities, like parents or siblings. Using this little inventory, he divvied up the available hours so that each man would have enough to feed his family and there were no layoffs.

However, the problems did not end with excess payroll. For Saville and the water department—and most other utilities—the bond market was crucial for maintaining operations and continuing with expansion plans. Sadly, the bond market in New York was in shambles. The inability to raise funds through bond sales threatened to severely crimp the work on the Barkhamsted Reservoir.

It is with this backdrop of hard times and deprivation that Saville pressed ahead with the great Barkhamsted Reservoir Project. First and foremost on his punch list was the continued acquisition of properties in the East Branch valley. With the power of condemnation on his side, the assemblage of vast acreage in a small river valley in northwestern Connecticut, in retrospect, looks like one big paper chase—trading cash for deeds. However, the hollows were not just oddly shaped parcels of real estate on surveyors' maps. They were the homes of fifth and sixth generation inhabitants in a remote corner of the state and represented a way of life that few people in Hartford could even imagine. In the end, the families in the hollows would become members of an exclusive club—folks without hometowns.

***

During the 1920s—America's prohibition years—life in northwestern Connecticut was an unhurried, blissful time. Composed almost completely of small Republican hamlets and crossroads towns, most families were farmers of one kind or another. But of all the lovely, bucolic areas of Connecticut, none could match the "forgotten by time" innocence of the small collections of humanity isolated along the streams and rolling hills of the Farmington River valley.

The Farmington River's two major branches are similar in that they share the same headwaters on the southern slopes of 2200-foot Becket Mountain in the Berkshires, but quite dissimilar in other ways. The East Branch is the smaller of the two branches and is fed by a watershed of approximately sixty square miles. Just on the other side of the west mountain of Hartland rushes the waters of the larger West Branch of the Farmington River, which drains a watershed of about 100 square miles. While the East Branch at one time had a few gristmills and other small manufactories along its banks, the larger industries were on the larger West Branch.

In the early part of the nineteenth century, there were many diverse manufactories taking advantage of the fabulous millseats on this western course of the river and the whole area was extremely prosperous. Almost on the Massachusetts line, there was a small town, Colebrook River, where Sawyer's Cotton Mill was constructed in 1840. The railroad brought the bales of cotton to Winsted and they were hauled to the mill by horse and wagon. Ultimately, workers transformed the cotton into tents and sails.

In the small hamlet of Riverton, a little farther down the West Branch, Lambert Hitchcock built a mill to manufacture chairs. The business was very successful from 1826 to the early 1840s but, after an unwise move to Unionville in 1844, it began a slow decline toward bankruptcy. Hitchcock died insolvent in 1852. The great bulk of the manufactories along the Farmington River declined in the mid-nineteenth century. The massive steam powered manufactories of the cities spelled the end of the company town along the small waterways of America. The backwoods businesses of the northwestern hills of Connecticut were no exception. The declining industrial valleys of the East and West Branches would serve another purpose now.

The East Branch of the Farmington River tumbled swiftly between the mountains and through the hollows of the northwestern part of Connecticut with the residents of the area giving it little thought. They fished it almost the year long, catching trout, small-mouthed bass and pickerel during lazy summer afternoons. Nights, bands of small boys would sneak up to the "black pool" near the Old Newgate Coon Club and fish for bullheads which, when cooked properly, tasted every bit as good as trout. In the winter, the preferred method of fishing was called "tunkin'." Anglers broke a hole in the ice and, using a sort of rake with bent-up tines, jerked skyward repeatedly until they speared a fish. No matter the method or the season, the East Branch of the Farmington River was a feast for the hungry.

The residents of the hollows built small bridges to ford the river, first with their oxen and wagons and later with their automobiles and pickups. Beyond that, it had all of the insignificance of a river passing through the heart of any other New England town. In the spring, it usually flooded its banks and kept both people and farm wagons close to home. The children loved it, for until the water receded, there would be little or no schooling.

Sometimes, however, the men carried the children over the high water on their shoulders to get them to the one-room schoolhouses. For most of the farmers though, it simply marked the beginning of another growing season. In addition to keeping dairy cows, sheep, pigs and chickens, they also raised tobacco, silage corn, potatoes, hay and a large market basket of vegetables in back yard gardens for their personal use. The farm wives canned prodigiously, using the wood stoves in their summer kitchens to put up as much produce as they could for the long winters.

South Hollow schoolhouse in Hartland Hollow circa 1925

There were two separate hamlets in the East Branch valley. On the south, there was Barkhamsted Hollow—a quiet little place, closely associated with the much smaller Barkhamsted Center just across the river to the west. In the north end of the valley was another collection of humanity—Hartland Hollow. Though each of these hollows was distinct in its own way, the flow of news from the outside world, dictated by the terrain, found its way up the river from the town of New Hartford, through Barkhamsted Hollow and, at length, up to Hartland Hollow.

The principal fixture of Barkhamsted Hollow was LeGeyt's Store, the only general store in the whole valley. It was located at the intersection near the East

Road (along the river) and the Washington Hill Road, which was the unofficial line between the north and south hollows of the village. The store was a tiny but surprisingly complete operation, selling household goods, meat and produce, as well as nails and general hardware items. As an adjunct to the produce and staples operation, it also had a fairly large feed and grain department. Should a customer receive " a call from nature" while on a visit to LeGeyt's, there were outhouses behind the building.

LeGeyt's Store (left) in Barkhamsted Hollow circa 1920.

A couple of people set up small stores in their front parlors, but LeGeyt's was the real center of commerce for the entire valley. In addition to the usual assortment of items associated with a general store, the building also contained the local post office with Charles LeGeyt's wife, Mae, acting as postmaster. Mail was routinely delivered farm to farm, but LeGeyt's had about fifty post office boxes in the store as well. The establishment had originally belonged to a man named Hubert Case who was shot to death at the store during a robbery in 1914. (The two drifters responsible were later hanged in Torrington.) Charles LeGeyt purchased it from the widow Case in 1918. When starting out, he and his family had to live over the store, but in just a couple of years, an unusual opportunity arose. Thanks to prohibition Merrill Tavern—owned by Hubert Case—was effectively out of business. Seeing the potential of the place, Charles and Mae LeGeyt turned the old building into a home for themselves. It was their first experience with indoor plumbing.

Charles LeGeyt was an active man who wanted the best for his family and other in the hollows. In the mid-1920's, he and a farmer friend, Harold Birden, approached the electric company's representative in New Hartford to secure electricity for the valley. However, the utility's salesman was not encouraging. The electric company, while anxious to sign up new customers, could not see the financial sense in installing poles all the way up the narrow roads of the valley. The number of new customers could never have justified the expense. So, in a last ditch effort to secure some electric power—and telephone service—the two men agreed to plant the poles themselves. Unfortunately for them, the soil of the valley floor was not easy digging and every chestnut pole was planted over the next few years through a heap of sweat and a mountain of frustration. Electricity and telephone service finally reached the valley in early 1927.

The East Branch valley was a place where people had to help one another and they did so gladly. In the annual reports of the towns of Barkhamsted and Hartland Hollows, the yearly expenses tell a story of innocence lost. Teachers were paid $100 a month, selectmen made $25 for the year and the local farmers took care of the roads in their off hours, billing the town at a rate of $4 a day. Firewood for the schoolhouses was purchased for $8 a cord and gasoline was 17¢ a gallon. Each of the hollows had a total annual budget of about $18,000, more than half of which went to educating the young.

Barkhamsted Hollow had a new schoolhouse built in 1926—the land cost $500, the school $3,245 and the outhouse $125. Beyond the commonplace work of repairing bridges and town buildings, each of the hollows recorded money spent on paupers and widow's pensions.

Mr. Day, the mail carrier, delivered groceries along with the mail as he made his way over to Barkhamsted Center and then up to Hartland Hollow. In return for his help with the grocery deliveries, Mr. Day could count on some fresh vegetables for his family, courtesy of LeGeyt's Store of course.

The first automobile in town was Harold Birden's 1920 Ford Model "T." Eventually, the LeGeyts would have one too, but for the time being, they relied on a red Reo "Speed Wagon." It was a tired, heavy-duty pick-up truck, used mostly for delivering groceries and feed to the local farms. Charles LeGeyt used his charm to get the farm wives off the party line and then called around the valley to see if anyone needed supplies.

Bridge over the East Branch of the Farmington River, connecting Barkhamsted Hollow on the east with Barkhamsted Center on the west.

Beginning in 1927, fourteen-year-old, pig-tailed Laura LeGeyt helped by driving the unwieldy truck to deliver sacks of grain up and down the valley. As long as there were men to offload the heavy hemp bags at their final destination, she muscled the aged Reo "Speed Wagon" along the dirt roads between the hollows making deliveries. Usually with fifteen to twenty sacks per trip, the tired Reo put in a long day with the unlicensed Laura at the wheel. If the farms needed vegetables or other groceries, she would bring them along as well.

All of the babies in the two hollows were delivered at home with a visit from the doctor as soon thereafter as possible. The physician might come out of either Winsted or New Hartford, the two slightly larger towns to the south of the hollows. For many years, it was the unflappable Dr. Chester English who drove his horse and buggy from New Hartford to the farms in the valley.

Mae LeGeyt organized "baby clinics" at her home, whereby all of the mothers could bring their children around and Dr. English would examine them. A Winsted nurse, Helen Van Meter, assisted him. The clinic was a magnet for the women and children of the hollows, but also for those from Pleasant Valley and Riverton, two small crossroads on the far western side of Barkhamsted.

Farther up the valley in Hartland Hollow, life was even quieter than life in Barkhamsted. All told, there were about twenty-five farms and private homes. Some sat on pieces of land as small as a few acres while others rivaled Augustus Feley's 345-acre spread.

Hartland was divided between three distinct sections—West Hartland at the top of the west mountain, East Hartland at the top of the opposite mountain and Hartland Hollow down in the valley between them. In the springtime, the beautiful rose-colored flowers of the trailing arbutus bushes blanketed the sides of both mountains. A town hall, two schools and a cemetery were contained within Hartland Hollow. The town hall was quite a bit more than the official building that the name conjures up. Rather, it was the center of almost all of the social activity of the town. Over the years, it hosted fairs, picnics and dances, as well as political meetings and elections. When bad weather kept the residents from driving their carriages up the west mountain to attend the Second Congregational Church in West Hartland, religious services were held at the town hall. It was a plain white clapboard structure, maybe thirty by fifty feet, but no building was more important to the people of the hollow.

Hartland Hollow itself was divided, if only by the vernacular of the day, between the north hollow—upstream of Route 20—and the south hollow—downstream. Route 20 descended the mountain from the west more gently than it did on the east—the beat up macadam road making almost a straight shot directly into the hollow. To do the same on the east side would have been lunacy. That road, commonly called Walnut Hill Road, was a ledge cut which snaked back and forth across the mountain between trees and boulders, until it finally straightened out for a quick run through a thirty-foot long covered bridge over the East Branch of the Farmington River. The young people in the hollow who thought they knew something, called it the "kissing bridge." It was washed out by spring floods a number of times and had been replaced as recently as 1920.

Hartland Hollow Town Hall, or Town House, as it was sometimes called.

One of the three town cemeteries was also in Hartland Hollow, on the west side of the river, and about a half mile up the road of the north hollow. For the education of the young people, there were two one-room schoolhouses—one in the north hollow and one in the south. With teachers making $100 a month, these jobs were coveted and some of the farm wives wrested them from more qualified outsiders. The farm children in the hollow would go to the little schoolhouses for grades 1 through 8 and then attend the Gilbert School in Winsted for grades 9 through 12. The post office, in the home of Lena Cables, made the hollow almost completely self-sufficient.

By today's standards, life in Hartland Hollow was harsh. There was no indoor plumbing and certainly no home heating except what could be furnished by wood-burning, cast iron box stoves. To keep warm at night, children wrapped a towel around a flat iron or a brick and took it to bed with them. When nature called, small "privies" sufficed. On Saturday nights, hot water was taken from a side tank on the wood stove and baths given in a galvanized tub. There was no electricity—therefore no radio, telephones or electric lights. Most people used kerosene lamps. Until the mid-1920s, amenities were few.

Almost all of the farmers kept dairy cows and eventually joined the Milk Producers Association whereby they "sold their milk out" to Bryant & Chapman in Hartford who collected it on a daily basis. The milk was stored in forty-quart cans with the average farm selling twelve to sixteen cans a day. Many of the farmers also grew broadleaf tobacco that, like all Connecticut grown tobacco, was used for cigar wrappers. The farm women tended coops full of chickens and their families either ate the eggs or exchanged them at LeGeyt's store in Barkhamsted Hollow for household staples.

In the springtime, farmers "set" quills—three to a bucket—in the huge sugar maple trees in the valley and collected sap for maple syrup. The pails were emptied into a vat atop an oxen-drawn bobsled and brought to the boiling pan, where the thick, gooey mess was reduced. Forty gallons of sap yielded one gallon of maple syrup. It was a tedious process, but ensured each family a sweet confection to put on almost everything they ate.

Tobacco farmers in Hartland Hollow

Six-year-old Pauline Emerick learned first hand how tough life could be in Hartland Hollow when fire swept through the family homestead in 1924. Despite the efforts of every able-bodied man and boy, throwing buckets of water on the blaze all night long, the structure burned to the ground. She, her five brothers and sisters, and her parents had to move in with her grandparents, Mary and Robert Stewart. Sadly, her parents had no fire insurance and the place was never rebuilt. When her family left Hartland Hollow in 1933 for a new home in West Hartland, it was from the farmhouse of her grandparents. At the time of the move, she was fifteen years old.

Although the Town of Hartland sent representatives to the Connecticut General Assembly, the same as every other town in the state, the average citizen was not well educated or knowledgeable in current affairs. As far back as 1913, the annual report of the water company was a public record that could be perused at the public library in Hartford if anyone had the time or the inclination. At the conclusion of the financial statements—and pasted inside the back cover—was a bundled up map. When completely unfolded, this document was perhaps twelve inches square. Not only did this map show the six existing reservoirs in West Hartford but also the proposed Nepaug Reservoir, complete with the compensating reservoir in Barkhamsted. Beyond all that though, it even showed the entire sixty-one square mile watershed *of the whole East Branch of the Farmington River.* Nonetheless, someone looking at this document in 1913 might not suspect trouble for the East Branch valley because Hartford was only growing at a rate of 3 percent a year. Keeping in mind that Hartland Hollow was almost eight miles north of the compensating reservoir in Barkhamsted, it is easy to see how the townspeople might have felt that they would be unaffected by any new water projects.

But after the Nepaug Reservoir was completed and the water company started buying farms in the East Branch valley—and particularly in Hartland Hollow—suddenly things looked very different. One can only imagine the conversations among the farmers in the hollow when they learned that the Robert Stewart Farm had been sold to the Hartford Water Works in late 1927. Undoubtedly, they had a sinking feeling when they realized—for the first time and without reservation—that it was only a question of time before the water company did to the East Branch valley what it had done to the Nepaug River valley just a few years before.

In 1927 though, who would have dreamed that a new and bigger reservoir was needed? After all, the Nepaug project had just been completed in 1922 and impounded ten billion gallons of water for a city of about 150,000 people. Wouldn't that be enough? It might have been if Caleb Saville, Charles Goodwin and the idea of the Metropolitan District Commission had not come along. Still, who in 1927 would have bet that a large regional water commission would have been accepted by the neighboring towns? After all, when it was first proposed, it faced stiff opposition. Even when it was finally accepted, the towns surrounding Hartford passed it by the slimmest of margins.

The only thing that could be said with any certainty was that it was a very unsettling time for the people living in the hollows. Though they would all be losing their farms, the experience was different for each family. Some sold early and bought new farms in other towns with hardly a look back. Others fought bitterly and even forced the water company's hand, winding up in condemnation proceedings. In the end, of course, everyone was forced to leave the beautiful valley.

***

As stated before, the water company began acquiring acreage in the East Branch valley in 1927, long before the state legislature was even close to granting permission to impound the waters of the Farmington River. Late that year, the Stewart Farm in Hartland Hollow was sold to the water company. The Stewarts, together with their son, daughter, and her six children were allowed to remain on the property for another six years, while they sought a new place to live. A month later, in November of 1927, Mrs. Joanne Carrier, sold her farm to the MDC and moved with her daughters to Riverton, in the valley of the West Branch.

During the second half of 1928 the water company bought three more farms. It was their intention to scoop up the biggest farms as early as possible, as this would hasten control of the area. Among the farms purchased at this time were the 220-acre Waldo Miller Farm and the 256-acre Wilber Miller property. The third property was only forty acres, but it was perhaps the most active forty acres in the valley. Walter and Lena Stewart and their four children lived on the west side of the East Branch where they kept horses, cows, pigs, chickens, and honeybees. Beyond the animals, every year they put out a huge vegetable garden. Most of these vegetables they sold as well as eggs, milk, honey and nuts. Models of industry, Walter and his two sons even maintained a trap line where they snared foxes, otters and raccoons. They sold the pelts to buyers who traveled regularly through the valley.

In July 1929, just as the General Assembly granted a charter to the new district commission, the MDC purchased J. Alfred Cables's 200 acres.

J. Alfred Cables's bucolic 200-acre farm.

The Cyrus Miller Tavern—and its twenty acres—followed. This particular purchase must have been a great blow to the people of Hartland Hollow because, in its day, the tavern was a centrally located gathering place and a very lively roadhouse. It sat on the Albany Turnpike (Route 20) very close to the road leading to the north hollow. (The structure was removed from the valley, board by beam, and lives on today as The Tollgate Inn of Litchfield.)

The MDC picked up Anna Schramm's eighty acres in April of 1930 and the Fred Stevens Farm (ninety-five acres) that same June. Near Christmas, they scooped up the forty-three-acre farm where young Pauline Emerick had watched her whole world go up in flames just six years before.

On July 1, 1930 the Metropolitan District Commission began full operation with Charles Goodwin elected as its first chairman, a post he held until his retirement in 1949. As if to remove any lingering doubts about the Barkhamsted Project, it was at this time that the East Branch Water Supply Act was passed by the state legislature, outlining every single part of the dam and reservoir in detail.

Whittled down to its basics, it allowed the Metropolitan District Commission to take the East Branch of the Farmington rivers "by purchase, condemnation or otherwise any lands, water rights, flowage rights, rights of way or easements . . . necessary," including building all of the necessary "dams, dikes, reservoirs, spillways, flumes, canals, aqueducts, wheel-pits, waste-weirs, races [&] buildings. . . ." Additionally, the water commissioners were saddled with the duty of supplying water "to any inhabitants of the towns through which the line of main pipes . . . shall pass, upon reasonable terms . . . ." Most importantly, the mechanism by which the water works would maintain the level of the Farmington River was spelled out in detail for the benefit of the downstream owners.

A crucial provision of the legislation granted to the board of the new MDC was the power of condemnation. They were not given this power during the building of the Nepaug Reservoir and the compensating reservoir. Caleb Saville had written in earlier reports, that during the course of the Nepaug project, "the necessary lands were acquired without excess litigation." However, the language of this new legislation seems to indicate that the new commissioners of the MDC felt it might not remain that way. After all, the amount of acreage and private farms needed for the Barkhamsted Reservoir project was many times that of the Nepaug project and the number of owners accordingly much higher. The right of condemnation would certainly dash the hopes of hardheaded landowners and invariably speed up the acquisition process.

Another thing that was striking about the legislation concerned the detail to which the lawmakers went, even spelling out the exact amount that the towns would be paid for their bridges and precise instructions for the relocation of the cemeteries and some of the doomed buildings of the hollows. The lawmakers realized, as Caleb Saville did, that the more matters cast in stone, as it were, the less controversy later. In any event, the water company's survey and land acquisition work continued without delay as the MDC exercised its new powers.

Initially, when the water board met with the riparian owners to hash out yet another deal regarding the flow in the river, Saville knew that there would be problems. As designed, the Barkhamsted Reservoir was to be built in the watershed of the compensating reservoir for the Nepaug Reservoir, thereby cutting off its supply. All the same, if the compensating reservoir were kept filled with water from the new reservoir above it, nothing would change. The riparian owners were having none of it though. They could see that if there were now two huge reservoirs—the Nepaug and the Barkhamsted—holding back water from the Farmington River, one compensating reservoir would not be enough.

The solution was the same as the one arrived at during the Nepaug negotiations—a second compensating reservoir. This time, the water company would build a dam over on the West Branch of the Farmington River—above the town of Riverton—and impound waters in a reservoir called the Hogback. The mill owners accepted this with one proviso—until the Hogback Reservoir was completed, the water company would be bound by law to release 13.6 billion gallons of water into the old compensating reservoir annually to keep the flow in the Farmington River constant. This would ensure a steady flow in the river and guarantee the rights of the riparian owners, at least for the time being.

While the MDC purchased the farms of Hartland Hollow in the late 1920s, they began negotiations in Barkhamsted Hollow as well. But, in the twenties, only a few Barkhamsted farms changed hands. It was during the thirties, the Depression years, that the great bulk of the sales transpired with a total of eighty properties falling into the hands of the MDC. The length of the buying spree in the entire valley, from the first sale in the twenties to the last sale in the early forties spanned a period of fifteen years.

From the very beginning, it was Saville's intention to buy up as much land around the Barkhamsted Reservoir as was humanly possible. Only in that way would they be able to insure that the water kept its pristine nature. Considering that they were buying farms in a depressed region in the middle of the nation's worst economic downturn—they were able to control the entire watershed almost to the Massachusetts state line.

Lands that would be underwater at the completion of the project had priority of course, but Saville was adamant about securing complete control of all the watersheds. Just as an example of the ongoing work involved in protecting watersheds, in 1928, six years after the completion of the Nepaug project, he convinced the commissioners of the MDC to purchase 273 acres around that reservoir and another ninety-three acres the following year. Saville understood better than anyone that the business of controlling—and thus protecting—watersheds was an ongoing process.

At the end of the 1931 school year in Hartland Hollow, enough families had already left the valley to allow the selectmen to close down the North Hollow schoolhouse. For the next two years, all of the children upstream of Route 20 would attend the South Hollow school.

Meanwhile, the MDC bought another 208 acres from Leon Dickinson in June 1931, and a month after that, the Clifford Cable's farm (140 acres). Soon thereafter, the MDC closed on another large piece of property—Byron Stratton's place—giving them 344 acres in one fell swoop. At the end of July the water commissioners acquired a property on which they were probably loathe to waste time. Frederick and Etta Stewart had a small house on the east side of the river in the southern part of Hartland Hollow. The Stewarts had no children, no barns or livestock and no fields of any kind. Frederick Stewart always hired out to others in the hollow and had little interest in anything except his honeybees. While necessary, such a small purchase must have highlighted the tediousness of the process for all concerned.

Conversely, it was a colossal blow for the people of the valley when the Talcott Banning Farm was surrendered. On the surface, it might have appeared like the loss of just another 160 acres, along with the usual cows, sheep,

*Leon Dickinson's Tobacco farm illustrates nicely why the
East Branch valley was perfect for a massive reservoir.*

chickens and honeybees, unless one knew about Talcott's little sideline—he ran an illegal distillery. Talcott's "still" did a land office business and, during those thirsty prohibition years, he produced enough hard cider and apple brandy for everyone in the hollows. It was an irony of unspeakable proportions that the whole valley had to suddenly go "dry" to slake the thirst of strangers twenty-five miles away.

Just before Thanksgiving, it was Augustus C. Feley's turn to surrender his land and he did it in a big way. A number of years earlier, in a property swap, he had picked up an extra farm. He sold his own place (345 acres), and the Robert Stewart, Sr. Farm, which was a bit smaller but highly productive all the same. The Feleys were a prosperous family and they had had the first telephone in Hartland Hollow. A. C. Feley was a practical man and, sensing the futility of a long exhausting battle (with a preordained outcome), he simply accepted the MDC's offer and moved on.

Just before the beginning of 1932, the Metropolitan District let the contract for the clearing of the site where the new Bills Brook Dam would be located. (This dam would eventually be named for Saville, but for the purposes of this story, the original name Bills Brook remains, reflecting its proximity to a small stream that spilled into the East Branch just below the construction site.) Most people who were alive at that time recognize 1932 as the stage when the full brunt of the Great Depression bore down on the country. During January of that year, the water board had an unusual meeting. This particular gathering was held at The Hartford Club, a posh "old boys" haunt on Prospect Street, and the mood of the times was captured quite nicely in the comments of the recording secretary—

> ... Chairman Charles Goodwin recommended that the removal of the cemeteries be undertaken very soon, to show that the [MDC] was definitely embarked on this project, and so remove the possibility of concerted opposition by cemetery authorities. [He also] spoke ... of ... a temporary halt in land purchasing. ...

Goodwin's concern with the ongoing land purchases stemmed from the horrendous condition of the bond markets in New York. Understating the case badly, investors were wary of all financial instruments, whether stocks or bonds. As a result, the bond offerings included the following language— "Principal and interest payable in gold coin of the United States of America of the present standard of weight and fineness." With this kind of distrust of paper instruments, was it any wonder that Franklin Roosevelt outlawed the ownership of gold in 1933?

With no one to purchase the MDC's bonds, it was highly unlikely that the money could be found to continue the enormous land purchases. Moreover, he felt that the board was paying too much for the land—considering the depressed economic times. Accordingly, the commissioners voted to stop all land purchases, withdraw all offers until further notice and contacted all property owners affected by the decision immediately.

But such a wide sweeping decision was bound to cause trouble. Would the MDC's decision to retract all of its offers be understood by the people of Barkhamsted and Hartland Hollows? Would they realize that the bond market in New York was in shambles? Or was it more likely that they would be confused by the mixed signals being sent by the water commissioners? Most likely, they would not be convinced that the board could not get the necessary funds to buy the remaining properties. More likely, they would feel that the water board was using this excuse as a bargaining tool to acquire the land at better prices.

Regardless of perceived motives, exactly two weeks after the board voted for a moratorium on land purchases, they received an offer of sale from the heirs of the Ford Brothers Farm. The property in question was the Dutton-Ford Brothers place. It was a 167-acre farm at the very north end of Hartland Hollow and was more of a lumbering operation than a farm. The Duttons had started the mill and, later, the Ford Brothers bought the place and continued the business. The Fords had the only horse-drawn hay baler in Hartland Hollow and they took it from farm to farm giving a hand to their neighbors at harvest time.

At the MDC's February 16 meeting—one short month after the decision to end all land purchases—the board was informed that an offer of sale had been received. At the same time, the members were read chief engineer Saville's comments—

> . . . [that] the immediate acceptance of [the offer], will allow the property to be purchased for $4000, and . . . the purchase at this time would be very advantageous. This purchase will clear up the northeast corner of the required area through which one of the main brooks runs. . . .

The board voted to consummate the deal, and despite their misgivings, they were back in the land acquisition business. They also voted to accept an offer by a company, whose mill was along the river close to the compensating reservoir, thus acquiring two more parcels. Later in the summer, an elderly widow named Mary French, died in Hartland Hollow. Quickly they snapped up her land as well. At the same meeting in August, they voted to purchase Sophie Luhrs' fifty-five acres for $8,300 and to accept eight acres from the Warner Brothers in Barkhamsted for $400. Not all land transfers ran so smoothly though. Two counter offers came before the board that showed recalcitrance on the part of the owners and it was voted, ". . . that the District Counsel be requested to take such steps as are necessary to obtain the (said properties) by condemnation." Sensing a losing battle, one of the two property owners had a sudden change of heart and agreed to the board's offer. They accepted his property a month later at the originally agreed upon price.

At their November 29 meeting at the end of 1932, the board had an ugly task facing them. There were four property owners in Barkhamsted Hollow who had chosen to be hardheads. Earlier, the board made final written offers, but they were rebuffed. It was voted unanimously, ". . . that the District Counsel be requested to institute condemnation proceedings at once . . . [against these four owners]."

One of the properties in question was LeGeyt's store. Charles was the secretary and treasurer of Barkhamsted and by all accounts a good-natured and reasonable man, but together with his wife, Mae, they had acquired about 120 acres, their home and store, and were determined to stay put. Still, the LeGeyt's hearts were not in it. They knew that, at the end of the day, any victory would be Pyrrhic. Nevertheless, Charles was a man with a strong sense of propriety and, in the end, he fought simply because he thought it was the right thing to do.

It has been a hotly debated question over these many years as to whether the MDC entered the hollows like a thief in the night and stole the people's farms or whether the prices paid were fair. On these matters, a number of different factors should be considered. To begin with, the land was not particularly good land, fetching about $27 a lightly wooded acre and about twice that for farmland, which was exactly what the water company was offering. Secondly, if an owner didn't like the offer, they could retain a lawyer and an appraiser, and enter into "binding arbitration." If that didn't work, and condemnation proceedings were instituted, the MDC paid $1 and waited for a court date. One way or another it was settled. Most people didn't fight, but it would be well to note that those who held out the longest did the best financially. The second source is Charles Goodwin himself who expressed his opinion at the January 1932 board meeting that the MDC was paying too much for the land.

Lastly, a valuable source of information on the matter is a former Judge of Probate for Hartland and past chairman of the Hartland Historical Commission, Stanley Ransom, who writes in his book, *History of Hartland*, the following—

> . . . When it became known for a certainty that Hartland Hollow and much of the area comprising the West Mountain was to be eventually acquired by the Metropolitan District for reservoir and watershed purposes, there were feelings of mixed emotions on the part of those inhabitants directly affected. Some congratulated themselves on their good fortune in having their land acquired *at above the average market price*, while others, whose roots ran deep in Hartland soil, were reluctant to relinquish their ancestral acreage. It was only a matter of a few years, however, before most of them had become reconciled to their fate, had disposed of their property and migrated to nearby towns . . . (Italics added)

To build on Stanley Ransom's remarks, it might be fair to say that for many people, no amount of money could compensate them for the loss of their homes and farms. How much money were Barkhamsted and Hartland Hollows worth? The answer, of course, would depend in large part on one's emotional ties to the land.

By the spring of 1933, the actual construction of the Bills Brook Dam began. (It is important to understand that the land purchases, the engineering and the construction work on the Bills Brook Dam overlapped one another. For simple clarity, the disparate elements of the Barkhamsted Reservoir project are discussed separately in these chapters.) By this time most of the properties in the two hollows had been acquired by the water company. Once they had "good and sufficient deed," the new owners—the MDC—could afford to be compassionate and perhaps rebuild their tattered image a little. It could not have been easy to ask people to leave property that, in some cases, had been in their families for many generations. People were allowed to remain on their farms under the most favorable conditions, while they looked for other accommodations. As previously mentioned, the Emerick family stayed for six years.

Long grace periods were actually easy to grant because the properties would be secured until it was time for demolition. The water company even offered to let families repurchase the dwelling house for $1 and move it to another site.

There were some takers. The McWade family took down their home and relocated it to Litchfield. In the end though, the torch was put to most of them.

For those who postponed the inevitable, it grew very lonely in the valley. By early 1933, almost all of the families had moved on to new farms in other towns and the wind whistled through the houses and barns, banging loose doors and shutters. A strange quiet—even an eeriness—had settled over the whole valley. When fifteen-year-old Pauline Emerick and her family left the valley in 1933, they were the last to leave Hartland Hollow.

Five miles away, in the center of Barkhamsted Hollow, LeGeyt's Store was holding its own. Unfortunately though for Charles LeGeyt, business had slowed to an occasional order from his friend, Harold Birden, another holdout. Young Laura LeGeyt, who had struggled with the Reo "Speed Wagon" delivering sacks of grain at fourteen, left the Hollow in 1930 to attend nursing school in Hartford. She was seventeen years old and only visited Barkhamsted Hollow a few more times after that. All of her life she would be haunted by her three favorite memories of the hollow—her father, Charles, making ice cream on Sunday afternoons, the oyster suppers at Marshall Case's home and the gorgeous blue forget-me-nots that grew along the sides of the narrow dirt roads throughout the valley.

True to the spirit of the protest, LeGeyt's Store remained open until November of 1934, when Charles and Mae finally sold. Charles' friend, Harold Birden, was made out of marginally stronger stuff and lasted until April of 1936. He was the last one to leave Barkhamsted Hollow.

Harold Birden driving a hay rake in Barkhamsted Hollow.

After everyone was out of the valley, in the early summer of 1936, the MDC hired S. J. Groves, a stripping company from Ridgefield, New Jersey, to clear over 1,100 acres. The valley was sloped in such a way that, at completion, the reservoir would have a depth of 120 feet at Barkhamsted Hollow, but only 40 feet in its northern reaches. In the basin where the water would rest, it was a scorched earth contract. The work began in November of 1936 and was completed the following August. Times were tough and local people were not too proud to work for Groves, sometimes stripping land formerly owned by their own kin, neighbors and friends. All together, the company fielded a crew of about seventy-five hands. Using two-man whipsaws, they felled towering hardwoods from morning to night. Ted Gillette, an old-timer from Winsted, set up shop in Charles and Mae LeGeyt's old house to sharpen the men's saws. Trees, brush, house parts, barn wood and old farm implements were stacked in an enormous pile in the center of A. C. Feley's tobacco fields. One of the workers, a local man, estimated the pile to be sixty feet tall by the time it was set ablaze. When it went up, the flames licked the clouds. Working through the long, cold winter, S. J. Groves completed the contract in nine months, after which time there was nothing left except empty cellar holes that would fill with water along with the rest of the valley.

Beyond the two hollows, there were other sections of the proposed watershed where people refused to heel. Real estate activity came almost to a halt as the practical people moved on and the hardheads dug in for a fight. During the years 1935 and 1936, there were considerably fewer land transfers and each individual property began to get special attention by the water board.

The Old Newgate Coon Club in Hartland Hollow was one of the last properties to go, perhaps because all of its decisions were made by committee— the same as at the MDC. Rather than try to describe the Coon Club from

Old Newgate Coon Club with some coon hunters.

such a distance in time, it is instructive to read the words of a writer working on the Federal Writer's Project in 1938, one of Franklin Roosevelt's "make work" agencies of the Great Depression—

> . . . the Old Newgate Coon Club, [is] one of the numerous such
> clubs in Connecticut . . . .Men, dogs, lanterns, and, invariably, a number
> of small boys, make up the usual . . . coon hunting party . . . The
> 'coon,' . . . is unaware of the hunt until he hears the bark of a distant
> hound. When the dogs bark 'treed' . . . the huntsmen . . . circle the tree,
> flashing their lanterns . . . to locate the coon by the shine of his eyes . . .
> Once found, the coon is . . . usually . . . shaken from his lofty perch . . .
> as the shouting huntsmen swing their clubs. The . . . meat is highly
> prized, and . . . becomes the main dish at a coon supper. . . .

The one hundred members of the Old Newgate Coon Club were mostly from
Granby with a smattering of men from the hollows. Pauline Emerick's father,
William, was a member and had a coonhound, Lady, who treed thirty-two
raccoons in a single season, a record in the mid-1920s. After considerable
negotiations, the Old Newgate Coon Club, together with its eighty-nine acres,
was sold to the MDC for $24,000. (The coon hunters used the money to buy a
new club farther to the west.)

When most of the property in the East Branch valley had been purchased,
Caleb Saville made plans for the next phase of the project. It was at this stage
that fatigue began to show in members of the land committee. These men had
grown tired of approaching disgruntled farmers with unwelcome buyout offers,
so they decided to bring in a third party to help with the wearying negotiations.
But who?

One of the lawyers in Charles Goodwin's law firm was his younger brother
F. Spencer Goodwin, who among his many accomplishments in life, had served
as the president of the Board of Water Commissioners for the old Hartford Water
Works during two separate terms—in 1913 and 1928. In addition to his past
experience with the water department, he also sat on a number of boards at
different Connecticut businesses including the Collins Company in Collinsville.
The owner of this company was a Yale-educated engineer and industrialist, H.
Bissell Carey. With a persuasive pitch by F. Spenser Goodwin, Carey agreed to
help the MDC acquire lands for the Hogback Reservoir on the West Branch of
the Farmington River. Oddly enough, the Collins Company was one of the
downstream riparian owners who held the water company's feet to the flame
during negotiations at the capitol for the new reservoir.

In December 1940, the board authorized the Collins Company to offer
$7,000 for the forty-acre "Bronson" parcel near the site of the new Hogback
Reservoir. Over the next decade, about half of the land needed for the Hogback
Reservoir was bought by the Collins Company and then deeded over to the MDC
later. On the transfer deeds in the land records of Colebrook, it is often written
that the transfer to the MDC was "without consideration." Whether this was
actually true or whether a commission was paid "out of closing" is anyone's

guess. Most probably, Carey's commission checks were cut separately so that the former property owners would not feel that he was profiting from their misfortune.

There was still some work to do in the upper reaches of the watershed of the new Barkhamsted Reservoir, but the MDC was already buying up the land over in the valley of the West Branch for the Hogback Reservoir. (The Hogback Dam was renamed for Charles Goodwin a year before it was completed in 1960, but for the purposes of this story, the original name will remain.)

As if he were a fortuneteller instead of a lawyer, Charles Goodwin had called the problems with the cemetery trustees as early as January of 1932. At that time, he had warned of the possibility of trouble with the cemetery officials and even expressing concern about ". . . opposition by cemetery authorities." Almost seven years later, they were still tussling with the representatives of the Barkhamsted Center Cemetery Association and the Hartland Hollow Cemetery.

At an October 1940 meeting of the board, a memo from Caleb Saville noted his displeasure with the progress of negotiations. In this note, he informed the board that all of the work was completed, but he could only fill the reservoir up to the old Rt. 20 in Harland Hollow because of a few nuisances. First, Hartland Hollow Cemetery and the town hall had not yet been moved, nor had the old dirt roads of the valley been abandoned. And lastly, the fate of the old Universalist Church and cemetery at Barkhamsted Hollow was still undetermined.

The land committee of the MDC met with the representatives of the cemetery association one last time to try to come to an agreement on the price to be paid for the Universalist Church property. Regrettably, their offers and counteroffers were not even close. The Barkhamsted representatives had lowered their offer to $5,000 and the board had raised theirs to $1,500. Beyond the simple matter of arriving at a dollar sum for the church and the cemetery land, there were contentious side issues. For example, there was the matter of a certain "Constitution Oak Tree."

In Connecticut, there exists an old legend that goes roughly as follows: King James II of England created the Dominion of New England in 1686, which effectively rendered all of the young states' charters invalid. To drive the point home, the King sent his representative around to the individual states to collect the original charters (documents). When he tried to collect the "Charter of 1662" at Hartford, it was squirreled away in a hollowed out oak tree. Thus, the legend of the Charter Oak was born.

The townspeople of Barkhamsted wanted an easement established so that the citizens of the town could walk down the side of the watershed to the old cemetery property and view the tree, which they claimed was a scion of the original charter oak. Unfortunately, the tree was not in a spot where that could be accomplished without scuba gear, so the MDC officials waved off the whole issue. In order to placate the representatives though, the board offered to give Barkhamsted a scion (in seedling form) of the original Charter Oak from its own nursery that could be planted in the new Barkhamsted Cemetery.

Still, the Barkhamsted Center Cemetery Association was not satisfied and so in April of 1941, the board voted to institute condemnation proceedings against them. At the same meeting, a similar recommendation was issued for the land of a farmer, Henry Gidman, who was by far the hardest of the hardheads in the valley. A month later, the board threw in the towel. They voted to give the Barkhamsted people $2,500 for the church and cemetery land and, in an effort to clear the slate once and for all, gave Henry Gidman $2,500 for his farm. This was considerably more than they had been giving for similar pieces of property, but they were tired of the whole affair and just wanted it settled. The MDC would continue to purchase property on the sides of the watershed for many years to come, sometimes swapping parcels with the state. However, at this point, the purchases needed for the reservoir itself had been completed.

Getting slightly ahead of themselves, the commissioners had already let the contract to the Bottinelli Monumental Company of New London ". . . for the removal and reinterment of the bodies, monuments, and etc." from the three cemeteries in Barkhamsted, as well as two small plots on private farms, to the new Barkhamsted Cemetery. Finally, three years later, the company could begin its work. The cost would be more than $52,000.

The Hartland Hollow Cemetery still had to be moved but the negotiations were going nowhere. In the interim, the board agreed to pay Hartland $25,000 for their town hall. Despite the irritation of the lengthy negotiations, they still agreed to allow the building to remain standing until a new one could be built somewhere else. The commissioners even went so far as to purchase a lot on the west mountain and one on the east, so that two new town buildings could be built. The members of the board were painfully aware that the reservoir would adversely affect the town of Hartland the most—in effect, it cut the town in half. Whereas Barkhamsted would have a scenic drive across the new dam to get to the other side of town, the people of Hartland would be forced to drive a ten-mile horseshoe around the north end of the reservoir to visit neighbors. There would be no picturesque causeway for them.

Despite the seriousness of the land transfers and the disruption of the lives of so many, humorous things still happened along the way. After Barkhamsted's First Selectman, Marshall Case, had negotiated the sale of a bridge and three schools to the MDC, he decided that the town should be compensated for another "Constitution Oak," which sat in one of the schoolyards. Upon closer inspection though, it was discovered that the tree in question was a pin oak while the time-honored legend was built on a white oak. So as not to ruffle any feathers, the water company simply gave Barkhamsted two more seedlings from its nursery and $100. After all the fuss, Charles LeGeyt and some other men paid the MDC $1 and moved the South Hollow schoolhouse to the top of Washington Hill—above the watershed lands—in an effort to preserve something of the past.

Wilbur Miller, Hartland's First Selectman finally came to an agreement with the board. The Hartland Hollow Cemetery property was transferred and at its next meeting on October 19, 1940, the contract for the removal and reinterment of the bodies was let. Again, the Bottinelli Monumental Company was the low bidder so the board awarded the contract to them. Most of the bodies would be reinterred in a new cemetery in West Hartland. At the request of the next of kin, some went to new gravesites in East Hartland and other towns. The cost to the MDC was $17,000.

While Caleb Saville's work was important, it created great hardships for the people in its path. His work had displaced upwards of a thousand people. Since most of the people wanted to buy new farms and start over, very few were able to stay in Barkhamsted or Hartland. After selling their land, they moved to Granby, Suffield, Winsted, New Hartford, Riverton, Pine Meadow, and Canton. They had to go where there were farms for sale and they tended to buy to the east of the valley. Based on what they now knew, any purchase to the west might necessitate another move later on.

Chapter 11
Completing the Barkhamsted Reservoir

The land committee of the MDC—thanks to an early start—had assembled almost 8,000 acres of land in the East and West Branch valleys by the end of 1931. The total climbed every year until, a decade later, the utility owned more than 20,000 acres in the towns of Barkhamsted, New Hartford, Hartland and Colebrook in northwestern Connecticut. In the East Branch valley alone, they had cobbled together 11,457 acres, the equivalent of more than eighteen square miles. This included land that began at the Richard's Corner Dam on the south end of the compensating reservoir in Barkhamsted and ran almost to the Massachusetts state line.

At a meeting of the commissioners of the MDC, a memo was read from chief engineer Saville, outlining his best guess for the time required to complete the initial phase of the Bill's Brook Dam work. He noted—

> . . . on account of the conditions at the [Bills Brook Dam] site, which must be thoroughly investigated, it would be at best the summer or fall of 1933 before actual construction could begin on the main works. . . .

The survey work at the dam site and in the valley, however, took much longer than he had estimated. As strange as it sounds, the original field surveys for the Barkhamsted Reservoir were not done by Saville's engineers but by R. H. Randall & Co. of Toledo, Ohio. Along with the usual trek up the valley shooting coordinates of everything extant, they also produced a map showing all the main roads, well defined forest and farm lanes, fences, walls, open fields, buildings, streams, marsh lands and the staked flow line of the new reservoir.

In 1934, another team of consulting engineers studied the Barkhamsted Reservoir Project and rendered opinions concerning the work. This team included J. Waldo Smith, associated for many years with the New York water supply system including work on the Ashokan, Kensico and Schoharie Reservoirs in the Catskills, Robert Ridgeway formerly in charge of New York's Catskills Aqueduct and Frank E. Winsor, chief engineer of the Boston water system. The plans for the dam, after approval by all of the consultants, were submitted—as required by law—to William G. Smith of Waterbury, a member of the State Board of Civil Engineers, under whose jurisdiction the dam was to be built. After repeated visits to the site and a thorough inspection of the plans, Smith issued his permit for the work to begin.

The original estimates for the capacity of the Barkhamsted Reservoir called for the impoundment of 23.5 billion gallons of water, while the finished reservoir actually contained 30.5 billion gallons. This is a shocking 29 percent more water than expected, pointing up nicely how difficult it is for even the most talented engineers to estimate the amount of water that will eventually settle into an amorphous valley, nine miles long and, in places, almost a mile wide.

The Bills Brook Dam was designed as an earthen structure almost 2,000 feet along the top and 137 feet off the bottom of the original riverbed. The dam faced southwest with its spillway on the western shore. The most remarkable thing about the dam was the seamless job that Saville did in making the new dam conform to the existing surroundings. His earlier work—the Nepaug Dam—was an impressive and imposing concrete structure, but the Bills Brook Dam was pure genius in its invisibility. It blended so beautifully with the natural surroundings that motorists could drive across the causeway without even realizing that they were atop a dam. Truly a remarkable feat.

The first phase in the construction of all dams is to find a way to divert the water source so that work can commence. To allow the East Branch to continue on its way, the plans called for an oval concrete conduit (17' x 21') to be built through the bottom of the proposed dam. At the completion of the work, this same conduit would allow for the transfer of supplies into the old compensating reservoir and also house the main aqueduct, which would flow to the Nepaug Reservoir. From there, water would descend to Reservoir No. 1 in West Hartford where the sand filtration beds were located.

The foundations for the dam and the diversion tunnel for the river were completed in August of 1934. Subsequently, the East Branch was diverted into the concrete conduit at the bottom of the Bills Brook Dam site. The contractor doing the work was hampered by a late spring and had to resort to working almost around the clock to complete the work in a timely fashion.

While the contractors worked at the dam site in the East Branch valley, engineers at Worcester Polytechnic Institute in Massachusetts were hired to do laboratory testing of the spillway for the dam. Using a model of the proposed spillway, which was actually only one-thirtieth the size of the one to be used at Barkhamsted, the engineers at the Alden Hydraulic Laboratory at W.P.I. ran a complete series of tests including the simulation of a flood of Biblical proportions. The tests allowed for certain aspects of the final spillway to be reduced in size, the savings more than compensating for the cost of the experiments. Model testing was not as novel in 1934 as it sounds. It should be noted that one of the first dams to use model testing was the Wachusett Dam outside of Boston, which of course Saville helped design and build between 1897 and 1905.

The core wall of the Bills Brook Dam was separated into two different contracts with as many as nine companies bidding on the work. As it turned out, B. Perini & Sons of Framingham, Massachusetts, was the low bidder on both contracts. Bonfiglio Perini was the quintessential hard-working immigrant who built a fabulously successful construction company out of nothing. Of all the men who worked with Saville on the Barkhamsted Reservoir Project, Saville got along best with Lou Perini, the oldest of Bonfiglio's three sons. Perini was a powerful personality and a self-assured, aggressive businessman, and Saville recognized a kindred spirit when he saw one. Beyond that, since Saville considered Boston the center of the civilized world, the fact that the Perinis were from Framingham didn't hurt. (In 1944, after completing the concrete work on the Bills Brook Dam, Lou Perini bought the Boston Braves baseball team, ousting Casey Stengel as manager in the process. With a new manager, Billy Southworth, the Braves won the National League pennant in 1948, but declining attendance eventually forced Perini to move the club to Milwaukee and then Atlanta. The team was sold to Ted Turner in 1976.)

Originally, Perini had 136 men working on the site but, as the structure rose and the work became more difficult, that number climbed steadily until there were 232 men jostling around the site like ants on an anthill. Perini's men laid up and stripped thousands of board feet of heavy wooden forms daily. Between July of 1935 and July of 1936—with a winter break from December until April—the men were able to pour the entire core wall. The concrete was poured in a crazy patchwork design that "locked" all of the separate pieces together and, at the same time, gave the new concrete time to cool and cure before more was added. The work progressed slowly, in part, because there was a shorter period of good weather in the northwestern hills than in the Connecticut River valley, but also because the concrete formwork was so complex and labor intensive. Aside from the backbreaking construction work, the men had to drive long distances to complete the job, shortening the workday for all concerned. After the corewall was poured and the concrete cured, earth was removed from the valley floor, upstream of the dam, and laid up on both sides of the structure at a slope of about forty-five degrees. The physics of moving earth up against a concrete corewall was child's play, but it was complicated greatly by a simple fact— trucks had not reached sufficient size to transport 1.8 million cubic yards of fill in an efficient manner. Just as with the concrete, the excavation and backfilling of the core wall moved at a snail's pace.

Besides the downstream aqueducts and the landscaping, the stonework on the causeway and upper gatehouse remained to be completed after Perini's men finished the corewall and it was backfilled. Both were finished in rough-cut granite blocks, which gave the whole project a rustic appearance. To complete the beautiful, natural look of the dam site, more than 9,000 plants, trees and shrubs were set along the sides of the downstream embankment and a groundcover of myrtle blanketed the whole downstream face of the earthen portion of the dam. Additionally, various flowering plants were set along the service road leading south from the causeway.

In May 1940, the Bills Brook Dam was completed, bringing the total cost of the reservoir and dam to $10 million. There were still a few matters to address at the northern end of the reservoir, but those were resolved by early 1941. Seven long years after the first spade of earth was turned and ten years after the preliminary survey work was done, the Barkhamsted Reservoir was finally finished. When one considers that the New York's Empire State Building was completed a few years earlier in about thirteen months, the completion of the Barkhamsted Reservoir was indeed a monumental task.

But Americans had more important things on their minds than dams and reservoirs. In Europe, a madman was loose. Adolph Hitler had already reoccupied the Rhineland, annexed Austria, grabbed the Sudetenland, conquered Poland and overrun Belgium and France. Though most people understood that it was only a question of time before the U.S. entered the war, many still felt— wrongly as it turned out—that America could stay out of the fighting.

Actually, long before the declaration of war, the United States had been feverishly preparing for the conflict. Lend-lease and the unprecedented defense appropriations of 1940-1941 transformed a depression-ridden nation into FDR's "arsenal of democracy." Within a year, over six million workers were reabsorbed into the nation's workforce and unemployment was virtually eliminated.

In Hartford, because of the city's particular industrial base, it was way ahead of the rest of the nation in wartime industries. Huge factories like Colt's Patent Fire-Arms, Billings & Spencer, and Pratt & Whitney Tool turned out vast quantities of metal and plastic products for the British and United States governments. The largest defense contractors in Central Connecticut were Pratt & Whitney Aircraft (engine builders) and Hamilton Standard (propeller manufacturers). In fact, so crucial to defense were Pratt & Whitney's vaunted piston aircraft engines that the federal government forbade the company from tooling up for the jet age until after the end of hostilities, giving rival General Electric a huge head start in the field.

With Hartford's rapid wartime industrial expansion came an unprecedented influx of people. The old trolley tracks were torn up so the steel could be used toward the war effort. The familiar blue and white Connecticut Company busses ferried passengers to and from an almost unlimited number of defense and war-related jobs. This massive new wave of humanity put the largest demand on the MDC up to that time. Both skilled and unskilled workers came from other parts of New England, from the industrial Midwest and from the rural South, straining all services to the breaking point, particularly housing. Different government-sponsored, low-cost apartments sprung up, but even those proved inadequate.

Hartford's highly industrialized manufacturing base caused some concerns though. The city's presumed vulnerability to enemy attack brought forth measures for civilian defense and precautions against enemy sabotage in the areas of crucial industries and resources, including the MDC's reservoirs and aqueducts. Around the clock guards patrolled the watersheds throughout the hostilities.

The war years were a difficult time to continue planning for the future, but as Hitler advanced his murderous conquest of Europe, the land committee of the MDC continued its exasperating negotiations with the farmers and town officials of the affected towns. Ever so slowly, they continued to assemble the pieces of the watershed in the reaches above the new reservoir and to acquire the necessary farmland for the Hogback Reservoir in the valley of the West Branch.

While Hitler laid waste country after country and visited his own personal brand of destruction on the world, Caleb Saville's new reservoir quietly filled with water. By the time World War II ended, the Barkhamsted Reservoir was still only 60 percent full. Or perhaps stated in an even more surprising way, the original watershed drawings of the East Branch valley were done before 1913, the Bills Brook Dam was completed in 1940, and water hit the top of the spillway for the first time in 1948. The period from 1913 to 1948 is thirty-five years, pointing up what colossal engineering projects dams and reservoirs really are.

As a further illustration of just how much longer the Barkhamsted Reservoir project took than expected, it is useful to revisit an earlier gathering of the commissioners of the MDC. At the same January meeting in 1932 when Charles Goodwin called a halt to future land purchases, Caleb Saville estimated for the board the time that it would take to fill the reservoir, based on his past experience and written papers by other hydraulic engineers. His memo to the committee stated that—

> . . . on account of the demands which must be met for the supply of water to mill owners, it is possible that from two to three years would be required to fill the reservoir after it is completed, depending upon rainfall . . . this would make the . . . reservoir available not before 1939 or 1940 . . . but on account of the amount required to fill the new reservoir, it might not be available for a year or so later than is now anticipated. [In fact, he thought the whole project, including the filling of the basin, could be finished by 1940 or 1941.]

This is not to slight Saville in any way. There were unforeseen delays of every kind during the course of the work, the vast majority of them beyond his control. In fairness, it must be remembered that massive reservoirs were new to America in the early years of the Great Depression. With only a handful of projects of this size to offer guidance, Saville was in very murky waters. Clearly, even the great hydraulic engineers who consulted with Saville were unable to put a completion date on the project.

Since it would take years to fill up the reservoir, Saville wasted no time in impounding the waters of the East Branch. By closing the aqueduct at the upper gatehouse, snowmelt and spring rains of early 1940 began collecting and the level of the water in the reservoir quickly amassed to about half way up the new dam. Because the valley floor was tipped, when water was halfway up the dam, it also began to encroach on Rte. 20, which was still the principal road from one side of Hartland to the other. Because the new Rte. 20—a horseshoe-shaped highway around the top of the reservoir—was not yet finished, the discharge gates at the dam had to be opened to let the water abate. By August, the new road was functional and the gates were closed once again, collecting the complete flow of the East Branch of the river. By the end of the year, the water was back up near the middle of the dam. Frustratingly, Saville was dogged by further setbacks. Dry weather caused the Farmington River to drop alarmingly, which in turn brought angry protests from the downstream mill owners. In consequence, the water had to be let out of the new reservoir a second time.

The Saville Dam and the Barkhamsted Reservoir(top), with the compensating reservoir(Lake McDonough) at the center.

Even when Saville was able to impound water again in early 1941, he had to let vast quantities pass right through the basin. Until the Hogback was completed on the West Branch of the river, he had no choice. Owing to a number of unrelated factors, the Hogback—which was to straddle the border of Hartland and Colebrook to the west—would not be completed until 1960. For the present, therefore, Saville had to adhere strictly to the terms of the bill passed by the

General Assembly and allow 13.5 billion gallons to slip through his fingers annually. Considering that this was more than 40 percent of the water that the new reservoir would eventually hold, it was a painful amount to lose each year. Accordingly, the Barkhamsted Reservoir filled at a pace that could only be described as positively glacial. The new reservoir filled so slowly that it was four years before any of its supplies made their way down the aqueduct to Hartford. But finally in 1948, water hit the top of the spillway for the first time and the Barkhamsted Reservoir was considered a done deal.

***

The Barkhamsted Reservoir turned out to be many things to many different people. For the farm families of the peaceful little hollows it represented a disruptive, even gut-wrenching, experience. The simple lives that they had either inherited or carved out for themselves, were gone forever. Those who were young enough to start over, accepted the MDC's money and bought elsewhere. The older folks just retired to nearby towns. Either way, it was a long and distasteful chapter in their lives.

For the residents who remained behind in the far eastern and western parts of Barkhamsted and Hartland, a tangled web of emotions lingered. Even though the law stated that the MDC had to supply water to these towns, the wording of the law was curious. It spoke of supplying water on terms agreeable to all parties. The cost of building pumping stations to lift water to the tops of all the hills in the affected towns made any connection to the system cost prohibitive.

Actually, Unionville, one of the towns along the route of the aqueduct, received water occasionally over the ensuing years when it experienced shortages—most notably from September 1941 until February of 1942. But the people of Barkhamsted and Hartland continued to use the same old wells while the reservoir in their midst eventually supplied water to 400,000 strangers, twenty miles away. In the end, none of the affected towns ended up receiving water from the MDC.

In the process of negotiating with the representatives of the MDC, the people of the small towns either were overlooked, or were simply unable to secure for themselves fishing and hunting rights within the watershed. There was some poaching, but it would make a fisherman's heart skip a beat to imagine the size of the fish in a nine-mile long reservoir after more than half a century.

Although there were certainly other inconveniences for the citizens of the region, one lasting bone of contention was taxes. Had the land within the watershed continued as homes and farms, the tax revenues collected by the towns would have been much higher than what they were for unimproved forestland. Accordingly, each homeowner was forced to pay higher taxes in order to maintain the same level of town services. As if this weren't bad enough, the MDC, a number of times, contested the tax bills. After reviewing the issue, very often a judge found in favor of the utility and the tax base of the town in question eroded further.

Conversely, for the employees and commissioners of the water company, it was the headiest of times. The construction of the Bills Brook Dam created an immense reservoir that was the crown jewel of the new regional supplier—the MDC. Hundreds of jobs had been created in the middle of the Great Depression and the new reservoir's maintenance, forestry and surveillance needs would keep an army of people employed as far as the eye could see. Lastly, the days when the supply was only a few hogsheads ahead of demand were over. The engineers at the MDC could relax.

For Caleb Saville, following on the heels of the Nepaug project, he had built the largest reservoir in the state and had added considerably to his reputation as a hydraulic engineer. The Nepaug and Barkhamsted Reservoirs would be a lasting monument to his genius, foresight and industry.

In sheer size, the Barkhamsted project was three times that of the Nepaug and very often required a special skill that Saville simply did not possess. Unlike the other disciplines, which he was able to master in his life—hydraulic engineering, hydrology, hydrography and riparian law, just to name a few—he was constitutionally unsuited for the give-and-take of dealing with politicians. In the course of large-scale projects, such as the Barkhamsted Reservoir, there was an unending amount of negotiations and just plain, old-fashioned politics. In these matters, he simply lacked the patience. He desperately needed the help of a skilled negotiator like Charles Goodwin. The well-connected lawyer could go to the State Capitol and horse trade with the best of them. As the old expression goes, "He knew where the bodies were buried."

He had another advantage over Caleb Saville. As chairman of the MDC, he received no remuneration of any kind. In the eyes of many, this completely eliminated the possibility of personal gain and gave him the mantle of a Solomon, a luminary, a true steward of the public good. With the calculus of personal gain removed from the equation, Charles Goodwin had secured the moral high ground. (Incidentally, no chairman or commissioner of the MDC has every been paid a cent in its seventy-five year history.)

The same year that the Barkhamsted Reservoir was filled to capacity, there was a poignant juxtaposition of events—just as the new receptacle was full, the manager and chief engineer of the Metropolitan District Commission, Caleb Saville, at 82 years of age, was depleted. He had given everything that he had to the water department, and had left the utility with more than twice the clean drinking water it needed. Actually, though it was not known at the time, he had probably left the capital region with enough water to last a century or more. Though he would continue working as a consulting engineer for the MDC until shortly before his death at 94, he retired as manager and chief engineer in the first week of January 1948.

Upper gatehouse at the Saville Dam.

Neither Caleb Saville, the engineering genius, nor Charles Goodwin, the well-connected aristocrat, could have built the Barkhamsted reservoir alone. Together though, they were able to guarantee millions of people clean drinking water for an unimaginable number of decades. To do this, they recreated the formula for success in almost all human endeavors down through the ages—the teaming of an engineering genius with a practical politician. Therefore, it was only fitting that they should bow out together.

In the year following the retirement of the MDC's first manager and chief engineer, Caleb Saville, the MDC's first chairman, Charles Goodwin, stepped down. He had given nineteen years to the water company and he had other responsibilities. At the same time that he was fighting the MDC's battles at the state capital, he was still the president of the State Savings Bank, a senior partner of Shipman & Goodwin and a trustee or board member of a dozen other companies, foundations and clubs. Retirement would give him more time for the sailing that he loved so much. After what amounted to a semi-retirement period of just five years, he died in 1954 at the age of seventy-seven.

Even before the entire Barkhamsted project was complete, including the Hogback Reservoir, the engineers at the MDC were looking for future water supplies. Most notably, they had in mind joining the two newest reservoirs with an aqueduct, allowing the West Branch's larger watershed to help recharge the huge basin on the East Branch. (Another compensating reservoir could be built to the north of the Hogback to appease the mill owners on the Farmington River.) In light of the legislative hurdles, a continuous quest for water supplies was only prudent. What no one seemed to sense at the time was that a massive population shift was underway, which would alter every forward-looking calculation of the MDC's engineers. Few saw it coming.

For the time being, abundant supplies meant that water would be taken for granted like never before. Forgotten were the days when the city was faced with water famines. Gone were the memories of the weeks and months at the end of the year when the reservoirs of West Hartford gave up the last of their water and the Connecticut River Pumping Station had to take up the slack. Never mind the times when the puny Lord's Hill Reservoir was the difference between the city's residents having water or not. All the unsettling struggles were ancient history once the Barkhamsted Reservoir was completed.

The MDC was not alone in this. The first six decades of the twentieth century was a golden age for hydraulic engineers in the United States. Men seized opportunities that came along once in a thousand years—building drinking water systems for the budding cities of a new nation. Fantastic projects were under construction in almost every major city. While there were a couple of dams of note built in the nineteenth century, the sheer number of dams and reservoirs constructed in the first sixty years of the twentieth century was unprecedented. This blessed time for engineers will probably never be duplicated since all of the major water companies in the country now have world-class systems in place. The great bulk of the work now will be in the area of maintenance, expansion of the existing systems and water purification improvements.

The largest water companies in the United States completed their building sprees in the 1960s. New York completed it last reservoir—the Cannonsville—in 1967. Boston finished the dam at its mammoth Quabbin Reservoir in 1939 and Providence built the Scituate in 1925. Farther down the east coast, Baltimore dammed the Patapsco River in 1956 thereby creating the Liberty Reservoir—their last. Seattle's Tolt River Reservoir began supplying the city with drinking water in 1964, and Portland's Bull Run Dam #2 was finished in 1962 (the city added Powell Butte Reservoir in 1981, but that is more of a distribution hub than a reservoir).

Denver actually did build a small catchment—the Strontia Springs Reservoir in 1983, but it was comparatively small when one considers that it holds only 1.5% of Denver's water supply. Conversely, the Dillon Reservoir, the real workhorse of the system—completed in 1963—impounds approximately thirty-six times as much water.

***

Caleb Saville had told the residents of Hartland Hollow that their town hall would be the last building demolished and he kept his word. The proud old building stood alone long after the other buildings had been destroyed and burned. The rest of the valley was now just a collection of cellar holes. The residents of the east and west parts of Hartland were having a difficult time deciding on which side of the reservoir to build their new town hall. The MDC's $25,000 settlement included two building lots and the suggestion that each side of Hartland build its own town hall, but the idea never gained a following. In the end, the residents decided that the new town hall would be on the east side of the reservoir and a new school building would be on the west. (Later, this school building was supplanted by a newer school east of the reservoir, as East Hartland became the more heavily populated section of town.)

Despite his best efforts to be gracious, the decision to demolish the Hartland Hollow Town Hall was eventually taken out of Saville's hands. It was now the end of 1940, the new dam was finished and the waste gates had been closed, allowing the reservoir to fill with water. Barkhamsted Hollow and the lower end of the valley had already slipped from sight and it would not be too long before the waters were lapping at the old tobacco fields in Hartland Hollow.

***

Almost seven years had passed since the last families had left the valley, and the MDC had used that time to build the Bills Brook Dam, demolish houses and clear the valley of trees, bushes, brush and anything else that might contaminate the new water supply. Adding together the buildings of the two hollows, they had burned down over two hundred houses, barns, and outbuildings.

Even though the valley was bare, the people of Hartland Hollow wanted to have their 1940 Halloween dance in the old building, and Saville acquiesced. The dance committee, in an effort to save money, talked one of the former residents of the hollow, Howard Feley, into being the caller. The son of A. C. and Leslie Feley and one of seven children, he was a good-looking twenty-five year old and a naturally gifted caller. The Silkey Boys band would back him up and a first class fiddler from Riverton, Eudean "Red" Pease, would play melody. Pease was a gentle giant of a farm boy, but also a remarkably gifted fiddler.

Helping with the arrangements was a newly married, twenty-two year old carpenter named Paul Crunden. Small and wiry, he had worked part-time when he was a teen for a farmer, John Nelson, who owned a dairy farm atop the west mountain. The 300-acre farm was typical of the operations in the area in that Nelson raised milking cows, grew silage corn and had a side business of cutting and selling cordwood. Because of this earlier tie to Nelson, the dance committee prevailed on Crunden to gather some firewood and build a fire in the box stove at the old town hall. It was Saturday, October 26, 1940, and the leaves were already off the trees in Hartland and the weather cold but dry.

Helping Crunden were Nelson's two nieces, Peggy and Loreen. Peggy was a gregarious, eighteen-year-old blonde while her sister was a shy brunette. After filling the car's trunk with seasoned hardwood logs, the three set off for the town hall. Soon the automobile was bouncing along the broken up asphalt road—Rte. 20—that would take them straight down into the hollow from the west. The load in the trunk pitched the nose of the car high into the air, as the three friends descended into the hollow.

In an alarmingly short period of time, they were riding smoothly along the valley floor. An eerie chill filled the car. Gone were the houses and barns where they had idled away their early years. Also gone were the large shade trees under which they had enjoyed church picnics and other less organized fun. The hollow was just a long empty basin made all the more grotesque as the headlights of the car disappeared into the miasma of nothingness before them. The only thing left was an odd collection of empty cellar holes, where the homes and farmhouses of friends once stood.

The only two structures left in the whole valley were the Hartland Hollow Town Hall, which needed a paint job badly, and the "kissing bridge," sagging from disrepair. Both would soon be gone. The moment was colored by another irony—the only thing that had not changed a bit was the peaceful East Branch of the Farmington River, which had unwittingly caused all the heartache. It moved briskly along, through just one more valley, on its eighty-mile journey to the Connecticut River and thence to the Atlantic Ocean.

One last item added a bit of ghoulishness to the Halloween Dance preparations. The MDC had just let the contract for the removal of the graves from the old Hartland Hollow Cemetery the week before and the work had not yet begun. Accordingly, not half a mile up the road of the north hollow, sat the small picket-fenced enclosure with its simple monuments. The wind blew stray leaves between the markers as its residents waited patiently for the movers.

Hartland Hollow Cemetery.

Peggy backed the car up to the rear door of the town hall and Crunden ran in to light one of the wall sconces. Using what little light the device threw off, the three of them spent the next quarter hour stacking the firewood inside the building. The town hall was actually just one big room with a ten-foot high ceiling. The lowest part of the walls were covered with vertical wainscoting that ran four feet up from the floor. The only daylight that ever reached the room came through six oversized windows—three on each side.

A forty-two-inch cast iron box stove near the center of the back wall would furnish the heat for the dance. On the walls on either side of the front door were wooden coat pegs where the revelers would hang their hats and coats. Between numbers, the dancers could rest on benches surrounding the room against the walls. The only other permanent fixture in the room was a closet in the right rear corner, used alternately as a storage room and a voting booth.

The dance committee had been busy, as long tables were set up against the north wall for the refreshments and orange and black crepe paper looped across the ceiling. In the corners of the room were bundles of corn stalks and pumpkins. Popcorn and cider would be delivered later.

Crunden set to work. Opening the door of the box stove, he placed a couple of the smaller logs on a pile of flash kindling and lit it. While the fire built to something trustworthy, he moved about the room filling wall sconces with kerosene and lighting them. After satisfying himself that the fire would not smolder out, he adjusted the damper and they all left.

Advertised as the last dance at the town hall, old neighbors and friends came from great distances to attend the affair. The names of the partygoers were the names of residents of the area going back a century or more. Joining the revelers from West Hartland would be folks from Riverton, the furniture town over in the valley of the West Branch. Families from East Hartland would be joined by some of the transplanted families now living in Granby and West Suffield.

Descending the west mountain road were Peggy and Loreen's parents, Mildred and Carl Nelson. Carl was a carpenter and woodchopper who hired out all around the valley. He had worked on the Cable's farm for many years along with Walter Stewart, and Lloyd and Perry Ransom. His wife, Mildred was a good-looking woman with short brunette hair who was a teacher at the south hollow schoolhouse in Hartland Hollow before it was closed down in 1933. Pauline Emerick had been in her last class. One last couple from the west mountain was Lillian and Raymond Hall. Ray was a builder and, before the MDC bought up Hartland Hollow, his wife, Lillian, delivered the mail.

From the south, and using the dirt roads along the river would be the people from New Hartford and Canton. Twenty-eight-year-old Herbert Case and his new wife, Yahne, drove up along the west river road past Barkhamsted Hollow where he had grown up. Having moved to New Hartford in 1934, he was appalled by the emptiness of the valley, which he had not visited since leaving. Disoriented by the complete absence of familiar trees and bushes and unable to make out the cellar holes in the darkness, he was powerless to show Yahne where his family's farm had been. It was an empty and forlorn feeling that he never forgot.

For the most part, the collection of automobiles around the town hall left no doubt about the rough economic times—old Fords, Chevrolets and Plymouths along with some rusty old farm pick-ups. Pauline Emerick was now married to Paul Crunden's brother, George, and they arrived at the dance in a brand new 1940 Hudson "Stinger." It was an unusually expensive car, considering the hard times, but car dealers were so hungry for sales that almost any terms could be arranged.

The dance was a family affair, with a couple of generations of each family represented. It was an unusual Halloween hybrid—a costumed square dance. While everyone had a good time square dancing, and enjoying the "round" numbers like "She'll Be Coming Round The Mountain," judges awarded prizes for the best costumes—a box of cigars for the men and a bottle of perfume for the women.

Paul Crunden's wife, Ethel, wasn't feeling well but she insisted that he tag along with his brother Clayton. Among the other dancers present were Howard Feley's family and the whole Stewart clan (Pauline Emerick's people). Alfred and Lena Cable were there as well. Though Alfred had lost a leg while coon hunting many years before, he never missed a day's work or a good party thereafter.

By eight o'clock, the dance was underway and everyone square-danced non-stop into the night, feasting on the popcorn and cider (and an occasional sip from a pint of "sneaky Pete"). Most of the former residents had made peace with the past. Many of them had sold their farms a decade before and started anew in other towns. Throughout the dance, there was no mention of old grievances, with folks only interested in having fun. Everyone let themselves go, enjoying a loud and unfettered good time in an otherwise empty corner of the world. The revelry lasted until midnight without a single mention of the MDC or the loss of their farms. What was done was done—simple as that.

The party broke up when Red Pease stopped fiddling at the stroke of midnight. Despite such an obvious hint that the dance was over, everyone was too keyed up to leave. All the same, by packing up his fiddle, Red made it clear that he was through for the night. While not exactly pleased, no one wanted the party to end on a sour note, so couples gathered their belongings and left. (Word got around the next day that someone had stolen Red's violin. Since the fiddle never surfaced, a good guess is that it rests under a rock in a cellar hole at the bottom of the Barkhamsted Reservoir to this day.)

As couples left that night, it was into a pitch-black world that they walked, for there were no lights of any kind—no streetlights, no houselights, not even the reassuring glow of the moon. But this may have been the biggest blessing of the whole evening. Without any lights, the partygoers couldn't see Hartland Hollow denuded of all the things that had, at one time, made it home. As they stumbled along in the darkness, for some it was this very moment when they realized—finally and at last—that Hartland Hollow was something else now. A small but vibrant town—with a collection of simple but interesting people—had been stripped from the world and reduced to a meaningless dot on outdated maps. Now it was just a rapidly fading memory of a time gone by—of warm summer afternoons when the only sounds were cow's tails swishing at flies, young boys 'kerplunking' into their favorite river pool and old Ford pick-ups rattling along rutted roads.

The older folks left the dance for home while the younger couples, behaving like all the young people who have ever lived, tried to locate private places in the valley where they had stopped before. As one man put it, "We just wanted to leave our footprints upside down on the dashboard one last time in the hollow."

Ten days later, men and women returned to the town hall building to vote in the presidential election of 1940. The box stove at the back of the hall was churning out welcome heat as the cold voters, one by one, streamed into the building. Like coon dogs, they headed straight for the comfort of the cast iron heater. Holding their hands toward the warmth, they chatted idly, catching up on local news and gossip.

Some, like Russell Hayes, voted for the first time that day. In an orderly fashion, they each took their paper ballots into the cluttered voting booth in the corner, penciled in their choices and then deposited the folded slips in an oak box just outside the closet. It went without saying that Hartland's local representatives would be Republicans, but with the economy still very sluggish and Hitler launching blitzkriegs all over Europe, the presidential vote was in doubt. When the ballots were counted after supper, Hartland once again delivered a Republican landslide, with Wendell Willkie getting 112 votes to Franklin Roosevelt's 52.

A short time later—and just ahead of the rising waters—Caleb Saville gave the order and the eighty-year-old town hall was burned to the ground.

***

It would have been small comfort for the people of Hartland Hollow (and Barkhamsted Hollow) to realize that they weren't the only people who had lost their homes to reservoirs over the years. But even though misery loves company, it would not have eased their sense of loss much. Indeed, almost seventy years since leaving the beautiful valley—and a simple, unhurried life—some residents still nurse grudges against the MDC. It is a hurt that will accompany them to their graves. Still, just exactly how many times had this happened in other places? How many people had surrendered their ancestral homelands to thirsty urban folks in far off cities?

Without sugar-coating it, New York and Boston were the biggest offenders when it came to chasing families off their land. When John Jervis agreed to build

New York's Croton Dam, Reservoir and Aqueduct, it was obvious to everyone that some property owners were going to lose their land. In the watershed of the Croton Reservoir and along the route of the aqueduct, there were about two hundred landowners who had to be bought out. However, in 1836—the year that work began on the project—no water company had ever attempted to force people to sell their property. Naturally, the people of Westchester County opposed the project wholeheartedly. They sent written protests to the legislature at Albany, contending that the act under which the water board of New York City was proceeding would deprive people of their property against their will and, therefore, violated the laws the State of New York and the Constitution of the United States.

Concurrently, they did everything in their power to stop the work. Surveyors were turned away at people's property lines and, when finally the engineers were able to shoot some coordinates, their pinning stakes mysteriously disappeared during the night. The workers were verbally abused and, in a few cases, physically assaulted.

The property owners claimed that the workers on the aqueduct had depreciated the value of their land with their drunkenness and malicious damage to crops and outbuildings. In the final analysis, one of the water commissioners, Steven Allen, estimated that the land for the Aqueduct had cost the city $166,000, when the original estimate had been only $37,000. Likewise, the land for the Croton Reservoir had cost $91,000, when the appraisal, before work began, was only $29,000.

The two hundred property owners dispossessed during the building of the Croton Aqueduct were only the first wave of landowners to lose their property to the thirsty throngs in New York City. When the second Croton Dam was built in 1885, it greatly expanded the Croton Reservoir and the village of Katonah had to be moved to higher ground. In Westchester and Putnam Counties, the New York Water system eventually built or annexed twelve reservoirs.

In 1907, the water board headed toward the Catskills to add to their supplies. Just north of White Plains, they found a perfect spot for a dam near the little hamlet of Kensico. As villages go, it was small, but had houses, stores, churches, a hotel, a railroad station and a couple of mills. To make way for the reservoir, 200 people were evicted.

The Ashokan Reservoir, built in 1915, backed up the waters of Esopus Creek more than twelve miles. In the process, it condemned eight villages—Shokan, Brodhead Bridge, Brown's Station, Olivebridge, West Hurley, Glenford, Olive and Ashton. Two thousand residents were displaced. Lessening the level of angst slightly, the water board was able to relocate four of the towns—Shokan, Olivebridge, West Hurley and Glenford. The Schoharie Reservoir, which was finished in 1927, evicted 350 residents of Gilboa and, lest the dearly departed be forgotten, 3000 graves were moved from thirty-two cemeteries.

As the water needs of New York grew, the water board turned to the Delaware watershed and completed two more reservoirs immediately after the World War II—the Rondout and the Neversink. This erased the villages of Eureka, Montela, Lackawack, Neversink and Bittersweet, forcing out another 1500 people. Following these two projects, construction began on the largest body of impounded water in the New York system—the Pepacton Reservoir, which flattened four villages—Arena, Pepacton, Shavertown and Union Grove. This scattered to the four winds another 974 people and caused 2371 graves to be moved.

New York's final water project of the Delaware system was the Cannonsville Reservoir, which required the destruction of five villages—Beerston, Cannonsville, Rock Rift, Rock Royal and Granton. The last New York residents to be forced off their lands—to date—amounted to an additional 941 rural residents.

Including the original land purchases in the late 1830s for the Croton Reservoir and Aqueduct, New York City's water board has demolished twenty-six towns and forced about 6500 people off their lands. Calculating the total number of houses, barns, businesses, schoolhouses, hotels, churches and cemeteries that were destroyed or moved could never be accomplished with any accuracy. Water companies—for obvious reasons—tend to lose track of these displacements.

Boston started much later than New York in the messy business of land acquisition for reservoirs. Strictly speaking, Boston had nothing to do with the sections of Winchester, Medford and Arlington in which the Mystic Lakes system sat and there are no records to indicate that any land acquisitions were necessary for the original aqueducts to be bedded. Even the Lake Cochituate Aqueduct was a fairly painless undertaking inasmuch as that work consisted solely of building an aqueduct from Long Pond (Lake Cochituate) to Brookline. Except to close off the outlet from the pond to the sea, the lake itself remained untouched. With tongue firmly in cheek, the water board tried to sell the idea that "Cochituate" was an Indian word meaning "water delivered to Boston by gravity."

However, things changed with the Wachusett project. When the Nashua River was dammed above Clinton to create the Wachusett Reservoir in 1905, it flooded six and a half square miles in four separate towns. The residents of Clinton, Boylston, West Boylston and, to a lesser extent, Sterling, were traumatized by the project according to old newspaper accounts at the Clinton Historical Society.

While building the Wachusett Dam, 378 homes, schools, churches and mills were demolished. It was the first time that the state had allowed the flooding of an inhabited area and landowners were shocked and disillusioned. Even before the Wachusett was completed, people came to believe that Frederic Stearns, the chief engineer of Boston Water, knew that the reservoir would only be able to supply greater Boston for about thirty years.

They were right. By the mid-1930s, Boston Water was looking toward the setting sun for additional supplies. They ended their quest in the valley of the Swift River. When their plans for a new reservoir were announced, the State of Connecticut took the Metropolitan Water District of Boston to court because the Swift River was a major tributary of the Connecticut River. In the end, Massachusetts was required to allow, in perpetuity, a fixed amount of water to flow into the Connecticut River from the Swift River valley.

That wasn't the biggest headache though. The engineers in Massachusetts faced a more delicate problem. By impounding the waters of the Swift River, they would have to buy up all of the land in the valley and erase forever the four towns of Dana, Enfield, Greenwich, and Prescott. All together they would displace 2700 people. Just as in Connecticut, they applied for and received the authorization from the state legislature, including the power of condemnation.

The dam was begun in 1936, and completed three years later. It took seven years to fill the Quabbin Reservoir and it became the largest man-made reservoir in the world devoted solely to drinking water supply. It held a stupendous, thirst-quenching 412 billion gallons of water.

The visitor's center at the Quabbin Reservoir maintains the vital records of the former residents of the four towns that were flooded by the new reservoir—all birth, death and marriage certificates. Photo albums display snapshots of the 650 homes that were demolished. For another 7,613 former residents, the Swift River valley did not prove to be their final resting place. Their remains—unearthed from thirty-five different cemeteries—were reinterred on higher ground. In effect, the visitor's center is the clerk's office for four ghost towns. A group of former residents meets every Tuesday for tea and a little chitchat about old times. They even publish a newsletter, *Quabbin Voices*. Just as in the case of the lost hollows in the Farmington River valley, memories die hard.

One of the strangest stories of displaced families concerns the town of Dillon, Colorado. Seemingly born under a wandering star, Dillon has moved or been moved four times in its history. A tiny town of only a few hundred people, it was located first on the banks of the Snake River. When the railroad laid tracks through the Rockies, residents decided to move closer to the Blue River where the rail lines passed. Later, it was moved to the foot of nearby Cemetery Hill, where the town remained for fifty years. Then, in the 1930s, Denver Water decided that the natural basin where Dillon was situated would make a fabulous reservoir and they quietly began buying up the surrounding lands. At long last, in 1956, Denver Water announced plans for the Dillon Reservoir. The residents were given five years to vacate their homes. The wandering residents of Dillon moved for the last time to land near the northern shores of the new reservoir. The Dillon Reservoir was completed in 1963.

Suffice to say the residents of the East Branch valley were not the first nor would they be the last to surrender their lands in the name of clean drinking water. Though they were not alone, they surely felt as if they were. Remembering that they were not well-educated people—and certainly did not know the water history of New York, Boston or any other city—it is easy to see how they assumed that their little corner of the world was a unique case. At the time, at least in their own minds, they felt as alone as treed coons.

Chapter 12
A Circle Within a Cycle

The end of World War II brought thousands of young servicemen back to America to pick up their lives. They were the flesh and bone catalysts behind the largest marriage and birth rates America has ever experienced. People began buying goods not available during the war, which fueled corporate expansion and created jobs aplenty. Suburban tract houses sprang up like weeds in empty fields and were filled with previously unaffordable appliances. To get the next generation of Americans around, the nation's automakers retooled for long-awaited peacetime models. People of all ages snapped up the new cars with abandon. Like the automobile, the development of the television had been interrupted by the war, but by the late 1940s, black-and-white sets, pulling in sometimes thirteen stations, found their way into one home after another.

By the late 1940s, the populations of the towns served by the MDC had grown significantly. From year to year, the rate of growth varied, but up to that time, it had always been above 10 percent. Suddenly, just as all those former GIs and their brides were buying homes and having babies, the growth rate dropped to 7 percent a year. As with most cities throughout the United States, Hartford itself was losing population at an alarming rate. Between 1950 and 1960, the city lost 8.5 percent of its residents. For a variety of reasons, people were leaving the city in droves. (From 1950 to 2000, Hartford's population dropped by almost 30 percent.) However, what no one had really foreseen was that the people leaving the city increasingly hopscotched over the surrounding communities and settled in towns that were not members of the MDC.

This trend was unsettling news for the water commissioners, but the situation was further exacerbated by another dilemma. Pratt and Whitney Aircraft (the engine builder) in East Hartford had always been the single largest water consumer within the Metropolitan District. During the supercharged production years of World War II, their use of water was awe-inspiring, but after the Japanese signed the surrender papers on the battleship *Missouri* in September 1945, its water consumption dropped to a fraction of its wartime level.

The commissioners tried to add towns to its roster of clients, but with limited success. The sticky non-compete clause in their charter barred them from encroaching on the territories of other water utilities. Unlike other companies with products to sell, their own charter circumscribed their sales area. The MDC had worked hard to build a fabulous water system and now they were powerless to increase their customer base. Worse, the legislature saw no reason to change the water company's charter.

Aside from the political considerations of expanding the MDC, there were the day-to-day exigencies of running a huge utility. Topping the list of unresolved problems was the new compensating reservoir on the West Branch of the Farmington River. Until the Hogback Reservoir could be built, the MDC was bound by law to discharge billions of gallons of water annually from the Barkhamsted, depleting hard-won supplies. The Hogback, as originally drawn, would impound another seven billion gallons of water on the West Branch of the Farmington River, ensuring a steady flow downstream.

The enormous cushion created with the completion of the Barkhamsted Reservoir—and with the MDC's customer base increasing at a slower pace than expected—there developed precious little incentive to finish the Hogback Reservoir in a timely fashion. The Barkhamsted project had taken thirteen years (not counting the filling of the reservoir). The Hogback Reservoir was one-fifth the size of the Barkhamsted, and yet it took twenty-two years (again not counting fill time.) Straddling the boundary line between Hartland and Colebrook, it would—the past as prologue—erase the old cotton factory village of Colebrook River.

Increasingly, the MDC relied on the services of H. Bissell Carey to purchase the properties of the valley of the West Branch. In hindsight, since the properties were bought in the name of the Collins Company—instead of the MDC—the idea of a "straw man" comes to mind. While the Collins Company was certainly successful enough to convince the locals that it had plans for expanded manufacturing facilities farther up the Farmington River, the idea that it tried to hoodwink the residents of Colebrook River is just not borne out by the facts.

First of all, there was no reason to believe that people of the area would sell their property any cheaper to an industrialist than they would to the MDC. It could be argued that exactly the reverse would have been the case, inasmuch as the MDC had the power of condemnation backing up its offers. Secondly, even if Carey sought to deceive the people in the valley of the West Branch, he would not have turned the acquired properties over to the MDC so quickly. Land records are public and such a ruse would have been discovered almost immediately. Besides, keeping in mind that purchasing the whole valley of the West Branch would take a decade or more, the "straw man" charade could not possibly have worked for more than a couple of months.

The final point is a little meatier—Carey had nothing to do with the MDC and, as such, had nothing to gain except a small agent's commission. True, he was a big help to men he knew in Hartford—who he bargained with during the riparian negotiations over the years—but that would not mean much when weighed against the amount of time that he would be required to invest in and around Colebrook River.

H. Bissell Carey was the president of the Collins Company, which produced axes, machetes and other hard-edged tools. However, he was quite a bit more than that. In addition to sitting on the boards of about a dozen companies including the Hartford Electric Light Company, Hartford Fire Insurance and Hartford Accident and Indemnity, just to name a few, he was also the president of Automatic Refrigeration and vice-president of the M. S. Little Manufacturing Company.

Of the firms where he functioned as a director, one was of particular interest—the D. N. Barney Company. His wife, Mary (Barney) Carey, was descended from one of the earliest families of Farmington. Her father, D. Newton Barney, married Laura Dunham, whose father, Austin C. Dunham— along with silent partners that included Hartford Mayor Morgan Bulkeley— established the Hartford Electric Light Company. (H. Bissell Carey's father-in-law eventually became the largest shareholder in Helco.) D. N. Barney & Co. was the trust that controlled all of Mary Barney Carey's shares and voting rights in that utility. As if his business interests were not enough to qualify him as a man of substance, he was also a member of the Hartford Golf Club, the most elite golf venue in the city, and the old boys' dining and social club on Prospect Street—The Hartford Club. To use a shopworn phrase, H. Bissell Carey knew all the right people.

Undoubtedly when Charles and F. Spencer Goodwin were discussing a better way to purchase the farmlands in northwestern Connecticut, the idea of a disinterested third party came up. Moreover, since the younger Goodwin was a director of the Collins Company, Carey was probably the first person he thought of. The industrialist was an extremely capable businessman who was as good as his word. Operating on behalf of the MDC, he went on a buying spree in and around sleepy, little Colebrook River, gathering up properties like some real life game of Monopoly. Generally in the afternoons, he drove his Cadillac out along the banks of the West Branch and struck deals with the farmers and townspeople of the area. The village itself was actually just one of four districts within the Town of Colebrook. In point of fact, it was the largest one, with more than half of the population of Colebrook living within its bosom.

Old postcards show Colebrook River as the quintessential New England village, quaint but quirky. On the east side of the river sat the Methodist Church, the Victory Grange Hall, Ives & Baxter's Store, The Colebrook Inn, Bettes' Garage and a two-story schoolhouse. The river was a wide—albeit shallow— body of slow-moving water, which had propelled the town to prosperity in the last half of the 1800s. Factories on both sides of the river used the water to power their machinery.

Over the years, there had been a cotton mill, scythe works, a tannery and a mill for carding wool. On a smaller scale, there had been the Lewis & Ives clock shop, which was run quite successfully by its two proprietors. In addition to all of this industry—and very much in keeping with the tradition of the area—there were farms of all sizes and descriptions.

Sawyer's Cotton Mill buildings in Colebrook River. During droughts, the steel bridge still "pops" out of the water at Colebrook River Lake.

Because people lived and worked on both sides of the West Branch, of necessity, the residents built four bridges across the river. Three were for farm wagons, livestock and automobiles while the fourth was a three-foot-wide, suspension-type, wood and cable pedestrian crossing. Walking east across the river on this swaying cable bridge deposited a person on the shoulder of Route 8 and diagonally across from the Methodist Church.

As picturesque as the village was, in truth, it was long past its heyday. Railroads and waterpower slowly lost their place as prerequisites for the successful operation of a manufactory and small mill towns like Colebrook River fell into decline. The strong farming base prevented the town from ever actually breathing its last, but its fortunes were definitely on a downward cant.

For Carey and the MDC, the timing, at first blush, seemed serendipitous. It has been said that, for the rural areas of Connecticut, the Great Depression really didn't end until the 1950s. This was certainly the case with Colebrook River. Money was tight and a windfall buy-out offer from the MDC was a blessing in disguise, or so it appeared. Too, after the Japanese bombed Pearl Harbor in 1941, a whole generation of the village's young men enlisted in the armed forces and the older folks were preoccupied with war production and rationing. The MDC bought its first parcel of land in 1938 for $10,000 when it came to an agreement with an aging farmer, Ed Seymore. When residents were willing sellers, the MDC dealt with them directly, but if they showed the slightest recalcitrance, H. Bissell Carey handled the negotiations.

The system worked reasonably well, although it was agonizingly slow. There were less than a hundred parcels to be acquired—farms on the hillsides, about seventy-five private homes and maybe a dozen businesses. With the Collins Company and the land committee of the MDC working steadily, it still took fourteen years to buy all of the patches of the quilt that would form the new reservoir and watershed.

Footbridge over the West Branch of the Farmington in Colebrook River.

Watching their neighbors on the East Branch surrendering their farms during the Great Depression, to some extent, had educated the residents of Colebrook River. Just as Charles LeGeyt and Harold Birden had stubbornly held onto their property in Barkhamsted Hollow for as long as they could, Colebrook River had its own pair of hardheads—Bill Bettes and Gene Bourquin.

Bill Bettes and his family lived at the corner of Route 8 and "the Tolland road," which led up into Massachusetts. Just to the south of his house was his garage. It was a small, eccentric garage, its main business the repair of farm machinery and automobiles. But Bill Bettes also did welding, fabricating and just about anything else that came up. He probably would have gone out of business if he had to depend on the little bit of money he made from the Shell gasoline he pumped each month. His friend, Gene Bourquin, inherited a farm from his father on the opposite side of the river but did little farming, choosing instead to work in a shop in nearby Winsted.

While the MDC thought the timing could not have been better for their buying spree, a number of things confounded their plans. To begin, the Great Depression had stolen America's innocence. People had come up against the kind of hard times that only a few years earlier seemed unthinkable. They had seen grown men in breadlines and children going to bed hungry. The inability of the government to turn things around made all forms of authority suspect. In short, people had lost their trust.

Add to this, the unconscionable aggression of the Axis Powers in Europe and the Japanese in the Pacific. World War II, like all wars before it, had put aggression under the microscope where it could be examined and despised anew. What was different about a water company forcing people to sell their ancestral homesteads under the threat of condemnation? From this point of view, the MDC had an uphill battle in Colebrook River.

Unfortunately the water board, both knowingly and unwittingly, compounded the problem. Somehow, during the very early going, the townspeople were led to believe that a wealthy New York family wanted to refit the cotton mill and resume making tents. There was a certain simple-minded logic to this story—wouldn't all those GIs need tents? Sorry to say, there wasn't an ounce of truth to it. Of course, anyone could have started the rumor, but who had the most to gain?

Compounding the first round of misinformation was an assertion made by some of the residents of the village—the MDC promised that land above the Spencer Bridge—which was at the extreme southern edge of the village—would never be touched. *If* this were said, it was a boldfaced lie, because all of the drawings of the proposed Hogback Reservoir—including some done in the late 1930s—showed the surface area of the new reservoir extending almost to the Massachusetts border. Colebrook River lay about a mile from the state line and would definitely have been underwater at the completion of the project.

Things got increasingly contentious, until the people of the whole northwestern corner of the state formed a corporation called Allied Connecticut Towns, Inc. The sole purpose of the organization was to stop the MDC from annexing Colebrook River and the surrounding farms. At a public meeting, the MDC's board members stated that they only needed 621 acres for the Hogback Reservoir when their own maps showed a watershed, on the Connecticut side of the border, which would encompass 3,000 acres in and around Colebrook River.

The MDC could hardly be blamed if it were a little cavalier in these matters. In 1945 and again in 1947 it had formally sought approval from the state legislature to impound the waters of the West Branch of the Farmington River. Both times, the bills were turned down. But after some concessions, the General Assembly finally passed a compromise bill in 1949—*An Act Increasing the Powers of the Metropolitan District Respecting Water*, granting permission for the water company to build the Hogback Reservoir. Considering all of the previous laws regarding additional water supplies, the language used in this piece of legislation was eye-popping—

> . . . the taxing, diverting and conveying…the waters of the main stream of the Farmington River, commonly referred to as the West Branch… to erect and maintain dam or dams on said river, *and take by purchase, condemnation or otherwise*, waters, water rights, flowage rights, rights of way or easements, or other right of property . . . necessary . . . *and if the district cannot agree with the riparian owners below the proposed dam as to the damages for diverting water, the district is given the power of condemnation.* (Italics added)

With these powers in hand, who could blame the MDC or H. Bissell Carey for asserting their wills with something short of the usual courtesies? From the point of view of the MDC, the matter was a *fait accompli*. After a little bothersome land acquisitions, their construction work could commence. Even with all of the cards though, the MDC wisely decided that a few concessions would clear the path faster than strong-arm tactics.

First, unlike their friends in the East Branch valley, the people living along the West Branch retained for themselves fishing and hunting rights in the watershed. A ramp was even built so fishermen could launch boats. Also, it was agreed that the right of eminent domain would never be exercised along or bordering the West Branch of the Farmington River. It is unlikely that the MDC felt it was giving away much with this second item because it could still *"...take by purchase, condemnation, or otherwise,"* whatever it needed. Such niceties though, kept meetings short and egos intact.

By 1951, the only properties left to be bought and leveled were those of the two hardheads—Bill Bettes and Gene Bourquin. They held out as long as they could, but it was a costly fight, especially for Bill Bettes, because his auto repair business slumped considerably once Colebrook River became a ghost town. He sold directly to the MDC in January of 1951. His friend, Gene Bourquin, turned his farm over six days later.

With the last of the land purchases in hand, the MDC's engineers put the final touches on the plans for the Hogback Dam. At the same time, the Bottinelli Monumental Company of New London attended to the last detail in the dismantling of a New England town. In 1953, they removed the bodies of almost 500 former residents, from what their kin had considered their final resting place, and reinterred them in the new Colebrook Cemetery. It was an odd collection with bodies removed from Colebrook River Burying Grounds, Spenser Cemetery and the Old Town Cemetery. Also there were three graves on the Alton Hurd property—including two infants—and two more on Anna Nixon's farm. Just as they did back in the hollows on the other side of the mountain, the remains of the graves were put into small boxes—15" x 15" x 36"—and piled unto the backs of pick-up trucks and reinterred on higher ground. A resident of Colebrook, who lived just outside of the proposed watershed, remembered in a macabre way, ". . . we always wondered who it was that was going by."

The way was now clear for the MDC to begin work on the Hogback Dam— another earthen structure with a concrete corewall. It would impound a much smaller body of water than either the Nepaug or the Barkhamsted Reservoirs— only seven billion gallons. Since the MDC already had in storage twice as much water as the capital region needed, and since this catchment was so much larger than the other compensating reservoir, the public was confused. It was beyond the imaginative skills of the average person to think like a hydraulic engineer. While the average citizen was provident after a fashion, it was rare to find one who planned thirty to forty years ahead. No argument could possibly be proffered that the water was needed then. Still, *someday* it would be. Fittingly, in the early writings of Caleb Saville is this cautionary idiom, "In water works . . . 'never' is a comparatively short time."

Trouble was the constant companion of this new project. The years of squabbling with the local residents had, of course, put the MDC way behind. Then a hurricane tore through New England, crippling the state from border to border. Immediately after Hurricane Diane was downgraded to a tropical storm in August 1955, she dumped anywhere from sixteen to thirty inches of rain over a thirty-six-hour period. It created the most devastating floods that the state had ever seen—before or since. Many towns—especially those near rivers—were reduced to a flooded pile of rubble with property damages estimated at over a billion dollars. Statewide, 103 people died and 30,000 were homeless. The northwestern hills were hit particularly bad. The spillway of the Saville Dam was damaged by the fearsome amount of water that cascaded through the concrete conduit, but the valley of the West Branch was battered much worse. Keeping in mind that the watershed area of the West Branch of the Farmington River was more than a hundred square miles, it's easy to see that a small river like the West Branch could not possibly have handled such a massive runoff. As the whole valley filled up with water, this wild cataract swept away houses, businesses, bridges and all of the timber and debris that was being cleared from the Hogback Reservoir site.

In Winsted, a few miles away, a couple of small streams disgorged such large amounts of water that the entire town was flooded to a depth of three feet. Though Caleb Saville was almost ninety years old by this time, and, technically, only a consultant to the MDC, one sentence in his earlier writings rang true again— "It is axiomatic in hydraulic engineering that the greatest floods and the most severe droughts will someday be surpassed." The disaster in the valley of the West Branch proved his theorem convincingly.

Not only did this flood send the engineers of the MDC back to their drawing boards, it awakened another group of people—the U. S. Army Corps of Engineers. They had been watching this area of New England since a similar flood back in 1938 had destroyed the valley and they had even completed a preliminary survey of the area. Owing to the size of the watershed above the valley of the West Branch, huge and uncontrollable floods were increasingly viewed as facts of life instead of isolated events to be expected once every hundred years.

For the MDC and the Army Corps of Engineers, it was time to put their slide rules together. The two groups met to compare notes. The men from the Corps explained that they had been watching the northwestern part of Connecticut for some time. Moreover, recent events had shot the West Branch watershed to the top of their "to-do list." Although there were several meetings over a period of years, it would be impossible to reconstruct exactly what transpired and when. This much is certain—a partnership emerged to control flooding in the area.

To the secret delight of the commissioners of the MDC, the Army Corps of Engineers wanted to build and operate a flood control dam and reservoir to the north of the Hogback giving the federal government control of a large swath of land in Massachusetts. Since ninety percent of the 104-square-mile watershed was in Massachusetts—and for this reason had always been an irritant for the MDC—naturally the Corps's decision pleased them immensely. The small Hogback Dam and Reservoir would not only be protected from the ravages of destructive floods, but it would also enjoy a steady flow from the much larger body of water that the Corps would create with its new dam and lake.

After the detailed calculations were completed, it was announced that the most desirable spot for the Corps's new dam was in the middle of what was to be the Hogback Reservoir. In common parlance, it could be said that the two separate projects would actually overlap one another at completion. Perhaps to improve relations with the locals and since Colebrook River would now be at the bottom of the flood control dam instead of the Hogback Reservoir, the Army Corps of Engineers named their project Colebrook River Lake.

The amount of water in this new lake varies throughout the year depending on the amount of rainfall, but it is generally kept at very low levels. (So low in fact that the steel bridge at now-demolished Sawyer's Cotton Mills pops up out of the lake in the autumn.) Should there be a storm of Biblical proportions though, Colebrook River Lake would fill up fast enough. In the process though, it would save the whole valley below from certain destruction and inevitable loss of life.

Even with this change of plans, when the Hogback Reservoir was completed in 1960, the MDC had added another four billion gallons of water to its coffers. Some felt that an aqueduct under the mountain to the east would be beneficial, allowing Hogback waters to flow directly into the Barkhamsted Reservoir. Regrettably, the MDC was sitting on so much water at the time that the aqueduct was impossible to sell to anyone.

Taking the larger view, the MDC decided that since the demand for water in the capital region had slacked off after the Second World War, the aqueduct could wait. What they didn't realize at the time was that as they waited, opposition mounted. In the face of a water glut, people could not be convinced to allow the building of an aqueduct connecting the two reservoirs.

Eventually, the connecting channel was reduced to a remote possibility. (Answering a reporter's question in 1990, the then-chairman of the MDC, Anthony Gallicchio, stated, "The tunnel [aqueduct], in my opinion, is a dead issue.") All the same, when the day finally comes when more water is needed in central Connecticut, it is a foregone conclusion that the MDC will be given the right to install the connecting aqueduct. In the interim, the reservoir would be used to compensate the riparian owners downstream exactly as it was originally intended.

While building the Hogback Reservoir, the board inadvertently created one of the premier trout streams in the Northeast because, even in the dry months, the West Branch is a wild, brimming and vibrant river. It is a favorite of canoeists and tubers as well. The partnership formed between the Corps of

Engineers and the water company has left many people confused about the meaning of the whole project, not to mention the sensitive issue of control. Should such questions arise, it would be wise for the puzzled to take a walk by the Colebrook River Lake and read the rustic sign installed by the Corps. It reads—

Operated By The U.S. Army Corps of Engineers
New England Division
In Cooperation With The
Metropolitan District Commission
State Of Connecticut

The U.S. Army Corps of Engineers worked on the Colebrook River project from 1965 until 1969, afterwards building an office at the facility to oversee the finished project. With the Army Corps's completion of Colebrook River Lake, the MDC was sitting on almost fifty billion gallons of water, with a treatment capacity of eighty million gallons of fresh drinking water a day.

In early 1960, the MDC took the controversial step of adding fluoride to the drinking water. Initially the board couldn't decide whether to let the towns vote on the issue or to make the decision themselves. In the end, the board reasoned that, since the science behind the fluoridation issue was fairly complex, they were the only ones who could make an informed decision. For the water commissioners though, one can't help but think they were skeptical of the whole voting process. Each of the members knew that when the vote was taken in 1929 on whether or not to create a Metropolitan District Commission, only one out of three registered voters bothered to show up at the polls. Why should they let such an important decision fall into the hands of an obviously indifferent constituency?

***

The story of fluoridation is an unusual one. Most people are under the impression that the practice of putting fluoride in drinking water to reduce dental caries was the result of exhaustive experimentation and superb lab work. Nothing could be further from the truth. Actually, in some regions of the United States, the water naturally contains *too* much fluorine, and that is where the tale begins. (Fluorine is the naturally occurring element from which sodium fluoride is made.)

In 1901, a newly graduated dentist from the University of Pennsylvania, Frederick McKay, moved to Colorado Springs, Colorado. His choice of towns wasn't an accident. In 1891, gold had been discovered at nearby Cripple Creek and people had flooded into the area. The population of Cripple Creek ballooned to over 50,000 and Colorado Springs swelled to more than 20,000. With such a mass of humanity, obviously a dentist could do well.

One of the first things Fred McKay noticed was that an inordinate number of his patients had unsightly and permanent stains on their teeth. It was sometimes light brown in color but more often was a "mottled brown," which in severe cases was darker than even the darkest chocolate.

Finding nothing in his textbooks that even remotely resembled this condition, he began casting about for the cause of the problem. The condition wasn't painful and, as he was to find out after examining thousands of children, it was closely associated with an almost complete absence of tooth decay. He questioned them about their habits, at last sensing that the culprit was somehow connected to the drinking water. But he couldn't prove it. Just when it looked like the problem would fester for decades, another dentist in Benton, Arkansas noticed the same problem with the children of nearby Bauxite, an Alcoa company town. Because Alcoa stood to lose everything if the mothers of America found out that aluminum pots and pans—made from bauxite—caused health problems, the company put their head chemist, H. V. Churchill, on the case immediately. Remembering an old scientific paper by Fred MacKay, he sent for water samples from Bauxite, and ran them through the most rigorous battery of tests ever run on drinking water up to that time. Among other things, he found that the water from Bauxite contained an unusually high amount of fluorine—13.7 parts per million.

Maddeningly, the information presented a tricky puzzle—since the fluorine was associated with fewer dental caries, was there some optimum level at which fluorine would prevent decay but not cause mottling? Of course, that level was eventually found to be one part per million.

By 1956, more than twelve hundred communities were fluoridating their water supplies, including Philadelphia, Pittsburgh, St. Louis, San Francisco, Milwaukee, Cleveland, Baltimore, Chicago, St, Paul and Washington D. C. However, fluoridation has always been a controversial issue with a sizable body of opponents, who believe sodium fluoride to be carcinogenic. Hundreds of studies have been done and the overwhelming evidence says otherwise, but the debate lives on. Many California cities, including Los Angeles, did not fluoridate until 1999.

***

In the same year that the Hogback (Charles A. Goodwin) Dam was dedicated, the attorney's longtime friend and co-worker, Caleb Mills Saville, died from arteriosclerosis. He was ninety-four. Reverend Charles Goodwin, the son of the former chairman, officiated at a private ceremony. The great engineer's body was then cremated and his ashes transferred to the Mt. Auburn Cemetery in Cambridge, Massachusetts. The ashes of his wife, Elizabeth, who had predeceased him by five years, had been held in storage until he could join her. Both of the urns were interred in February 1960, among the famous politicians and Brahmins of the greater Boston area. Presumably, the fact that he and his wife were very proud of their ancestry forbade him from accepting a resting place any less grand than Mt. Auburn. In fact, after Saville purchased the plot in Mt. Auburn, upon the death of his wife in 1955, he used to quip to co-workers at the MDC—

Born in Boston,
Educated at Harvard,
Buried at Mt. Auburn.
What more could a mortal want?

This way, the Savilles would spend eternity next to Henry Wadsworth Longfellow, Oliver Wendell Holmes and Winslow Homer, just to name a few of the luminaries buried at Mt. Auburn. In hindsight, it was so fitting that just as the last piece of the puzzle dropped into place, Caleb Saville's life ended. He had come to Hartford when the water company had a few small, hand-grubbed reservoirs and he contributed to the construction of six major dams that impounded enough water to last for a century or more.

After his wife's death, Saville sold the house on North Beacon Street and moved into the Heublein Hotel. The once-elegant building stood at the corner of Gold and Welles Street (near present day Bushnell Towers). Right up to the last, his driver still picked him up early in the morning and brought him to the MDC's headquarters—in the old Rossia Insurance Building—on the corner of Broad Street and Farmington Avenue. At lunchtime, instead of a bowl of chowder at Honiss's Oyster House, he now ate at the University Club on Lewis Street. He arrived daily at exactly 11:30, and at 11:55, took his place at his customary table, always ordering the same sandwich and coffee. To complete this inflexible regimen, he ate with the same friend each day.

In 1960, newspapers assumed a euphemistic tone in their remarks about deceased members of the community. Therefore, one can't help but be taken aback by the comments in the *Hartford Times*. The newspaper characterized Caleb Saville as having ". . . a brusque and frequently domineering personality that made it difficult to work with him." Conversely, they went on to say that he ". . . was an apostle of thoroughness, of integrity, of diligence."

Caleb Saville, it is fair to say was a tough individual. He was indeed loud and domineering at times. On the other hand, he could be a very considerate and kind-hearted man. He was difficult and authoritative, but he just could not have built a first-class water system without the hard work, diligence and single-mindedness of purpose that he demanded of himself and those around him. In life, it seems, a community rarely gets a person of genius and industry without receiving some irritating qualities in the bargain.

By the end of 1960, the construction period of the water company had come to a close. The four billion gallons of water collected in the Hogback Reservoir was the last to be impounded. Judging by the difficulty other water companies have had in the building of new reservoirs, the Hogback might well be the last for the MDC. As one engineer commented wryly, "The reservoirs could never be built today. One 'snail darter' would bring us to our knees."

In the process of providing for the drinking water needs of the people of the capital region, the Metropolitan District Commission wound up owning more than half of the Town of Barkhamsted, one quarter of Hartland and about one-fifth of Colebrook. By virtue of its reservoir holdings, it owns smaller amounts of New Hartford, Burlington, Canton, West Hartford, and Bloomfield.

Hiram Bissell

Just as any story about water represents a variation on the theme of the deceptively simple hydrologic cycle, the story of Hartford's water company is no different. Its history, or at least that part of its history that deals with its construction years, is also a human circle. As a member of the first Board of Water Commissioners in 1854, Hiram Bissell, the brick mason, oversaw the construction of the Lord's Hill Reservoir, a glorified swimming pool, yet Hartford's first successful attempt to impound drinking water.

Eighty-five years later, his grandson, H. Bissell Carey, helped to purchase the land for the water company's final reservoir. The construction years of the water company spanned more than a century, from 1854 until 1960, and these two men, by contributing their time and skills, completed the circle. Assisting with the purchase of the village of Colebrook River and all of the surrounding farmlands, H. Bissell Carey helped the MDC assemble the entire watershed for the Hogback Reservoir.

Could he have known that the Hogback would be the water company's last reservoir? Of course not. Did he know about his grandfather's battle with the city's Whigs over the Trout Brook plan in the 1860s? Or about the enervating door-to-door campaigns to convince the residents of Hartford to abandon the Connecticut River for the pristine upland sources? Yes, he knew it all.

H. Bissell Carey was twenty-four years old and had already graduated from Yale's engineering school when his grandfather, Hiram Bissell, died in 1910. The older man's obituary—highlighting his contribution to the water works of Hartford—was displayed prominently in both of the city's newspapers.

Therefore, when given the chance to help the MDC, H. Bissell Carey, undoubtedly felt compelled to do so.

In the period between 1960 and 2004, the water company has built no new reservoirs. Owing to the industry of a simple brick mason, Hiram Bissell, his friend and steel merchant, Ezra Clark, Jr., and the engineer Caleb Mills Saville, the water supply for the Hartford metropolitan area is secured possibly as far into the future as 2100. (The date is anyone's guess because the water supplies are subject to such diverse variables as population expansion, industrial growth, conservation and even acts of God.)

H. Bissell Carey

With the passing of the years, the astute decisions made as the water company struggled to gain a toehold are lost on the average consumer of this all-important daily need. What, for example, would the drinking water be like in the capital region today if the *three-fifths majority* had not been obtained in the fourth and final vote for the Trout Brook plan in July 1865? Would the water company still be dependent on river water as are so many other cities? Is that what the future came down to—the votes of 132 people? (Actually if only half of the 132 voters—67 to be exact—had chosen to stay with the Connecticut River water, then that might be the source of the drinking water in the capital region today.)

A greater matter for speculation revolves around the collapse of the dam of the first reservoir on Trout Brook in 1867. What if the ignominy of the collapse had forced the champions of the upland sources to give up and return to the Connecticut River for supply? Would someone have had the moxie to step forward at some future date and reach into the far-off hills for the pristine uplands sources? Difficult to say.

As if the reservoirs in West Hartford did not cause enough heartache at the outset, what if the long drought of the 1870s had caused the public to waver. When Reservoir No. 1 gave up the last of its water in September 1873, what if the general public had felt that Trout Brook was a costly mistake? Could the water board not have been forced to retreat and rebuild their operations around the old Connecticut River Pumping Station?

A more interesting question, in light of the size of the reservoirs today, centers on the 1911 hiring of Caleb Mills Saville. What if Shiras Morris had managed to hogtie John Dower and another engineer had been given the job. Would he have done as good a job as Caleb Saville? And if not, would the reservoirs have been completed in a timely fashion, thus avoiding a water drought? An imponderable, at best.

Today, in addition to distributing drinking water to its eight member towns, the MDC also supplies water to a number of other communities including parts of Cromwell, East Granby, Farmington, Glastonbury, South Windsor, Manchester, Portland and Windsor Locks (including Bradley International Airport). All together, the MDC serves about 400,000 customers who consume a little over 50 million gallons daily. That number was as high as 62 million gallons in 1990, but has since declined a bit. With 1.6-gallon toilets, low-flow showerheads and more efficient dishwashers, it may be a long time before maximum water utilization is reached—if ever.

That having been said, the quest for new supplies is the *raison d'etre* of a water company. A good hydraulic engineer thinks of little else. It is with this in mind, that the MDC initiated a pilot program in the early 1990s—the drilling of deep wells. In South Glastonbury, not far from the Shingle Hollow birthplace of Hiram Bissell, the water company ran a pilot program to see if groundwater could increase supplies in the future. Approximately two-dozen test borings were done using 2½" casings. Sometimes the auger bit hit solid rock at 20 feet and other times the boring continued to depths of over 90 feet. Although the MDC decided against pursuing wellfields as an immediate source of supply, it was determined that the aquifer—small and un-consolidated though it be—could deliver a safe yield of between ten and twenty million gallons per day. In reality, the MDC had repeated the test borings done by the old Hartford Water Works in 1910—just a little farther down river. Once again though, the water company chose not to pursue groundwater as a source of supply, though the option remains.

On a happier note, the limitations on the MDC's customer base—as outlined in its charter—may be in the initial stages of a sea change. Because of the growing costs of laboratory testing and engineering, small community water companies are feeling the pinch. Add these burdens to the public's insatiable demand for top quality water at affordable prices and it is little wonder many of these smaller water utilities are increasingly choosing to buy their water—raw or treated—from the large regional suppliers or turn their water systems over completely to larger utilities. Undoubtedly, there will be a period of consolidation in which every community water company will be faced with tough choices. The final outcome is anything but certain. However, it would not be unreasonable to assume that the large regional suppliers—like the Metropolitan District Commission—are only in their infancies.

Afterword

This book took considerably longer than I anticipated, and had I known at the beginning that this volume would consume five years of my life, I might never have written it. So said, it should come as no surprise that I had my doubts along the way. During the worst periods—particularly when vital information simply could not be found—I used to take a break from my work and drive to Cedar Hill Cemetery in the southwest corner of Hartford. There, I visited the grave of Hiram Bissell. A writer probably should not pick a favorite character in his story, but I found Hiram Bissell an inspiring person. True, Ezra Clark was an honorable man who fought disastrous financial troubles to serve Hartford and the water department for many years and Caleb Saville was the prototypical driven genius, but Hiram Bissell was my favorite. From his humble beginnings to his unyielding integrity, great native intelligence and unfailing resilience, he was an inspiration.

Cedar Hill is easily the most gorgeous cemetery I have ever visited. It was designed in 1863 by a Swiss-born architect, engineer, and landscape designer, Jacob Weidenmann, who also designed Hartford's Bushnell Park. Hiram Bissell, as one of the original directors of the cemetery, was able to secure for himself and his family a very desirable spot in Section One.

Viewed from above, Cedar Hill resembles a pretzel on steroids, with miles of narrow, heavily bowered roads, gently twisting their way around small patches of ground, each with its own impressive collection of mammoth hardwoods, exploding foliage and imposing monuments. This breathtaking Eden is the final resting place of dozens of notables of every social, ethnic, political and religious persuasion—America's elusive dream brought to life—in death.

The headstones of Hiram and Nancy Bissell are small, flat rectangles almost flush with the earth, as are those of Hiram's brothers, Sylvester and Martin, and Hiram and Nancy's daughters, Isabelle and Ella Louise. Almost all of the Bissells' grandchildren and great-grandchildren are buried in the family's ample plot. Curiously enough, the only two stones that stand up in profile against the lush backdrop of lilac, azalea, forsythia and rhododendron are the two little markers of the Bissells' sons, George and Samuel, both of whom died young. About twenty yards to the south of Hiram Bissell's grave is that of Charles R. Chapman, Hartford's mayor when Bissell finished his long run at the head of the water board. To the north are the final resting places of Nathan Starkweather, the first engineer that Bissell hired, and Henry Tryon, his cousin and first partner in the masonry business, and the man who did so much construction work for the water department.

A stone's throw away are the graves of Samuel Ward and James Goodwin, two of the Whigs who were constant thorns in Bissell's side. On a brighter note, to the northwest is the tall, gun barrel monument of Samuel Colt, who used his fabulous wealth to frighten off Ward, Goodwin and the other Whigs a few months before the new water works first began pumping Connecticut River water to the top of Lord's Hill in October 1855.

Also to the north is the outsized monument of Eliphalet Bulkeley who, together with William Hungerford, nearly succeeded in killing the water works by denying Bissell the legal wherewithal to bed the long aqueduct from Reservoir No. 1 at Trout Brook into Hartford.

Of course, not all of the characters, whose exploits crowd the pages of this book, are buried in Cedar Hill, but enough of them to make a walk around its lanes and monuments a nostalgic trip back into the water works' long and involved history.

The luxurious, rolling lawns of Cedar Hill, for all their beauty, are now the great common denominator, the leveling field for men who sometimes worked together for the common good and, other times, fought rancorously for the right to see Hartford rise up according to their own vision. Now, friend and foe alike, rest for all eternity cheek by jowl.

Cedar Hill has three lakes and Hiram Bissell's resting place faces the smallest one, Llyn Lilly, which is, appropriately enough, about the size of the original Lord's Hill Reservoir. Nothing could dissuade me from believing that Hiram Bissell picked this site for its beautiful view of the water.

K.M.
Wethersfield, CT
January 2004

Notes

Chapter 1

Pg. 1   *In the spring of 1836...*, The Hartford Courant, October 1, 1910, p. 11

Pg. 1   *Bissell was a tall, wiry young man...*, Commemorative Biographical Record of Hartford County, J.H. Beers & Co., Chicago, 1901, p. 108

Pg. 1   *...known colloquially as Shingle Hollow...* The information about the Tryons of South Glastonbury and the Shingle Hollow section of that town came from the following people: Frances Tryon Barker, Shirley Tryon Fuller, Arlene Dilts, Russ Shemstone, Richard Chapman, Howard Horton, Jr., John Heagle and Bill & Sue Duffert. Also of help was Bayless Earle, Sexton of the Still Hill Cemetery (where Chester and Prudence Bissell were laid to rest), Jim Bennett of the Historical Society of Glastonbury and Marjorie McNulty, Glastonbury Town Historian.

Pg. 1   *In addition to farming...* Commemorative Biographical Record of Hartford County, J.H. Beers & Co., Chicago, 1901, p. 108

Pg. 1   *Bissell's father, Chester,...* Ibid. pg. 107-109

Pg. 1   *Her father had a fondness...* Most of the information regarding the "Bissell place" was supplied by the present owner of the property, Adrien Tetreault, and the engineer, John Heagle, who lived in the hollow at one time. Supplementary information was found at the Glastonbury Hall of Records.

Pg. 1   *Not long after William Tryon's death...* U.S. Census Data, 1830 and Vital Statistic at the Glastonbury Hall of Records.

Pg. 1   *By 1833, when the Bissell's last child...* U.S. Census Data, 1850.

Pg. 2   *The Tryons of South Glastonbury...* Historical Society of Glastonbury, maps and genealogical information.

Pg. 2   *...even a "forceful character"...* The Hartford Courant, October 1, 1910, p. 11

Pg. 2   *...a man "whose advise was ...",* The Hartford Courant, October 1, 1910, p. 11

Pg. 2   *Two of Hartford's leading masons...,* Genealogical research records of Frances Tryon Barker and Geer's City Directory, 1836, State Archives, Connecticut State Library, Hartford.

Pg. 2   *...he hired Bissell for a four-year...* The Hartford Courant, October 1, 1910, p. 11.

Pg. 2   *In 1836, there were a little over 11,000 people...* The information about the City of Hartford in 1836 was assembled from a large number of reference works and other source material including, but not limited to, the following:
Secretary of State's Office, State of Connecticut, Census figures
Glenn Weaver, Hartford: An Illustrated History of Connecticut's Capital, Connecticut Historical Society; Windsor Publications, Inc., Woodland Hills, California, 1982
Ellsworth S. Grant, The Miracle of Connecticut, published by the Connecticut Historical Society and Fenwick Productions, (no date)
Ellsworth Strong Grant & Marion Hepburn Grant, The City of Hartford 1784- 1984 - An Illustrated History, Connecticut Historical Society, 1986

Albert E. Van Dusen, The History of Connecticut, New York: Random House, 1961

Marion Hooper & Lewis Browne, Life Along the Connecticut River, Brattleboro, VT: Stephen Day Press, 1939

Lewis Sprague Mills, The Story of Connecticut, West Rindge, NH, Richard R. Smith Publisher, 1953

Charles W. Burpee, A Century In Hartford, Pub. by the Hartford County Mutual Fire Insurance Co., 1931

Edmund Delaney, The Connecticut River: New England's Historic Waterway, Chester, CT: The Globe Pequot Press, 1983

Geer's City Directory, 1836, State Archives, Connecticut State Library

Pg. 3 *...The river became completely...*, The Connecticut Courant, January 20, 1836, p. 3

Pg. 3 *Just north of the wharfs...*, George E. Wright, Crossing the Connecticut, Hartford: Smith-Linsley Co., 1908, pp. 1-10

Pg. 3 *...was one of only two public bridges...*, Marguerite Allis, Connecticut River, New York: G.P. Putnam's Sons, 1939, p. 105. Note: The first bridge across the Connecticut River was built in 1808, connecting Enfield with Suffield.

Pg. 3 *A woman recalled taking the trip...*, Helen Post Chapman, My Hartford of the Nineteenth Century, Hartford: Edwin Valentine Mitchell, 1928, p. 62

Pg. 4 *The cheapest room...*, From a United States Hotel brochure of the late 1830s, Hartford Public Library, Hartford Room.

Pg. 4 *A signature springtime meal...The Hartford Daily Times*, April 26, 1853, p. 2.

Pg. 4 *Merchants kept their shops...The Hartford Daily Times*, January 16, 1852, p. 2.

Pg. 5 *Eerily quiet, this elegant...*,The description of the Universalist church was taken from an 1825 engraving of the southern side of Meetinghouse Square and accompanying description which can be found in Burpee's History of Hartford County, Volume 1, Published by the S. J. Clarke Co., Hartford, 1928.

Pg. 5 *Unlike Boston, New York...*, Nelson Blake, Water for the Cities – A History of the Urban Water Supply System in the United States. Syracuse University Press, 1956, pp. 13-14.

Pg. 5 *(...one armed Billy)...*, Newton C. Brainard, The Hartford State House of 1796, Hartford: The Connecticut Historical Society, 1964, p. 2.

Pg. 5 *His first lodging...*, Geer's City Directory, 1836, State Archives, Connecticut State Library and U.S. Census, 1840.

Pg. 5 *His employer, Eldridge Andrews*, Geer's City Directory, 1836, State Archives, Connecticut State Library.

Pg. 5 *Mary Buckley's home...*, U.S. Census, 1840

Pg. 6 *...Mr. Hartshorne's warm...The Connecticut Courant*, July 6, 1830, p. 2.

Pg. 6 *There were other builders...*, Geer's City Directory, 1836, State Archives, Connecticut State Library.

Pg. 6 *...insisting that her students speak only...*, Helen Post Chapman, My Hartford of the Nineteenth Century, Hartford: Edwin Valentine Mitchell, 1928, p. 37.

Pg. 6 *While he learned the masonry...*, The Hartford Courant, October 1, 1910, p. 11.

Pg. 6 *For the whole first season...*, Ibid. p. 11.

Pg. 6   *The second, third and fourth...,* Ibid. p. 11.

Pg. 7   *One aspect of city life...,* The Connecticut Courant, March 6, 1797, p. 1 and
Charles W. Burpee, A Century In Hartford, Pub. by the Hartford County
Mutual Fire Insurance Co., 1931. (Hartford's Old Bell-Tower, for signaling
fires, was erected in September 1867 (The Times, September 7, 1867, p. 2),
behind the old Sack & Bucket Company's house on Pearl Street at which time it
was scheduled to receive "a steel bell weighing two tons." When the bell was
finally installed on the seventy-five foot high tower, the bill for the bell was $9,
091. It struck for the last time on May 25, 1921, when sirens replaced the
existing system.)

Pg. 7   *By 1836, Hartford had been...* Ibid, p. 1.

Pg. 7   *Fire. About half past nine...,* The Connecticut Courant, December 23, 1836, p.
3.

Pg. 8   *The firemen submerged the ends...* The History of Hartford County, 1633-1928,
Charles W. Burpee, Vol. 1, pub. by The S. J. Clark Publishing Co., Chicago,
1928, pp. 370-2. (Between 1789 and 1850, the city built twenty-one of these
fire cisterns under the streets of Hartford.)

Pg. 8   *Just 100 miles to the northeast, ...,* Nelson Blake, Water for Cities – A History
of the Urban Water Supply System in the United States, Syracuse University
Press, 1956, p. 64.

Pg. 8   *In addition to Boston's great success...,* Ibid, pp. 64-67.

Pg. 8   *...people knew that New York...,* Ibid, p. 44.

Pg. 8   *They also knew about Philadelphia's...,* Ibid, pp. 18-43.

Pg. 8   *...and Baltimore's water company...* Ibid, pp. 219

Pg. 9   *The genesis of the first water...,* Hall of Records, Hartford.

Pg. 9   *...a most wonderful well...,* Auburey, Travels, Hartford, (self-published),1781,
State Archives, Connecticut State Library.

Pg. 9   *With the help of the couple's...,* Vital Statistics, State Archives, Connecticut
State Library, Hartford.

Pg. 9   *...Elisha printed the American Mercury...,* Geer's City Directory, State
Archives, Connecticut State Library, Hartford.

Pg. 9   *... "famous well on the Dolly Babcock farm... ",* J. Hammond Trumbull, The
Memorial History of Hartford County: 1633-1884, Boston: Edward L. Osgood
Publisher, 1886, p. 456.
Trumbull uses the word "probably" when writing about Babcock and Hull
tapping the spring on David Clark's farm, while *The Hartford Daily Times*
(November 28, 1866) states it as a fact. However, if only 200 people used the
aqueduct system, it seems unlikely that the water from David Clark's farm was
ever needed.

Pg. 9   *Sensing that the water could be...,* Private Laws of Connecticut, State Archives,
Connecticut State Library, Hartford.

Pg. 9   *Accommodating the pair, the state legislature ...,* J. Hammond Trumbull, The
Memorial History of Hartford County: 1633-1884, Boston: Edward L. Osgood
Publisher, 1886, p. 456.

Pg. 9   *To further their plan...,* Ibid, p. 456.

Pg. 9   *... "pine logs with 2 ½ inch bores. ",* Ibid, p. 456.

Pg. 9   *... "about two hundred persons used... ",* Ibid, p. 456.

Pg. 9   ... "mainly for drinking water...", The Hartford Daily Times, Nov. 28, 1866, p. 2.

Pg. 9   Though the spring on the farm of David Clark..., Ibid, p. 2.

Pg. 9   ...required to pay an annual tax..., The Connecticut Courant, July 13, 1801, p. 3.

Pg. 9   Chauncey Gleason and Elias Cowles..., The Connecticut Courant, June 9, 1800, p. 3.

Pg. 10   A Contract..., The Connecticut Courant, November 9, 1801, p. 3.

Pg. 10   According to the 1801 bill..., Public Records of Connecticut, 1801, p. 311-2, State Archives, Connecticut State Library.

Pg. 10   After suffering under the onus..., Public Records of Connecticut, May 1803, p. 3213, State Archives, Connecticut State Library.

Pg. 10   ...all connection in trade... The Connecticut Courant, June 8, 1803, p.2

Pg. 11   The third and final..., Public Records of Connecticut, May 1830, State Archives, Connecticut State Library.

Pg. 11   (Damon was not new to Hartford...), Michael C. DeVito, Connecticut's Timbered Crossings, Warehouse Point, CT, pub. by DeVito Enterprises, 1964.

Pg. 11   Atop Cedar Hill were..., The History of Hartford County, 1633-1928, Charles W. Burpee, Vol. 1, pub. by The S. J. Clark Publishing Co., Chicago, 1928, pp. 370-2.

Pg. 11   Cast iron pipes eventually..., Nelson Blake, Water for the Cities – A History of the Urban Water Supply System in the United States, Syracuse University Press, 1956, p. 83, 220.

Pg. 11   The original method..., Ibid, p. 38, 58-59, 61, 106, 122, 128.

Pg. 11   As an etymological curiosity... Webster's Encyclopedic Unabridged Dictionary of the English Language, Gramercy Books, New York, 1996, p. 2148.

Pg. 12   However, in 1842 when..., Nelson Blake, Water for Cities – A History of the Urban Water Supply System in the United States, Syracuse University Press, 1956.

Pg. 12   He went off on his own..., The Hartford Courant, October 1, 1910, p. 11.

Pg. 13   In an attempt to expand..., Ibid, p. 11.

Pg. 13   Her name was Nancy Sheldon..., Vital Statistics, State Archives, Connecticut State Library.

Pg. 13   Nancy Sheldon's father, Samuel,..., Geer's City Directory and Death Records, State Archives, Connecticut State Library, Hartford.

Pg. 13   Two years after her husband's..., Hall of Records, Hartford.

Pg. 13   Building Lots For Sale..., The Daily Times, July 22, 1844, p. 1

Pg. 14   Since Nancy's mother, in due course,...U.S. Census records, 1850.

Pg. 14   Paying $700 for the land..., Hall of Records, Hartford.

Pg. 14   Constructed of red brick..., (The house still stands.)

Pg. 14   On July 28, 1844..., U.S. Census Data and Marriage records, State Archives, Connecticut State Library, Hartford.

Pg. 14   In fact, the city's growth was..., The Hartford Daily Times, July 28, 1851, p. 2.

Pg. 15   Both were active in Democratic..., William N. Hosley, Colt: The Making of an American Legend, Amherst, University of Massachusetts Press, 1996.

Pg. 15   ...did a substantial amount..., Ellsworth S. Grant, The Colt Legacy: The Colt Armory in Hartford: 1855-1980, Providence, R.I., Mowbray Co., 1982.

Pg. 15   *Bissell even acted as...,* Hall of Records, Hartford.

Pg. 16   *By 1848, the engineer Ellis Chesbrough...,* Nelson Blake, Water for the Cities: A History of the Urban Water Supply System in the United States, Syracuse University Press, 1956, pp. 199-218.

Pg. 16   *One resident even made reference...,* Hartford Daily Times, Nov. 6, 1851, p. 2.

Pg. 16   *This, in spite of the fact...,* Nelson Blake, Water for the Cities – A History of the Urban Water Supply System in the United States, Syracuse University Press, 1956, pp. 15-16.

Chapter 2

Pg. 17   *Hartford might never...,* There are a number of volumes published over the years which record Hartford's history in scholarly detail. The following is a list of the volumes used in researching this book:
Glenn Weaver, HARTFORD- An Illustrated History of Connecticut's Capital, Connecticut Historical Society; Windsor Publications, Inc., Woodland Hills, California, 1982.
Ellsworth S. Grant, The Miracle of Connecticut, published by the Connecticut Historical Society and Fenwick Productions, (no date)
Ellsworth Strong Grant & Marion Hepburn Grant, The City of Hartford 1784- 1984 - An Illustrated History, Connecticut Historical Society, 1986.
Albert E. Van Dusen, The History of Connecticut, New York: Random House, 1961.
Charles W. Burpee, History of Hartford County, Connecticut: 1633-1928 (3 Vol.), Hartford, S. J. Clarke Pub. Co., 1928.
Marion Hooper & Lewis Browne, Life Along the Connecticut River, Brattleboro, VT: Stephen Daye Press, 1939.
J. Hammond Trumbull, The Memorial History of Hartford County, Connecticut: 1633-1884 , Boston: Edward L. Osgood Publisher, 1886.
William DeLoss Love, The Colonial History of Hartford, Centinel Hill Press & The Pequot Press, Inc., 1974.

Pg. 17   ... *"to seeke out a convenient place. ",* William DeLoss Love, The Colonial History of Hartford, Centinel Hill Press & The Pequot Press, Inc., 1974, p. 1.

Pg. 19   *Its voters were Irishmen...,* Ellsworth Strong Grant & Marion Hepburn Grant, The City of Hartford: 1784- 1984 - An Illustrated History, Connecticut Historical Society, 1986, p. 14.

Pg. 20   *After their marriage...,* Records of Births, Deaths and Marriages, State Archives, Connecticut State Library, History and Genealogy Department; Real Estate Records, Hall of Records, Hartford.

Pg. 20   *In 1846, their first child...,* Birth, Death and Marriage records, State Archives, Connecticut State Library, History and Genealogy Department. All of the information regarding the births and deaths of Hiram and Nancy Bissell's children come from the Vital Statistics records of the State Archives, Connecticut State Library, Hartford and their monuments in Cedar Hill Cemetery.

Pg. 20   *Outdated medical texts...*, Paul Drake, JD, What Did They Mean By That: A Dictionary of Historical Terms For Genealogists, Bowie, MD, Heritage Books, 1994.

Pg. 20   *For goods of a pressing nature...*, Information about businesses in Hartford and the extent of their merchandise was culled from a wide variety of newspapers published by *The Hartford Daily Courant* and *The Hartford Daily Times* in the early to mid- 1850s.

Pg. 21   *Hartford was a peaceful...*, Census Records, Secretary of State's Office, State of Connecticut.

Pg. 21   *People had always enjoyed simple concerts...*, The Hartford Daily Times, July 2, 1851, p. 2 and *The Hartford Daily Times*, July 7, 1851, p. 2.

Pg. 21   *...the law of this state...*, The Hartford Daily Times, May 22, 1851, p. 2

Pg. 21   *Jenny Lind, the Swedish nightingale...*, The Hartford Daily Times, July 2, 1851, p. 2.

Pg. 21   *Twelve hundred people paid...*, The Hartford Daily Times, July 7, 1851, p. 2.

Pg. 22   *Traveling orchestras gave concerts...*, Glenn Weaver, Hartford: An Illustrated History of Connecticut's Capital, Connecticut Historical Society; Windsor Publications, Inc., Woodland Hills, California, 1982, p. 73.

Pg. 22   *Though it was a small city...*, U.S. Census Figures, 1850.

Pg. 22   *The roads were a combination...The Hartford Daily Times*, May 7, 1852, p. 2

Pg. 22   *There were twenty houses of worship...*, Geer's City Directory, 1850, State Archives, Connecticut State Library, Hartford.

Pg. 25   *In 1840, a twenty-five-year-old...*, Elias B. Sanford, A History of Connecticut, Hartford: The S.S. Scranton Co., 1922, pp. 405-412.

Pg. 26   *The Thames had become...*, Peter Ackroyd, London: The Biography, New York: Nan A. Talese, Doubleday, 2000, p. 338.

Pg. 27   *(When Mark Twain moved to Hartford...),* Information on Mark Twain's life can be obtained in any number of biographies, but a tour of the Clemens's home in Hartford is infinitely more informative.

Pg. 27   *In May of that year...*, Legislative Acts, State Archives, Connecticut State Library, Hartford.

Pg. 27   *In a cruel quirk of fate...*, Death records, State Archives, Connecticut State Library, Hartford.

Pg. 27   *A seemingly all-inclusive ensemble...*, The thirty-six signatories of the original incorporation document were checked as to occupation, &c, through Geer's Hartford Directory, 1851, State Archives, Connecticut State Library, Hartford.

Pg. 27   *...a one-time ship's captain...*, J. Hammond Trumbull, The Memorial History of Hartford County, Connecticut: 1633-1884 , Boston: Edward L. Osgood Publisher, 1886, p. 662.

Pg. 27   *The petition also included the signatures...*, From the original 1851 incorporation document, State Archives, Connecticut State Library, Hartford.

Pg. 28   Besides Mayor Flower..., *The Hartford Daily Times*, May 7, 1852 and May 29, 1852 (Just two examples among many.)

Pg. 28   *Ignoring the superb examples...*, Nelson Blake, Water for Cities – A History of the Urban Water Supply System in the United States, Syracuse University Press, 1956.

Pg. 28   *By May 1851, Colt...* William N. Hosley, Colt: The Making of an American Legend, Amherst, University of Massachusetts Press, 1996.

Ellsworth S. Grant, The Colt Legacy: The Colt Armory in Hartford: 1855-1980, Providence, R.I., Mowbray Co., 1982.

Pg. 28 *One oddity of life in Shingle Hollow...*, This information on the water supply in Shingle Hollow was first unearthed by Frances Tryon Barker in an interview that she conducted with Amy Tryon Benton (her aunt), who lived in that area of South Glastonbury. As difficult as it is to believe, the "Bissell place" did not procure its own water supply until a little after 1965—about 140 years after Hiram Bissell's father built the place—when the property changed hands and the new owners were given three years to drill a well.

Pg. 29 *...The winter of 1851-2 will probably...*, The Hartford Daily Times, January 21, 1852, p. 2.

Pg. 29 *...regard a home investment...*, The Hartford Daily Times, March 6, 1852, p. 2.

Pg. 30 *Letters poured into the newspapers...*, The Hartford Daily Times, March 15, 1852, p. 2.

Pg. 30 *...it was plainly to be seen...*, The Hartford Daily Times, May 13, 1852, p. 2.

Pg. 30 *First, they scheduled...*, The Hartford Daily Times, May 19, 1852, p. 2.

Pg. 30 *...let a corporation get the...*, The Hartford Daily Times, May 29, 1852, p. 2.

Pg. 30 *The Courant referred to Dr. Hunt...*, The Hartford Daily Courant, May 3, 1889, p. 4.

Pg. 31 *On a bitter cold night...*, The Hartford Daily Courant, January 29, 1853, p. 2. The Hartford Gas Light Company began to install streetlights in 1849, generally starting in State House Square and working outward, until there were over 1000 streetlights by 1880, at which time the conversion to electric models began.

Pg. 31 *Built one block north of State House Square...*, The descriptions of the inside layout of city hall were culled from Geer's City Directories, 1850-1855.

Pg. 31 *The Courant described the meeting...*, The Hartford Daily Courant, January 29, 1853, p. 3.

Pg. 31 *Mayor Ebenezer Flower presided...*, The Hartford Daily Times, January 29, 1853, p. 2.

Pg. 32 *...that water be introduced from the Connecticut River...*, The Hartford Daily Times, January 29, 1853, p. 2.

Pg. 32 *The Water Project in New Haven...*, The Hartford Daily Times, March 28, 1853, p. 2.

Pg. 32 *As was expected, Hartford's public...*, The Hartford Daily Times, July 19, 1853, p. 2.

Pg. 33 *Three weeks later, they appointed...*, The Hartford Daily Times, August 9, 1853, p. 2.

Pg. 33 *Pure Water! The door-keeper of the House placed...*, The Hartford Daily Courant, June 25, 1853, p. 2.

Pg. 33 *Frustratingly circumspect ...*, The Hartford Daily Times, March 3, 1854, p. 2.

Pg. 34 *As the city's denizens waited...*, The Hartford Daily Times, November 3, 1853, p. 2.

Pg. 34 *The Hartford & New Haven ...*, The Hartford Daily Times, November 10, 1853, p. 2.

Pg. 34 *Just prior to the April elections ...*, The Hartford Daily Times, March 29, 1854, p. 2.

Pg. 34 *On Monday, April 10, 1854...*, The Hartford Daily Courant, April 11, 1854,

p. 2.

Pg. 35   *The following day, The Courant lamented...*, The Hartford Daily Courant, April 13, 1854, p. 3.

Pg. 35   *The newly elected water board...*, The Hartford Daily Times, April 25, 1854, p. 2.

Pg. 35   *Within four months...*, The Hartford Daily Times, August 12, 1854, p. 2.

Pg. 35   *Precipitated by what the Whigs...*, The Hartford Daily Times, August 15, 1854, p. 2.

Pg. 35   *"...I suppose you will see in the papers... "*, Letter dated April 16, 1851, Clark Family Collection, Watkinson Library, Trinity College, Hartford, CT.

Pg. 35   *Nevertheless, Clark was the most ...*, The Hartford Daily Times, September 26, 1896, p. 2.

Pg. 36   *At last, realizing that...*, The Hartford Daily Times, May 25, 1855, p. 2.

Pg. 36   *(Of the 39 towns...)...*, The Hartford Daily Times, April 3, 1855, p. 2.

Pg. 36   *After the election...*, The Hartford Daily Times, May 25, 1855, p. 2.

Pg. 36   *Beyond that, he would...*, The Hartford Daily Times, October 1, 1910, p. 2.

Pg. 36   *His future was crowded...*, Hall of Records, Hartford.

Pg. 36   *In time, his interests expanded...*, Geer's City Directories, State Archives, Connecticut State Library, Hartford.

Pg. 36   *Bissell was the only member...*, U. S. Census data, 1850, 1860.

Pg. 36   *Rum and Water...*, The Hartford Daily Times, August 3, 1854, p. 2 (repeat and retort to article in *The Hartford Daily Courant*)

Pg. 37   *First of all, in 1852...* Hall of Records, Hartford and Geer's City Directories, State Archives, Connecticut State Library, Hartford.

Pg. 37   *...his brothers—Sylvester and Martin...*, U.S. Census, 1850; Geer's City Directory, 1852-3.

Pg. 37   *Though Sylvester was the youngest...*, U.S. Census, 1850 and Geer's City Directories from 1852-1860 and Hartford Vital Statistics, State Archives, Connecticut State Library, Hartford.

Pg. 37   *In due course, Sylvester...*, Geer's City Directories and Vital Statistics, State Archives, Connecticut State Library, Hartford.

Pg. 37   *He worked steadily for his brothers...*, Geer's City Directories, 1850-1875 and Hartford Vital Statistics, State Archives, Connecticut State Library, Hartford.

Chapter 3

Pg. 38   *From the mid-1840s, slavery...*, Once again, the political movements in Connecticut are derived from the books listed in the bibliography at the beginning of Chapter 2.

Pg. 38   *Springing from this tension were...*, The Hartford Daily Times, April 4, 1854, p. 2. The newspapers of the day used the words "fusion" and "union" interchangeably when referring to these political amalgams.

Pg. 38   *In the peak year...*, Bernard Christian Steiner, History of Slavery in Connecticut, Baltimore: Johns Hopkins Press, 1893, Appendix, p. 84.

Pg. 38   *In Nook Farm, the barn behind...*, Horatio Strother, The Underground Railroad in Connecticut, Middletown, CT: Wesleyan University Press, 1962, pp. 143-4.

Pg. 38   *As The Times enjoyed chiding...,.The Hartford Daily Times*, April 4, 1854,

p. 2.

Pg. 39   *In early April 1854...*, The Hartford Daily Times, June 16, 1854, p. 2.

Pg. 39   *The most effective configuration...*, The Hartford Daily Times, May 7, 1855, p. 2.

Pg. 40   *...This combination has already...*, The Hartford Daily Times, May 7, 1855, p. 2.

Pg. 40   *Either in an open landau...*, Helen Post Chapman, My Hartford of the 19th Century, Hartford: Edwin Valentine Mitchell, 1928, p. 63.

Pg. 40   *By late summer, Hiram Bissell...*, The Hartford Daily Times, May 25, 1855, p. 2.

Pg. 41   *A few months before Bissell's...*, The Hartford Daily Times, Dec.12, 1854, p. 2.

Pg. 41   *...had landed the contract for all...*, William N. Hosley, Colt: The Making of an American Legend, Amherst, University of Massachusetts Press, 1996, p. 106.

Pg. 42   *...The former board, ...,* Report of the Board of Water Commissioners, April 23, 1855.

Pg. 42   *Punctuating the problems...,* Report of the Board of Water Commissioners, April 23, 1855.

Pg. 42   *Spending most of 1854...,* Report of the Board of Water Commissioners, April 23, 1855.

Pg. 42   *Slade was not from Hartford...,* Geer's Hartford City Directory, 1854-5, 1855-56.

Pg. 42   *He had, on a number of occasions...,* The Hartford Daily Times, Sept. 9, p. 2.

Pg. 42   *Yet, when Hiram Bissell and Ezra Clark...,* Report of the Board of Water Commissioners, April 1855.

Pg. 42   *...Bissell dismissed him as chief...,* Ibid

Pg. 42   *(Unfortunately, until Congress...),* Abraham Lincoln declared Thanksgiving a national holiday in 1863. Before that time, the governor of each state would designate a date—almost always the last Thursday in November—for the celebration. Not until Franklin Roosevelt proposed fixing the holiday as the fourth Thursday in November (to lengthen the Christmas shopping season) in 1938 was the idea considered. Congress passed the appropriate legislation in 1941.

Pg. 43   *In the late fall of the previous year...,* The Hartford Daily Times, Dec. 20, 1853, p. 2 and Geer's City Directory.

Pg. 43   *Except for some preliminary...,* Hall of Records, Hartford and Report of the Board of Water Commissioners, April, 23, 1855, p. 7.

Pg. 43   *In approximate numbers...,* Geer's New Map of the City of Hartford, 1858.

Pg. 43   *However, at the end of June...,* Hall of Records, Hartford.

Pg. 44   *In any event, for $5,190...,* Hall of Records, Hartford.

Pg. 44   *...a hundred men had dug...,* The Hartford Daily Times, October 25, 1854, p. 2.

Pg. 44   *Clay was used to "puddle"...,* Report of the Board of Water Commissioners, April 23, 1855.

Pg. 44   *Chief engineer Slade...,* Ibid.

Pg. 44   *At the bottom of this pit...,* Report of the Board of Water Commissioners, Jan. 1, 1856 and *The Hartford Daily Times,* October 1, 1855, p. 2.

Pg. 44   *"Once in about one-quarter... "*, Ibid. , p. 2.

Pg. 44   *As if the slides were not enough...*, Report of the Board of Water Commissioners, April 23, 1855.

Pg. 45   *Only days after that vote...*, *The Hartford Daily Courant*, July 21,1853, p. 3 and July 23, 1853, p. 3 and Aug. 6, 1853, p. 3.

Pg. 45   *...The various kinds of service pipe...*, Report of the Board of Water Commissioners, April 23, 1855.

Pg. 45   *...the pipes did not pass...*, *The Hartford Daily Times*, Oct. 20, 1854, p. 2.

Pg. 46   *...was a colossal expense...*, Report of the Board of Water Commissioners, Jan. 1, 1856.

Pg. 46   *The Cornish engine...* Asa Briggs, The Power Of Steam : An Illustrated History of the World's Steam Age, Chicago: University of Chicago Press, 1962, pp. 163-166.

Pg. 47   *In early 1854, when the city...*, *The Hartford Daily Times*, April 9, 1853, p. 2.

Pg. 47   *His talents were so extraordinary...*, Ellsworth Strong Grant & Marion Hepburn Grant, The City of Hartford: 1784- 1984 - An Illustrated History, Connecticut Historical Society, 1986, p. 9.

Pg. 47   *At a meeting of the Common Council...*, The Hartford Daily Times, Feb. 28, 1854, p. 2.

Pg. 48   *In its place, Root recommended...*, Ibid. , p. 2.

Pg. 48   *Since he could not afford...*, Ibid., p. 2.

Pg. 48   *The council replaced the ...*, *The Hartford Daily Times*, March 14, 1854, p. 2 and Geer's City Directory, 1854-5.

Pg. 48   *...approved a contract with R. P. Perrott...*, *The Hartford Daily Times*, April 13, 1854, p. 2.

Pg. 48   *Although the matter would have...*, *The Hartford Daily Times*, July 25, 1854, p. 2.

Pg. 48   *Making the case for the water board...*, *The Hartford Daily Times*, Sept. 9, 1854, p. 2.

Pg. 48   *The Common Council—and others...*, Ibid., p. 2.

Pg. 49   *At seven o'clock on a Friday...*, Ibid. p. 2.

Pg. 49   *In the United States...*, Ibid., p. 2.

Pg. 49   *Philadelphia, he pointed out, was using...*, Ibid., p. 2.

Pg. 49   *The following night, Lucius Robinson...*, *The Hartford Daily Times*, Sept. 11, 1854, p. 2.

Pg. 49   *"...a failure in the engine... "*, Ibid., p. 2.

Pg. 49   *The next night, without...*, *The Hartford Daily Times*, Sept. 12, 1854, p. 2.

Pg. 49   *Oddly enough though—according...*, *The Hartford Daily Times*, Sept. 13, 1854, p. 2.

Pg. 50   *The council's next move, however, ...*, *The Hartford Daily Times*, Oct. 10, 1854, p. 2.

Pg. 50   *The ill-fated James Slade and the ...*, Ibid., p. 2.

Pg. 50   *That same month, the council...*, *The Hartford Daily Times*, Sept. 14, 1854, p. 2.

Pg. 50   *Soon thereafter, a firm was engaged...*, *The Hartford Daily Times*, Oct. 10, 1854, p. 2.

Pg. 50   *On January 10, 1855, The Times...*, *The Hartford Daily Times*, Jan. 10, 1855, p. 2.

Pg. 50   *...to "consider the subject... "*, Ibid, p. 2.

Pg. 50   ...*it is broadly hinted that an effort*..., Ibid, p. 2.

Pg. 50   ...*to appoint a blue-ribbon committee*..., *The Hartford Daily Times*, Jan. 16, 1855, p. 2.

Pg. 51   *Astute businessman that he was*..., Ibid, p. 2.

Pg. 51   ...*would buy $5000 [worth of] water bonds*..., Ibid, p. 2.

Pg. 51   *Samuel Woodruff, a Whig member of the*..., Geer's City Directory.

Pg. 51   *In March 1855,...*, *The Hartford Daily Times*, March 27, 1855, p. 2.

Pg. 51   *To avoid the appearance of*..., *The Hartford Daily Times*, Jan. 22, 1855, p. 2.

Pg. 51   ...*and Democrat, James Bolter*..., *The Hartford Daily Times*, April 17, 1855, p. 2.

Pg. 51   *As the spring rains fell*..., *The Hartford Daily Times*, April 18, 1855, p. 2.

Pg. 51   *Eight of the nine-mile network*..., Ibid, p. 2.

Pg. 52   *The city had already expended $177,000*..., Ibid, p. 2.

Pg. 52   *Nathan Starkweather was a* ..., *The Hartford Times*, January 17, 1902, p. 2.

Pg. 52   *"...a large portion of the street pipes*..., Report of the Board of Water Commissioners, April 23, 1855.

Pg. 53   *Starkweather only stayed*..., Geer's City Directory, 1855, 1856.

Pg. 53   *In early May when Messrs*..., *The Hartford Daily Times*, May 7, 1855, p. 2.

Pg. 53   *At the same time, the playbill*..., *The Hartford Daily Times*, Nov. 3, 1853, p. 2. This is but one date featuring the announcement of the play "Uncle Tom's Cabin," but almost any edition of The Times throughout the 1850s contained a mention of Dr. Wyatt's Lyceum.

Pg. 53   *With startling indelicacy, privies*..., *The Hartford Daily Times*, May 16, 1855, p. 2.

Pg. 54   ....*Let the seats only be placed*..., Ibid, p. 2.

Pg. 54   *The majority of these*..., *The Hartford Daily Times*, Sept. 6, 1855, p. 2.

Pg. 54   *"...after the middle of next week."*..., *The Hartford Daily Times*, Sept. 11, 1855, p. 2.

Pg. 54   *"...in such a state of forwardness..."*, Ibid, p. 2.

Pg. 54   *Crews were even attaching* ..., Ibid, p. 2.

Pg. 54   *Democratic Alderman James Bolter—*..., *The Hartford Daily Times*, Sept. 11, 1855, p. 2.

Pg. 55   ..."*believed there was a cat under the meal."*..., Ibid, p. 2.

Pg. 55   *When Alderman Abner Church, a rope manufacturer*..., Ibid, p. 2.

Pg. 55   *Councilman Lawson Ives,*..., Ibid, p. 2.

Pg. 56   ... *"especially the president pro tem..."*, Ibid, p. 2.

Pg. 56   ..*refused to pay $962.50 in accumulated*..., Ibid, p. 2.

Pg. 56   *The hastily written note*..., Ibid, p. 2.

Pg. 56   *Therefore, at the next council*..., *The Hartford Daily Times*, Sept. 25, 1855, p. 2.

Pg. 56   ..."*approving all of his acts..."*, Ibid, p. 2.

Pg. 56   ..."*Clark should have used the council..."*, Ibid, p. 2.

Pg. 57   *They apparently had the last word*..., Report of the Board of Water Commissioners, January 1856.

Pg. 57   ...*he shows up as one of the commissioners*..., Ibid, p. 4.

Pg. 57   *By 1860, there were 139 water delivery systems*..., Nelson Blake, Water for the Cities – A History of the Urban Water Supply System in the United States, Syracuse University Press, 1956, p. 267.

Pg. 57   *On a Saturday night at the end...*, The Hartford Daily Times, Oct. 1, 1855, p. 2.

Pg. 57   *..."moistened this artificial bed..."*, Ibid, p. 2.

Pg. 57   *..."to supply the water by the middle of this month..."*, Ibid, p. 2.

Pg. 57   *As workmen descended on the troublesome...*, The Hartford Daily Times, October 9, p. 2.

Pg. 58   *Each year, trains from Springfield...*, Ibid, p. 2.

Pg. 58   *One of the most popular attractions...*, Ibid, p. 2.

Pg. 58   *Workmen labored daily on the...*, The Hartford Daily Times, Oct. 20, 1855, p. 2.

Pg. 58   *...The high water prevents, at present, ...*, Ibid, p. 2.

Pg. 59   *The water is likely to be introduced...*, Ibid, p. 2.

Pg. 59   *It was a two story brick affair...*, Geer's City Directories, 1856-1860.

Pg. 60   *At noon on Tuesday, October 23, 1855, ...*, The Hartford Daily Times, Oct. 26, 1855, p. 2.

Pg. 61   *...a mechanic referred to as Mr. Smith...*, The Hartford Daily Times, October 25, 1855, p. 2.

Pg. 61   *True, the water department...*, Report of the Board of Water Commissioners, April, 1861, p. 4.

Pg. 61   *With a few mechanics looking on expectantly...*, The Hartford Daily Times, October 25, 1855, p. 2.

Pg. 61   *...The good new spread like wildfire...*, The Hartford Daily Courant, October 24, 1855, p. 3.

Pg. 61   *A Final Triumph...*, The Hartford Daily Times, October 24, 1855, p. 2.

Pg. 61   *Over the next few days, the engines...*, The Hartford Daily Times, October 25, 1855, p. 2.

Chapter 4

Pg. 63   *"...the work "gives general satisfaction...*, Report of the Board of Water Commissioners, Jan. 28, 1856.

Pg. 63   *Few cities in the United States...*, The Hartford Daily Times, Dec. 12, 1855, p. 2.

Pg. 64   *For years, the Firemen's Balls...*, The Hartford Daily Times, Dec. 12, 1855, p. 2.

Pg. 64   *"...the ice makes a great...,"* The Hartford Daily Times, Feb. 28,1856, p. 2.

Pg. 64   *One of Bissell's little annoyances...*, The Hartford Daily Times, Feb. 26, 1856, p. 2.

Pg. 64   *After the stone walls...*, The Hartford Daily Times, April 2, 1856, p. 2.

Pg. 64   *The jets are so arranged...*, The Hartford Daily Times, April 28, 1856, p.2.

Pg. 64   *The Times tried to help, ...*, The Hartford Daily Times, May 1, 1856, p. 2.

Pg. 65   *...expense of laying the dust...*, The Hartford Daily Times, May 1, 1852, p. 2.

Pg. 65   *After almost a month of haggling...*, The Hartford Daily Times, May 27, 1856, p. 2.

Pg. 65   *For sheer publicity value...*, The Hartford Daily Times, July 5, 1856, p. 2.

Pg. 65   *...to the delight of everyone, 15 or 20 fountains, ...*, The Hartford Daily Times, July 3, 1856, p. 2.

Pg. 66   *The Hartford Water Works was...*, The Hartford Daily Times, July 5, 1856, p. 2.

Pg. 66   *At one o'clock, a powerful...*, The Hartford Daily Times, July 5, 1856, p. 2
Pg. 66   *The two... [carriages]...containing...*, The Hartford Daily Times, July 5, 1856, p. 2.
Pg. 66   *The storm cleared in time...*, The Hartford Daily Times, July 5, 1856, p. 2.
Pg. 66   *...displays, created by EDGE & Company...*, The Hartford Daily Times, July 5, 1856, p. 2.
Pg. 66   *The Lord's Hill reservoir erased...*, The Hartford Daily Times, August 21, 1856, p. 2.
Pg. 67   *New Haven's death-grip competition...*, The Hartford Daily Times, Feb. 27, 1856, p. 2.
Pg. 67   *The premier event...*, The Hartford Daily Times, Oct. 4, 1856, p. 2.
Pg. 67   *On February 26, 1857, John Brown...*, The Hartford Daily Times, Feb. 27, 1857, p. 2 and The Hartford Daily Courant, Oct. 25, 1914, quoting from its files.
Pg. 67   *A slight check to the increase...*, Report of the Board of Water Commissioners, March 22, 1858.
Pg. 67   *Less cheerfully, he noted that,...*, Ibid.
Pg. 68   *Actually, Bissell had reached this conclusion early on...*, Report of the Board of Water Commissioners, March 23, 1857.
Pg. 68   *Worse, the water rent for the average...*, Report of the Board of Water Commissioners, March 22, 1858.
Pg. 69   *...and Baptist ministers still paraded...*, Helen Post Chapman, My Hartford of the Nineteenth Century, Hartford: Edwin Valentine Mitchell, 1928, p. 12.
Pg. 69   *Young people dismissed it as...*, Ibid, p. 10.
Pg. 69   *In the early 1850s, when Rev. Horace Bushnell...*, 48th Annual Report of the Park Commissioners of the City of Hartford, Hartford, Connecticut, The Smith-Linsley Co., 1908, p. 8-17, State Archives, Connecticut State Library, Hartford; Bushnell Park was accepted by the voters in 1854, but not officially dedicated until 1868.
Pg. 70   *... "shavings, leather cuttings,...*, Ibid.
Pg. 70   *... "projected their outhouses...*, Ibid.
Pg. 70   *... 'We give such help as we can.' "...*, Ibid.
Pg. 70   *... "assured not only of the perfect...*, The Hartford Daily Times, May 30, 1860, p. 2.
Pg. 71   *... "a nauseous taste. "*, The Hartford Daily Courant, December 5, 1854, p. 3
Pg. 71   *Boston's preeminent chemist...*, Ibid. p. 3.
Pg. 71   *Among many things dredged up, they found...*, The Hartford Daily Times, Jan. 17, 1855, p. 2.
Pg. 71   *"...people around the pond... "*, Ibid, p. 2.
Pg. 71   *...that there was slave insurrection...*, The Hartford Daily Times, October 17, 1859, pg. 2.
Pg. 71   *... "that the telegraph wires had been cut... "* Ibid.
Pg. 72   *Business had slackened...*, The Hartford Daily Times, October 22, 1859, p. 2.
Pg. 72   *Getting about the city was about...*, Ellsworth Strong Grant & Marion Hepburn Grant, The City of Hartford: 1784- 1984 - An Illustrated History, Connecticut Historical Society, 1986, p. 32.
Pg. 72   *..."not highly ornamental"*, The Hartford Daily Times, Nov. 11, 1859, p. 2.

Pg. 72   ... *"pipe doesn't connect because...*, *The Hartford Daily Times*, Sept. 19, 1860, p. 2.

Pg. 72   ... *"nice blocks of clear transparent...*, *The Hartford Daily Times*, Jan. 4, 1860, p. 2.

Pg. 73   *The river opposite Colt's factory...*, Ibid.

Pg. 73   *"...and for twelve hours poured up a stream...*, *The Hartford Daily Times*, February 23, 1860, p. 2.

Pg. 73   *Towards the end of February...*, *The Hartford Daily Courant*, February 29, 1860 and *The Hartford Daily Courant*, March 6, 1860, p. 2. Also, some of the information about Lincoln's visit was culled from Merrill H. Dooey, Famous Visitors and Distinguished Guests of Hartford, Mss. For A Thesis, Trinity College, May 14, 1938, p. 44 ; Note: *The Hartford Daily Times* had nothing good to say about Abraham Lincoln who they dismissed as an Abolitionist.

Pg. 73   *The oddest part of Lincoln's visit...*, Helen Post Chapman, My Hartford of the Nineteenth Century, Hartford: Edwin Valentine Mitchell, 1928, pp. 25-26.

Pg. 73   *...the new President later stated...*, Merrill H. Dooey, Famous Visitors and Distinguished Guests of Hartford, Mss. For A Thesis, Trinity College, May 14, 1938, p. 44.

Pg. 73   *A further coincidence, though...*, Ibid, p. 36.

Pg. 74   *In April, 1860, a little more than a month later...*, *The Hartford Daily Times*, April 17, 1860, p. 2.

Pg. 74   *The Water Works have triumphed...*, Ibid.

Pg. 75   *By the end of May, the council produced,...*, *The Hartford Daily Times*, May 22, 1860, p. 2.

Pg. 75   *The following afternoon, a lovely,...*, *The Hartford Daily Times*, May 30, 1860, p. 2.

Pg. 76   *Crude though they were, the estimates...*, Report of the Board of Water Commissioners, March 25, 1861, p.7 and *The Hartford Daily Times*, June 13, 1860

Pg. 76   *Undeterred by the wildly...*, *The Hartford Daily Times*, June 12, 1860, p. 2

Pg. 76   *Never one to miss a business opportunity...*, *The Hartford Daily Times*, June 13, 1860, p. 2.

Pg. 76   *By the end of June...*, *The Hartford Daily Times*, June 13, 1860, p. 2

Pg. 77   *Some parties, at least of the determined...*, *The Hartford Daily Times*, June 26, 1860, p. 2.

Pg. 77   *By this time, the water works...*, Report of the Board of Water Commissioners, March 26, 1860

Pg. 77   *Then they "asked the water commissioners...",* *The Hartford Daily Times*, July 24, 1860, p. 2.

Pg. 77   ... *"he would not bathe in because...",* Ibid, p. 2.

Pg. 78   *"Base grounds...*, *The Hartford Daily Times*, Sept. 12, 1860, p. 2.

Pg. 78   *Under the New England Base Ball Rules,...*, *The Hartford Daily Times*, Sept. 14, 1860, p. 2.

Pg. 78   *One of the most popular pastimes...*, Helen Post Chapman, My Hartford of the Nineteenth Century, Hartford: Edwin Valentine Mitchell, 1928, p. 51.

Pg. 78   *Still, one popular summer...*, Ibid, p. 55.

Pg. 78   *The Maine Law—forbidding...*, *The Hartford Daily Times*, Nov. 11, 1859, p. 2.

Pg. 78　*The Drama begins...., The Hartford Daily Times*, Dec. 21, 1860, p. 2.

Pg. 78　*The newspaper went on to remark...*, Ibid, p. 2.

Pg. 79　*The blackest day ever seen by America..., The Hartford Daily Times*, April 13, 1861, p. 2.

Pg. 79　*During the Civil War, Colt's...*, Edmund Delaney, The Connecticut River: New England's Historic Waterway, Chester, CT: The Globe Pequot Press, 1983, p. 95.

Pg. 79　*Concurrently, war fever was..., The Hartford Daily Times*, April 13, 1861, p. 2.

Pg. 80　*Running twenty-five pages, ...*, Report of Benjamin Silliman, Jr. to the Board of Water Commissioners of the City of Hartford, August 30, 1861.

Pg. 80　*"...[The] waters...proposed to be used..."*, Ibid, p. 13.

Pg. 80　*The opinion which [we] have...expressed...*, Report of the Board of Water Commissioners, March, 1862.

Pg. 81　*In overwhelming numbers, [the rebels]..., The Hartford Daily Times*, April 8, 1862.

Pg. 81　*The Hartford Soldiers' Aid ..., The Hartford Daily Times*, April 26, 1862, p. 2.

Pg. 81　*When sick and wounded soldiers..., The Hartford Daily Times*, April 26, 1862, p. 2.

Pg. 81　*In response to the mounting..., The Hartford Daily Times*, Sept. 17, 1862, p. 2.

Pg. 81　*Reflecting the make-up of the council...*, Ibid, p. 4.

Pg. 82　*In October, H. & S. Bissell won the ..., The Hartford Daily Times*, Oct. 1, 1862, p. 2.

Pg. 82　*"...all persons held slaves..., The Hartford Daily Times*, January 1, 1863, p. 2. This article is simply a re-quote of some of the document, which can be found in any encyclopedia.

Pg. 82　*"...your committee express themselves..."*, Report of the Joint Standing Committee on Water Works, released February 23, 1863 to Common Council, p. 4.

Pg. 82　*Moreover, they suggested that the mayor...*, Ibid, p. 5.

Pg. 82　*The water franchise had been...*, Report of the Board of Water Commissioners, March 28, 1864.

Pg. 83　*As expected—considering that Silliman, ..., The Hartford Daily Times*, April 14, 1863, p. 2. The actual vote was held on April 13, 1863.

Pg. 83　*As Trout Brook meandered...*, Atlas of Hartford & Tolland Counties, Pub. by Barker & Tilden, Hartford, CT, 1869, p. 34.

Pg. 83　*...gristmill operation, which was the oldest in West Hartford...*, Nelson R. Burr, From Colonial Parish to Modern Suburb: A Brief Appreciation of West Hartford, written for the Revolutionary Bicentennial Commission, 1976; Pub. by Noah Webster Foundation & The Historical Society of West Hartford, Inc., 1976, p. 4; Also, William H. Hall, West Hartford, West Hartford: Published by the West Hartford Chamber of Commerce, 1930, p. 40.

Pg. 83　*Together with his wife, Sarah, ...*, The information on Childs Goodman and his family comes from the records of the First Congregational Church of West Hartford, Census Records of 1850 and 1860, and Childs Goodman's Obituary in *The Hartford Evening Press*, Sept. 15, 1866, p. 3. All of this material is at the State Archives, Connecticut State Library, Hartford.

Pg. 83 *His dander up, in early December 1864, ...,* J. Hammond Trumbull, The Memorial History of Hartford County: 1633-1884, Boston: Edward L. Osgood Publisher, 1886, p. 459 Note: Trumbull names the man who secured the first injunction against the water commissioners as "Childs Goodwin." However, an obscure document from the Board of Water Commissioners, an "Appendix" attached to nothing and dated May 8, 1865 identifies the miller by his correct name, Childs Goodman.

Pg. 83 *... "stopping or interfering with the natural..."* Annual Report of the Board Of Water Commissioners, Appendix, May 8, 1865.

Pg. 83 *... "any prosecution of the preparatory work..."*, Ibid, p. 42.

Pg. 83 *The only hitch was that the ...,* Private Laws of Connecticut, State Archives, State of Connecticut, July 1, 1863, p. 539.

Pg. 84 *Conversely, the gas company,...,* Ellsworth Strong Grant & Marion Hepburn Grant, The City of Hartford, 1784- 1984 - An Illustrated History, Connecticut Historical Society, 1986, p. 32.

Pg. 84 *...the horse railroad company...,* Ibid, p. 32.

Pg. 84 *Even the bridge crossing the Connecticut...,* George E. Wright, Crossing the Connecticut, Hartford: Smith-Linsley Co., 1908, pp. 1-10.

Pg. 85 *As a direct result of a shameless...,* The Hartford Daily Times, July 8, 1863, p. 2

Pg. 85 *...It is much to be regretted...,* Report of the Board of Water Commissioners, March 28, 1864.

Pg. 85 *This time, they chose William Worthen...,* J. Hammond Trumbull, The Memorial History of Hartford County: 1633-1884, Boston: Edward L. Osgood Publisher, 1886, p. 458.

Pg. 86 *...I would not recommend the construction...,* W.E. Worthen, Report to the Water Commissioners of the City of Hartford, Undated, but received by the water board in 1863.

Pg. 86 *...an expenditure of $230,000...,* Ibid, p. 12.

Pg. 86 *Full of vim and vigor, the new council...,* J. Hammond Trumbull, The Memorial History of Hartford County: 1633-1884, Boston: Edward L. Osgood Publisher, 1886, p. 459.

Pg. 86 *While Mayor Deming had declared that...,* The Hartford Daily Times, April 17, 1860, p. 2.

Pg. 87 *... "whole bredth from Connecticut river...,* William DeLoss Love, The Colonial History of Hartford, Centinel Hill Press & The Pequot Press, Inc., 1974, p. 116.

Pg. 88 *...Touro Hall was for sale...,* The Hartford Daily Times, October 19, 1863, p. 2.

Pg. 88 *In October 1863, it was announced...,* The Hartford Daily Courant, Oct. 16, 1863, p. 2.

Pg. 88 *...former Mayor Timothy Allyn, who began his...,* Hartford Connecticut as a Manufacturing, Business and Commercial Center, Pub. by the Hartford Board of Trade, 1889, p. 81-82.

Pg. 89 *Mr. Booth is one of the few who succeed...,* The Hartford Daily Times, October 19, 1863, p. 2.

Pg. 89   *The Times noted that, Atlanta...", The Hartford Daily Times*, Sept. 5, 1864, p. 2.

Pg. 89   *Tragically though, on September 10, 1864,...*, Vital Records, State Archives, Connecticut State Library, Hartford.

Pg. 89   *On the day following her passing..., The Hartford Daily Times*, Sept. 11, p. 3 and *The Hartford Daily Times* 12, 1864, p. 3.

Pg. 89   *His daughters were a concern...*, Census Records, State Archives, Connecticut State Library, Hartford.

Pg. 89   *...an Irish domestic servant, Catherine,* Census Records, State Archives, Connecticut State Library, Hartford.

Pg. 90   *A total ballot count of 2018..., The Hartford Daily Times*, Oct. 4, 1864, p. 2.

Pg. 90   *When Professor Silliman studied...*, Report of Benjamin Silliman, August 30, 1861, p. 11.

Pg. 90   *They swiftly cobbled together five adjacent parcels...*, Hall of Records, Town of West Hartford, CT.

Pg. 90   *On the edge of this rapidly..., The Hartford Daily Times*, July 31, 1865, p. 2.

Pg. 91   *Critics like The Times..., The Hartford Daily Times*, July 31, 1865, p. 2.

Pg. 91   *The ringleaders of this plot..., The Hartford Daily Courant*, March 24, 1865, p. 2. Of interest here is that *The Courant*, of course, does not list these two men as the :ringleaders" but, of the men mentioned, these two Yale educated lawyers stick out like sore thumbs. (The other men were wool dealers and dry goods merchants, &c.)

Pg. 91   *Almost all of the men behind the injunction...*, Original handwritten 1851 petition of the thirty-six original incorporators of The Hartford Water Company— the private, for-profit venture. Connecticut State Library, Hartford.

Pg. 91   *Bulkeley was sixty-two...,* Commemorative Biographical Record of Hartford County, J.H. Beers & Co., Chicago, 1901, p. 69.

Pg. 91   *Highlighting Bulkeley's enormous brainpower,...,* Ibid, p. 69.

Pg. 92   *Teamed with this brilliant pied piper...,* Ibid, p. 1488-1489.

Pg. 92   *"His manner, though not awkward...",* Ibid, 1488-1489.

Pg. 92   *By plying selected members of the state's..., The Hartford Daily Times*, July 31, 1865, p. 2.

Pg. 92   *Moreover, The Times reported that," they have already..., The Hartford Daily Times*, March 27, 1865, p. 2.

Pg. 92   *Exactly a week before the council...,The Hartford Daily Courant*, March 24, 1865, p. 2. Though none of Hartford's newspapers give the date when the injunction was actually granted, they all indicate that it was around March 23 or 24, 1865.

Pg. 92   *...to spend $120,000..., The Hartford Daily Times*, March 14, 1865, p. 2. The 20" cast iron and concrete pipe from the Patent Water & Gas Pipe Company of Jersey City—required by the water works—was $4.95 a lineal foot, bringing the cost (without peripherals to $118,800).

Pg. 92   *It forbade Bissell or anyone else from...,* J. Hammond Trumbull, The Memorial History of Hartford County: 1633-1884, Boston: Edward L. Osgood Publisher, 1886, p. 459.

Pg. 93   *On April 4, fellow Republican Charles Beach...,* Report of the Board of Water Commissioners, "Appendix," May 8, 1965.

Pg. 93   *News of the surrender reached Hartford...*, All of the information regarding the celebration after the surrender at Appomattox Court House is taken from *The Hartford Daily Courant* and *The Hartford Daily Times* of April 10, 1865, p. 2.

Pg. 94   *In exchange for allowing the Hartford Water Works...*, Private Laws, State Archives, Connecticut State Library, Hartford. Note: The original law, which allowed Hartford to sell water bonds to build the water works, contained a detailed description of the water works. In this legislation, it was stated the water would come from the Connecticut River. The act for the additional supply from Trout Brook in West Hartford was, at last, signed into law on July 21, 1865. This is the Private Law that includes the troubling language "within a reasonable distance of the aqueduct." The Private Law that forced the Hartford Water Works to supply the whole of West Hartford was enacted on March 13, 1913.

Pg. 94   *In the last paragraph of the Private Law...*, Private Laws (July 21, 1865), State Archives, Connecticut State Library, Hartford.

Pg, 95   *The Times ran long articles...*, *The Hartford Daily Times*, July 22, 25, 27, 28 & 31, 1865 (p. 2 in all).

Pg. 95   *The legislature enacted the law...*, *The Hartford Daily Times*, July 25, 1865, p. 2.

Pg. 95   *The Post reported the following day...*, *The Hartford Evening Post*, July 25, 1865, p. 2.

Pg. 95   *"...that the mayor would call a meeting...*, Ibid.

Pg. 95   *Though not necessarily conspiring with...*, Ibid.

Pg. 96   *At the request of several gentlemen, ...*, *The Hartford Daily Times*, July 25, 1865, p. 2.

Pg. 96   *At the meeting, held at Central Hall, ...*, *The Hartford Evening Post*, July 26, 1865, p. 2.

Pg. 96   *"...the clique who are fighting...*, *The Hartford Daily Times*, July 25, 1865, p. 2.

Pg. 96   *"...the examinations [were] made...*, *The Hartford Daily Times*, July 31, 1865, p. 2.

Pg. 96   *Two days before the vote, ...,* *The Hartford Daily Courant*, July 27, 1865, p. 2

Pg. 96   *...Depend upon it, there is a ...*, Ibid.

Pg. 97   *As a disingenuous gesture of fairness...*, *The Hartford Daily Courant*, July 29, 1865, p. 2.

Pg. 97   *At five in the afternoon, ...,* Descriptions of the counting of the ballots comes from the Monday, July 31 editions of *The Hartford Daily Times*, *The Hartford Daily Courant* and *The Hartford Evening Post*. (p. 2 in all).

Chapter 5

Pg. 99   *On the Tuesday following the ...*, *The Hartford Daily Times*, Aug. 2, 1865, p. 2.

Pg. 99   *"would be universally regarded...",* *The Hartford Daily Times*, Aug. 2, 1865, p. 2.

Pg. 99   *As soon as was practicable...*, *The Hartford Daily Times*, August 8, 1865, p. 2.

Pg. 99   *Inside of three weeks, the contracts...*, The Hartford Daily Times, August 28, 1865, p. 2.

Pg. 99   *Clyde specialized in contracting...*, Geer's Springfield City Directory, 1865, State Archives, Connecticut State Library, Hartford.

Pg. 99   *Supplying and bedding the four miles...*, The Hartford Daily Times, August 28, 1865, p. 2.

Pg. 99   *...went to Camden Iron Works...*, The Hartford Daily Times, August 28, 1865, p. 2.

Pg. 99   *(For unspecified reasons, Walker was...)*, The Hartford Daily Times, August 28, 1865, p. 2 and Report of the Board of Water Commissioners, March 1, 1867, p. 11.

Pg. 99   *Henry Tryon, Bissell's cousin, ...*, The Hartford Daily Times, August 28, 1865, p. 2.

Pg. 100   *Bissell chose a well-respected...*, Report of the Board of Water Commissioners, March 1, 1866, p. 10.

Pg. 100   *Marsh was by nature and training...*, The Hartford Daily Times, May 1, 1866, p. 2.

Pg. 100   *As a result, only about a mile...*, Report of the Board of Water Commissioners, March 1, 1866, p. 9-10.

Pg. 100   *On the brighter side, Milton Clyde...*, The Hartford Daily Times, November 13, 1865, p. 2

Pg. 100   *The dam was a simple earthen structure...*, There are countless references to the dimensions of the dam and the configuration of the aqueduct, waste pipe and sluiceway and, not so surprisingly, the best descriptions are contained in the post-mortem analysis after the collapse of September 6, 1867. *The Hartford Daily Courant* of September 7, 1867 and *The Hartford Daily Times* of September 6 and 7, 1867 are the two best sources for this material.

Pg. 100   *As early as 1631 a dam...*, Norman Smith, A History of Dams, The Citadel Press, Secaucus, NJ,1971, p. 148.

Pg. 101   *While the contractors had been slowly...*, Commemorative Biographical Record of Hartford County, J.H. Beers & Co., Chicago, 1901, p. 108.

Pg. 101   *...a farmer, Dorus Barnard, who died of "confluent smallpox...",* Geer's City Directories and Vital Statistics, State Archives, Connecticut State Library, Hartford.

Pg. 101   *...leaving her with three small children...*, Commemorative Biographical Record of Hartford County, J.H. Beers & Co., Chicago, 1901, p. 108.

Pg. 101   *The American Hall still hosted...*, The Hartford Daily Times, August 1, 1865, p. 2 and *The Hartford Daily Times*, Sept. 11, 1865, p. 2

Pg. 101   *The Times estimated that to rent...*, The Hartford Daily Times, June 14, 1866, p. 2.

Pg. 101   *The Connecticut State Billiards...*, The Hartford Daily Times, Nov. 12, 1866, p. 2.

Pg. 101   *The theater was also host to the Beethoven...*, The Hartford Daily Times, Nov, 8, 1866, p. 2.

Pg. 101   *For gamblers, the Hartford Trotting Park...*, The Hartford Daily Times, August 30, 1865, p. 2.

Pg. 101   *In the summer of 1866, the Charter Oaks...*, The Hartford Daily Times, July 25, 1866, p. 2.

Pg. 102   ...*Mr. Bassett will make a balloon ascent...*, The Hartford Daily Times, Sept. 7, 1865, p. 2.

Pg. 102   *Counterfeiting of currency was rampant...*, The Hartford Daily Times, April 2, 1866, pg. 2; June 26, 1866, p 2; July 26, 1866, p. 2; July 27, 1866, p. 2.

Pg. 102   *During the Civil War...*, A. Barton Hepburn, History of Coinage and Currency in the United States and the perennial Contest for Sound Money, New York, The Macmillan Company, 1903, p. 177-205; also Irwin Unger, The Greenback Era: A Social and Political History of American Finance, 1865-1879, New Jersey, Princeton University Press, 1964, p. 13-19.

Pg. 102   *Postal Money Orders made...*, The Hartford Daily Times, August 18, 1865, p. 2.

Pg. 103   ... *"the demands of the war..."*, The Hartford Daily Times, September 4, 1866, P. 2.

Pg. 103   *Women's fashion even took a welcome...*, The Hartford Daily Times, Aug. 22, 1866, p. 2.

Pg. 103   *For all the innovative fashions...*, The Hartford Daily Times, Sept. 20, 1866, p. 2.

Pg. 103   *Soon after a moderate rainstorm...*, The Hartford Daily Times, Oct. 23, 1865, p. 2.

Pg. 103   *The struggle now became fearful...*, Ibid, p. 2.

Pg. 104   *The following April, the spring...*, The Hartford Daily Times, April 4, 1866, p. 2.

Pg. 104   ... *"drawing it off and letting it fill again..."*, Ibid, pg. 2.

Pg. 104   *The water works suffered another setback...*, The Hartford Daily Times, May 1, 1866, p. 2.

Pg. 104   ...*it is said that he became sick...*, Ibid, pg. 2.

Pg. 104   *After the Governor's Foot Guard...*, Report of the Board of Water Commissioners, March 1, 1867, p. 10 and Census Data, State Archives, Connecticut State Library, Hartford.

Pg. 104   *June was the month of graduation...*, The Hartford Daily Times, June 18, 1866, p. 2.

Pg. 104   ...*in 1823 by Catherine Beecher...*, Information on the Beecher family and the Hartford Female Seminary was supplied by Nook Farm in Hartford and Geer's City Directory, State Archives, Connecticut State Library. The information on the class trip is in *The Hartford Daily Times*, June 18, 1866, p. 2.

Pg. 105   *Reservoir No. 1 only covered...*, Report of the Board of Water Commissioners, March 1, 1867

Pg. 105   *Throughout the year 1866, Milton Clyde's...*, Ibid.

Pg. 105   *In August, 1866, Hartford's Sanitary Board...*, The Hartford Daily Times, August 18, 21, 1866, p. 2 in both papers.

Pg. 105   *By early October, the city...*, The Hartford Daily Times, Oct. 11, 1866, p. 2.

Pg. 105   *At the end of October—with the ...*, The Hartford Daily Times, October 24, 1866, p. 2.

Pg. 106   *While the contractors from...*, Ibid, p. 2.

Pg. 106   *In order to break the logjam...*, Ibid, p. 2.

Pg. 106   *In one case, the water board...*, Ibid, p. 2.

Pg. 106   ... *young miller, Giles London...*, The Hartford Daily Courant, Sept. 7, 1867, p. 4 and Census Data, State Archives, Connecticut State Library, Hartford.

Pg. 106 *In the second case...*, The Hartford Daily Times, October 24, 1866, p. 2.

Pg. 106 *Sadly, Childs Goodwin did not live...*, The Hartford Evening Press, September 15,1866, p. 3. Note: The dam and millpond that powered Childs Goodman's gristmill is still in working order and located on the west side of North Main Street, ¾ of a mile north of West Hartford Center.

Pg. 106 *...Childs Goodman's wife, Sarah...*, Vital Records and Records of the Congregational Church of West Hartford, State Archives, Connecticut State Library, Hartford.

Pg. 106 *...award was $1500.*, The Hartford Daily Times, October 24, 1866, p. 2.

Pg. 106 *When the gate to the aqueduct was closed...*, The Hartford Daily Times, October 24, 1866, p. 2.

Pg. 106 *...at 212 million gallons of water...*, The Hartford Daily Times, October 31, 1866, p. 2.

Pg. 107 *The great merit of the West Hartford...*, The Hartford Daily Times, October 31, 1866, p. 2.

Pg. 107 *The city elections of April 1866...*, The Hartford Daily Times, April 10, 1866, p. 2.

Pg. 107 *When the question of the second...*, The Hartford Daily Times, Nov. 14, 1866, p. 2.

Pg. 108 *Accordingly, the crew platted three...*, Report of the Board of Water Commissioners, March 1, 1867.

Pg. 108 *Bissell may have had an easier...*, The Hartford Daily Times, July 5, 1867

Pg. 108 *"...we beg leave to give notice...",* Ibid, p. 2.

Pg. 108 *In January of 1867, almost four years...*, Report of the Board of Water Commissioners, March 1, 1868, p. 9-10.

Pg. 109 *In February, Bissell ran an experiment...*, Report of the Board of Water Commissioners, March 1, 1868, p. 8-9.

Pg. 109 *Actually, by the late 1860s, meters...*, Ibid, p. 8.

Pg. 109 *Considering that Hartford's system...*, Yesterday and Today: One Hundred Years of Water Supply, (In House Pub. of MDC), 1955, p. 14.

Pg. 109 *From less than ten miles...*, Report of the Board of Water Commissioners, March 1, 1868, p. 6.

Pg. 110 *In one short decade, there sprung...*, Geer's City Directories, State Archives, Connecticut State Library, Hartford.

Pg. 110 *...a large stream is running...*,The Hartford Daily Times, Jan. 26, 1867, p. 2.

Pg. 110 *As the cold and confining winter...*, The Hartford Daily Times, March 19, 1867, p. 2.

Pg. 110 *By early April, another citywide...*, The Hartford Daily Times, April 9, 1867, p. 2.

Pg. 110 *The gate at the reservoir's...*, The Hartford Daily Times, May 22, 1867, p. 2.

Pg. 110 *Nevertheless, by the time the good...*,The contractor's name only surfaced later in *The Hartford Daily Times* issue of September 6, 1867, p. 2.

Pg. 111 *On May 1, the regular Election Parade...*, The Hartford Daily Times, May 2, 1867, p. 2.

Pg. 111 *In June, President Andrew Johnson...*, The Hartford Daily Times, June 22, 1876, p. 2.

Pg. 111 *Now that the war was over, steamboat...*, The Hartford Daily Times, June 24 and 25, 1867, p. 2 in both papers.

Pg. 111   *Communications between metropolitan centers...*, *The Hartford Daily Times*, August 10, 1867, p. 2.

Pg. 112   *...the Connecticut River was more then...*, *The Hartford Daily Times*, August 19,1867, p. 2.

Pg. 112   *"The rain has beat with..."*, *The Hartford Daily Times*, August 23, 1867, p. 2.

Pg. 112   *"...The main dam, a sort of earthwork,...*, *The Hartford Daily Times*, September 6, 1867, p. 2.

Pg. 112   *... "For some time now water...*, *The Hartford Daily Courant*, September 7, 1867, p. 4.

Pg. 113   *In the first part of September 1867, Lobdell...*, Report of the Board of Water Commissioners, March 1, 1868, p. 11.

Pg. 113   *On September 5, a Thursday...*, *The Hartford Daily Times*, September 6, 1867, p. 2.

Pg. 113   *The rain began in the late afternoon...*, In their editions of September 6,1867, *The Hartford Evening Press* records that the rain began at 3 P.M. and ended at 8 P.M., while *The Hartford Daily Times* reported that it rained from 6 P.M. until midnight. Because the thunderstorms came in waves, the exact time period of the rains will always be in dispute.

Pg. 113   *In the first few hours of the storm...*, *The Hartford Evening Press*, September 6, 1867, p. 3.

Pg. 113   *... "down the hillside from the Farmington Road...*, Report of the Board of Water Commissioners, March 1, 1868, p. 11.

Pg. 113   *Uncertain what to do, he...*, *The Hartford Daily Times*, September 6, 1867, p. 2.

Pg. 113   *When the messenger finally ...*, The details of Hiram Bissell's ride out to and back from Reservoir No. 1 on the night of September 5, 1867 are an amalgam of newspaper reports and other reference works including: *The Hartford Daily Times* September 6 & 7, 1867, p. 2 in each paper, and *The Hartford Daily Courant*, September 7, 1867, p. 4, and the Atlas of Hartford & Tolland Counties – 1869, Pub. by Parker & Tilden, Hartford, CT., 1869, Map, p. 34, State Archives, Connecticut State Library, Hartford.

Pg. 114   *Gas streetlights...*,The Hartford Gas Light Company was incorporated in 1848 and had been installing street lights throughout the city since that time.

Pg. 114   *The last enclave of people...*,The 140 acre site of Nook Farm was purchased from William Imlay, after his first bankruptcy in 1851. Imlay was the wealthiest man in Hartford (after Jeremiah Wadsworth, whose son, Daniel, established the Wadsworth Atheneum in 1842), but his business interests were so far flung as to be unmanageable. He was forced to declare bankruptcy a second time in 1857,and he died about a year later.

Pg. 114   *Nook Farm was considered so far from the rest...*, Helen Post Chapman, My Hartford of the Nineteenth Century, Hartford: Edwin Valentine Mitchell, 1928, p. 25.

Pg. 115   *As he shuttled along...*, Report of the Board of Water Commissioners, March 1, 1868, p. 11, Note: Hiram Bissell in his annual report to the Common Council states specifically that, "During the evening of the fifth of September, a portion of the dam of the upper reservoir [No. 2]...was swept away...," indicating that the catalyst for the ensuing problems had been triggered even before he arrived at Reservoir No. 1, just before midnight.

Pg. 115   *"...the water began...soaking...*, Report of the Board of Water Commissioners, March 1, 1868, p. 12.

Pg. 115   *...he instructed the engineer, Samuel Gray...*, The Hartford Evening Press, September 7, 1867, p. 4.

Pg. 115   *Over the next hour and a half,...*, The Hartford Daily Times, September 6, 1867, p. .2

Pg. 115   *At 1:30 in the morning...*, Ibid, p. 2.

Pg. 115   *By 9:00 the following morning...*, Ibid, p. 2.

Pg. 116   *In twenty-two minutes...*, Report of the Board of Water Commissioners, March 1, 1868, p. 12.

Pg. 116   *...tore a 125-foot yawning chasm...*, The Hartford Daily Courant, Sept. 7, 1867, p. 2.

Pg. 116   *...disgorged its 200 million gallon load...*, Report of the Board of Water Commissioners, March 1, 1868, p. 12.

Pg. 116   *...bystanders compared it to an earthquake...*, The Hartford Evening Press, September 7, 1867, p. 4.

Pg. 116   *... "two or three hundred feet wide and...*, The Hartford Daily Times, September 6, 1867, p. 2.

Pg. 116   *The first mill flattened...*, The Hartford Daily Courant, September 7, 1867, p.2

Pg. 116   *... "a solid structure and was..."*, The Hartford Evening Press, Sept. 7, 1867, p. 4.

Pg. 117   *Along with it went 5,000...*, Ibid, p. 4.

Pg. 117   *The gristmill contained a half ton...*, Ibid, p. 4.

Pg. 117   *...jammed into a mass under the mill...*, The Hartford Evening Press, Sept. 7, 1867, p. 4.

Pg. 117   *The first farms devastated were...*, The Hartford Evening Press, Sept, 7, 1867, p.4.

Pg. 117   *... "covered with dirt, rocks and rubbish..."*, The Hartford Daily Times, Sept. 7, 1867, p. 2.

Pg. 117   *...the farms of Deacon Josiah Griswold and...*, The Hartford Daily Times, Sept, 6. 1867, p. 2.

Pg. 117   *Five of John Griswold's dairy cows...*, The Hartford Daily Courant, Sept. 7, 1867, p. 4.

Pg. 117   *The high water rushed toward...*, The Hartford Daily Times, Sept. 6, 1867, p.2

Pg. 117   *... "a vast tumbling, boiling wave...*, Ibid, p. 2.

Pg. 117   *...the destructive mass swept away his millpond...* Atlas of Hartford and Tolland Counties, Hartford, Pub. by Baker & Tilden, 1869, p. 24. This 1869 map shows clearly the gristmill and millpond owned by C.(Chester) C. Goodman, Childs Goodman's son.

Pg. 117   *... "not one stone [was] left upon another...*, The Hartford Daily Times, Sept, 6, 1867, p. 2.

Pg. 118   *As the surging, foaming water...*, The Hartford Daily Times, Sept. 7, 1867, p. 2.

Pg. 118   *The bridge at Gilbert's Corner...*, The Hartford Daily Courant, Sept. 7, 1867, p. 4.

Pg. 118   *Later in the day, there was a tremendous...*, Ibid, p. 4.

Pg. 118   *In the first accounts of the breach,...*, The Hartford Daily Times, Sept. 6, 1867, p. 2.

Pg. 118   ... *"walked into the stream..."*, Ibid, p. 2.

Pg. 118   ... *"The man who was supposed to have been drowned...*, The Hartford Daily Times*, Sept. 10, 1867, p. 2.

Chapter 6

Pg. 119   *In the days following the devastation...*, The Hartford Daily Times, Sept. 8, 1867, p. 2.

Pg. 119   *"...in buggies, on horseback and on foot..."*, The Hartford Daily Courant, Sept. 9, 1867, p. 8.

Pg. 119   ... *"plans, red tape and fuss,"*, The Hartford Daily Times, Sept. 8, 1867, p.2

Pg. 119   *In some cities, they would whistle...*, The Hartford Daily Times, Sept. 21, 1867, p. 2.

Pg. 119   *Topping the list of ruined...*, Annual Report of the Board of Water Commissioners, March 1, 1868.

Pg. 119   *One of the men was Nathan...*, Annual Report of the Board of Water Commissioners, March 1, 1868

Pg. 119   *Added together, the losses to the farmers, ...*, Ibid.

Pg. 119   *Bissell's choice to help with...*, Ibid.

Pg. 120   *During October, November and December...*, Ibid.

Pg. 120   *Former soldiers, with missing limbs, ...*, The Hartford Daily Times, May 22, 1869, p. 2.

Pg. 121   *In order to protect...*, The Hartford Daily Times, Dec. 21, 1867, p. 2.

Pg. 121   *Eventually, the mayor issued...*, The Hartford Daily Times, Dec. 8, 1869, p. 2.

Pg. 121   *This problem was eventually solved...*, Helen Post Chapman, My Hartford of the Nineteenth Century, Hartford: Edwin Valentine Mitchell, 1928, p. 30.

Pg. 121   *The greatest amusement after the war...*, The Hartford Daily Times, Feb. 13, 1869, p. 2 and Ellsworth S. Grant, The Miracle of Connecticut, published by the Connecticut Historical Society and Fenwick Productions, (no date)

Pg. 122   *...hundreds of young men...*, The Hartford Daily Times, March 29, 1869, p. 2.

Pg. 122   *...the Hartford Ice Company...*,The Hartford Daily Times, April 21, 1869, p.2

Pg. 122   *The Hartford Gas Light Company had fifty miles...*, The Hartford Daily Times, March 8, 1870, p. 2.

Pg. 123   ... *"he counted on one side..."*,The Hartford Daily Times, Feb. 12, 1870, p. 2.

Pg. 123   *"There were two runaways today..."*, The Hartford Daily Times, Oct. 13, 1869, p. 2.

Pg. 123   *"The runaway today was a milkman's...*, The Hartford Daily Times, March 8, 1870, p. 2.

Pg. 123   *...the different halls in the city...*, The Hartford Daily Times, Sept. 15, 1867, p. 2.

Pg. 123   *"...for many years, Allyn Hall..."*, Helen Post Chapman, My Hartford of the Nineteenth Century, Hartford: Edwin Valentine Mitchell, 1928, p. 12

Pg. 123   *Even before the new Opera House...*, The Hartford Daily Times, Jan. 6, 1869, p. 2.

Pg. 123   *After Robert's Opera House opened, ...*, The Hartford Daily Times, May 7, 1867, p. 2.

Pg. 123   ... *"Patrons will please remove..."*, Helen Post Chapman, My Hartford of the Nineteenth Century, Hartford: Edwin Valentine Mitchell, 1928, p. 16.

Pg. 124   *Charles Dickens had come...*, *The Hartford Daily Times*, Jan. 16, 1868, p. 2.

Pg. 124   *He was not considered...*, *The Hartford Daily Times*, Feb. 19, 1868, p. 2.

Pg. 124   *A month before Dickens spoke...*, *The Hartford Daily Times*, Jan. 25, 1868, p. 2

Pg. 124   *"Mark Twain was in town...",* *The Hartford Daily Times*, Jan. 25, 1868, p. 2.

Pg. 124   *In June 1853, John Hooker...*, Hall of Records, Hartford and J. Hammond Trumbull, The Memorial History of Hartford County: 1633-1884, Boston: Edward L. Osgood Publisher, 1886, p. 665.

Pg. 124   *After the purchase, John and his wife...*, Joseph S. Van Why, Nook Farm, Hartford: The Stowe-Day Foundation, 1975, p. 7; The reference to Octavius Jordan, the architect, comes from information supplied by the Connecticut Historical Society. Also, there have been a number of books written about Nook Farm and information about the enclave and its occupants is readily available at the Stowe-Day Foundation and the Mark Twain House in Hartford.

Pg. 124   *...hired Octavius Jordan...*, Information supplied by the Connecticut Historical Society, Hartford.

Pg. 124   *(Since Octavius Jordan had a business relationship...),...,*Anne Crofoot Kuckro, Hartford Architecture, Volume Two: South Neighborhoods, Hartford Architectural Conservancy Survey, 1980. Note: Octavius Jordan was born in England, worked in Hartford for a decade and died shortly after moving to New York. At his insistence, he was buried in Hartford. (see *The Hartford Daily Times*, August 23, 1870, p. 2)

Pg. 125   *Mr. John C. Day, son of Calvin...*, *The Hartford Daily Times*, June 18, 1869, p. 2.

Pg. 125   *Calvin Day, the father of the groom...*, J. Hammond Trumbull, The Memorial History of Hartford County: 1633-1884, Boston: Edward L. Osgood Publisher, 1886, p. 670-1.

Pg. 125   *...in the mid-1850s, he joined...*, Ibid.

Pg. 125   *Sam Clemens married his "Livy"...*, Joseph S. Van Why, Nook Farm, Hartford: The Stowe-Day Foundation, 1975, p. 52.

Pg. 125   *...the wealthiest city in America...*, Geoffrey C. Ward and Dayton Duncan, Mark Twain, New York: Alfred A. Knopf, 2001, p. 88.

Pg. 125   *...the common council annually expended $400...*, *The Hartford Daily Times*, Aug. 25, 1868, p. 2.

Pg. 126   Hiram *Bissell was paying laborers...*, *The Hartford Daily Times*, Oct. 17, 1868, p. 2.

Pg. 126   *...he wanted fifty more workers...*,Ibid,

Pg. 126   *Improvements to the dam included...*,*The Hartford Daily Times*, March 28, 1870, p. 2.

Pg. 126   *Contributing to this last category...*, *The Hartford Daily Times*, May 1, 1869, p. 2.

Pg. 126   *Packing the hydrants in straw...*, *The Hartford Daily Times*, Dec.4, 1868, p.2

Pg. 126   *In the spring of 1870, information...*, *The Hartford Daily Times*, May 30, 1870, p. 2.

Pg. 126   *... 'cracked and warped by drought.'* Ibid.

Pg. 126   *..."a remarkable scarcity of water.",* Ibid.

Pg. 127   *However, the year before the Democratic landslide...*, *The Hartford Daily Times*, July 11, 1870, p. 2.

Pg. 127   *(His company was finally acquired...),* City Directories, State Archives, Connecticut State Library, Hartford.

Pg. 127   *First in the gubernatorial...,* The Hartford Daily Times, July 11, 1870, p. 2

Pg. 127   *...trying to replace Hiram Bissell...,* The Hartford Daily Times, July 11, 1870, p. 2.

Pg. 127   *... "On one occasion when Mr. Bissell...,* The Hartford Daily Times, July 8, 1870, p. 2.

Pg. 128   *...Alderman Lawrence—also a water commissioner—...,* The Hartford Daily Times, July 12, 1870, p. 2.

Pg. 128   *In July 1870, President Grant...,* The Hartford Daily Times, July 25, 1870, p. 2.

Pg. 128   *When Nellie Grant arrived at the school...,* Information supplied by Susan Tracy of Miss Porter's School, Farmington, Connecticut.

Pg, 128   *..."I shall die if I must stay here."...,* Ibid.

Pg. 128   *"Miss N. Grant went away last week—..."...,* Ibid.

Pg. 128   *"This is an unparalleled summer... ",* The Hartford Daily Times, July 23, 1870, p. 2.

Pg. 128   *...the upper reservoir at Mine Brook...,* The Hartford Daily Times, Aug. 8, 1870, p. 2.

Pg. 128   *Hiram Bissell advised the papers that...,* Ibid.

Pg. 129   *... "ancient and fish-like" smell...,* The Hartford Daily Times, August 29, 1870, p. 2.

Pg. 129   *Even "one-armed Billy" at the northwest corner...,* The Hartford Daily Times, Sept. 12, 1870, p. 2.

Pg. 129   *... "plenty pure and sweet"...,* The Hartford Daily Times, Ibid.

Pg. 129   *Opening stopcocks all over town...,* The Hartford Daily Times, July 11, 1870, p. 2.

Pg. 131   *... "a menace to the town... ",* Helen Post Chapman, My Hartford of the Nineteenth Century, Hartford: Edwin Valentine Mitchell, 1928, p. 21.

Pg. 132   *One would think that Ezra Clark's...,* Information on the life of Ezra Clark and his family was gathered from a number of sources including: *The Hartford Daily Times,* Sept. 26, 1896; *The Hartford Daily Courant,* Sept. 28, 1896; Geer's City Directories; J.H. Beers & Co., Commemorative Biographical Record of Hartford County, Chicago, 1901, p. 72; Annual Reports of the Board of Water Commissioners, the land records of Hartford and East Granby and the Clark Family Letters at the Watkinson Library at Trinity College, Hartford.

Pg. 138   *In 1871, Ezra Clark was re-elected...,* The records of the water works are missing for the year 1871. Information published in The Hartford Daily Times makes it clear that Clark was working closely with Bissell on the water board in 1871. (see The Hartford Daily Times, July 8, 1871, p. 2).

Pg. 139   *After the Chicago fire...,* Glenn Weaver, Hartford: An Illustrated History of Connecticut's Capital, Connecticut Historical Society; Windsor Publications, Inc., Woodland Hills, California, 1982, p. 87.

Pg. 140   *The drought of the 1870s...,* Records of precipitation are fuzzy during this period of time. A Canton, Connecticut resident, G. J. Case, kept laborious records of rainfall as a pastime and the water works relied on his records— running from 1859 until 1914 and showing an average precipitation of 50.21" annually. However, records kept at Reservoir No. 1 by the Hartford Water

Works from 1868-1914 showed the average precipitation of 44.06" a year. The percentages and calculations in this book are based on the records of the water company since they are closer to the numbers that are experienced today.

Pg. 140   Smaller boats like the Silver Star..., The Hartford Daily Times, Sept. 1, 1875, p. 2.

Pg. 141   "...to take out the greater portion...", Annual Report of the Board of Water Commissioners, March 1, 1870.

Pg. 141   "...both personally and officially..., Annual Report of the Board of Water Commissioners, March 1, 1873.

Pg. 141   "...delay in the work has not been satisfactorily..., Ibid.

Pg. 143   ..in favor of confirming him [Clark]..., The Hartford Daily Times, April 15, 1873, p. 2.

Pg. 143   ... "including the castings for the St. Louis water works...", The Hartford Daily Times, April 15, 1875, p. 2.

Pg. 144   On Friday evening, September 26,..., The Hartford Daily Times, September 26, 1873, p. 2.

Pg. 144   ..."pumps just set."..., Ibid.

Pg. 144   ...houses be "...strong, safe and...", The Hartford Daily Times, June 11, 1873, p. 2.

Pg. 144   During June, July and August of 1873..., The Hartford Daily Times, June 11, 1873, p. 2 and The Hartford Daily Times, June 13, 1873, p. 2.

Pg. 145   As the installation of the new pumps..., In his annual report in March 1874, Ezra Clark states that the new pumps were installed September 27, 1873. Since, in the 1877 report, engineer Seth Marsh wrote that, "...the fact that we escaped a water famine should be attributed more to the good qualities of an engine and boiler, which have been in service over twenty years, than to any other cause...," one has to conclude that, while the engine and boiler may have been overhauled in 1873, the only new parts installed by Hartford Foundry and Machine Company were the four new pumps.

Pg. 145   ...We had a taste of Connecticut River water..., The Hartford Courant, September 29, 1873, pg. 3.

Pg. 145   ...the amount flowing in a day..., Ibid.

Pg. 147   At this juncture, the water works..., Information on the hydraulic engineers working in the United States during the 19th and 20th centuries was obtained directly from the fifty largest water companies in the country, their websites and other books and periodicals.

Pg. 149   ...a local engineer, Seth Marsh., Annual report of the Board of Water Commissioners. March 1, 1875.

Pg. 150   "...sickness [typhoid fever] was occurring...," Annual report of the Board of Water Commissioners. March 1, 1879.

Pg. 150   ... "...all good citizens to be as economical..., The Hartford Daily Times, Sept. 25, 1878, p. 2.

Pg. 150   ... "...if there be waste,...,Ibid, p. 2.

Pg. 150   In the mid-1870s, the long competition..., Glenn Weaver, Hartford: An Illustrated History of Connecticut's Capital, Connecticut Historical Society; Windsor Publications, Inc., Woodland Hills, California, 1982, pp. 98-100 and The Hartford Daily Times, July 11, 1879, p. 2 and The Hartford Daily Times, October 13, 1879, p. 2.

Pg. 150   *In 1880, however, the city went Republican again...,* Information on Morgan
          Bulkeley can be obtained from many sources including: Richard Hooker,
          Aetna Life Insurance Company: Its First Hundred Years, Hartford, 1956 and the
          Encyclopedia of Connecticut Biography (Boston, 1917), IV, pp.172-173.

Pg. 151   *The introduction of electricity into Hartford...,* Glenn Weaver, The Hartford
          Electric Light Company, Hartford, Published by The Hartford Electric Light
          Company, 1969, pp. 15-17.

Pg. 151   *While the water works flirted with the concept...,* Geer's City Directories

Pg. 152   *More importantly, in the late 1870s...,* Annual Report of the Board of Water
          Commissioners, 1878-79-80.

Pg. 153   *As the city street department...,* The Hartford Daily Times, Oct. 1, 1874, p. 2.

Pg. 153   *Two local men brought...,* The Hartford Daily Times, May 5, 1873, p. 2.

Pg. 153   *...the races always bring to our city...,* The Hartford Daily Times, Aug. 19,
          1878 , p. 2.

Pg. 153   *Two local men brought home...,* The Hartford Daily Times, May 5, 1873,
          p. 2.

Pg. 153   *...displayed a 60 pound bass...,* The Hartford Daily Times, May 22, 1878,
          p. 2.

Pg. 153   *...This morning we noticed...,* The Hartford Daily Times, Oct. 23, 1874 , p. 2

Pg. 154   *..."100,000 rare, novel and interesting curiosities,"...,* The Hartford Daily
          Times, April 28, 1873, p. 2.

Pg. 154   *Barnum mounted five shows in two days...,* The Hartford Daily Times, April 29,
          1873, p. 2.

Pg. 154   *At Robert's Opera House, Buffalo Bill...,* The Hartford Daily Times, Nov. 7,
          1878, p. 2.

Pg. 154   *His little mule kicked...,* Ibid.

Pg. 154   *The riverboats were doing...,* The Hartford Daily Times, July 2, 1878 , p. 2.

Pg. 154   *By 1884, the water works completed...,* Annual Report of the Board of Water
          Commissioners, March 1, 1885.

Pg. 154   *However, on November 23, the Sunday before Thanksgiving...,* The Hartford
          Daily Times, November 24, 1884, p. 8.

Chapter 7

Pg. 156   *From the standpoint of inventions...,* Memories of Hartford, sponsored by
          Phoenix Mutual Life Insurance Company, series of interviews.

Pg. 156   *In addition to a large collection...,* Geer's City Directories, 1885, 1886.

Pg. 156   *The dirt streets continued to...,* Memories of Hartford, sponsored by Phoenix
          Mutual Life Insurance Company, series of interviews.

Pg. 156   *Children walked the railroad tracks...,* Ibid, *passim.*

Pg. 156   *When the young German Immigrant...,* Ellsworth S. Grant, The Miracle of
          Connecticut, published by the Connecticut Historical Society and Fenwick
          Productions, (no date) and Geer's City Directory, 1847.

Pg. 157   *Not long after Gershon Fox...,* Hartford in 1912: Story of the Capitol City,
          Published by The Hartford Post, 1912.

Pg. 157   *..."The Big Store"...,* The Hartford Times, July 4, 1896, p. 4.

Pg. 157 *First class fare was only $1.25...*,Geer's City Directories, State Archives, Connecticut State Library, Hartford.

Pg. 157 *Prices ranged from $75...*, The Hartford Times, (Pope's advertisements of the 1880s).

Pg. 158 *However, at the end of Ezra Clark's...*, Annual Report of the Board of Water Commissioners, March 1895.

Pg. 158 *...The principal sources of waste...*, Annual Report of the Board of Water Commissioners, March 1877.

Pg. 158 *Up to this time, the total cost...*, Annual Report of the Board of Water Commissioners, March 1885.

Pg. 159 *Even with the existing five reservoirs...*, Annual Report of the Board of Water Commissioners, March 1892.

Pg. 159 *All by itself, the Tumbledown...*, Annual Report of the Board of Water Commissioners, March, 1892.

Pg. 159 *In 1892, repeating a now familiar cycle...*, Annual Report of the Board of Water Commissioners, March 1893.

Pg. 159 *That same year, there were 200 men...*, Annual Report of the Board of Water Commissioners, March 1893.

Pg. 159 *To speed up the work...*, Annual Report of the Board of Water Commissioners, March 1894.

Pg. 160 *Merchants shuttered their stores...*, Memories of Hartford, sponsored by Phoenix Mutual Life Insurance Company, series of interviews.

Pg. 160 *Toward this end, Ezra Clark...*, The Hartford Daily Times, September 26, 1896, p. 1.

Pg. 160 *Col. Pope's interest, however, lay...*,The information on Col. Albert Pope's bicycle manufactory can be found in the following books:
Glenn Weaver, HARTFORD- An Illustrated History of Connecticut's Capital, Connecticut Historical Society; Windsor Publications, Inc., Woodland Hills, California, 1982.
Ellsworth S. Grant, The Miracle of Connecticut, published by the Connecticut Historical Society and Fenwick Productions, (no date).
Ellsworth Strong Grant & Marion Hepburn Grant, The City of Hartford 1784-1984 - An Illustrated History, Connecticut Historical Society, 1986.

Pg. 161 *The purity of the water supply...*, Annual Report of the Board of Water Commissioners, March 1885.

Pg. 161 *After stepping down from the water board...*, The Hartford Daily Times, September 26, 1896, p. 1.

Pg. 161 *Ezra Clark's daughter, Fanny...*, Ellsworth Grant, The Club on Prospect Street: A History of the Hartford Club, Htfd. Imprint, 1984.

Pg. 161 *Unfathomably, the man who succeeded...*, Annual Report of the Board of Water Commissioners, March 1896.

Pg. 162 *Ezra Clark continued to live...*, The Hartford Times, September 26, 1896, p. 1.

Pg. 162 *State Street was paved in 1895...*,The Hartford Times, September 17, 1896, p. 6.

Pg. 162 *While a group of entrepreneurs...*, The Hartford Times, September 17, 1896, p. 5.

Pg. 162 *... "twelve of the handsomest... "*, The Hartford Times, September 19, 1896, p. 4.

Chapter 8

Pg. 173   *A brief description of the canal...*, David G. McCullough, The Path Between The Seas: The Creation Of The Panama Canal (New York: Simon & Schuster, 1977).

Pg. 173   *When Saville left for the canal...*, Biographical Notes on Caleb Mills Saville by Thorndike Saville, March 1961.

Pg. 174   *The Saville's fourteen-year-old...*, Telephone Int. with Thorndike Saville, Jr., January 4, 2001.

Pg. 174   *By August 1907, the Stegomyia fasciata...*, David G. McCullough, The Path Between The Seas: The Creation Of The Panama Canal (New York: Simon & Schuster, 1977).

Pg. 175   *Caleb and Elizabeth Saville's son...*, Telephone Int. with Thorndike Saville, Jr., January 4, 2001.

Pg. 175   *All of Caleb Saville's life, he kept...*, Evidenced by his voluminous correspondence kept at the MDC, Hartford, CT.

Pg. 175   *The man responsible for bringing...*, Hartford in 1912:Story of the Capitol City, Published by The Hartford Post, 1912.
Advertisements for Dower and Cosgrove, The Hartford Times, 1906-1911

Pg. 176   *Dower was first made aware...,The Hartford Times*, Dec. 27, 1911, p. 1.

Pg. 176   *Dower wired an invitation to Saville...*, The details of Caleb Saville's hiring are interwoven from accounts in accounts in *The Hartford Times*, Dec. 23, 26, 27, 29, 1911 and *The Hartford Courant*, Dec. 21, 29, 1911.

Pg. 176   *While there, Saville took the train...*, Int. with Gerry d'Avignon, January 8, 2001.

Pg. 176   *(Strangely enough, forty-one years later...)*, Int. with Gerry d'Avignon, January 8, 2001.

Pg. 179   *There has always been a persistent...*, Int. with Gerry d'Avignon, January 8, 2001.

Pg. 180   *...The investigation which I have...*, Annual Report of the Board of Water Commissioners, March 1913.

Pg. 180   *Beyond the tedious chore...*, Ibid.

Pg. 180   *With his tremendous organizational ...*, Annual Report of the Board of Water Commissioners, March 1912, Diagram V.

Pg. 181   *Frederic Stearns was born...*, National Cyclopaedia of American Biography being the History of the United States, The James T. White & Co., 1910, p. 306-7.
Catherine Mulholland, William Mulholland and the Rise of Los Angeles, University of California Press, Berkeley, Los Angeles, London, 2000, picture captions in center of book.

Pg. 181   *John Freeman was also...*, National Cyclopaedia of American Biography being the History of the United States, The James T. White & Co., 1910, p. 11-13.

Pg. 182   *Caleb Saville was born...*, Biographical Notes on Caleb Mills Saville by Thorndike Saville, March 1961.

Pg. 182   *The Savilles were proud of their lineage...*, Biographical Notes on Caleb Mills Saville by Thorndike Saville, March 1961.

Pg. 182   *At one time, he even ...*, Letters of Caleb Saville (1948-9).

Pg. 183   *Work on the Quabbin...*, Boston Water History: Ware River & Quabbin Reservoir, 4/29/00
http://www.mwra.state.ma.us/water/html/hist5.htm

Pg. 183   *Initially, they rented a home...*, Geer's City Directory, 1912, 1913, 1914; Also, Hartford City Land Records, Hall of Records, Main Street, Hartford.

Pg. 183   *...Since Elizabeth Saville was not...*, Motor Vehicle Registrations, 1920, State Archives, Connecticut State Library, Hartford.

Pg. 183   *When the Savilles finally decided to purchase...*, Hall of Records, Hartford.

Pg. 184   *One of Saville's idiosyncrasies...*, Int. with Gerry d'Avignon, January 8, 2001

Pg. 184   *To begin with, the water commissioners...*, Legislative Acts, Special Laws of Connecticut, Increasing the Powers of the Board of Water Commissioners of the City of Hartford, August 2, 1911, pp. 389-395, State Archives, Connecticut State Library, Hartford.

Pg. 185   *On a slightly lighter note...*, Annual Report of the Board of Water Commissioners, March 1914.

Pg. 185   *The maintenance of the existing...*, Annual Report of the Board of Water Commissioners, March, 1913.

Pg. 186   *Serving as a constant reminder...*, Annual Report of the Board of Water Commissioners, March, 1913.

Pg. 186   *Before the passage...*, Annual Report of the Board of Water Commissioners, March, 1913.

Pg. 186   *A grisly item on the board's punch list...*, Annual Report of the Board of Water Commissioners, March, 1916.

Pg. 186   *...To make the Nepaug Reservoir...*, Annual Report of the Board of Water Commissioners, March, 1913.

Pg. 187   *A story, perhaps apocryphal...*, Int. with Gerry d'Avignon, January 8, 2001

Pg. 189   *In Caleb Saville's writings...*, Letters of Caleb Mills Saville (1947-48).

Pg. 190   *Up to this time, the water company...*, Annual Report of the Board of Water Commissioners. March, 1915, Table VI.

Pg. 190   *By the end of 1913, the water ...*, Annual Report of the Board of Water Commissioners. March, 1914.

Pg. 190   *In 1915, Saville estimated...*, Annual Report of the Board of Water Commissioners. March, 1915.

Pg. 190   *While the work progressed ...*, Annual Report of the Board of Water Commissioners. March, 1915.

Pg. 190   *Beginning in late 1916...*, Annual Report of the Board of Water Commissioners. March, 1917, p. 70.

Pg. 190   *The Richard's corner Dam...*, Annual Report of the Board of Water Commissioners, March, 1916, p. 54.

Pg. 191   *As an unwelcome reminder...*, Annual Report of the Board of Water Commissioners, March, 1919.

Pg. 191   *What the board—and even Caleb Saville—...*, Erie County (New York) Water Authority, Annual Report 1999, pg. 4

Pg. 192   *The fall of 1919 was a time...*, Annual Report of the Board of Water Commissioners, March, 1920, p. 45.

Pg. 192   *With the Lord's Hill Reservoir...*, Annual Report of the Board of Water Commissioners, March, 1923, p. 42.

Pg. 192   *Also in 1919, with the largest chunk...*, Dictionary of American Biography, Vol. IX, Sewell-Trowbridge, Ed. By Dumas Malone, Chas. Scribner's Sons, New York, 1936, p. 542-3.

Pg. 192 *Six second-hand, ...*, Annual Report of the Board of Water Commissioners, March, 1920, p. 64.

Pg. 192 *In reality, the water company's...*, Annual Report of the Board of Water Commissioners, March, 1916, p. 65-6.

Pg. 192 *In the end, they settled on special...*, The Metropolitan District, Drinking Water, Water Treatment, About the Sand, http://www.themdc.com/mdch2o.htm

Pg. 193 *In 1922, eight huge sand...*, Annual Report of the Board of Water Commissioners, March, 1922, p. 60-61.

Pg. 193 *What was never revealed...*, William R. McCurdy, The Origins of the Metropolitan District of Hartford County, (In-house Publication) 32pgs., pg. 10.

Chapter 9

Pg. 194 *After the completion of the Nepaug...*, Annual Reports of the Board of Water Commissioners and from Int. with Gerry d'Avignon and Paul McCarthy (former MDC employees who knew and worked for Saville).

Pg. 194 *Saville had a deep interest...*, Caleb Saville's personal habits, likes and dislikes are collected from interviews with a number of different people including: his grandson, Thorndike Saville, Jr., Gerry & Paulette d'Avignon, Paul McCarthy, Richard Phillips, Stanley Johnson, Arthur W. Sweeton III, Mrs. Malcolm McInnes (widow of Saville's second driver, "Mac" McInnes), and from a collection of newspaper articles in *The Hartford Courant* and *The Hartford Times*, December, 1911. Also, information was gathered from Saville's personal notes and letters.

Pg. 195 *Oystering was one of Connecticut's...*, Ellsworth S. Grant, The Miracle of Connecticut, Pub. by The Connecticut Historical Society and Fenwick Productions, (no date), p. 11.

Pg. 196 *In the mid-19th century...*, Geer's City Directories & Advertisements in The Hartford Daily Times during this period.

Pg. 197 *It has been said by more than one...*, Interviews with Gerry d'Avignon, January 2, 2001 & January 8, 2001.

Pg. 197 *Tony Fornabi, Saville's last driver...*, The Hartford Courant, August 26, 1990, Northeast Magazine Section.

Pg. 197 *On the other hand, when Saville's son...*, Raleigh News and Observer, September 11, 1921 & Int. with Paulette d'Avignon, June 2002.

Pg. 198 *It was natural for Saville...*, Annual Report of the Board of Water Commissioners, 1913.

Pg. 199 *In 1919, a pipe was laid for the Wolcott...*, Annual Reports of the Board of Water Commissioners, 1910 & 1920.

Pg. 199 *Several other towns surrounding...*, William R. McCurdy, The Origins of the Metropolitan District of Hartford County, (In-house Publication) , pg. 10-12.

Pg. 200 *As a direct result of the horrendous pollution...*, Legislative Acts of 1925, State Archives, Connecticut State Library, Hartford.

Pg. 200 *Due largely to the popularity of the automobile...*, Census Figures, Secretary of State's Office, Hartford.

Pg. 200   *In much the same ham-fisted way...*, William R. McCurdy, The Origins of the Metropolitan District of Hartford County, (In-house Publication) 32pgs., pg. 2-3.

Pg. 201   *...Sources adequate for greater Hartford...*, Annual Report of the Board of Water Commissioners, March 1926.

Pg. 201   *In the mid-1920s, when he took up Saville's.....*, Information on the life of Charles Goodwin was collected from a number of sources including: Encyclopedia of Connecticut Biography (Boston, 1917); The History of Hartford County, 1633-1928, Charles W. Burpee, pub. by The S. J. Clarke Publishing Company, Chicago, Hartford & Marion Hepburn Grant, The Fenwick Story, The Connecticut Historical Society, 1974; *The Hartford Courant*, October 8, 1954, p. 1; Hall of Records, Hartford, CT & In-house publications of the Metropolitan District Commission.

Pg. 204   *In the mid-1920s, the state legislature...*, William R. McCurdy, The Origins of the Metropolitan District of Hartford County, (In-house Publication).

Pg. 205   *It could be argued that...*, Boston, City of, History: Early Boston. Early Boston Water System 4/29/00
http://www.mwra.state.ma.us/water/html/hist2.htm

Pg. 205   *As a direct result of a devastating typhoid...*, New York, City of, History of the Water Supply System. New York
City's Water Supply System: History   5/5/00
http://www.ci.nyc.ny.us/html/dep/html/history.html

Pg. 205   *Chicago has always been described...*, Chicago Public Library, Down The Drain: Typhoid Fever City,
http://www.chipublib.org/digital/sewers/history3.html

Pg. 205   *When discussing regional suppliers...*, William Mulholland, A History, William Mulholland: The Man Who Built the Los Angeles- Owens River Aqueduct, Los Angeles, City of, Water Supply Fact Sheet. 4/29/00
http://www5.dwp.ci.la.ca.us/water/supply/facts/index.htm

Pg. 206   *However, the most impressive example...*, Providence, City of, History of Providence Water and the Scituate Reservoir. 5/2/00
http://www.provwater.com/history.htm
Providence, City of, Providence Water Facts 6/7/00
http://www.provwater.com/pwsbfact.htm

Pg. 206   *The new plans called for the demolition...*, Annual Report of the Board of Water Commissioners, December 1926.

Pg. 207   *For the city, the biggest bone of contention...*, William R. McCurdy, The Origins of the Metropolitan District of Hartford County, (In-house Publication).

Pg. 207   *...we doubt seriously if Hartford...*, William R. McCurdy, The Origins of the Metropolitan District (in-house publication of the MDC).

Pg. 207   *...as for the people of Hartford...*, William R. McCurdy, The Origins of the Metropolitan District (in-house publication of the MDC).

Pg. 208   *In early May 1929 the state Senate...*, Legislative Notes, State Archives, Connecticut State Library, Hartford.

Pg. 208   *The bill, An Act Creating...*, Legislative Acts, State Archives, Connecticut State Library, Hartford.

Pg. 208   *For a bill with such sweeping authority...*, William R. McCurdy, The Origins of the Metropolitan District of Hartford County, (In-house Publication).

Pg. 209   *At the first meeting of the MDC, Charles Goodwin...*, William R. McCurdy, The Origins of the Metropolitan District of Hartford County, (In-house Publication).

Pg. 209   *What very few people knew at the time...*, Land Records, Barkhamsted and Hartland, Connecticut.

Pg. 209   *Fewer people still knew....*, Annual Report of the Board of Water Commissioners, December 1927.

Pg. 210   *...near the end of 1929...*, Annual Report of the Board of Water Commissioners, December 1929.

Pg. 210   *...preliminary study on the proposed...*, Annual Report of the Board of Water Commissioners, December 1928.

Chapter 10

Pg. 212   *From October 1929 until the market bottom...*, George E. Mowry, The Urban Nation, New York: Hill and Wang, 1981, p. 66.

Pg. 212   *In Hartford, insurance companies cushioned...*, Daniel Hawthorne, The Hartford of Hartford, New York, 1960, p. 228.

Pg. 212   *When delinquent water rents...*, Int. with Gerry d'Avignon, Jan.2, 2001.

Pg. 213   *The Farmington River's...*, Information about the Farmington River and its watersheds was collected from Annual Reports of the Board of Water Commissioners.

Pg. 213   *While the East Branch at one time had a few gristmills...*, Irving E. Manchester, The Colebrook History (1935).
          William H. McNeill, Colebrook: A Historical Sketch, With Maps and Other Assistance by Robert Grigg, The Colebrook Historical Society (1990).

Pg. 213   *They fished it almost the year long...*, All information about life in the Barkhamsted and Hartland Hollows was gathered from interviews with former residents of the area. Chief among them – Paul Crunden, Pauline (Emerick) Skaret, Loreen (Nelson) Pfaefflin, Joan Schramm, Virginia Lewis, Ken Church, Bertha (LeGeyt) Warner, Robert Hart, David Gidman, Laura (LeGeyt) Merrill, Herbert Case and Doug Roberts.Also contributing to the information base were local officials and members of the local historical societies. Chief among these people were: Joan Stoltze, Marianne Holthan, Betty Hillbrect, Mandy Nurge, Karen McNulty, Walt Landgraf, Nancy Winn, Charles Lynes, Sharon Neumann-Lynes and Harriett Winchenbaugh.

Pg. 215   *The establishment had originally belonged...*, Richard G. Wheeler, & George Hilton, ed., Barkhamsted Heritage - Culture and Industry in a Rural Connecticut Town, (Barkhamsted Historical Society,1975) p. 147.

Pg. 216   *In the annual reports of the towns...*, Annual Reports of Barkhamsted and Hartland, CT, 1927-1933, State Archives, Connecticut State Library, Hartford.

Pg. 217   *Beginning in 1927 fourteen-year-old...*, Int. with Laura (LeGeyt) Merrill, May 9, 2000.

Pg. 217   *Farther up the valley in Hartland Hollow...*, Pauline Emerick Skaret, Hartland Hollow...The Doomed Town (Hartland Historical Society, 1991. Descriptions of all of the properties in Hartland hollow are from this book.

Pg. 219 *As far back as 1913...*, Annual Report of the Board of Water Commissioners, March 1913, map.

Pg. 220 *Nonetheless, someone looking...*, Census Figures, Office of the Connecticut Secretary of State, Hartford.

Pg. 220 *As stated before, the water company began...*, Information regarding land sales comes from the Hall of Records in the Town Halls of Barkhamsted, Hartland and Colebrook.

Pg. 221 *In July 1929, just as the...*, General Statutes, May 20, 1931, State Archives, Connecticut State Library, Hartford.

Pg. 223 *The mill owners accepted this with one proviso...*, Annual Report of the MDC, December 1930.

Pg. 223 *Just as an example of the ongoing...*, Annual Report of the Board of Water Commissioners, December 1928, p. 13.

Pg. 224 *Conversely, it was a colossal blow...*, Pauline Emerick Skaret, Hartland Hollow...The Doomed Town, (Hartland Historical Society, 1991).

Pg. 224 *During January of that year...*, Notes from January 8, 1932 meeting of the MDC commissioners.

Pg. 225 *Still, exactly two weeks after...*, Notes from February 16,1932 meeting of the MDC commissioners.

Pg. 225 *...[that] the immediate acceptance of [the offer]...*, Notes from February 16, 1932 meeting of the MDC commissioners.

Pg. 226 *To begin with, the land was...*, Richard G. Wheeler, & George Hilton, ed., Barkhamsted Heritage - Culture and Industry in a Rural Connecticut Town, (Barkhamsted Historical Society,1975) p. 164.

Pg. 227 *When it became known for a certainty that Hartland Hollow...*, Stanley A. Ransom, History of Hartland (Hartland Bi-Centennial Committee, 1961) Printed by The Dowd Printing Company, Winsted, CT, p. 139.

Pg. 228 *True to the spirit of the protest...*, Int. with Laura (LeGeyt) Merrill.

Pg. 228 *After everyone was out of the valley...*, Int. with Paul Crunden , May 27, 2000. Also, Annual Report of the MDC, December, 1937, p. 46-7.

Pg. 228 *After everyone was out of the valley...*, Int. with Paul Crunden; also, Annual Report Of the Board of Water Commissioners, Dec. 1936.

Pg. 229 *The Old Newgate Coon Club...*, Hartland Land Records ; Pauline Emerick Skaret, Hartland Hollow...The Doomed Town, (Hartland Historical Society, 1991), p. 2-3.

Pg. 230 *...the Old Newgate Coon Club...*, Federal Writers Project, Connecticut, 1938.

Pg. 230 *One of the lawyers in Charles Goodwin's...*, Annual reports of the Board of Water Commissioners covering the years 1913 and 1928.

Pg. 230 *The owner of the company ...*, The Hartford Times, June 17, 1967, p. 5.

Pg. 231 *At an October 1940 meeting of the board...*, Notes on the October 19, 1940 meeting of the MDC Commissioners.

Pg. 232 *Getting slightly ahead of themselves...*, Notes on the October 19, 1940 meeting of the MDC Commissioners.

Pg. 232 *In the interim, the board agreed to pay...*, Notes of the October 19, 1940 meeting of the MDC Commissioners.

Pg. 232 *After Barkhamsted's First Selectman...*, Notes of the June 1941 meeting of the MDC Commissioners.

Warner, Robert Hart, David Gidman, Laura (LeGeyt) Merrill, Herbert Case and Doug Roberts.

Pg. 245 *The MDC had just let the contract...,* Notes of the October 19, 1940 meeting of the MDC Commissioners.

Pg. 247 *The revelry lasted until midnight...,* Int. with Pauline (Emerick) Skaret, April 18, 2000.

Pg. 248 *When the ballots were counted...,* The Hartford Courant, November 6, 1940, p. 1.

Pg. 248 *Without sugar-coating it, New York and Boston...,* Information about the water projects and displacement of people and towns was obtained directly from the individual water works themselves, as well as books previously mentioned.

Pg. 249 *In the watershed of the Croton Reservoir...,* Nelson Blake, Water for the Cities – A History of the urban Water Supply System in the United States (Syracuse University Press, 1956) p. 148-9.

Pg. 249 *The property owners claimed...,* Nelson Blake, Water for the Cities – A History of the urban Water Supply System in the United States (Syracuse University Press, 1956) p. 150.

Pg. 249 *The Ashokan Reservoir, built in 1915...,* About CWC (A Brief Watershed History),
http://www.cwconline,org/about/ab_hist.htm

Pg. 249 *...lest the dearly departed be forgotten...,* Catherine Mulholland, William Mulholland and the Rise of Los Angeles, University of California Press, Berkeley, Los Angeles, London, 2000, Preface, p. xv.

Pg. 250 *Strictly speaking, Boston had nothing to do...,* History: Early Boston, Early Boston Water System,
http://www.mwra.state.ma.us/water/html.hist2.htm

Pg. 250 *However, things changed with the Wachusett...,* The Worcester Telegram & Gazette, Wachusett Reservoir Work Upset Central Mass. Towns: The Sacrifices Were Many, July 9, 2000, Telegram & Gazette Staff Writer, Dave Greenslit

Pg. 251 *By impounding the waters of the Swift...,* Boston, City of, History: Quabbin and Ware. Ware River and Quabbin Reservoir 4/29/00
http://www.mwra.state.ma.us/water/html/hist5.htm

Pg. 251 *They even publish a newsletter, ...,The* Hartford Courant, Dec. 13, 1999, A Valley of Memories. Courant Staff Writer Lynne Tuohy.

Chapter 12

Pg. 253 *From year to year...,* Census Figures, Connecticut Secretary of State's Office
Pg. 254 *Increasingly, the MDC relied...,* Hall of Records, Colebrook, CT.
Pg. 254 *The final point is a little meatier...,* The Carey family lived in Farmington, CT, and as such were 'associate' members of the MDC. Therefore, H. Bissell Carey was not eligible to be a water commissioner, and there simply is no evidence anywhere that he had anything to do with the water company (witness his obituary in *The Hartford Times,* June 17, 1967, p. 5).

Pg. 255 *His wife, Mary (Barney) Carey, was a descendant...,* Interview with Austin Carey Jr. February 18, 2001.

Pg. 255 *The village itself was actually just...,.*Irving E. Manchester, The Colebrook History, (1935) William H. McNeill, Colebrook: A Historical Sketch , With Maps and Other Assistance by Robert Grigg, The Colebrook Historical Society, (1990).

Pg. 255 *On the east side of the river sat...,* Interviews with past residents, Juanita Dustin and Mildred Church.

Pg. 255 *Over the years, there had been a cotton mill...,* Irving E. Manchester, The Colebrook History (1935) William H. McNeill, Colebrook: A Historical Sketch , With Maps and Other Assistance by Robert Grigg, The Colebrook Historical Society (1990).
Irving E. Manchester, The Colebrook History (1935).

Pg. 256 *The MDC bought its first parcel...,* Hall of Records, Colebrook, CT.

Pg. 257 *Just as Charles LeGeyt and Harold Birden...,* Hall of Records, Colebrook, CT. & Interview with Mildred Church.

Pg. 257 *Bill Bettes and his family lived...,* Interview with Mildred Church.

Pg. 257 *Somehow, during the very early going...,* Interview with Joyce Nelson, Juanita Dustin, Mildred Church and other former residents of Colebrook River.

Pg. 258 *They said that the representatives of the MDC...,* Interview with Joyce Nelson, Juanita Dustin, Mildred Church and other former residents of Colebrook River.

Pg. 258 *Things got increasingly contentious, until the people...,* Steven M. Jones, What The Metropolitan District Wants...The Metropolitan District Gets, A Paper, January 1977.

Pg. 258 *But after some concessions...,* Records of the Connecticut State Legislature, State Archives, Connecticut State Library, Hartford.

Pg. 259 *First, unlike their friends in the East Branch valley...,* Steven M. Jones, What The Metropolitan District Wants...The Metropolitan District Gets, A Paper, January 1977.

Pg. 259 *By 1951, the only properties left...,* Hall of Records, Colebrook, CT.

Pg. 259 *At the same time, the Bottinelli Monumental Company...,* Annual Records of the MDC, December, 1953.

Pg. 259 *A resident of Colebrook, who lived...,* Edie Clark, The Town That Disappeared, (Yankee Magazine Aug. 1984) p. 62- 76, 152-158, Article about Colebrook River, Connecticut.

Pg. 259 *Fittingly, in the early writings...,The Hartford Courant,* August 29, 1990, Northeast Magazine Section.

Pg. 260 *The years of squabbling with the...,* Annual Report of the MDC, December, 1955.

Pg. 260 *Immediately after Hurricane Diane...,* Flood '55: New England's Greatest Disaster, Compiled, Edited and Published by Interstate Press, Hartford, Sept, 1955.

Pg. 260 *...It is axiomatic in hydraulic engineering...,* Papers of Caleb Mills Saville, State Archives, Connecticut State Library, Hartford.

Pg. 260 *Not only did this flood send the engineers...,* Annual Report of the MDC, December, 1955.

Pg. 261 *After all of the detailed calculations were completed...,* Annual Report of the MDC, December, 1956.

Pg. 261 *Perhaps to improve relations...,* Personal observation and map references.

Pg. 261   *(Answering a reporter's question...)...*, Comment by Chairman Anthony
           Gallicchio, The Hartford Courant, August 8, 1990, Northeast Magazine Section.

Pg. 262   *With the Army Corps's completion of Colebrook River...*, Annual Report of the
           MDC, December, 2000.

Pg. 262   *In early 1960, the MDC took a controversial...*, Annual Report of the MDC,
           December,1960.

Pg. 262   *In 1901 a newly graduated dentist...*, Donald R. McNeil, The Fight For
           Fluoridation (New York, Oxford University Press, Inc.,1957).

Pg. 263   *In the same year that the Hogback (Goodwin) Dam...*, The Hartford Courant,
           February 15, 1960, p.1 and Caleb Saville's Death Certificate,
           Hartford vital records.

Pg. 264   *The ashes of his wife, Elizabeth, had predeceased him...*, Notes of Thorndike
           Saville, circa March 1961; Records of Mt. Auburn Cemetery.

Pg. 264   *Born in Boston, Educated at Harvard...*, Int. with Paulette d'Avignon, June 15,
           2002.

Pg. 264   *After his wife's death...*, Int. with Gerry d'Avignon, Jan. 2, 2001.

Pg. 264   *In 1960, newspapers assumed a euphemistic tone...*, The Hartford Times,
           February 15, 1960, p. 1.

Pg. 265   *As one engineer at the MDC commented...*, Int. with MDC engineer Stanley
           Johnson, June 11, 2000.

Pg. 265   *In the process of providing for the drinking water...*, Land Records of the towns
           mentioned.

Pg. 265   *Eighty-five years later, his grandson, H. Bissell Carey...*, Hiram Bissell's
           younger daughter, Ella, married Frank Carey, who began his working career as
           a mail boy for *The Hartford Courant* and rose to vice-president and treasurer.
           Ella and Frank Carey had three children – Hiram Bissell, Harold Dearborn and
           Ruth Bissell (who died young).

Pg. 265   *H. Bissell Carey was twenty-four years...*,*The Hartford Times*, June 17, 1967, p.
           5 (obit).

Pg. 267   *Today, in addition to distributing...*, Annual Report of the MDC, December,
           2002.

Pg. 267   *In South Glastonbury, not far from the Shingle Hollow...*, Int. with MDC
           engineers Stanley Johnson and Jim Randazzo, June 2000.

Index